In The Nation:

1932-1966

In The Nation:

1932-1966

by Arthur Krock

McGraw-Hill Book Company

New York   Toronto   London   Sydney

To James Sayler,
the Librarian of the Washington Bureau
of *The New York Times*,
and to Laura Waltz,
my secretary.
Their constant encouragement,
and their toil in assembling the material for this book,
are greatly responsible for whatever merit it may have
as a day-by-day chronicle of the revolutionary change
over the past three decades in the social,
economic and political directions of the United States
at home and abroad.
A. K.

CONTENTS

FOREWORD
by Tom Wicker

Arthur Krock came to Washington from Kentucky in 1910 as a correspondent for Henry Watterson's Louisville *Courier-Journal,* but his connection with public life in this country began when he watched William
Howard Taft nominated for President in 1908. Mr. Krock was elected
to the Gridiron Club in 1913, later went back to Louisville to run the
Courier, suffered the slings and arrows of outrageous ownership and departed for New York, became assistant to the Publisher of the *World,*
shifted to Adolph Ochs's *New York Times,* took over the *Times* Washington bureau in 1932, covered everything in sight and a good deal that
wasn't, influenced men and affairs, won three Pulitzer Prizes and earned
himself an honored place among the handful of newspapermen to whose
work history will find itself indebted.

But let biographers deal with that and let readers sample for themselves the value and flavor of his work in Washington, much of which
can be read in the following pages. For my part, I only want to say a
few good words for my friend, Mr. Krock.

Even this is presumptuous, for I have known him only at the evening
of his career. I crept into the Washington bureau of *The Times,* thoroughly awed and fearful of my plain inadequacies, in early 1960; by
then, Mr. Krock had turned the bureau over to Scotty Reston and was
devoting himself to writing his column, "In The Nation," three times a
week. For nearly thirty years he had been terrorizing and edifying official Washington, to say nothing of *Times* readers all over the world, and
there I was, fresh in from North Carolina and Tennessee, green, scared
and working in the same office.

It would be nice to relate that Arthur Krock, after the usual polite introduction, took me under his wing and encouraged me. As a matter of fact, nothing intimidated me more than his Olympian majesty. He would stalk through the office, carrying a statesman's girth with more aggressive dignity than anyone in Washington, his head cocked back to allow his gaze to play scornfully on the gods, a Churchillian cigar cocked toward his hatbrim like a banner of war. In full steam, Mr. Krock caused hardened reporters to leap rabbit-like from his path; as for me, I could only pray that he might never notice that so lowly a creature was in the office.

On one of these impressive passages, Mr. Krock swept by my obscure desk with a tread more fierce than his accustomed stately pace. I cowered, but it was not in quest of me that those footfalls rang so martially on the littered newsroom floor. A hapless copyboy had some-how acquired temporary charge of the maze of plugs, sockets and cords on the telephone switchboard; he made of it a hopeless mess in a few moments; and office communications collapsed.

Mr. Krock descended on the quivering offender like a dreadnaught beating down on Jutland. "Mr. Jones," he pronounced (at such mo-ments, Mr. Krock would never "thunder" or "roar" or "bellow"; he pronounces, and it is merely devastating); "Mr. Jones," he pronounced, "you may someday make a great editor. But you will *never* make a switchboard operator."

Whereupon, he executed a perfectly gauged wheel to the left, emitted two conclusive mushroom clouds from the cigar, and returned to his office; I fancied that the building trembled.

(I was not then as aware as I am now of one of Mr. Krock's great distinctions—his wit. He is one of the funniest men I know and at its best his published humor is either openly hilarious or subtly designed to take someone's hide off in the dark. He once wrote of Harry Hopkins, for instance, that he "may, at times, have thought that something the President said or did was not perfect. If so, he suppressed the unworthy thought with ease." It could as aptly be said of some of Washington's current *haut monde*. For readers of this volume, I might suggest, as random samples, the discussion of John L. Lewis's literary style, the classic tale of how Lyndon Johnson brought a camel-driver from Pakis-tan to "Kennedy the King," and a picture of Harry Truman pondering whether to run again in 1952 that takes the form of a parody of Ham-let's lament, and begins:

"To run or not to run, that is the question:
Whether my grand designs—foreign and domestic—

Can safely be entrusted to another * * *"
and in fine iambics observes:
"Thus politics makes wobblers of us all.")

Months passed, years even. I began to write something about politics,
a small impingement on the Krockian demesne. Perhaps Mr. Krock
noticed my Southern accent; he was ever partial to the mushmouth
cadence. A story or two may have caught his eye and raised my status.
One morning, it happened. I had turned, I thought, a rather nice lead on
a story about one of Washington's great characters, Judge Howard
Smith of Virginia.

Mr. Krock paused for a moment at my desk. I quaked within and
without. "Hrrrumph," he said. "Mr. Wicker." The great cigar was removed with a Roman fling of the arm. A finger tapped the short paragraph of my cherished lead. "That's the way to do it," he said. And off
he went to his office, the turgid air of the newsroom curling away from
his prow.

Well, since that day, I have believed that I had some small right to be
in Washington and might possibly stay the course. Mr. Krock would
occasionally talk politics with me, and I listened avidly; how many people who saw William Howard Taft nominated and every President
since, can you find? Then, too, Mr. Krock found me a receptive audience for the inexhaustible stock of stories and anecdotes that enlighten
and enliven his long memory. Like President Johnson and many other
Southerners, he is a great storyteller and firmly believes that Southern
men not only tell them best but enjoy them most. We agreed early to
disagree about civil rights. And not long after Mr. Johnson became
President, Mr. Krock finally admitted me to his shocking secret. He
could be jolted from Olympus; he was only mortal.

Some months earlier, he had published a controversial article in Fortune, discussing in stern tones what he saw as the efforts of President
Kennedy to win the press by wining and dining reporters and otherwise
soliciting favor by appealing to journalistic vanity—a commodity in
oversupply in these parts.

President Johnson, then reaching out as rapidly and as often as possible to anyone who might be of assistance to him, called Mr. Krock to
the White House one day for an interview. As then often happened, the
"interview" turned into a luncheon in the private Presidential quarters,
rambled on for three or four hours, and ended in what was then a typical White House ceremony. Mr. Krock found himself standing at attention and being crowned with a pearly white, five-gallon LBJ hat with
the brand of the LBJ ranch emblazoned on the interior band.

The next day I was summoned to Mr. Krock's office.

"Mr. Wicker," he informed me gravely, "I am in deep trouble. You must help me."

I was only too happy. "Mr. Wicker," Mr. Krock said, after telling me of the luncheon and coronation, "I could not refuse the President's gift. But I could only think of those men sitting out there in the press lobby. I could only think of them watching me pass through, wearing my LBJ hat. Or carrying my hat box. Mr. Wicker, after my article in *Fortune,* I could not do it."

In desperation, Mr. Krock had found his way through the White House corridors to a secretary's desk. Presenting her with the explosive hat box, he had said: "Young lady, you must hide this for me. And you must never let your boss know."

Now, he informed me, it was my job to get that LBJ hat out of the White House in deepest secrecy. I did, with no difficulty, being without scruple in such capers. I don't know how he felt about it but since then I have been able to look at Arthur Krock as a colleague, a friend, "one of us," and few relationships in my life have been more rewarding.

When Mr. Krock stops by my desk now, as he often does, I know that something useful, thoughtful or funny—or probably all three—is going to be said. He is more interested in public affairs and *The New York Times* than some reporters half his age; his counsel is sound; his news judgment is undiminished; and not much happens that he has not seen before, and upon which his great experience can shed no light.

From a vacation house at Newport, he once wrote that "a shore from which the ocean stretches unbroken to an unseen landfall in the other hemisphere is perhaps the place where a vacationing Washington observer of the ways of Government is most likely to keep them, however unwillingly, in mind. For, like the ocean as seen from such a shore, only their surface changes. In the depths, there is no change."

That is one reason why I think Mr. Krock's articles in "In The Nation" are immensely valuable, albeit they infuriate a lot of people who think the ocean depths only exist at Newport or Cape Cod or Rehoboth. He can be as wrong, and as wrong-headed, as anyone, and often is, but like Uncle Joe Cannon he has "seen it all" and knows that "rain don't always follow the thunder."

Perhaps not as an entirely unbiased witness, I think Mr. Krock also reflects in his articles the last, firm, proud expression of the best of the Old South—a South that is gone now, I suppose rightly and inevitably, but none the less sadly. I mean a South that was, however the expression may have been perverted in recent inglorious years, a way of life

—flawed like all ways of life, but still a manner of living in which men knew and loved their tradition and therefore could speak of and believe in honor and pride and courtesy and repose—in which the endless shimmering summer days and the murmurous evenings and the quiet of pine woods and the dark waters barely flowing to the sea gave men a sense of continuity, an assurance of belonging, a oneness in a shared fate with their neighbors of whatever color. The Old South had little but a way of life to share and bequeath; now it is all gone, for some a good riddance, for others a bitter sacrifice to the demonic force of change. But Arthur Krock is still here, still speaking, and the Old South lives yet awhile.

And again: amid the triumph of pragmatism, this man writes straight down the line of a hard-earned, time-tried point of view—a line of principles, if you will, that to him are as immutable and everlasting as the blue depths of that Atlantic laving Newport with its transient surface. I am not myself, in that sense, "a man of principle"; I am a child of an age of change and I will not curse my time or generation, however they wound my heart. But I think we need to listen to someone who will ignore the surface, who is, in President Kennedy's phrase, "willing to take the long look, undisturbed by prejudices and slogans of the moment, who attempts to make an honest judgment on difficult events," who seeks to "distinguish the real from the illusory, the long-range from the temporary, the significant from the petty."

And a final, personal word. Mr. Krock and I probably agree, on matters of public policy, about as seldom as men can. He thinks I am a backslid Southerner and he is quite right, and he thinks I am soft on politicians and he may be right about that, too. But no man of great experience and superb attainment could differ with a junior with more courtesy, deference, respect for what my life has made of me, or plain regard for the worth of another human being. I commend that attitude to some who differ with him or with anyone; and while Arthur Krock can say, as he once did, that "the most fortunate of my fates is that I have always been an employe of gentlemen," it ought to be said that it takes one to know one.

Tom Wicker

Washington
May 1, 1966

The Roosevelt Years

For almost 40 years after Adolph S. Ochs bought *The New York Times,* he maintained the foundation of impersonal journalism on which he had raised the paper from a parochial to a national institution. The privilege of signing dispatches was rarely bestowed. Any expression of an attitude toward the news was strictly reserved to the anonymity of the editorial page. And, since interpretation and analysis of events and the policies of government must inevitably reflect something of the writer's bent of mind, this also was banned, even to those *Times* reporters whom Mr. Ochs completely trusted to strive for the objectivity in the news columns which was his First Commandment.

The stern standard involved a commercial risk because, when Mr. Ochs imposed it, the newspapers produced by his principal competitors —Pulitzer, Hearst and Bennett—were successful examples of the contrary. But as their rivalry intensified, so did the consciousness of the reading public that no axes, especially that of the owner, were being ground on the news touchstone of *The Times*. So that, in due course, the risk of pitting its impersonal journalism against the then entrenched and exciting personal variety, was canceled by a public preference for news as uncolored as honest effort could make it.

Mr. Ochs lived to see this preference take on the durability which has enabled *The Times* increasingly to collect and publish more of the news, from more points of origin, than any other journal in the history of the

3

press. But his satisfaction in this emphatic proof of the commercial, as well as the ethical, soundness of his concept of the kind of paper he wanted to publish was acutely diminished by the contemporaneous shrinkage of the New York morning newspaper field. Of Hearst's *American*, of Bennett's *Herald*, of Pulitzer's *World*, only their names, in hyphenated mast-heads, survive.

Yet they had left the mark of personal journalism on the trade, and by none of them was it more deeply impressed on the reading public throughout the country than by *The World*. Failing to induce the owners of *The World* to await the outcome of his effort to finance its purchase by its employes (with his substantial underwriting), Mr. Ochs turned to consideration of what *The Times* could do to fill something of the void without in the least relaxing the objectivity of its news columns.

The first and for some years the only *Times* feature that conceivably could have been the product of this review was my signed Washington column on the editorial page.

It was by no means the first space in the paper given over to critical appraisal of public matters and events. The customary newspaper departments in which books, dramatic and musical performances, and so on, are reviewed and their quality evaluated, as it appears to the individual who reviews them, were present in *The Times* from its beginnings. The staff members and outsiders whom the Sunday editor chose to write the articles in the weekly magazine and book-review sections were not inhibited in the expression of editorial opinion. And for years the editorial page itself had carried a column, "Topics of The Times," which was a series of light essays on all manner of human activities. These essays, written over a long period by Frederick Craig Mortimer and his successor Simeon Strunsky, were distinguished examples of those *causeries* that rate the classification of literature. But, though no restraint on the expression of opinion was imposed on the anonymous authors, their columns touched only lightly and casually on the politics, actions and policies of Government.

But when mine, which specifically and directly did, and was written under signature at the seat of Government, was first introduced to

Times readers in the issue of May 4, 1933, the column was not as originally contemplated by Mr. Ochs. He had come slowly and dubiously to
the decision that something of the kind—a very vague something—was
desirable. But it required the patient and constant efforts of his chief of
staff, Arthur Hays Sulzberger, to persuade him to (a) put the decision
in practice and (b) accept the format of a signed critique as well as an
exposition of the acts and personnel of the Government in Washington.

Even after Mr. Ochs agreed to the concept of a signed Washington
column on the editorial page, he envisaged it as "a letter" to an imaginary "Aunt Hattie." And Mr. Sulzberger risked and perhaps incurred
Mr. Ochs's displeasure in finally arguing him out of this design. This
relieved me of the necessity of explaining that I could not in good heart
and conscience have undertaken the assignment in that fixed form. And
it gave me the opportunity to try to demonstrate favorably to the readers of *The Times* in general, and Mr. Ochs in particular, that such a
column could strike a fair balance between information and critical
analysis, and between rigidly impersonal journalism and the opposite
kind.

But, since I was venturing onto *terra incognita,* insofar as *The Times*
was concerned—and *terra periculosa* as well—I began the venture with
the guide which had led the paper to the pinnacle of the American press.
I was convinced that eventual acceptance of my credentials for critical
analysis would depend on prior establishment of the column as primarily a source of information, reliable and, as the trade jargon now goes,
"in depth." Also, I was acutely aware that on this primacy Mr. Ochs's
judgment of the value of the product would be based.

The introducing article, therefore, was an exposition of the economic
theory of the New Deal "brain trust" by one of its formulators whom I
identified as "The Professor." It was a form of presenting the news that,
in those days on *The Times,* was still unacceptable in the news columns
—even if signed by one of the few byliners whose number was beginning
very slowly to increase. And it deliberately supplied no clue to my personal attitude toward the proposition as set forth by "The Professor,"
because this seemed to be the best way to test what Mr. Ochs really

wanted a signed column on the editorial page to be like. Time enough to give the new, experimental feature the color and movement which I believed the readers would have reason to expect in such a departure from anonymity on the page.

Since any value it might develop for the reader, beyond the full record of events of the day that was lavishly spread before him in the news columns, depended on selection of the subject, the choice inevitably reflected a personal point of view. Hence choice was necessarily an editorial decision. But, except for that aspect, the introductory article was wholly informative—a synthesis of the economics of the New Deal. The only suggestion of a point of view was oblique—a query by the writer to "The Professor": "The millennium, then, is in sight?"

Today's newspaper reader, who accepts presentation of the news in outright editorial terms by the writers of Washington columns as a general journalistic canon, may be astonished to learn that the inclusion of this query was rather venturesome on *The New York Times* of that era. As I tapped it out on my typewriter I wondered whether this mildly intrinsic editorializing would prejudice Mr. Ochs against the new project. But I decided that if the new editorial page feature was to justify its placement in the paper it should indicate a point of view. The only way to discover whether Mr. Ochs was amenable to this concept, if not pursued to the point of dominating the informational content (which I had and have no intention of doing), was to ease into it.

I was gratified to learn that, though Mr. Ochs was not enthusiastic about the subject matter of the column, he made no other criticism. With this encouragement, though negative in character, and favorable comments from readers on the positive side, what began as a *Times* experiment soon became a durable fixture. I had joined, from a quarter where it was least expected by the press of the period, the then small contingent of what has grown into a battalion of Washington commentators on the news.

But, engaged as I now was on contributing four interpretations of the news to the daily editorial page and one for the "Sunday Review Of The Week," the editorial character inherent in the selection of subjects was soon automatically established. For example:

When the Supreme Court made a ruling which, set in parallel with previous opinions, was a reversal of its settled construction of a statute and the Constitution, and the majority nevertheless insisted it was not, the new *Times* Washington column would point out and document the inconsistency. In that period, to make the point was not permissible in the news report of the action, on the ground that this would amount to "editorializing" by the reporter. The same standard applied to turnabouts in Administration policy that were officially and untruthfully asserted to be consistent with the past; also to positions taken by members of the political branches of the Government that were clear repudiations of positions they had taken before.

But then as now, more than thirty years later, I endeavored to keep these implicit criticisms impersonal. A good deal of impact on the reader was forfeited thereby, a deficit which has been more than made up in the last few years as *Times* columns of opinion have proliferated. Expressions of plainly personal viewpoints, directly or through the employment of conclusive adjectives and the open advocacy of selected officials and policies, are now standard practice in the commentaries from Washington. These are published as written, and widely distributed in this country and abroad through the agency of newspaper syndicates.

The facts that some syndicated commentators are plainly influenced by personal likes and dislikes, and recommend the adoption of their personal foreign and domestic policies by the Government, seem to have increased rather than impaired the degree of their acceptance by the subscribing publishers of daily newspapers. But Mr. Ochs's three successors as publisher—Arthur Hays Sulzberger, Orvil E. Dryfoos and Arthur O. Sulzberger—have, in my judgment, maintained, while greatly relaxing it, much of the substance of his precept for the signed semi-editorial commentary he reluctantly admitted to the paper. This precept is that the viewpoint of the writer toward the subject he has selected is the least important element in a product which is justified primarily by the additional information and deeper background that in the news columns would breach the stern canon of straight reporting.

It chanced that I was in an especially advantageous position to decide what questions of information, background and personal and political motivation were left unanswered in the reader's mind by the purely factual reporting of news to which the reader is entitled, but was the function of the editorials alone to supply. I was in this position by reason of being "The Washington Correspondent of *The New York Times*," the traditional title of the head of its bureau in the Federal capital. In this capacity for 21 years I was responsible for the collecting, editing and dispatching to New York of the news produced by a large staff of reporters. Hence, from them and from independent news-gathering of my own, I was reasonably well informed of the background of Government actions and policies that are inappropriate for use in straight news reports if the standard of objectivity is to be maintained. This information, however, is legitimate grist for the mill in which signed editorial Washington columns are produced, when clearly identified as such to the reader.

My assignment as The Washington Correspondent came about by chance. Richard V. Oulahan, who for many years had been the outstanding member of the press corps in the capital, died unexpectedly, after a brief illness, in December, 1931. It happened that, of those members of the staff in New York who were considered for replacement, only two were previously experienced in the field, Harold Phelps Stokes and myself, both members of the Editorial Board. Neither of us aspired to the transfer—Stokes, because he was a born New Yorker, with deep roots there, and devoted to his work as editorial writer on the affairs of his native city and State; I, because working on *The Times* in New York at my level represented the summit of my professional ambition, and because I savored the life in the metropolis at that time with the special relish of the newcomer.

When Stokes prevailed on Mr. Sulzberger to accept his preference, the immediate field was reduced to me. My respect, and my professional and personal admiration, for Mr. Sulzberger, who had persuaded Mr. Ochs to import me from *The World* in 1927, combined with his expression of confidence induced me to accept the assignment. So, in January, 1932, when the Hoover Administration had 14 months to go, I took over the Washington Bureau. The job was not only administrative; I also ex officio wrote many of the daily news dispatches designed for page one. The assignment of the four-day-a-week and Sunday column was made by Mr. Ochs 15 months after I took over the Washington Bureau, and President Hoover had been out of office for about 60 days.

A periodic responsibility of the Washington Correspondent (which was mine from 1932 through 1948) was to write in the New York office the "lead" account on page one of the results of the biennial general elections. It first devolved on me when the voters chose Franklin D. Roosevelt for President over the incumbent Herbert Hoover. In a re-portorial account of the causes for Roosevelt's 1932 election is this passage which serves to key in the following group of articles on the evolution of the New Deal's socio-economic philosophy:

A political cataclysm, unprecedented in the nation's history and produced by three years of depression, thrust President Herbert Hoover and the Republican power from control of the government yesterday, elected Governor Franklin Delano Roosevelt President of the United States, provided the Democrats with a large majority in Congress and gave them administration of the affairs of many States of the Union.

The country was voting a national grouch against three years of business stagnation, against farm foreclosures, bank failures, unemployment and the Republican argument that "things could have been worse." The President's single-handed fight to sustain his record, his warnings against Democratic changes in the Hawley-Smoot tariff and efforts to impress the country with fear of a change of administration were as futile in the final analysis as straw votes and the reports of newspaper observers had indicated it would be.

THE NEW DEAL

I suspect that weeks before President-elect Roosevelt took office, March 4, 1933, he realized that the economic Depression was so deeply implanted that he would be obliged to reverse the policy commitments of the platform on which he was elected. Among its pledges, which he had promised to carry out in good faith, were a 25 per cent retrenchment in the annual costs of the Federal establishment. And reform of the abuses of the capitalist system, that had reached a peak in the money markets of the twenties, was given priority in the platform over Federal programs for economic "recovery."

In any event, it was not long after becoming President that Roosevelt found it necessary to reverse the priority and concentrate on the pump-priming measures which thenceforth dominated the activities of the New Deal. The about-face was in full practice by the end of The Hundred Days in which Congress approved the reforms of the stock and security markets as rapidly as the President could send the legislative drafts to the Capitol—sometimes even before the drafts were completed. When the Senate, knowing that a piece of paper which Majority Leader Joe T. Robinson of Arkansas was flourishing was not the text of the major piece of legislation it was represented to be, "passed" it anyhow, two new conditions were apparent:

The 1932 Democratic platform was a dead letter. And Congress, reflecting the overwhelming sentiment of the country, had become the

11

eager and willing agent of the Executive's conclusion that the emergency
required him to seek and exercise "dictatorial" powers.

The conclusive nature of the President's decision to abandon the conservatism of the 1932 platform for planned economic recovery was revealed in a vast public works program. But what established the change
was a proposition so radical, in the political thinking of the time, that
the news of it was widely disbelieved. This proposition took form in the
National Recovery Act, but when its outlines were first reported in my
Washington dispatch that immediately follows (my source was the late
Senator Robert F. Wagner of New York) the President was hotly challenged at a news conference to say it wasn't so.

Although I had carefully attributed the origin of the plan to "the
President's closest advisers," and written merely that they "hoped to
persuade him to adopt it," the publication came before Roosevelt had
had time to soften up the opposition he knew the plan would engender.
So he threw cold water on the dispatch by telling his news conference
questioners he knew nothing of such a plan and otherwise disparaging
any inference that it was under serious consideration. Accordingly,
Mark Sullivan, the eminent columnist and intimate of former President
Hoover, was only one of several Washington commentators who assured
his readers in print that they need not apprehend this violent laying on
of Government's hand to the free enterprise system.

But not long afterward the N.R.A., in the form described in the dispatch that follows, was legislated by Congress at Roosevelt's request
and set in operation by him under General Hugh Johnson:

'WAR BOARD' PROPOSED
April 13, 1933

A plan to mobilize private industry under the government for expansion
in the production of articles and materials in normal demand, this expansion to be coeval with the administration's public works activities, is

being developed by the President's closest advisors and they hope to persuade him to attempt it.

Certain types of industry, under the plan, would be assembled and regulated by a government agency reminiscent of the War Industries Board. Competition would be regulated: hours of work and minimum rates of pay would be fixed; and some of the proponents of the idea also would have the government guarantee manufacturers against loss in resuming or increasing the manufacture of prescribed articles and materials.

The thought behind the plan is that a public works program standing by itself, even if five billions is expended upon it, will not sufficiently reduce unemployment or make use of the new purchasing power. It is contended that private industry must, at the same time, be put in a position to absorb the new purchasing power, composed of the billions which the government will be putting in the hands of citizens all over the United States. To do this, it must resume manufacture, and that will restore many to private employment in the factories themselves and in the retail establishments which will dispose of the products of these factories. This will, in turn, give purchasing power to those privately as well as those governmentally employed. A part of the billions will then flow back to the Treasury in various forms of taxation.

The argument which seems to have been most effective in bringing the administration to support the public works appropriations is that the deflationary policy has cut down the purchasing ability of the country by seven billions. Of this five billions is in the closed banks, one billion in the budget savings and another billion in reductions made by the several State governments.

The vast public works program having been definitely agreed upon, with the probability that it may involve an expenditure of as much as five billions, it soon became evident to the architects of administration policy that this plan needed a companion.

It was all very well to balance the budget, and, with government credit thus established, to borrow billions for roads, buildings, flood control and the like. But this question remained: How could private industry get the full use of those billions for purchase? Without some form of government stimulation and aid, it was felt that manufacturers of ordinary consumers' commodities would wait to clear their stocks, while retailers were clearing theirs, and when the manufacturers did resume production, they would simply proceed at "depression pace."

The result of these considerations was the plan to set up a government agency to induce industrial expansion, to quicken and regulate it meanwhile, to protect it against loss and perhaps even to fix the prices of labor's product as well as the wage of labor itself. The general philosophy back of the idea and a warning that it might be applied, was expressed by the President in his inaugural address in this language:

* * * If we are to go forward, we must move as a trained and loyal army, willing to sacrifice for the good of a common discipline, because, without such discipline, no progress is made, no leadership becomes effective.

We are, I know, ready and willing to submit our lives and property to such discipline because it makes possible a leadership which aims at a larger good.

This I propose to offer, pledging that the larger purposes will bind upon us all as a sacred obligation with a unity of duty hitherto evoked only in time of armed strife.

During the last period of "armed strife," industry moved as an array under a common discipline enforced by the War Industries Board and submitted to an allotment of product, fixed prices, strict competitive regulation and other details in a paternalistic regiment. The new government agency would have similar powers, modeled to suit the new economic circumstances. If the plan is adopted it will be incorporated in a measure submitted along with those which will compose the public works expenditures legislation.

It would add an impressive unit to the administration's program designed not simply for "holding the line," but for rebuilding the economic structure of the country and of the world.

———

A month after the disclosure of the intent to set up the N.R.A. there appeared the first of my editorial page columns (previously alluded to). On even cursory examination of "The Professor's" description of the economic philosophy of the President's "brain trust," it was as apparent—then as now—that the mobilization-for-recovery of private industry the Administration had undertaken was well within the pattern of this philosophy:

'PROFESSOR' CHARTS
'BRAIN TRUST'
May 3, 1933

The Professor drew a circle on a sheet of paper. He had been asked what was the economic philosophy of the President's "brain trust."

The Professor is not yet a resident member of that interesting group. He still retains his connection with a university far from Washington and comes here for periods of conference only. But he is the architect and builder of the foundation and framework of one of the major pieces of administration legislation, and his opinions are sought and carefully weighed at grand headquarters. He could be a steady member of the inner council if he lived in the capital.

After drawing the circle the Professor explained that it represented the structure of capitalism as we long have known it in this country: finance, industry, politics, social intercourse, education, literature, and the rest. Then he drew, from the top of the sheet, a broad shaft which penetrated the circumference at a certain point.

"That is individualism," he said, "the unrestrained individualism that has permitted money and power to be concentrated into the hands of a very few."

The Professor extended the shaft within the circle until it had reached its centre. From the bottom of the sheet he drew a similar shaft, the head of which collided with the first one at the centre.

"That is organized labor and similar collective movements for toilers," he said. "These two, pushing steadily at each other, will destroy the circle. If the shaft of individualism destroys the other, the eventual result will be anarchy. The triumph of the shaft of workers' organization will be syndicalism. It is in an effort to avert both eventualities that what you call the 'brain trust' is bringing this other shaft to the centre of the circle, there to balance it and preserve it, though in somewhat reduced circumference."

This third shaft, when drawn from the two sides of the sheet by the Professor, was labeled "government control." It forced its way between the two others where they impinged. He explained that if the trend it represents in present lawmaking is permitted to continue, a benevolent form of State socialism will be the outcome, averting the evils and terrors of syndicalism and anarchy, which, he contended, would soon be the inevitable result of the thrusting-contest between the other two shafts.

The "brain trust," said the Professor, is constructing American civilization with a long view ahead. Some of the measures it proposes are temporary, but the basic idea is fixed. Fifty years would not be too long to set the foundation firmly. He said that the economic philosophy represented in the farm relief bill was the idea in its essence. He did not believe, he said to the friend to whom he was making this explanation and for whom he was drawing his chart, that the mass of the people will be willing to continue, or satisfied to revert, to the uncontrolled battle between capital and labor which was the bequest of the nineteenth century to the twentieth.

It was clear, said the Professor, to those who had been studying the new problems of government and who hope to make a better world hereafter, that wasteful and merciless trade competition, enforced by anti-trust laws and the like, long working hours and uncertainty of employment by the individual must be replaced by controlled and rationed trade practices, the short week with a spread of work, the minimum wage and security for those who labor. The immediate objectives he and his associates seek are a rise in commodity prices throughout the world and, of course, disarmament and the preservation of peace among the nations. But beyond and beneath that their quest is for improvement of living conditions of the masses who will dwell in the peaceful new world, exchanging goods on a profitable basis.

This is a general, somewhat technical and idealistic summation of the social aims of the "brain trust" as this non-resident member understands them. But it is at least an answer to a question that has been asked more and more in Washington as the administration's legislative program has emerged, and as increasing interest has been expressed in the fact that many former educators have been busy in formulating the program.

The Professor did not assert to his friend that the President accepts the thesis and all its details, or hopes to make unbreakable plans for so distant a prospect. For example, the President has not yet accepted the items in that plan to mobilize and control business known as the "National Industry Act." But the Professor did say that the President is wholly sympathetic toward what is sought, and he pointed out that in the farm bill and other measures the President has actively sponsored some of the basic ideas.

"The millennium, then, is in sight?"

The Professor stopped at that. The factor of human nature, he feared, prevented that assurance. Cynicism blocks the path. But he said that the struggle, with more powerful political backing than ever before in this country, will proceed.

The subjoined excerpts from my editorial page columns (1934–37) with headings indicative of their contents are offered in the hope that they will somewhat recreate, subject to the limitations of contemporary journalism as history, the course and the atmosphere of the New Deal through the period of its judicial obstructions and great political triumphs that encouraged the President to attempt the ill-fated venture of packing the Supreme Court.

FULL SPEED AHEAD
March 11, 1933

The sensation in Washington for a week has been like that which a person bent on a life-and-death errand thousands of miles away would experience when he changed from an ox-cart to Frank Hawks's airplane.

There is danger in the pace, and we know we may not land precisely where we intend to. But we are getting somewhere. And if swift decision and action, vast political power and the willingness to use it are the chief prerequisites in the pilot, Franklin D. Roosevelt in a week has displayed them all.

Never was there such a change in the transfer of a government. At any rate, no one in Washington remembers the like, and there has been neither leisure nor encouragement afforded for the production by the learned of historical similitudes.

Gone is the dying, functionless Hoover government, though many of its most important members—temporarily and patriotically absorbed into the new one—still labor here.

Gone is the fortress that was the White House; the formal, uneasy place that was the Executive Office; the wild-cat cage that was Congress. Gone, at any rate, for the present. While the President retains his present ways and mood, and his mastery of Congress, these things will remain absent.

It seems hardly likely—so wholly different from the dour and disappointed mood of the last days of the Hoover administration is this driving, confident, optimistic, informal one—that the methods of Mr. Roosevelt and his aides will change.

If he runs into trouble by losing political prestige, or through some other misfortune, it appears improbable that the administration's approach will be any different. The difference would lie in what happens on Capitol Hill.

But for the moment the President is the boss, the dynamo, the works. From the time he arrived here—about forty hours before he was inaugurated—the resistless, endless stream of energy which his body houses poured forth.

At the end of a week so swift-moving and momentous that it contained as many major events as have occurred in the entire administrations of some Presidents, Mr. Roosevelt was strong, cheerful, more than hopeful. When some of the calmest men about him were worrying themselves threadbare, the President kept his shirt on.

During the campaign, and the painful interregnum period, Mr. Roosevelt was much criticized for his smile, for what many believed or feared was innocence of what it is all about. That kind of talk is not heard in Washington today.

Even those who think his remedies desperate admit that the national situation requires such measures. The feeling is spreading that the "leadership" which was promised, and for which so many people voted, has arrived.

Everything so far is on a basis of realism. Completely vanished is that furtive, fearful dealing with unpleasant economic facts which characterized so many members of the Hoover administration.

An example of "the new deal" which has particularly impressed me is the manner in which the President's messages have been dealt with. Aside from the glorious virtues of being short, well-written and clear, the messages have been rapidly prepared after conferences which have lasted for hours.

The President writes a sentence, reads it to those whom he has called in to advise him, takes or rejects a suggestion, writes another sentence and gets through.

The President's first press conference, of which much has been written, was conducted on the same rational basis. Used to the rough-and tumble of press questioning, knowing what he wants to tell, the President puts no limit on the questions, nor asks that they be prepared in advance. He is a veteran of these wars, and this week he showed his medals.

But the observer must always revert to the energy, the cheerfulness and the courage which the President has displayed since the oath was administered a week ago today. He is perfectly aware that his rôle is Blondin on the tightrope above Niagara. But it is necessary to get to the other side, and he is the man who has to make the trip. So Mr. Roosevelt is simply making it.

A review of what he has done since he got here Thursday week is amazing in its revelation of decision and action.

All Thursday afternoon and evening he steadfastly said "No" to the urging of the Hoover administration that he take joint responsibility for the issuance of a proclamation declaring a national bank holiday and laying an embargo on gold.

All Friday and Friday night he continued to resist, saying that he would take what action he considered proper when he had the power to take it. He agreed only to advise the Governors of Illinois and New York that the suggestion made to them of State Bank holidays was sound.

Saturday he went through the ceremonies required of new Presidents of the United States.

The ceremonies ended, he summoned his Cabinet, had it sworn in en bloc and immediately took up the banking crisis. He let it be known that he would immediately summon Congress in extra session and ask for dictatorial powers to deal with present emergencies. By the end of the week they were his, or soon to be his.

Next day, Sunday, Mr. Roosevelt issued two proclamations, one calling Congress for Thursday, the other asserting war-time powers to embargo gold, declare a four-day banking holiday, prescribe prison for hoarders, and full capital liquidity on new deposits.

Monday the President worked steadily on the emergency banking legislation for Thursday. But he did many other things and, as before, saw many people. Tuesday he agreed to abandon the national scrip idea and to accept the new Federal Reserve banknote issue, non-redeemable in gold.

The same high-pressure activity was visible Wednesday. That night the President read his banking bill to the leaders of Congress and got their pledge to pass it the next day so that—as he then hoped—"a large number of banks" could open Friday.

Thursday was like a cyclone: the assembling of Congress, the banking message, the passage of the bill, the extension of the bank holiday by proclamation when the President found that the Treasury and the banks were not ready, and the White House night meeting at which leaders bound themselves to give the President powers usually exercised only by Congress to cut half a billion from veterans' costs and the civil list.

Somewhere in the midst of all this was evolved the "work relief" plan of the $500,000,000 bond issue for Muscle Shoals, flood control and the Boulder Dam. To the last hour of the week the pace was the same.

If leadership and action are what the public wanted, the public now has them.

ENTER THE KEYNESIAN THEORY
June 4, 1934

Never was so well-publicized a man so neglected by the Washington newspaper corps as was John Maynard Keynes, who spent five or six days here last week. If a report in usually well-informed circles is accurate, that was poor judgment on the part of the correspondents. The British economist is credited with having persuaded the President to step up greatly what is called "inflationary spending."

Mr. Keynes is represented by those who talked with him here, and students of his writings on American recovery policy, as firmly convinced of the necessity of the government spending policy. He is a believer in the theory, which was one of the parents of NRA and PWA, that (a) spreading money about the country increases purchasing power; (b) that this increase must be effected before recovery can come, and (c) that therefore it is economically unwise to pay any attention just now to economies or the balancing of the budget.

This theory is buttressed by his belief that in months when the government was the peak of inflationary spending conditions generally showed improvement, and that when inflationary spending lagged the signs of recovery decreased. From this it is an easy step for a convinced logician to argue that the government must augment its spending and keep it up.

If the newspaper group had followed Mr. Keynes's movements with the interest they now seem to have deserved, they would have found that he was much entertained at dinner . . . and that, before the President departed for Gettysburg and the review of the fleet, the British economist was granted a long interview. What was said at this interview is not known, although presumably Mr. Keynes advanced his spending theory. But what followed the interview is significant, and it provides the base for the report among persons who usually know what they are talking about that Mr. Keynes won the President once more to his policy.

Before Mr. Keynes saw the President, the Deficiency Appropriation Bill had been drafted to carry $1,172,000,000 for relief and rehabilitation during the next fiscal year and to turn over a limited amount of unexpended RFC and PWA 1933 balances for the President's use. But the committee was disposed to limit the amount as well as to earmark it for certain purposes. The remainder was to go to the credit of the Treasury, and, as a result, prevailing opinion was that the ten billion dollar deficit, envisaged by the President for June 30, 1935, would be substantially reduced.

But the day after the Keynes-Roosevelt interview, Chairman Jesse Jones of the RFC paid a visit to Chairman Buchanan of the House Appropriations Committee. He told the chairman, and authenticated it, that he came at the President's request. He asked that, in the Deficiency Appropriation Bill, all the RFC unexpended balances for the year be allocated to the President without earmarking for "relief and rehabilitation purposes" during the next fiscal year. The same request was made on behalf of PWA.

In that form the measure was duly reported, and in that form it was passed by the House today. The Senate is expected to follow suit. While the Republicans fear the results on their Congressional candidates of the use of this vast relief fund in the hands of the administration, they as politicians feel that it would be even more disastrous for them to resist the arrangement. After all, they can claim that they helped make it possible for this huge sum to go to their constituents.

The existence and spread of the drought, on which the administration plans to spend $500,000,000 and probably more, helped to accelerate the action of Congress. Members are not such firm believers as Mr. Keynes is reputed to be in the recovery effects of passing out money to the general public (this does not bear, of course, on direct relief—every one is for that). But it is re-election year, and the voices of economy and budget-balancing are so low in Congress as to be almost unheard. Even though the Republicans mutter about the allocation as a Democratic "slush fund," they believe they cannot oppose it safely on that suspicion alone. Thus the President had a set-up.

Chronology is definitely on the side of the report that Mr. Keynes won the President to his spending theory. If that is true, the British writer should now be equipped with a load of coals of fire to carry back to London with him.

PRESS INTERVIEWS FASHIONED ON ROOSEVELT'S METHODS
November 12, 1934

Infused by the President with a spirit of reverent emulation, most of his New Deal executives have gone in for frequent and at least apparently candid press conferences. When General Hugh S. Johnson was running the NRA, the audiences he gave to the press at times rivaled those at the White House. But with the General's retirement the only approach to Presidential competition disappeared, and with it a gift for salty comment that was sui generis.

Nevertheless, there are some worthy pupils of the President among his administrators, and outstanding among these are Secretary Ickes and Federal Relief Administrator Hopkins. They answer questions freely and often pungently, and they do not often prevent publication by labeling a reply "off the record." The President is obliged to do this more frequently than his aides, but he has permitted more to be published of conference material than any of his predecessors.

To conduct press interviews satisfactory to the captious gentlemen— and eager ladies—who represent the newspapers, several important qualities must be in the equipment of the one interviewed. Humor and good nature are appreciated. But what newspaper men value above the rest are candor, clarity, courage and an ability to turn the laugh against the questioner when that is an expedient thing to do. The advantage, of course, lies with the public official, surrounded as he is by the dignity and power of his office and favored by the fact that the questioners are his guests. But even that circumstance doesn't make it easy to hold the upper hand without recourse to pompousness or downright refusal to answer.

The President was a past-master in the art of press audiences before he came to Washington, and he has learned even more since he came. So skilled is Mr. Roosevelt in seeing ahead in newspaper fashion what the effect of a publication will be that his auditors were astonished the other day when he got himself into a jam about Senator Copeland. He read a written endorsement of Governor Lehman's candidacy—the only one he uttered. Reminded that there were others on the Democratic State ticket in New York, he evaded a direct reply.

He said that some people would be surprised to know how often he had voted the Republican ticket, and he refused three opportunities to say that he favored Senator Copeland's re-election. Because of the President's keen knowledge of how to spread an impression without definite commitment, the newspaper men assumed there must be a purpose in his evasion. Therefore they wrote speculatively about it. The result was that the President, arriving next day at Hyde Park, felt obliged to give out a statement that he was for Mr. Copeland, too.

But at the first press conference the President summoned on his return, he showed that he doesn't make the same mistake twice. He was asked specifically if he would comment on the defeat of Governor Ritchie for a fifth term in Maryland. "No," he replied. There was a rustling among the notebooks. Before the busy pencils could fly, the President added that his auditors need not go away and "write a lot of stories about how this refusal to comment was 'fraught with significance.' " He said he simply had not and would not comment on the election or defeat of anyone. That killed in embryo repetition of the Copeland business.

As has been said, Mr. Hopkins and Mr. Ickes are the President's brightest pupils. Their manner invites certain efforts at competitive wise-cracking by the press, but they rarely suffer in the exchange. Mr. Ickes had one experience when, asked about total PWA expenditures, he said he wasn't sure, that every time he went out the door somebody asked him for ten or fifteen millions. "And you usually give it to them, don't you?" tartly remarked an interviewer who did not think the question had been dodged with the skill worthy of the New Deal.

Excerpts from a recent Hopkins press conference illustrate the entertaining character of these encounters. Here is a bit:

Q.—"I hear the Western cattle aren't behaving right?"

A.—"The Western cattle are not? Aren't they having any calves'

Q.—"Are any State relief directors paid by you out of Fe' funds?"

A.—"Yes, Oklahoma and Massachusetts."

Q.—"The reason I ask is that the Republicans are makin' on —— ——, claiming he gets two salaries."

A.—"That is ridiculous. You know it is a funny thing in this office about politics. These people telegraph in here saying so and so is happening. Nobody around our office knows who these fellows are. Then it develops that they turn out to be a candidate for Governor somewhere or other."

A FAMILIAR POLITICAL AUTOPSY
November 13, 1934

The annual concentration of politicians in Washington has begun, and their chief topic of conversation is the future of the Republican party. Many Democrats, some Republicans and practically all radicals seem convinced that the Republican party is dead. Most Republicans do not appear to think that.

They give arresting reasons. One is that the country's long devotion to the two-party system is not demonstrable by the recent election returns as having been succeeded by a preference for one great, dominant party and a group of small rivals. Conceding that the Republican Right and Centre were destroyed by the Democrats last Tuesday, they insist that the land is full of recruits.

Another reason offered is that the President is fostering no successor and that, when he has served two terms, there will be no Democrat to bend the bow of Ulysses, while the Republicans have all that time in which to produce a leader. The hitherto inexorable swing of the pendulum of public preference is also mentioned by Republicans who insist they are not dead. Even as they admit that their party is not, for the present, national in the sense of holding power in all sections, they insist that it held dominance for years without Southern representation and can keep enough strength for recovery during the period when it must do without the Mississippi and the Missouri Valleys.

But oftenest of all, Republicans point to previous false accounts of their party's demise as proof that it is tougher than the Democrats ever admitted. Among the quotations used is this from Henry Watterson in 1912:

The truth is that Roosevelt has made as great a wreck of Republicanism in 1912 as Yancey made of Democracy in 1860. The Republican party seems to be going to pieces as the Whig party went to pieces in 1852. Wilson and Marshall may come in as Pierce and King came in, four States alone dissenting.

As it turned out, the Taft ticket held two States that year, Vermont and Utah. But the Republican party did not die.

There is force in all the reasons given, but exceptions to the logic can be noted. The man whom Watterson credited with probable destruction of the Republican party in 1912 was a Republican, Theodore Roosevelt. The man who is said to have killed it in 1934 is a Democrat, Franklin Roosevelt. Family fights are fiercer than fights with outsiders. But they are more quickly and easily made up. An illustration of this is the fact that the virtual certainty in 1919, when Theodore Roosevelt died, was that he would be nominated by the Republicans for President in 1920.

Whether Franklin Roosevelt has killed the Republican party, which its partisans deny, is something only the future can answer. Certainly he has reduced it to a small Congressional minority, and few States, counties and cities are ruled by Republicans. It is also true that he has surrounded its Left Centre, as in the instance of Senator Vandenberg, who had to promise New Deal support to get himself re-elected in Michigan; and that he has made fast allies of its Leftists and its Progressive stepchild in Wisconsin. In doing all this he has presented to the Republican leaders, as they admit in every conversation, this grave and difficult problem, on the solution of which its future existence depends.

Naturally, there are many conflicting [views] given in the Washington discussions. Some hold with the insurrectos of the Missouri Valley that liberalization of policies and the development of a radical leadership will drive the President and the Democrats Rightward and defeat the Democrats as the conservatives of 1938. But the large majority of the consultants at the anguished patient's bedside express a growing certainty that warm-blooded conservatism maintained for four years of adversity, will bring back the Republican party to health and power. It is a guessing contest at which anyone can play, and the dishes on the tea and dinner tables of the capital are rattling with it these days.

The spectacle of strong men in grief is one to moisten the eyes of the most heartless. It is particularly affecting when one remembers how ʌ customed the Republicans grew to national supremacy in the years 1860 to 1932.

After long debate, the wearied eye of Republicanism se͡ always to Michigan and Vandenberg in the hope that t͡ show the party how to be both for and against the N͡ re-elected.

FARM STATES TURN DEMOCRAT
December 7, 1935

The wind that sweeps north and west from the prairies into Lake Michigan will have important tidings for Franklin D. Roosevelt Monday if he can read the message of the wind. It comes from areas vital to him in his quest for re-election, the farms and cities of the Midwest.

When the President addresses the Farm Bureau convention in the hall just vacated by the finest, fattest cattle the Midwest has seen in many years, he will be conscious of the significance of his words about the farm program. This great and populous area, of which Chicago is the metropolis, hangs eagerly on those words.

Town and country, it is booming. In Chicago both heavy industry and the retail trade are reaching peaks. The department stores, for the first time in many years, advertised no August clearance sales because their shelves were empty. The steel community of Illinois and Indiana is working at 65 per cent of capacity against a national average of 57 per cent.

Farm prices are soaring. A recent hog quotation adding the processing tax, was $12.05–20, as contrasted with $7.50 to $8.30 a year ago. Corn is lower (around 59, as against 94 last year) because it is a new crop. But farmers are feeding it to the hogs and cashing in on the high pork prices. Wheat, on the same day as these other quotations, was 96¼ (40 last year), and cattle registered a high of $11.75, as compared with $9 a twelvemonth since. Butter was up and milk was rising.

In November Montgomery Ward & Co., one of the largest mail order houses in the United States, reported the largest month in its history—30,910,000 sales, an increase of 4,009,000, or nearly 15 per cent. Farmers bought most of those goods, and workers in private industry, on WPA projects and on relief are responsible for most of the city's Christmas trade.

Even though business men and financiers here generally echo their Eastern confreres in attacking the President and his policies, and ascribing recovery to the downfall of his policies (NRA) rather than their triumph, the President will come Monday to a forum roaring with new prosperity.

It may be that private industrial workers can be persuaded by the

Republicans during the campaign, as those who hire them are already persuaded, that recovery has come in spite of the New Deal. It may be that the farmers, who as late as this week have been grumbling at the livestock show, in the hearing of this writer, about "relief waste" and "regimentation," will turn away from the administration. But, unlike their brethren in the East, those in this region who hope for the repulse of the President at the polls next year are not very hopeful of these things.

After only a day in the prairie airs, chatting with people along the country highroads and city streets, hearing from habitués of those "well-warmed and well-stocked clubs" of which the President spoke so scornfully at Atlanta, the change from the attitude of the East is to this writer startlingly visible and audible. The same groups in Chicago and the farm region around it want to see the New Deal swept from office. But, assaying the factors calmly, in the way these people have, putting aside their bitter prejudices, as so many financiers and industrialists in the East never seem able to do, they generally agree that the forecast for 1936 in this part of the country is still favorable for Mr. Roosevelt.

The farmers are grumbling over imports of farm products under the New Deal. In small communities everyone knows who is on relief, and farmers say that the government has been providing for shiftless ones who don't want to perform honest labor.

The activity of Federal agents in the AAA program irks them also. They don't like to be checked up on by Washington, even though they signed agreements that this should be done. If the Republicans can devise some way to produce the same farm prices, and do away with the domination and inspection of Washington, they will have made a move toward getting their natural areas back in the party fold. But that miracle has not yet even been put in rehearsal.

For months in Chicago and the smaller adjacent cities, according to my informants, alarm and resentment have been developing as a result of the piling national debt. The President, pounded on this point by the three largest Chicago newspapers, has been losing ground among growing numbers who want spending curtailed and a formula as to how the bill is to be paid.

To overcome the political lead which the President still holds out here, and to assure that the rate at which he is slipping will be maintained or even accelerated, the Republicans must do a number of difficult things. They must rebuild their party organization, shockingly damaged, for example, in Illinois. They must build up a standard-bearer, for only Senator Borah and Mr. Hoover have any renown in this part of the country. They must select their candidate in harmony, for the Democrats are more united here than in the East.

No one pretends to know what the great masses on the West Side of Chicago, concerned over the rising cost of living, think about the administration of the nation's affairs. But the strength of the Democratic machine operated by Mayor Kelly, with its down-State affiliations, gives Illinois Republicans the blues. The small cities and the farming areas are reverent of the constitutional tradition, they feel certain. And if the Supreme Court should turn thumbs down on the Guffey Law, the Social Securities Act, the Wagner Bill and the Holding Company measure, they believe the Midwest farms will rise against Roosevelt, AAA and all.

Of course, hastily add these lookers-into-the-future, the Republicans must be ready with constitutional forms of social security and farm and labor relief. They may as well realize, too (saith this deponent), that the dream of a clean Republican sweep to the eastern shore of the Mississippi is still a dream.

F.D.R. AS BR'ER FOX
May 16, 1935

Perhaps it is because a combination of political factions and mass groups elected the President that he has permitted and even encouraged his key men publicly to pursue conflicting policies and argue over them in the newspapers. Anti-Hoover Republicans, Progressive Republicans and independents joined with Democrats in giving the President his great electoral and popular vote in 1932, and, reflecting this, his official and advisory groups include men and women of widely differing minds.

One of the most conspicuous examples of this division of opinion is the running public controversy over proper methods of reviving foreign trade. The protagonists, each of a different plan, are the Secretary of State, Cordell Hull, and the Special Adviser to the President, George N. Peek. They are far apart from the standpoint of economic procedure. The President, while he has left action with the State Department in so far as making trade agreements is concerned, has encouraged Mr. Peek to issue a number of statements inferentially belittling the department's activities. It is a matter of actual fact that Mr. Peek, before every publication he has made, has shown his documents and tables to the President and has been specifically authorized to release them "to promote wholesome discussion."

Briefly put, Mr. Hull's view is that the barriers of quotas, tariffs and other obstacles to the free flow of international trade must be swept away before the depression can be conquered. This must be accompanied by other agreements, such as stabilization, but he regards the elimination of trade obstacles as a sine qua non. Reciprocal trade treaties are being negotiated and made by the department as a means to the end. The Hull policy is based on the unconditional favored-nation arrangement, which means that any trade or tariff concession extended to the signatory of any reciprocal treaty must be extended to all other countries.

Except for the reciprocal treaty neogtiated with Cuba, Mr. Peek holds the entire State Department activity barren. His view is that he is a realist, Mr. Hull an idealist, in a severely factual world. Neither by precept nor example, in Mr. Peek's opinion, can the United States change that which is, and he deplores that, just as the rest of the world came in 1922 to the conditional favored-nation arrangement, the Harding administration abandoned it in favor of the unconditional. The method he favors is bilateral negotiation—not bilateral balancing, as has been charged to him—on the conditional favored-nation plan.

The contention that we remain a great creditor nation is wrong, being based on uncollectable war debts and obsolete investment appraisals, according to his figures, which he got from the Department of Commerce. Therefore, the United States should revise its trade policies in the light of the facts. As often as Mr. Peek urges this, Mr. Hull proceeds to invoke the other arrangement, and the President looks on and says nothing at all.

Mr. Peek's office was created by the President under NIRA, which expires June 16 unless it is specifically extended. He is instructed by the President to "keep me informed with respect to our foreign trade"; to bring any trade proposals he may see fit before the proper department; and to collect statistics and compile them for the President's information and use. An understanding of what Mr. Peek has been trying to accomplish can be gained from the following extract from one of his letters:

"Goods for goods" does not necessarily mean a balanced trade with every individual country, for there are some countries, notably suppliers of raw materials, from which we can afford to take far more than we sell them, just as there are other countries which can absorb more of our goods than we can buy from them. * * * At the same time it is to be observed that multilateral or triangular trade must in the first instance rest upon healthy bilateral trade relations. A trade relation in which one party is not paid directly or indirectly for the goods he sends is not a healthy one.

The Special Adviser added that his efforts to correct this condition and put the bilateral relationships on a "paying basis has been interpreted in some quarters as an insistence that trade be balanced country by country, which * * * is far from the fact."

Carpe diem, says Mr. Peek; we need not wait on currency stabilization to "resort to the common-sense principle of Yankee trading, country by country," with a return to the conditional favored-nation plan. No important or permanent revival of foreign trade can thus be attained, says Mr. Hull, and only the unconditional favored-nation plan can reduce tariffs and other barriers to trade.

All foreign trade activities of the government should be unified, says Mr. Peek. Provided the State Department runs it, that is agreeable to me, says Mr. Hull. Among nations pursuing nationalistic policies, like our own, says the Special Adviser, the State Department method belongs in wonderland. To accept nationalism as the world practice, means that we cannot restore foreign trade, says the Secretary.

If he cannot effect his program with this administration, Mr. Peek may respond to such Republican applause as has come recently from Senator Vandenberg, a possible candidate on the other side. As he has said, "I am in politics for agriculture, not in agriculture for politics." He would have a chance to demonstrate his singleness of purpose if the Republican platform of 1936 has a Peek plank.

Meanwhile, in the White House, Br'er Fox he jist lays low.

HUEY LONG'S PROGRAM
January 9, 1936

Once upon a time, according to the fable, the mice met in convention to decide on steps to protect themselves from the cat, and it was decided that a bell should be placed around her neck to warn the mice of her stealthy approach. But none could be found among them to bell the cat.

Senator Huey P. Long's approaches are not stealthy. He proclaimed from far-off New Orleans his intention to address the Senate on the

patronage issue in Louisiana between him and the administration. But it
is more and more evident in Washington that many Democrats feel he is
getting ready to pounce upon their party and absorb all or a large part
of it in 1936, and they would like to hang a bell, or preferably a can,
upon the Senator to protect their electoral votes. This may seem in the
East a fantastic worry. But it is real enough. And up to tonight no
Democratic Senator had been found who felt able to bell the Louisiana
cat after his attack on the administration this week.

In discussions whether there shall be an official party reply to Mr.
Long the sentiments expressed have been reminiscent of the debate
among the mice on the fabled occasion. It may be that Senator Robinson or another will soon arise to attempt the task. But what a very
prominent Democratic Senator said after dinner the other night represents the general attitude of his colleagues toward Senator Long:

"He is brilliant and dangerous. He is industrious and has much
capacity. The depression has increased radicalism in this country—
nobody knows how much. Long is making every preparation to unite it
politically in 1936. Any attempt to squelch him adds to his foundations.
We are obliged to propose and accept many things in the New Deal that
otherwise we would not because we must prevent a union of discontent
around him. The President is the only hope of the conservatives and
liberals; if his program is restricted, the answer may be Huey Long."

The man who said this has rugged political experience, and is a
conservative except when dealing with the leading product of his own
State. Among those who listened and gave general assent were other
prominent legislative followers of the President. No one knows better
than Huey Long how large he has come to bulk in the administration's
plans for 1936. He has a national platform and program ready, and
while he insists that he "probably will not lead a third party" himself,
he firmly asserts that his ideas will be carried under an independent
standard in that campaign.

To this correspondent today—and to a radio audience late tonight—
the Senator gave the outlines of his program. It is based on the thesis
that the national wealth, with curbs largely lifted on production, is
about 500 billions. His "share-the-wealth" plan will cost, he estimates,
about 10 billions a year and "can be put in operation within sixty
days." Under it the Senator predicts there will be "many more million-
aires than now," but it will be practically impossible to be a multi-
millionaire.

The first section of the plan involves an annual capital levy on assets
beyond a million dollars net. Citizens would pay 1 per cent levy on from

1 to 2 millions, 2 per cent from 2 to 3, 4 per cent from 3 to 4, 8 per cent from 4 to 5, 16 per cent from 5 to 6, 32 per cent from 6 to 7 and 64 per cent from 7 to 8. Beyond that capital holdings would be confiscated. Thus, no one could retain more than 3 millions of capital.

Under the second section are regulations of incomes. Higher general income taxes would prevail and no income could legally be retained above 1 million dollars net. On inheritance there would be imposed the same limit. In these two ways the Senator would get his 10 billions to run the country.

And how would he run it? He would devote 3,600 millions a year to social security measures—old-age pensions; guarantees of college or vocational education for everyone "under the Louisiana plan"; a home for every family, and a government pledge that all crops would be taken and surpluses stored by the government. When certain crop surpluses got beyond a certain point, the growers would have to stop growing, and public work would be found to replace their incomes. Also, work-hours would be reduced as a guarantee of employment for all.

In Senator Long's Utopia, billions would be spent on impounding all surplus water—to prevent floods—and releasing it—to prevent droughts. In this and other particulars he marches with the New Dealers. But his "share-the-wealth" tax plan is thus far his very own.

Before readers find themselves laughing too heartily over the Long plan, it may be sobering to record his assertion that he receives as high as 50,000 letters a week, nearly all of them endorsing what he has to propose. Perhaps it is also worth reiterating that a number of major legislative moves being made in Washington these days are made with a weather eye on the Senator's national program.

THE PARAMOUNT ISSUE: ROOSEVELT
April 10, 1936

Men are nearly always, if not always, the campaign issues in this country. Now that the Presidential choice of 1936 grows nearer, the fact becomes increasingly apparent. Many abstract issues are being debated —regimentation as opposed to free industry and a free society; the old guard against the new liberals; the "American way" as contrasted with the New Deal—but more and more surely a man and a personality will dominate the mind of the voter as he goes to the polls on Nov. 3. That man will be the President.

In the campaign of 1932 the nadir of the depression had come to mean Herbert Hoover to the mass of the voting population of the United States. Fair or unfair, he symbolized it in the public mind. In 1934 the beginning of recovery had come to mean Franklin Roosevelt. Fair or unfair, he symbolized it in the public mind. Now in the campaign of 1936 the issue is once more incarnated by the President in this way: Shall he be re-elected as a reward for good sevice and future promise, or defeated as a protection for the budget and against "un-American" tendencies charged to him?

It is only necessary to go into a newsreel theatre to realize how completely this is so. Many members of the audience have read their morning newspapers containing speeches of the candidates. They have glanced over statistics and excerpts from the files purporting to show how each candidate has repudiated a promise or a professed principle of several years ago. Then a face appears on the screen and a voice is heard. It is Alfred M. Landon. Applause or boos, or both. Another figure and another voice—the President. Applause or boos, or both.

* * *

The repeated demonstration that Americans vote on men as they embody issues rather than on the issues themselves, poses the question: are the two ever separable? It would not seem that they are separable any more than hydrogen and oxygen are separable if there is to be water. Men become issues in politics through their personalities and records if in office, and through their personalities and promises if they are contesting for office. The abstract issues are but backgrounds. The actual conditions of life when the campaigns are fought are the platforms on which candidates really stand.

It would seem, then, but surplusage for the Democratic political managers to devote so much time and toil on more than these activities: strengthening the local organizations to bring out the vote; trying to fix in the public mind their own campaign conception of the man who is the basic issue. But in an American political campaign, more than four months of intensive effort is required by custom. In July, August, September and October the interest of the voters must be stimulated. There must be speeches and other forms of public discussion. In the very effort to keep the voter mindful of the candidate, or to divert his thought away from the candidate to an abstract issue (should that be the better strategy) millions of words must be uttered, special trains must dash across the continent, newspaper pages must be filled with attack and defense. Out of this requirement and necessity come what are more commonly called the campaign issues—long rows of words in definition of promise and criticism.

*   *   *

The people, in the Congressional elections of 1934, were given an opportunity to pass judgment on the President. By general agreement the issue in that year was whether Mr. Roosevelt should be encouraged to proceed with the New Deal, as thus far disclosed, in his own way. The answer, in seats in the House and Senate, was overwhelmingly in the affirmative. . . . Such is the Democratic statement of the situation and outline of the 1936 issue.

The Republicans decline to acknowledge the point about the elections of 1934. They insist that the language and type of certain promises made in the platform and campaign of two years before that required meticulous observance of men of honor, and could have been kept without damage to the national welfare. Mr. Hoover (they contend) told only the simple truth when he said that he was conquering the depression at the time the Democrats nominated Mr. Roosevelt, and the country could still have withstood the election result of the following November if the President-elect had been willing to cooperate with President Hoover when the banking crisis became acute in January, 1933.

His refusal to do so made the final crash inevitable, and this represents the flaw in his character from which spring all the other faults attributed to him.

This is the crystallized form of the Republican argument, the reduction of the situation to the basic issue of the campaign, in whatever words it may be stated: the President's personality. For if he is an unreliable, impulsive, mentally dishonest, politically selfish man, much reason is provided for a vote against him. The more voters who can be persuaded that this is a fair appraisal of the President personally— presaging a greater setback to hard-won recovery than prosperity suffered in 1929–32—the better will be Mr. Landon's chances of election.

*   *   *

But Republicans have a broader formula with which to present the issues, and this is how they are roundly stated for the decision of the people:

Mr. Hoover, without abandoning the gold standard, had licked the depression by the Spring of 1932, and had sufficiently recognized new social tendencies and economic needs by the establishment of the Reconstruction Finance Corporation and other forms of Federal relief. The 15,000,000 who voted for him in the following November represented the most responsible members of the American community and those upon whom the progress of the nation largely depends.

When these became aware that nearly 22,000,000, including the irresponsible, unpropertied and radical elements of the people, were certain to defeat Mr. Hoover and elect Mr. Roosevelt, a psychological fear attacked them which brought back the depression in more violent form.

In the month before he took office Mr. Roosevelt accentuated this condition, for the purpose of justifying the New Deal, by refusing to cooperate with Mr. Hoover and thus save the country from the banking crashes. Shortly after he took office he began to attempt to turn the country into a collectivist State, to regiment industry and the individual, to repudiate the national honor, to waste the public funds in un-American experiments and political forms of public relief, and thus to retard the natural forces of recovery.

* * *

From this compression of the voters' case, as separately presented by the spokesmen of the two major parties, it can be seen how definitely and completely Mr. Roosevelt will be the issue on Nov. 3. True, there has been a tremendous publicity build-up for Governor Landon as a simple, honest, frugal, common-sense executive, with precisely the type of ability needed in a job of rehabilitation. But this is partly for the purpose of making a desired contrast between his personality and that of Mr. Roosevelt, and the very motive once more stresses the fact that the President is the inevitable issue whom both sides are recognizing.

Their tactics appear to have been sufficiently successful to presage a far lower popular majority for Mr. Roosevelt if re-elected than he had in 1932, and to forecast certain Republican gains in the House of Representatives which will cancel most of the controverted items in the New Deal.

Should that be the outcome of the struggle, there are many men of

long vision who believe it would be the best fate for the Republican
party at this time and would assure its recapture of the government—
first through the House in 1938 and then through the Presidency in
1940—a period when a clear course can be charted and followed.

* * *

What type of man is this Franklin D. Roosevelt who, if the foregoing
be a truthful estimate of the popular choice, embodies and transcends all
the public questions growing out of his record and his prospect? Opinions differ as widely as the verbal campaign lithographs.

The Republicans say officially that the President is an impulsive, un-
informed opportunist, lacking policy or stability, wasteful, reckless,
unreliable in act and contract. In their speeches and pamphlets Mr.
Roosevelt seeks to supervene the constitutional processes of government,
dominate Congress and the Supreme Court by illegal means and regiment the country to his shifting and current ideas—a perilous ego-
maniac.

The Democrats say officially that the President is the greatest practical humanitarian who ever averted social upheaval, the wisest economic
mechanician who ever modernized a government vehicle to meet new
conditions of road and hill, savior and protector of the American way—
including the capitalistic system—and rebuilder of the nation. In their
campaign documents, and in the sincere belief of many in his organization, Mr. Roosevelt has constructed, with daring and fortitude, a sound
bridge from the perilous past to the secure future.

He is not wholly either, and he is certainly something of both. In the
opinion of this writer he is much more of the latter than the former.

F.D.R. RENOMINATED
June 27, 1936

Under a cloud-veiled moon, in skies suddenly cleared of rain to a mass
of more than 100,000 people gathered in the stadium of the University
of Pennsylvania, and by radio to unnumbered millions all over the nation and world, Franklin Delano Roosevelt tonight accepted the renomination of the Democratic party for President of the United States and,

avoiding personalities of any description, defined the issue of this campaign as it appears to him.

The President said that, as the fathers of the Republic had achieved political freedom from the eighteenth-century Royalists, so it was the function of those who stand with him in this campaign to establish the economic freedom they also sought to establish, and which was lost in the industrial and corporate growth of the nineteenth and twentieth centuries.

The arrival of the President in the stadium was greeted by a real demonstration, as distinguished from the artificial efforts of conventions. One hundred thousand people rose and roared unmistakable acclaim as Mr. Roosevelt entered the platform on the arm of his eldest son and clasped the hand of Vice President Garner while "The Star-Spangled Banner" was sung.

If the high tenor of his speech can be taken as an indication of what sort of campaign he will conduct, Postmaster General Farley's prediction of the "dirtiest" contest of recent times will not be realized, so far as the chief protagonists of the parties are concerned, for Governor Alf M. Landon has implied the same tactics.

The only conceivable reference to Alfred E. Smith and other Democrats who have attacked him that the President made was when he said that some had grown weary of the struggle and relinquished their hope of democracy "for the illusion of a living." The crowd roared approval.

Informed by Senator Robinson that the administration "has vindicated the faith of plain people in the processes of democracy," and confounded those who demanded a dictatorship in 1933, the President took up this major theme, which is also sounded in the Philadelphia platform.

The following is a summary of the President's speech, which was more of a rededication of the New Deal to obtain and secure "economic freedom" than an acceptance speech, outlining a definite program, according to custom:

This occasion is for dedication to a simple and sincere statement of an attitude toward current problems. The speaker comes not only as party leader and candidate for re-election, but "as one upon whom many critical hours have imposed and still impose a grave responsibility."

Fear, which was the most dangerous foe in 1933, has been conquered. Yet all is far from well with the world. The United States is better off than most, but "the rush of modern civilization" has created problems for solution if both political and economic freedom are finally to be attained.

The eighteenth-century Royalists sought to perpetuate their special privileges from the British Crown. They regimented the people in labor, religion and the right of assembly. The American Revolution was fought to win political freedom, and political tyranny was wiped out at Philadelphia July 4, 1776, when the Declaration was penned.

But modern industry and invention have raised new forces that produced new royalists and new dynasties, with new privileges which they seek to retain. Concentration of economic power pressed every citizen into service, and economic freedom—the twin ideal, with political freedom, of Jefferson and Washington—was lost again.

Small business men, with the worker and the farmer, were excluded from this new royalty. "New mercenaries sought to regiment the people."

The collapse of 1929 revealed the new despotism for what it was. In the election of 1932 the people gave to the present administration a mandate to end it. It is being ended.

"The brave and clear platform * * * to which I heartily subscribe, sets forth the inescapable obligations of the government: protection of family and home, establishment of equal opportunity and aid to the distressed."

This generation of Americans has a rendezvous with destiny. Some who have long fought for freedom have wearied and yielded their democracy. Success of the New Deal can revive them. The war is for the survival of democracy, to save "a great and precious form of government for ourselves and for the world."

The President accepts the nomination and is enlisted "for the duration of the war."

SPLIT IN THE HOUSE OF LABOR
July 23, 1936

Each new exchange of defiances between William Green and John L. Lewis, the respective defenders of the crafts and the mass production unions in organized labor, accentuates the fact that in a time when all bodies of normally common thought and interest are dividing, workers offer no exception. Social and political labels all over the country are breaking under the strain of trying to hold dissonant groups together, and the trade-mark of organized labor is surely no stronger than these.

It is now clear that Mr. Green, as president of the American Federation of Labor, faces the gravest decision ever to confront a man in his position. The Committee for Industrial Organization, sponsored by Mr. Lewis, represents a large and highly important percentage of the ranks of organized workers, and no sign is lacking of its determination to effect mass production unions in the industries where it deems them essential to achieve wages-and-hour demands against employers nationally united. Thus far the words spoken by Mr. Green have been equally firm.

But he is beset with risks and disadvantages which do not trouble Mr. Lewis, at least in the same degree. Over the opposition of the C.I.O. he must, if he proceeds, claim for the federation council a power which the Lewis faction insists belongs only to the A.F. of L. convention itself— discipline by suspension or expulsion. If Mr. Green should move the council on Aug. 3 to take a disputed step, his administration must take responsibility for the most serious split ever known in labor ranks, which, if carried through, will mean the break-up of the A.F.L. Thus, the course threatened by Mr. Green will mean a crippling division in the labor group at a time when its most important requirement is unity.

These are the intramural aspects of the controversy between the two outstanding chieftains of organized labor. But there are two others of great weight in attempting to approach a conclusion as to how the strife will end. One relates to the personalities of the two leaders. The other is the political element in a year when everything in American life has a direct connection with politics.

Mr. Lewis is resolute, dominating, a bold and forceful leader of men, pursuing an idea in which he feels a deeper conviction of wisdom and righteousness because it is so largely his own. The union leaders who support him (Sidney Hillman is an example) are the strongest men and have many of the best minds in the organized labor movement.

Mr. Green is not so resolute, cannot be called dominating, and in debate with Mr. Lewis is at a disadvantage. The cabinet supporting him is not as strong, and certainly not as sure, as those around Mr. Lewis.

The President's administration naturally is preserving neutrality in the dispute. To win the election the President must poll the vast majority of the votes of organized labor, and among those supporting Mr. Green are persons who would like to see him defeated and would be quick to avail themselves of the slightest indication that the President is taking sides.

Nevertheless, there are ways known to politicians of taking sides while "preserving neutrality," though this must be done with stealthy skill if more damage than good is not to be the result. The Democratic campaign management is fully aware that Mr. Lewis and his group are almost unanimously—if not wholly that—behind the New Deal and its electoral candidates. This knowledge, if it has no more affirmative effect, at least makes it certain that no administration stone will be placed across the bold path being trod by Mr. Lewis.

Yet conciliation and compromise are so definitely in the interest of all concerned—save those employers who value the immediate advantage they see for themselves, if labor splits, over the probable injury to the general welfare it would entail—that this outcome would reasonably be expected. After all, as Huck Finn realized when he heard the Child of Calamity and the other braggart on the raft tell what they would do to each other—and didn't—the most-publicized impasses are those which are surest accommodated. Yet this one looks less soluble in an era of realignments.

WHY THE CITIES
TURNED DEMOCRATIC
October 19, 1936

Ever since what may have been a million people filled the streets of Chicago to see and hear the President several days ago, the political forecasters have been speculating on the reasons for the size and demeanor of the mass. One widely held opinion, which seems to be soundly based, is that Chicago is peculiarly devoted to the Chief Executive whose administration is coeval with the city's comeback from the deepest gulf in which the depression plunged any American community, with the exception of Detroit.

Chicago's credit had failed with its resources, and for many months its employes went unpaid. Schoolteachers whose pay had long ceased were in the habit of sharing their lunches with children even more distressed than they. Unemployed thousands milled about the streets. The temper of the community was ugly, and those in public and private life who were the leaders of the community were in real fear of the honest violence of the starving.

Quietly the Police Department was prepared for trouble. The station houses were arsenals. An attempt by the late Mayor Cermak to float

three millions of city bonds had failed, less than half having been privately subscribed. About this time Mr. Cermak called at the Chicago
Club a meeting of the leading citizens. What happened at that meeting
has never been published in detail. But one who was present said today
that these things occurred:

Mayor Cermak told the important bankers, lawyers, industrialists,
clerics, labor leaders, journalists and others present that he accepted his
responsibility for maintaining order and civilization in the town. He
said he owed this duty to the propertied class before him, but he owed it
also to the destitute. He explained the city's financial situation and then
gave a brief but alarming description of the mood of the masses. His
narration was supported by others.

Up rose Silas Strawn, leading lawyer and president of the Chamber of
Commerce of the United States. Just previously Daniel Willard, president of the Baltimore & Ohio Railroad, had been quoted in the press as
saying that if his family were starving and he could not find work, he
would get them food if he had to obtain it by violence. Mr. Strawn, his
normally ruddy countenace pale, his manner impressive by its gravity,
echoed that sentiment for himself and appealed to those present to
underwrite the remainder of the bond issue. In a short time there were
more bids than bonds.

Some time afterward Mr. Roosevelt became President and Washington began to relieve cities in Chicago's general condition which had discovered the difficulties of self-sustenance in such times. The RFC
changed its policy and, visited by a Chicago committee, agreed to buy
Chicago relief bonds (these it later sold at a premium to banks which
had refused to buy them from the city). The dawn of recovery appeared, and the light of hope grew swiftly into the midday of renewed
business activity. Chicago still has relief problems, slums, poverty and
great groups of the unemployed. But the difference between present conditions and those when the city's representative citizens met with Mayor
Cermak is the difference between black and white.

It is the opinion of many that the people of Chicago generally associate the President's recovery and relief policies with that change. Conceding his mistakes, they are grateful for his achievements and resentful of
the newspaper attacks which, led by the Hearst press and The Chicago
Tribune, and less frenziedly by Colonel Knox's Daily News, here have
reached a crescendo of bitter bias.

Another factor of great strength for Mr. Roosevelt here, which doubtless was reflected in the size of last week's throng, is the sympathetic attitude toward him of the eminent Catholic hierarchy in this city and State, chief of whom is Cardinal Mundelein. He and several of his Bishops are represented as believing that Mr. Roosevelt's re-election is necessary definitely to rout the forces of social radicalism.

F.D.R. ASKS AUTHORITY
TO NAME NEW JUSTICES
February 6, 1937

The President suddenly, at noon today, cut through the tangle of proposals made by his Congressional leaders to "bring legislative and judicial action into closer harmony" with a broadaxe message to Congress recommending the passage of statutes to effect drastic Federal court reforms.

The message—prepared in a small group and with deepest secrecy— was accompanied by a letter from the Attorney General and by a bill, drawn at the Department of Justice, which would permit an increase in the membership of the Supreme Court from nine to a maximum of fifteen when judges reaching the age of 70 declined to retire; add a total of not more than fifty judges to all classes of the Federal courts; send appeals from lower-court decisions on constitutional questions direct to the Supreme Court, and require that government attorneys be heard before any lower-court injunction issue against the enforcement of any act of Congress.

Avoiding both the devices of constitutional amendment and statutory limitation of Supreme Court powers, which were favored by his usual spokesmen in Congress, the President endorsed an ingenious plan which will on passage give him the power to name six new justices of the Supreme Court.

Under the provisions of the bill drawn by the Department of Justice for Congress, if the six now-sitting justices who are more than 70 years of age do not resign, the President is empowered to name a new member for each justice in that category. These are the Chief Justice and Justices Brandeis, Van Devanter, Butler, McReynolds and Sutherland. Thus, after the passage of the bill, which is generally expected, the court will number anywhere from nine to fifteen justices.

Although the message—an unusually long one for the President— was a general criticism of the effects upon government and private

litigants of overburdened courts and superannuated judges and stressed
a general plea to Congress to make provision for "a constant and syste-
matic addition of younger blood" to "vitalize the court," Congress instantly recognized its outstanding feature and purpose.

Although the message outlined basic defects in the administration of
justice in the United States, and contained many reforms to which no
exception will be taken, Congress quickly sensed that the President had
hurdled the present majority of the Supreme Court on his way to the
goal he outlined in his opening message of the session. This, as he stated
it, is to find "means to adapt our legal forms and our judicial interpretation to the actual present needs of the largest progressive democracy in
the modern world."

While all of the legislative and executive personnel of the government
and the press gallery buzzed all day with discussion of the President's
imitation of Alexander the Great and the Gordian knot, the justices of
the Supreme Court, in public at any rate, maintained complete and dignified silence.

It was noted that once more the magic number six finds favor in the
President's mind. He used to talk of cutting the Cabinet down from ten
to six. Then he approved the Brownlow committee's recommendation of
six executive assistants "with a passion for anonymity." Today it is the
Supreme Court which is to be increased by six if the bill passes, and the
justices now over 70 years of age are all alive and refuse to resign.

It was also noted that the President announced his plan a few days
before arguments on the Wagner act begin in the Supreme Court, and in
a week when a judicial order—in Flint, Mich.—has been disregarded
both by government and by the private parties to the controversy which
produced the writ.

THE DEEP SCARS
OF F.D.R'S DEFEAT
July 24, 1937

The President has taken a terrible beating from the Senate in the controversy over enlarging the Supreme Court. He staked his leadership
upon this "objective" and he had to permit the complete surrender of
his leaders—for this session at least—to the combination of Democrats
and Republicans who refused to follow him.

This is the plain statement of facts of major consequence to the future influence of Franklin D. Roosevelt in administrative and political affairs, and therefore of supreme bearing on the course of the nation in the immediate, and possibly the distant, future.

The chief blow was to the President's prestige, and, as in the case of any political leader, prestige is a wide and deep source of power. In asking for legislation to recruit the Supreme Court with six appointees of his own, the President took a sudden and surprising initiative and followed it with two aggressive speeches. For months, when the opposition was willing to compromise on fewer justices—thus, with the change in the court's legal philosophy, completely achieving his "objective"—he had been unyielding as to method.

When the rising tide of resistance forced him to yield on method, he backed a substitute of the same general tenor, and upon the sudden death of Senator Robinson reassumed the leadership in an effort to hold the narrow majority Mr. Robinson had acquired.*

In every particular, therefore, the issue was between the President and the opposition and that is why the defeat was personal. Thus, it must be assayed in personal terms. But, since the individual is head of the Republic and the Democratic party, and is perhaps the world's most powerful statesman, the personal equation affects the nation and the world.

As soon as the abandonment of the plan for this session was an accomplished fact, efforts began on several sides to make it appear that the President's leadership has not been seriously affected.

Intertwined in these arguments is generally counsel to the President that he announce his surrender to Congress on Supreme Court enlargement, and the prophecy that, if he does this, no important damage to him will have been inflicted.

The President does not believe in open concessions. Should he never return to his crusade it will not be on such a statement of the case. It will come from one of these reasons:

More retirements of elderly justices, which will achieve his objective indirectly, and persuade him he could never make the "country" support legislative enlargement (which might bring him to the method of an amendment).

Persuasion that he cannot "rally the country" to give him a specific

* Senator Joseph Robinson, Democrat from Arkansas and Senate Majority Leader, led efforts in the Senate to approve the Court-packing legislation.

mandate, and a resultant conclusion that he had best not risk the remainder of his prestige in such a cause. Indications of a turn in this direction seemed visible at Friday's press conference.

Should the retirements come, it is entirely probable that the Senate's
action this week will not have taken from the President his administrative or political leadership. On every hand people would say "Well, he
got what he was after, anyhow," and laugh admiringly. That attitude
might well repair the effect of the demonstration that the President can
be beaten in a public issue and that his threats do not cause instant
political death.

But if Mr. Roosevelt openly abandons, or permits to dissipate in mere
words his reiterated position that the Supreme Court must be changed
by statute to enable him to deal with conditions presaging new crises,
the nation and Congress are full of men and women who will strike at
him again in a determination to be rid of his influence and his program.
Having proved him vulnerable in a battle to which he brought all his
weapons and a reputation of invincibility, their next assault, if well-
chosen, will be easier.

Only if, through retirement or death in the Supreme Court, the President wins can he hope to regain the full measure of his leadership
while consigning his legislation to words written for posterity.

If the President accepts this view, which is widely held by political
observers, he will—barring developments in the court personnel—
resume his battle on some field and by some tactics as yet undisclosed.
That was his intention on the night when his leaders, their lines shattered by Mr. Robinson's death, told him of their necessity to surrender.

When a report spread that the President himself was an active principal in the program of abandonment, I asked someone very near him,
physically and otherwise, if that were true. The answer, after inquiry,
came as a quotation: "Never as long as he lives!"

In the court fight there was assembled an odd combination of liberals
and conservatives, banded together partly because of their dislike of the
proposed legislation, partly because some of them want to check the
President, partly because some of them want to check future Presidents
with designs on the two other coordinate branches.

On all points of the Roosevelt legislative program that combination
will not hold. But on the point of future Democratic party control
enough liberals are now in a mood to stand with the conservatives to
balk any Presidential move which can be construed as an effort to repair
political damages to the administration with 1938 and 1940 in mind.

F.D.R.'S PHILOSOPHY
AND POLITICS

It seems incredible, at this distance from the event, that Roosevelt, only a few months after his overwhelming re-election, could have provided such grievous evidence of a fundamental fact of politics in a democratic society. This is that, however deeply entrenched in popular favor a politician may be, he is as vulnerable as the least of his breed to the disaster of miscalculating his own strength. Roosevelt did this when he decided to replace the current Supreme Court majority with a majority of his own choice, in the hope that it somehow would find constitutional warrant for his proposed legislation—legislation that might be quite dubious on that score.

Roosevelt eventually attained the worthier substance of his objective. Deaths, resignations, and brilliant leadership by Chief Justice Hughes of a retreat, by several of the Brethren, from the concept that the Constitution permitted no flexibility of interpretation—by these developments the Court majority was changed from obstructive to sympathetic toward the inventive legislative programs of the New Deal. And I have always thought the President might have had his will of the Court almost immediately if he had not resorted to trickery so transparent that many in Congress who shared his objective were left politically defenseless from its opponents.

But the President was fully aware in the early stages of the battle that he had undertaken an unpopular venture in which even he, despite

46

his almost unanimous re-election, could suffer deep and lasting damage as the leader of the nation. He was in that mood when, in the week of February 27, 1937, I proposed he grant me an interview for publication. In this, I suggested, he could take note of charges that he sought to be a dictator in fact and was already making plans for election to a third term.

Roosevelt agreed. The dispatch which follows records the first and only interview authorized for publication, including direct quotes, that he gave in the 13 years of his Presidency. It was submitted to him beforehand, and, though he suggested that the headline should be "quiet," he made only a few minor changes of the language.

THE PRESIDENT DISCUSSES
HIS POLITICAL PHILOSOPHY
February 27, 1937

"When I retire to private life on Jan. 20, 1941," the President this week has been saying to his friends, "I do not want to leave the country in the condition Buchanan left it to Lincoln. If I cannot, in the brief time given me to attack its deep and disturbing problems, solve those problems, I hope at least to have moved them well on the way to solution by my successor. It is absolutely essential that the solving process begin at once."

This is his answer to those who have contended that the President has a third term in mind, and would remake the Supreme Court majority for a period of submissive cooperation with the other Federal divisions that will exceed the precedental time for chief executives. And it is his answer also to those who insist that nothing in the present condition of the country calls for new haste in an attack on problems, and that nothing will be lost by awaiting the long process of a constitutional amendment. Doubtless he will make these responses in detail for himself before the argument about the Supreme Court is ended by triumph, defeat or compromise.

Responses from him are expected, for, though it is only a few weeks since the Presidential election of 1936, the cry of "dictator" once more is heard. The provocation is Mr. Roosevelt's recommendation to Con-

gress of a statute whereby all Federal judges—including those of the
Supreme Court—must retire at the age of 70 or have a judge of equal
powers appointed to supplement them.

Since the effect of the President's proposal would be to supervene the
present Supreme Court majority with his own appointees if judges eligible to retire refused to do so, or to nominate a new majority if they did,
he has been widely accused of intending to supplant the Federal system
of checks and balances with one-man government, assure decisions upholding any legislation he might propose and offer to some future
dictator a precedent with which, with the approval of Congress, he
could, by changing the age-limit, wholly remake the Supreme Court
when he took office or increase it to the size—and reduce it to the
futility—of a mass meeting.

In discussing with the President these charges and the proposals
which produced them, the writer became conscious of Mr. Roosevelt's
complete certainty that the accusations are all founded in a misconcep-
tion of his aims and their consequences, in a total lack of understanding
of the crisis which confronts the country and calls for drastic remedies,
and in a failure to appreciate how sincere and sure is his labor to maintain democracy rather than to suspend it or undermine its future foundations.

In the President's view—and discussion with him makes it clearer—
the Supreme Court issue is but part of a larger problem: how to make
democracy work in a world where democracy has in many lands been
subvented. He believes that within the American democratic machine
are all the essential devices. He feels they must be boldly grasped and
employed to save democracy itself. Far from agreeing that recourse to
statutes, within the plain permissions of the Constitution, to sweep away
barriers to orderly progress and modern needs is an encouragement to
future dictatorships, he is firm in the faith that this method stamps out
the dictatorial seed. His belief is that legalistic or other obstructions to
"action by our form of government on behalf of those who need help"
are the real incentives to revolutions from which demagogues and
dictators emerge. What he has done and is doing are to him the definite
solvents of democracy.

The President believes it is necessary not only for the Federal Government to be able to regulate against overproduction and underproduc-
tion, to regulate against unsocial types of employment and against the
making of prices by speculation, but that it is also necessary for the
Federal Government to have some authority to compel collective bargaining and to enforce the maintenance of contracts both by employers

and employes. He feels that, today, there is real danger to the nation because any law passed by the Congress to provide national remedies is open to constitutional doubts if the language of the present Supreme Court majority is literally followed. In this connection, the President compares present conditions to a dead-end street.

The President, by reading and observation, and by tried and unusual familiarity with the attitude of Americans toward their public men, sees a future far more dangerous if he is balked of his solutions than if they are adopted. He sees a growing belief among the underprivileged that judicial supremacy is certain to cancel the progressive and humanitarian efforts of Congress and the Executive. He sees this belief easily firing into a desperate conviction, and he does not doubt that, should this happen, a leader will arise to tread down democracy in the name of reform.

The President has not forgotten Huey P. Long. While he does not say so in precise words, he entertains the opinion that one important reason why the Louisiana dictator was not able to extend his dominion further during his lifetime was because he was fortunately co-existent with wiser and more sincere remedies for the conditions which produced Long. In other words, had public opinion against the Hoover administration not been sufficiently formed by the elections of 1932, and had Mr. Hoover therefore been re-elected, the President believes that Huey Long would immediately have become a great menace to the democratic process.

Now, finding—from his viewpoint—essential, legal and democratic Federal action obstructed by the Supreme Court majority, or held in long uncertainty that has the effect of balking both preventive and remedial measures for what Mr. Roosevelt thinks ails the country, he sees the possibility at least that a new, more appealing and even more ruthless demagogue may arise to abolish American democracy for years. Whether a listener agrees with the President in his course and in his estimate of future menace, that listener notes in his words and tone no other primary objective than, as Mr. Roosevelt sees it, the preservation and the restoration of democracy.

Although there are many manifests of recovery, the number of the unemployed and the national relief bill impress the President with the certainty that much remains to be done if social dangers shall be averted and economic stability be attained. In averting social dangers and attaining economic stability, the President sees the assurance of continued democracy. That is what he is determined to assure, and he finds as natural attendant circumstances a better spread of income, steady work for the employable, a good standard of living, protection for the aged, opportunity for the young, and national action. The program to effect these benefits, which the President never thinks of save as human rights, is, to his mind, the program to keep American democracy working. At times the President is faced with this sort of problem in moving his program:

For one reason or another, a measure of national action which to him is essential to safeguard democracy comes newly into council and therefore has not been included in any specific mandate. Do the people expect him, and does fair dealing require, that he seek a popular referendum before proceeding?

If the President is convinced that the measure is effective, and that time is of its essence, he goes ahead. Since all such enterprises—this being a democracy—must first pass the Congressional test, the President sees in Congress itself a sufficient referendum in vital instances. It is true that Congress is made up of politicians, and, since 1932, that it has been dominated by members of the political group of which the President is party leader. But in conversation Mr. Roosevelt points out also that, being largely politicians, with district or State responsibility, members of Congress, if only for political self-preservation, submit his proposals to the test of public opinion, and to the further test of the democratic process. These tests, in conjunction with the full and free debate which is the privilege of the Senate, seem to the President to answer the charge that in any legislative request he ever tries "to put anything over" on the people.

He points out, for example, that many of his proposals to the Congress during the past four years have been either rejected by the Congress or have been so amended as to change them greatly—i.e., social security, bonus, $4,800,000,000 relief bill, &c.

He has been moving, through the medium of civil service reform, to withdraw political patronage from the Federal equation, and this will be well out of the sphere of Presidential influence over Congress if and when the government reorganization plan is adopted. Therefore, in the view of Mr. Roosevelt, the response of Congress to his recommendations is more and more a clear reflection of its free opinion as to the degree to which he represents wide and accredited popular leadership.

The President comes to the issue of the mandate with which he has been entrusted by the people with recent experience strongly in mind. He found it necessary, after taking office in 1933, to divert the course plotted by the party platform on which he was elected because of a change in conditions between June, 1932, and March, 1933—a change which all economic research and statistics reflect. In the Congressional campaign of 1934 this diversion was made an issue by the Republicans, and in return Democratic candidates for Congress offered the President himself as the only issue. "Shall Franklin D. Roosevelt's course thus far be approved and he be given a Congressional majority to proceed with the New Deal?" was the question as the people went to the polls in 1934. Overwhelming documentation of this is available in the political writings and oratory in that campaign. The answer was overwhelmingly in the affirmative.

In 1936 the President's diversion of course was again made an issue by the Republicans, who also pointed out that, if re-elected, he would probably have several new appointments to the Supreme Court. The age of many justices, if nothing else, was used to illustrate the certainty that, if re-elected, the opportunity to change the court majority would come to Mr. Roosevelt. Whether or not the voters troubled themselves much on that point the President does not know. But he does know that once again his course was given high majority approval, and 27,000,000 voters decided to put the country's fate in his hands for four more years.

The Philadelphia convention had promised "a clarifying amendment" to the Constitution if problems arising in the Supreme Court could be disposed of in no other way. The President, in December, 1936, decided that the amendment process requires too much time for the country's needs and security. He feels that, by the general permissions of 1934 and 1936, he was given ample mandate to attempt what upon mature consideration, and even altered method, he thinks is best. Therefore, he does not for a moment believe that the majority which has supported him in full measure in three national elections shares the feeling that he has exceeded his permission. Nor does he consider that the American majority expected him to have been able, in what he views as a shifting and perilous time, to chart in detail and in advance the measures he might finally employ to achieve the end stated and, as he is certain, desired by the people.

Furthermore, the President by no means discards into finality "a clarifying amendment" as mentioned in the Democratic platform. Such an amendment, he argues, would be necessary if the problems cannot be disposed of otherwise. He takes the view that the great majority of both houses of the Congress, including many Republican members, believed in passing the New Deal bills of the past four years and that these bills were constitutional. He holds, as he stated in this year's annual message to the Congress, that the Constitution definitely permits the Congress to legislate in regard to the production of crops and the production of manufactured articles which enter generically as products into commerce between the States. It is his contention that the Constitution does not forbid regulation of railroads or communications or trade practices and that, if the same rules were applied in the case of commodities of all sorts, unwieldy crop surpluses, starvation wages and unfair trade practices could be eliminated with the objective not only of improving social conditions but also of averting future panics.

If newer and younger blood in the Federal courts does not result in decisions which accord with the views of the majority of the members of the legislative branch and the views of the President, he is then wholly willing to admit that a clarifying amendment to the Constitution will be necessary.

In a time of public controversy, "so much," the President has said, "depends on what newspaper you read." Which is another way of saying that one's mental approach to an argument often forecloses the effect of that argument on one's conclusion—an indisputable fact. The President takes as an example of mental approach and inflection the wide use made on Feb. 22 of extracts from Washington's Farewell Address against his Supreme Court program.

Suppose, he says, the reader begins his perusal with remembrance that Washington wrote the words in 1796 before the Supreme Court had attempted to override an act of Congress without the specific warrant of the Constitution. It is, then, in his opinion, wholly logical to read the warning words of the Father of His Country against usurpation as a criticism of the course the Supreme Court has followed in many decisions since it assumed the power of invalidating. Why, he asks, does not this passage more forcibly apply to the majority reasoning in the AAA or Guffey Act cases (denounced by minority members of the court itself) than to any act of the Executive since 1796:

"It is important, likewise, that the habit of thinking in a free country should inspire caution, in those entrusted with its administration, to confine themselves within their respective constitutional spheres, avoiding in the exercise of the powers of one department to encroach upon another," &c.

From the time he entered public life, the President has maintained as his goal the preservation of the American form of democracy. He thinks it still needs preserving, not from his forms or persuasions, but from those who have prospered most under it and returned least. He believes that his program stopped the descent of the capitalist system, threatened by enemies within and without. He wants to raise and firmly buttress it against the attacks of these enemies by the time he leaves office "on Jan. 20, 1941."

A RECEDING POPULARITY

Implicit in this exegesis of his political philosophy, this pragmatic vision of the United States he hoped to leave as his monument, was Roosevelt's awareness that his honeymoon with Congress and the electorate was coming to an end. It had been less than four months since the people registered the largest endorsement of a President in the history of the Republic. But Roosevelt had overreached himself; he knew it; and he was engaged in repairing his damaged leadership.

In 1937, Roosevelt's very real popular majority of 1936 was patently receding. The vast powers over the economy which all groups of the people had urged upon him in 1933 and confirmed to him in the 1936 elections, and which he had used beyond limits theretofore found in the Constitution, had failed to accomplish actual economic recovery. Deficit, largely "make-work," spending was rising in company with the unemployment percentage, whereas the New Deal economic theory was that, as the first rose, the second would fall.

The great Depression of 1929-1933 had settled into a stubborn recession. Roosevelt's awareness of deepening trouble which was implicit in the February, 1937, interview was verified in the Congressional elections of 1938.

As reflected in the three dispatches which follow, the Congressional Democratic dissenters from the New Deal political theology had been emboldened by the President's defeat in his attempt to pack the Su-

53

preme Court. The legend that he was invincible in any undertaking had been badly damaged. So Roosevelt decided on a bold venture in party politics to restore it. This venture was to challenge the renominations of selected leaders among the dissenters by urging their rejection in speeches in their home constituencies, the famous and ill-fated "purge" in the spring and summer of 1938. Among the six he chose to eliminate from Congress were Senators Millard Tydings of Maryland and Walter F. George of Georgia, both deeply entrenched in States where a charge of "outside interference" in party primaries was traditionally a source of deep popular resentment.

As the event proved, this reached even to intervention by a most powerful President of the United States and leader of the national Democratic party. Of the six Democrats he had marked for "purging," only Rep. John O'Connor of New York City, the chairman of the Rules Committee, was denied renomination by his constituents. And the bitter intra-party division the President engendered was a contributing factor to the loss of Democratic seats in 1938, as James A. Farley had prophesied in his vain effort to dissuade Roosevelt from intervening personally and directly in the party primaries.

BELIEVERS AND UNBELIEVERS
January 8, 1938

One hundred and twenty-three years ago today Andrew Jackson won a battle against the British which was fought only because neither side knew peace had already been declared. As his party descendants celebrate the victory at New Orleans, some of them are accused of reversing Jacksonian history by fighting a battle to prevent a declaration of peace, because they know the terms would be unfavorable to them.

That battle is the revived policy struggle—produced by the business recession—between two groups of Democrats influential in public affairs. While each group is subdivided, they roughly represent the main division of the argument. It is not very illustrative to call them the Right and the Left, since nearly all of them are pretty well Left of pre-1932 Democracy with respect to methods of carrying out general objectives which nearly all profess. Perhaps for one writing they can be called the Believers and the Unbelievers.

The Unbelievers—so called because they reject the thesis of a selfish "capital strike" to cancel the social progress of the last few years—ascribe the recession largely to a lack of confidence in the stability and competence of the government. They propose fundamental modification of the tax laws; more frugal Federal housekeeping; localizing of the relief distributions; extension of the Hull tariff policies; equal treatment of labor with capital; consolidation rather than extension of New Deal activities; retirement of the government from competition with private industry; a moratorium on happy thoughts of favored White House economists; and suppression of the "hate" psychology.

The Believers—so called because they think government must be active and disciplinary on many fronts to stabilize recovery—have an entirely different program. They think big business has influenced little business to join with it in a capital strike in an effort to regain the brutal immunities of 1929. They deny all responsibility for a basic lack of confidence. They have decided the conduct of big business has been such that it is time to try the O. M. W. Sprague economics of 1933. These envisaged a non-monetary series of direct approaches to each economic problem, such as forcing housing and other construction by driving down material and labor costs and founding revival on the heavy industries.

The sincere Believers—for many of them are politicians who do not think what they say, when they think at all—are convinced that government must crack down to force a period of high production volume and low prices. By the latter they do not mean bringing all prices down to the present lowest level in consumers' goods. They want to raise some of the lowest ones and reduce nearly all of the highest ones, merging the price lines at a certain level on which increased factory employment, they are certain, will comfortably rest.

To accomplish their design means renewed government activity—at a time when the Unbelievers are calling for less—for correlation of supply and demand in all fields, particularly agrarian production, under Federal auspices or through light Federal supervision; for reorganization of government agencies so as to produce a neater pattern of policy, and for legislation to eliminate very low wages and very high hours everywhere in the United States.

Their immediate weapons are litigation against those heavy industries which they charge with collusion in keeping up the price of building materials, and pressure on labor to revise disproportionate wage scales in these trades. Litigation would take the form of anti-trust suits striking at high price levels and stagnant capital.

In the present state of industry the Believers have convinced the President they are right, and his policy is undergoing a definite transition in the direction of theirs.

Basic in this policy is what Assistant Attorney General Robert H. Jackson said in his radio debate this week with Wendell L. Willkie. He contends that private enterprise always has had concealed subsidies, that it has never been self-supporting. Land grants, the tariff, World War orders which stimulated growth of plants, and surpluses which were exported and paid for in foreign loans: these and other hidden subsidies, as important New Dealers see it, have always existed to support private enterprise. The alternative is to make it self-sustaining through open subsidies, the aim being increased volume and low prices.

Private enterprise, thus openly subsidized by government to bring it to the goal of sustaining itself, must then, of course (in this philosophy), accept government discipline. Upon business's honest and intelligent conduct the degree of that discipline will depend. Meanwhile the log jam on prices, production and employment should be broken by resort to enforcement of the anti-monopoly statutes, amending them after an inquiry to determine what amendments would make them more effective for free competition. This is the nub of Mr. Jackson's economic program, and it is widely supported in the government group.

Last March Dr. Leon Henderson, one of the topmost of the President's economists, in accurately predicting the recession to some textile men, endorsed the direct, non-monetary approach to national problems. He advocated "full use of government powers to prevent excessive price increases in the monopolistic industries; the use of the tariff; the use of taxation powers" and legislation to fortify purchasing ability in the low-income groups. "To maintain democratic processes and avoid authoritarian controls," he said, the government must "control credit through its monetary mechanisms, proceed against the most vicious of the monopolies * * * and there must be a considerable drawing off at the top and putting in at the bottom of purchasing power."

'HISTORIC CONVERSATION' BETWEEN F.D.R. AND THE MAYOR
November 7, 1937

It has been one of the more modest claims of a favorite clairvoyant that she can reveal what goes on within any four walls while it is happening. Accordingly in shameless disregard of several sets of ethics, on the pretext that it was an obligation he owed to the reporting of contemporary history, this correspondent repaired at 2:30 o'clock Thursday afternoon of last week to the mystic Harlem headquarters of Madame Tussaud.

Madame was at home and entirely willing, for the usual consideration, to demonstrate her occult powers. She readily agreed to link her spiritist recording device to a house in Sixty-fifth Street, just off Park Avenue, where a recently re-elected Mayor was about to confer with a less recently re-elected President.

It appeared, however, that before the ears of a client could be attuned to spiritual vibrations it was necessary for him to drain a foaming draught prepared by Madame Tussaud herself.

Skeptics will probably insist that what this correspondent then heard, and hereafter sets down, was a message received in a dream. But dream or reality, it was the following:

The President: Glad to see you, Fiorello, my old, old friend. I knew you could do it, and it's great for the undernourished third.

The Mayor: Thank you very much, Mr. President.

The President: You know Harry here, and good old Jim.

The Mayor: Put it there, Harry. Yes, I certainly know Jim.

Harry and Jim: Congratulations, Mr. Mayor.

Jim: You can see the fix I was in, Mr. Mayor.

The Mayor: I can see the fix you are in, Jim, yes.

Harry and Jim: Well, good luck, Fiorello. (*They depart.*)

The President: Fiorello, that was a wonderful victory for us. The voters in the greatest city in the country agreed with me—and with you, too, I mean—that the word is "forward." You knew, of course, I was with you all along.

The Mayor: Well, I heard something about it, but I wasn't sure. There was Bob Wagner saying labor owed its votes to Democrats only, and Bob has a strong voice with labor and he is known as your devoted friend and supporter. There was Herbert Lehman saying that he, not me, was responsible for the city's sound credit. And there was Jim— good old Jim—saying that a vote for Mahoney was a vote for you.

The President: Now listen, Fiorello, that was just politics. You know how it is. You are an irregular in politics, and I'm glad of it. But you can't afford to be that in a State or a national race. You've got to stand by a party label. Jim and Herbert and Bob, in their names and in mine, have asked the Democratic organizations for support time and again. They've got to give it in return, or what becomes of our party system and our organization? Jim wants to be Governor and there's 1938 to remember, and 1940.

The Mayor: Hum. Yes. There's certainly 1940. I wonder where we'll both be then, Mr. President.

The President: Why, helping to nourish the undernourished third, helping to house the ill-housed third, helping to get jobs for the unemployed third, Fiorello, as we are doing now.

The Mayor: Who'll be helping who? Will you be helping me silently, as you did this time, or audibly, as I have been supporting you all along? And will the firm be Roosevelt & La Guardia, as it is now, or La Guardia, formerly Roosevelt & Son?

The President: It'll be all right. Everything is going to be all right. The country will be all right. The party—our party—will be all right. John Lewis will be all—

The Mayor: Did you see what happened in Detroit?

The President: Indeed, I did, Fiorello. A good lesson for some people. It will teach them to support me—I mean us—in our names instead of trying to run the thing themselves. Now look at your election. My labor party came through and elected you. That was right. That was just. I assure you now that we'll stand by you as long as you stand by us for the best interests of the country.

The Mayor: Who is "us"? Do Bob, Herbert and Jim come in as "us"? If they had their way I'd be back in Yorkville.

The President: It was politics made them do that, as I explained. We'll have the situation all ironed out by 1940. You know Bob hated to do it. And Herbert wouldn't have done it if you hadn't been nominated by the Republicans. As for Jim, you know how faithful he is to me. I tell him sometimes he is as faithful as a dog.

The Mayor: Yes, that reminds me of something Senator Ollie James of Kentucky once said to Senator Owsley Stanley of Kentucky. Stanley's chief henchman was opposing James for re-election, and Ollie complained to Owsley about it. "Why, he's a fine fellow," said Stanley.

"He's my dog." "I know," said Ollie, "but why does your dog bite me?"

The President: Well, it worked out all right, didn't it? And remember I was always for you and stopped the boys from doing lots of things they wanted to do after the battle got hot. Jim was just pinning a rose on Mahoney. He had to do it. I always knew you would win.

The Mayor: Oh, you did? Well, of course, I wouldn't suggest such a thing. But if you always knew I was going to win, wasn't it better you kept out of the fight and got some of your boys to lay off? Naturally, such an idea never entered your head. But if it had—mind you, I say *if* it had—considering what may happen in the next four years, the party shifts and all that, you would have been a fox to act that way. Everybody says you are a fox. That would surely be being one.

The President: Ha-ha. That would have been slick, Fiorello, wouldn't it? But, as you say, I never thought of it. I was just thinking of the undernourished, ill-housed—

The Mayor: I know you were. And thanks for being for me all the time. It's nice to think we can go on working together, for a while, anyhow.

The President: Years more, Fiorello.

The Mayor: Yes, sir, for a while, anyhow.

The President: I think you'll find I'm right when I said "years more." I'm young yet. When I get through sharing the wealth, preserving individual enterprise, balancing the budget and seeing that farmers and laborers get their just dues from the taxpayers, we'll have another talk about what I'm going to do about you. Don't worry. You'll know where I'll stand.

The Mayor: What's all this I hear about cutting down relief and WPA and PWA? New York City has got a social and unemployment problem, the biggest there is.

The President: Everything will be all right. The country will be all right. You'll be all right. And I'll see that Bob and Jim will be all right again, though I can't answer for Herbert any more, I'm sorry to say. Such ingratitude!

Something must have happened to the spiritist wires at this point, or the effects of the draught must have worn off. At any rate, this correspondent suddenly found himself in his own office, at his own typewriter, pounding away as if his fingers had been in the control of celestial forces.

THE WHITE SUPREMACY ISSUE
August 24, 1938

The relapse of the Democratic primary campaigns in South Carolina and Georgia into the depths of the "white supremacy" issue is a natural and inevitable result of the President's attempt to dictate Senatorial and other nominations in that part of the country. Destructive and noxious as are the present brands of Southern defense, Washington must take part responsibility for them.

The President's personal influence, addressed to the defeat of a Democrat in a party primary, is prodigious. The political methods of his organization, employed to make that influence prevail, are ruthless. The vote-purchasing power of relief is great.

Therefore when a Southern politician finds himself in the path of such a machine, intent upon his destruction, he is inclined to take what ammunition lies closest and best to hand. Senator Tydings, in Maryland, and Representative O'Connor, in New York City, may rely upon the general issue of whether a Democratic legislator or the President shall represent his constituency. But in the South, where cruel economics and historical misadventure have held poverty and illiteracy over a larger popular mass, and where this mass naturally considers the President its first friend, the need to find a more emotional argument is greater . . . So "white supremacy," which has served often before to repel the ideas and powers of citizens of other sections, is being invoked again.

What has made that now both possible and expedient? There are two things, one flowing from the other. The first was the deliberate and successful capture of the Northern Negro vote by the Democrats in the campaign of 1936, an attempt worked out by Senator Guffey of Pennsylvania and executed by National Chairman Farley. The second was the Anti-Lynching Bill, to pass which nearly every Democratic legislative influence in the Northeast and Middle West was twice employed.

The virtually 100 per cent capture of the Negroes by the Democrats in 1936 swung the balances in enough great, populous States to give to the President the unwieldy portions of his majority in votes and in electors. If the Negroes had maintained any goodly part of their normal Republican allegiance the election would have been reasonably close, might even have been doubtful. Southern politicians noted this shift of votes at the time and began to wonder what effect it would have on administration policies. Being politicians also, they did not strike at the relief establishment—one administration activity of naturally great importance to the new Negro Democrats—because they wanted their own part of the swag.

But they came to life with the renewed pressure for the Anti-Lynching Bill and for months made a record against the administration for use at home if some political necessity, as they saw it, arose. Now, in their opinion, it has arisen, and the old, wretched, destructive issue— which may lose to the South much ground it has lately gained in the areas of tolerance and order—is being shouted again.

The Anti-Lynching Bill, which held county officers financially responsible for such outrages, was defeated again in 1938 by a Senate filibuster. Southern Senators were the most numerous in the bloc, but its intellectual leader was Senator Borah. The bill, pressed by Senators Wagner and Guffey, was opposed on several grounds, some spoken and some unuttered. Senators George and Connally made typical arguments against it as an unconstitutional invasion of State sovereignty and recalled the Reconstruction Era where the Federal power supplanted the State power by force. Others relied merely on the baser argument that to pass the bill would encourage Southern Negroes to "insolence" and crime.

But Mr. Borah tore the Federal bill to pieces legally and traditionally. He cited numerous Supreme Court decisions to prove that one sovereignty may not interfere with the machinery of another. He showed how a State itself—Illinois—could legally hold its peace officers responsible for damages incurred by mob violence and ended by saying he would always resist the encroachment of arbitrary power. When sufficient political demonstration had been made, proponents let the bill be laid aside, and the President made no protest. But the material for a "white supremacy" campaign had been gathered for use whenever the administration moved wholly to annex the legislators of the South. The move was made, and the material is being discharged accordingly.

TO KEEP THE PEACE

At the harvest of many errors, the gloomy assizes of 1938, the Republicans made great gains in the House, presaging the formation of the bipartisan alliance of conservatives and moderates which remained in control of Congress until shattered by the great Democratic sweep in the 1964 elections when President Johnson, the radicals of the party and their chief affiliates—organized labor and the Negro voters in the North—were established in firm control of the political branches of the Federal Government. The Supreme Court majority had already found constitutional warrant for the legislative programs these blocs proposed.

The 1938 setback to Roosevelt and the New Deal philosophy would probably have deferred for years this consequence of 1964, perhaps for a future measured in half-centuries, had not the Second World War intervened. In the heavy shadow cast on the United States by the outbreak of the Second World War in 1939, Roosevelt was able to make the covert and unexampled maneuvers by which he was nominated for his third term. And his fourth term was made inevitable by the fact that in 1944 this country was a co-belligerent of three years' standing.

These political consequences for Roosevelt mark an extraordinary irony of politics. For, from 1936 until he adopted a militant policy toward Japan (1941), the President made numerous attempts to avert the war in Europe and Asia that assured his third and fourth terms in the White House. The two subjoined dispatches deal with Roosevelt in this role of attempted restorer of the peace.

The first dispatch (published under my signature on page one of *The Times* of Aug. 26, 1936) is an authorized report of a conversation with Roosevelt at Hyde Park. Since he was then a candidate for re-election, and some of the details of his plan (getting Stalin and Hitler to the same table—which they did, nonetheless, in 1939) exposed him at the time to Republican charges that he was encouraging hopes he knew were false, Roosevelt replied to all demands for verification of my dispatch with "no comment." I had conditioned use of the conversations on his promise not to deny the story, however it was publicly received. He kept the letter of the compact. But when some of his own associates joined the Republicans and press critics of his plan to prevent the war, Roosevelt encouraged Henry A. Wallace, his Secretary of Labor, to cast heavy doubt on my professional integrity and/or reportorial capacity.

Emerging from the President's private railroad car, during a campaign tour, Wallace told the reporters he had "discussed" the article with the President and "did not believe" it was "true." When I informed Wallace of the facts, he apologized—but only in private, to me.

The second subjoined dispatch the President denied outright. He said it was "interesting and well-written" but "untrue." I was in the familiar position of reporters—my sources had imposed anonymity as the price of using a statement Roosevelt had made to two of them in person, and Mrs. Roosevelt had confirmed to the third. But confirmation came eventually, from Prince Franz Ferdinand, a grandson of the Kaiser, and others whom the President had enlisted as go-betweens with Mussolini and Hitler, in that order.

Here are the articles of Aug. 26, 1936, and of April 27, 1939:

POSSIBLE PEACE CONFERENCE
August 26, 1936

The President is seriously considering a plan—his own—in the event of his re-election to propose a joint conference soon thereafter with the heads of the most important nations in an effort to assure the peace of the world. He has mentioned his idea to a few intimate friends, stressing the fact that, while he has not definitely decided upon the plan and has thought out but a few details, he is earnestly weighing the possibilities.

The conference, to meet in the place considered fittest by those participating, would include the President, King Edward VIII, Joseph Stalin, Benito Mussolini, Adolf Hitler, President LeBrun of France, effective representatives of Japan and China and a few others. It would be small in numbers, which the President considers important for its impressive functioning. He believes that, in view of the power and prestige of the conferees, and because of the fact that detailed programs and commitments would not be asked, retinues of economic experts and diplomats —the usual accompaniment of international conferences—could be dispensed with.

As the President has outlined his idea thus far, the eminent members of the conference would generally discuss the prospects and hopes of disarmament and peace, consider the seeds of war, and unite in a proclamation of personal purpose to use all their influence to prevent war in any part of the world. Public opinion would be expected to take more vigorous and definite form behind the conferees than it has attained on the present separate nationalistic basis. While carefully refraining from assuming for the United States any obligation or responsibility for militant action for peace in the Eastern Hemisphere, and making no requests of any foreign States to assume these, the President would point to conditions in the Western Hemisphere and urge the Pan-American agreements as a model.

In such a conference the administration policy, pursued by Secretary of State Hull, for international trade agreements, the leveling of tariff barriers and the elimination of quotas would naturally be discussed with a view to extending the policy, and the importance of economic causes of war would be stressed.

The President has said to his friends that, if he is re-elected over the intense opposition he is facing, he believes he will be in the best position any American President has ever been to promote the cause of world peace, and he has given several reasons. One is that his prestige will have been greatly increased, which will lend additional weight to his initiative in the matter of a conference. He will have entered upon a new term of office, of fixed duration, in the course of which he can greatly assist in any peace efforts on which the conference may agree.

The President, as he considers his plan, has concluded that King Edward VIII and President LeBrun, rather than political heads of their states, will be the more representative and effective conferees. The King, as he sees it, symbolizes the entire British Commonwealth of Nations, which no other Briton can do. The President of France is a fixture over a period of years and is the symbol of the Republic.

Stalin, of course, is the effective head of the Soviet State and the proper member of such a group, as are Hitler and Mussolini. If the plan comes to fruition the conference which will assemble will number the most powerful group since the eighteenth century meetings at Vienna and Berlin which settled the affairs of the Continent. But it will be much more powerful because of its world-wide character and because it will be intended as a focus of public opinion instead of designed to draw a military cordon around the vanquished.

Whether the President will make known his plan in general or in detail before the election is not known to the few persons with whom he has discussed it. They are equally uncertain whether he will go through with it, even if elected, because he is not sure himself. But the concept has fascinated him; he returns to it often; and it would not be difficult to convince him that he has made a new discovery in world leadership for what he considers the greatest cause of mankind.

One reason which may restrain the President, even if he decides definitely on his idea, from making a detailed public statement in advance of the election is the certainty that the Republicans will classify it as a campaign device. They will say, he has told his friends, that it is an attempt to gain re-election on the Wilson issue of 1916, "he kept us out of war," and probably deride the plan as a romantic gesture, certain to yield barren results. The Hearst press and the *Chicago Tribune*, he apparently believes, will view the project as certain to involve commitments abroad and as the forerunner of an international policy more objectionable to them than membership in the League of Nations. He is not certain whether, in the heat of a campaign, he can completely demonstrate the value of the idea and the non-political atmosphere in which he feels it was born.

F.D.R. SOUNDS OUT DICTATORS
April 27, 1939

President Roosevelt sounded out Benito Mussolini, and through him Adolf Hitler, on a plan to meet him at sea, or near some neutral island such as one of the Azores, and they rejected the idea.

The President's purpose was to learn from the dictators at first hand their minimum terms for pledging lasting peace and, if he found these practicable, to offer his services as intermediary.

This disclosure completes the evidence that, far from provoking the situation in Europe, the President was prepared to risk his political future in the interest of world peace.

On behalf of the President it was suggested that each of the three statesmen board a naval vessel and come privately together for the unprecedented conference. The message was delivered to Signor Mussolini through an agent of Mr. Roosevelt. It is understood here that the Duce transmitted it and was informed that the Fuehrer could not arrange to leave Europe for that purpose even if he believed a settlement could come of it.

The President's exploratory tender was made some months ago, probably between the May and September crises. Diligent inquiry has failed to produce the exact dates and other details, because those to whom the President communicated his effort and its failure took fright when these details were sought. They were willing, however, to confirm that the President had made this extraordinary effort for peace.

The probability is that Mr. Roosevelt sounded out the dictators while the Munich crisis was in formation and before he resorted to the alternative of his cabled appeal to Herr Hitler and Signor Mussolini to avert war over the Sudeten issue. Unquestionably it was done before he began the series of speeches which have so greatly irritated the German and Italian Governments, culminating in his second—but sterner—message to the dictators asking for a ten-year guarantee of the status quo in Europe and offering a subsequent world "economic concession conference" in return for that guarantee.

Whatever Herr Hitler may have to say before the Reichstag tomorrow, he cannot—in the light of this publication—truthfully depict Mr. Roosevelt as preferring truculent speech and policy to peaceful adjustment, in which adjustment the President was even willing to serve as intermediary and to take the political risk of getting its terms at first hand. For it was not until the Fuehrer had declined the personal meeting and proceeded on an increasingly aggressive course that the President began to counter it.

Mr. Roosevelt's thought of a personal interview is the outgrowth of an idea that he conceived in 1936 and that was published in a dispatch by this correspondent in *The New York Times* Aug. 26 of that year. This publication was followed by numerous denials (the President's, however, not among them).

His belief then was that, in event of a crisis leading to inevitable and immediate war, he could summon a small conference and possibly avert the conflict. Among the conferees he had in mind the German and Italian dictators, the British King, the French President and himself. He played a bit with the idea of having Joseph Stalin at the same table, but on reflection abandoned that as impracticable and perhaps unnecessary.

At that time he viewed the British King and the French President as more stable conferees than the Prime Ministers of Britain and France because these latter are subject to political recall at any time.

In later reviews and private discussions the President altered his concept several times until it baked down to a meeting among himself, Mussolini and Hitler. To insure the requisite privacy and make a meeting physically possible without damaging advance notice, the plan of coming together at sea seemed best to him.

So long as he remains President, unless war shall come meanwhile, or an enduring peace formula be otherwise discovered, Mr. Roosevelt will probably continue to nurse his idea, despite its rejection by the dictators.

———————————

But, of all the efforts Roosevelt made to avert the war which, by a supreme irony of politics, virtually assured the third term that successful intervention would in all probability have denied him, his activities in behalf of the disastrous "settlement" at Munich are outstanding.

The part he played, which members of his Administration jubilantly described to Washington reporters as having "laid the foundations" for the Chamberlain-Hitler agreement—a pact they predicted would surely halt the drift of Europe into war—was proved by bitter and swiftly subsequent events to have been a gross miscalculation.

There is no attempt here to pass final judgment on Roosevelt's Munich role. The long-range view of history may be that Hitler would have kept open the negotiations with Chamberlain, and Chamberlain would have surrendered to Hitler's terms, even if Roosevelt had stayed wholly aloof in the crisis. But when Hitler plunged Europe into the Second World War less than a year after Munich, the President's friends did what they could to dull remembrance of Roosevelt's praise of the "settlement." And they were effective to some degree: for example, his participation is little known to the present younger generations of Americans.

The following dispatch under my signature, dated September 30, 1938, indicates, however, that this participation was not unanimously regarded at the time as meriting the claims being made for it by Roosevelt's aides, friends and admirers.

A LITTLE EARLY
FOR LAUREL WREATHS
December 30, 1938

War is hideous, and peace is beautiful, and there are no two ways about that. Responsible statesmen who make any contribution to the preservation of peace are deserving of grateful thanks from their fellow-men, and that cannot be argued. But reasonable question can lie against the pacifist creed, which is being so widely and automatically voiced in these times: that under no circumstances can war assure long periods of peace, that never is war a necessary final expedient.

It is true that the World War settled nothing; that there were no victors. But much of the reason for that result can be traced to the punitive peace of Versailles, the treaty compulsorily signed by the Germans, which produced Hitler and most of the world's present political and economic ills. It can honestly be argued, though it cannot be proved, that a wise and just peace would have endured far longer in Europe. And men can love peace and abhor war, yet still feel with Mr. Chamberlain: "If I were convinced that any nation had made up its mind to dominate the world by fear of its force I should feel that it must be resisted."

Mr. Chamberlain obviously reached the conclusion that such is not the purpose of Hitler or modern Germany. If he is right, then the Sudeten settlements made with the Fuehrer by the representatives of Great Britain, France and Italy will inaugurate a long period of peace in Europe.

But if this should prove the beginning instead of the end of war clouds and wars in Europe arising out of the current application of self-determinism, if war is demonstrated to have been postponed instead of averted, then the judgment of the contemporary world and of history will be different. In view of the minority questions still affecting several nations of Europe, the moods and methods of Hitler and Mussolini, and the constant need of dictators to win victories, it is early to say that peace has been firmly established by the concessions made by the democratic powers. Therefore it might be well to await the events of the next few months before too much credit is claimed for those statesmen who made contributions to the settlement of the Czech crisis.

This comes to mind when reading of the feeling among certain of the President's friends and admirers that he has repaired all recent political losses by his peace activities, and their belief that he "laid the foundation" for the settlement. The latter statement is rather extravagant considering that Mussolini, at the request of the British, had already got Hitler's promise to wait before Ambassador Phillips handed him the President's appeal, and he so informed the Ambassador. It is impaired also by the fact that the formula of Munich was as different from the President's, stated in his second note, as anything could be.

But remembering that claims like these are made with an eye to domestic politics, they can be regarded tolerantly. In the inner circle at Washington those New Dealers who want Mr. Roosevelt to run again have long told each other that by procuring peace in Europe the President could overcome the tradition against a third term. It is natural for them to try to take over the role of the Duce and the Prime Minister, particularly since the Congressional elections will soon be held.

But long before 1940 it is possible that the President's enthusiastic friends will not want to claim anything beyond the actual record, so far as Munich is concerned. They might even want to forget that part of the record in which Mr. Roosevelt told the Fuehrer that, if he would keep negotiations open, "the world would recognize your action as an outstanding historic service to humanity." If the crisis is soon revived through complications growing out of the Polish, Hungarian and Rumanian minorities situation, the consequences may not justify that expressed opinion.

One needs only to read certain newspapers—both their editorials and their inspired Washington and foreign dispatches—and note analyses made by the White House secretariat and others, to realize that some persons intend to give to the President chief credit for halting the German march on Wednesday. While this will require an astigmatic reading of the record of chronology and personnel as to Munich, few who are familiar with Washington will doubt that this presents an obstacle. It is stated in Berlin dispatches that the President's second note helped to persuade Hilter he could afford to wait and still get what he demanded. That should be sufficient for the moment, and it probably has the virtue of truth.

But prudence impels the suggestion that even this credit should not be too greatly stressed until there has been some opportunity to determine how enduring is the new peace monument. Between now and the date of the Congressional elections may not be time enough. From Washington and other New Deal points, however, the outlines emerge of an intention by some persons to attempt to link the President's valiant and splendid efforts against war with domestic political programs.

MR. WILSON'S SUMMONS
A STROKE OF POLICY
November 15, 1938

The deliberate action of Secretary Hull, after full consultation with the President, in giving public notice of the summons home to Ambassador Wilson in Berlin was a diplomatic method of expressing our high displeasure with what is going on in Germany. Whatever Berlin may say officially or semi-officially, the Wilhelmstrasse knows perfectly well what has happened and doubtless will not withhold the implications from the Fuehrer.

The involved policy is in consonance with the wish of the United States Government to remain the "question-mark" in world affairs. That is, the President and Mr. Hull intend that none of the autarchies shall take it for granted that under no circumstances will the United States assume a world position and implement it. One of the reasons for Munich was Hitler's confidence that the British would not go to war over Czechoslovakia. The government at Washington proposes that Berlin, Rome and Tokyo shall never be certain they can go to any length without the forceful intervention—not necessarily war—of the United States. In his Pilgrims' dinner speech, Ambassador Kennedy delivered that very message. The summons to his Berlin colleague is in the spirit of that utterance.

This, in the opinion of diplomatic officials, is sure to have two important effects on the German Government, even though it keeps the people in continued ignorance. One will be on Nazi economy, for that government has been anxious to negotiate a commercial agreement with the United States and Mr. Wilson is reported to have been sympathetic to the idea. The other will be to stiffen the democracies of the world in their protests and counteractions. This was already visible in the British and French press today.

Germany has strong allies now—Italy and Japan—and economic domination over Central and Eastern Europe. Also Germany, by threat of force, has been able greatly to expand its territory and material possessions. But all is not smooth sailing in the Reich, economically and otherwise. When Hitler was counting on complete United States passivity, the result of isolationist and pacifist sentiment in this country, his problems were lessened. And doubtless he was flattered by the words in the President's pre-Munich note ("an outstanding historic service to humanity") into thinking that, if he just wouldn't move troops, he could do anything else without a hampering move of any sort from the United States.

Since diplomats understand each other and work under a code, the significance of the summons home of Mr. Wilson is well understood by the Fuehrer's ministers of state. If they can convey its implications to him, he will probably not feel as sure as he did, especially just after Munich, that the most powerful nation in the world will venture nothing more than notes of protest.

Officially Mr. Wilson has been called home, not "recalled," for the purposes of consultation and information. But the existence of the transoceanic telephone is open knowledge, and the Ambassador has been reporting voluminously on the latest outbursts of Nazi violation of all law, human and humane. Veterans around the State Department today could not recall an exact precedent for the summons, or a more definite notice of high displeasure to what is called a "friendly nation."

Incidentally, administration claims of credit for the "Peace of Munich" have died away.

FOR THE DURATION

In the tumult which, as I write, is shaking every continent and the socio-economic structure on which the United States rose to unexampled military power and internal affluence, the dissensions that engaged the American people politically in the period between Munich and the 1940 elections have been deeply submerged in my recollections. So have the points of difference over Roosevelt's conduct of the American military forces in the Second World War, and over the clash of political philosophies in the management of our wartime economy.

The shock of the Japanese attack on Pearl Harbor on December 7, 1941, remains vivid in my memory. And time in its turbulent passage has not dimmed my remembrances of the 1940 Democratic convention which nominated Roosevelt for the third time; and of the Republican gathering in the same years from which Wendell L. Willkie emerged as the nominee for President of a party with which he had only just affiliated. Among them:

• "The voice from the sewer"—of Mayor Kelly's Commissioner of Sanitation, located in the cellar of the convention hall in Chicago—that, constantly and thundrously reiterating "We want Roosevelt," unnerved those Democratic leaders and delegations who came to the convention resolved to make a finish fight on the issue of No Third Term.

• The organized and highly effective gallery demonstration at Philadelphia, which was a successful employment of the same psychology, implying a popular demand for Willkie that swept away the resistance of the old-line Republicans.

72

• The strategic errors of the Willkie campaign, of which the best example was his stubborn refusal to concentrate his appeal on the voters in the populous States wherein lay his only chance of victory, and the diffusion of his energies instead in nationwide speaking tours.

• The political neutralization effected by Roosevelt when he assigned the responsibility of our industrial mobilization for war to Republicans such as William N. Knudsen and Edward R. Stettinius. Restricted thereby from confirming, as they were able to do, Willkie's charge that under Roosevelt the United States had drifted unprepared to the verge of war—which was Willkie's major issue—they maintained during the campaign the silence on this subject they felt their offices imposed on them.

To the day of his death Willkie believed that if Knudsen and Stettinius had not, by their silence, enabled Roosevelt to persuade the country of a condition of preparedness which was flagrantly contrary to the facts in 1940, he would have been elected. Others attributed Willkie's defeat more directly to the diffusion of his physical campaign activities, as noted above. But I believed then, and still do, that, even if he had been able to prove his charge with official statistics, and even if he had concentrated his on-the-spot speeches to the populous States, Roosevelt would have won anyhow. For the international situation in 1940, when both the President and Willkie were pledged to resist the growing pressure on the United States to enter the European conflict as a belligerent, lent itself to effective Democratic exploitation of Lincoln's counsel to the people in his wartime re-election campaign in 1864: ". . . it is not best to swap horses while crossing the river."

NOMINATION OF WILLKIE:
A COUNTER-ATTACK ON DICTATION
June 29, 1940

Democracy worked this week, at a time when triumphant war machines have been erected on its ruins in nearly all the rest of the world. The nomination of Wendell L. Willkie by the Republican National Convention was not only the climax of an American political revolution, and the achievement of a miracle; it was a notice that, as ever before, the Democratic system here furnishes a man for the exigent hour and traditional molds are burst to effect his entrance.

In the light of all political experience Mr. Willkie's nomination was impossible. He has voted the Republican ticket for only four years, and has been registered with that party for only one. He has never been in politics, or sought or held a public office. His claims to this nomination were not submitted to any party primary or convention before this one met. He is an executive in the utilities business, which the New Deal has chosen as its especial example to prove the needs for drastic regulation of industry. He is a director of the First National Bank of New York, a "Wall Street" bank. And not until the day before this convention met did Mr. Willkie form a professional political group to pilot his campaign.

Against Mr. Willkie were arrayed two sets of seasoned professional politicians and two candidates with impressive commitments from large delegations. One, New York County's crusading young District Attorney, had the color which it was felt the party needed; a large sum of money had been spent to project his personality across the country; and expert politicians were playing for great personal stakes in his name. The second, Ohio's junior United States Senator, son of a Republican President and Chief Justice, had what his backers conceived to be the "solid" qualities required to appeal to voters who have not found them in the New Deal.

There were other candidates of strong party appeal.

All of these had been months in the battle. It was only forty-eight days ago when Mr. Willkie decided that his friends were not kidding him, that every sign of a popular uprising in his behalf was to be seen. Prior to that, for a year, he had been casually mentioned as Presidential timber. On the impulse of an impromptu speech in New York by General Hugh S. Johnson, two young volunteers—Oren Root Jr. and Russel Davenport—had abandoned their affairs, the one to circulate petitions for Mr. Willkie, the other to create publicity for him.

But he did not throw himself seriously into the contest until it became plain that, without accepting contributions, on the basis of articles and speeches on the issues and successful resistance of New Deal encroachments on his utilities field, his volunteer organizations were getting widespread support. From that time on the clamor for his nomination grew until it culminated early yesterday morning in this city.

The galleries at Philadelphia demanded this nomination of the delegates. But these galleries were only the reflected image of a vast national gallery, as a deluge of telegrams, letters and telephone calls to the delegates quickly proved. An attempt was made by his competitors to ascribe this deluge to "paid propaganda," to a vast, secret "Wall Street fund." But their sincerity and spontaneity were unmistakable. Against every tried political device—whispering campaigns, an attempted combination between the leaders for Mr. Dewey and Senator Taft, an effort to hold the line with boss-led delegations from Southern States which can help to nominate Republicans but never elect them—this demand of the "galleries" prevailed.

For this and other reasons the candidate was able to say to the convention, when he spoke to it yesterday, that he owed no pledge, commitment or understanding to any man. And it is true. Hundreds of volunteers helped him. Among them the names of Governors Baldwin, Stassen and Carr, of Representative Halleck, of Mr. Root and Mr. Davenport, of Roy W. Howard are prominent. But Mr. Willkie nominated himself, and not one who assisted fails to realize that his contribution was a minor one.

The rare statement can be ventured that all these auxiliary efforts were made because the doers believed they were serving a great national need and in full knowledge that Mr. Willkie's future cannot be bought or sold.

What drew together this heterodox throng seemed to be the feeling that the present Administration's social-economic policies bar the prompt erection of an effective national defense, and that Mr. Willkie is the man to do this while restoring domestic economy behind the barricade. So far as this convention's action is concerned, they triumphed.

My dispatches from Washington that follow were written during the immediate prewar period and in the aftermath of war that ended with V-J Day.

The courses of government that were the dominant topics of my dispatches in the year 1942 are representative of the issues which engaged a much longer period: the Second World War, after the entrance of the United States as a belligerent, and the postwar era which was pre-Eisenhower. This accounts for the imbalance between the use in this book of dispatches written in 1942 and those in the succeeding decade.

The range of the subjects is: the part played by union labor in the political phases of the war; the uses and abuses of what was officially termed "voluntary censorship" of itself by the United States press, but had deliberately built-in compulsions; the shortcomings of President Roosevelt as an administrator; the wartime politics of the professional politicians; the up-and-down phases of the public morale; the shortages of war supplies due to maladministration, with rubber the typical commodity involved and North Africa the typical afflicted area.

In the 1942 collection which follows there are also commentaries on the Administration's connective with the disaster at Pearl Harbor; individuals whose activities were of paramount importance; the neglect of inflation until it got out of hand; and a survey of the results of the Congressional elections of 1942, in which public dissatisfaction was registered by a substantial reduction in the Democratic membership.

STEP FORWARD
FROM A FIRESIDE SPEECH
June 16, 1941

When Boston newspaper men today approached Dr. Herbert Scholz, the German Consul there, they heard him say:

I have been in this country seven years, but if orders came from Berlin I should be forced to return to Germany.

The United Press news ticker, which brought these piteous words to the capital, where Dr. Scholz was long a member of the German Embassy staff, did not reveal whether the plaint was uttered in a tone of surprise, of reproach, or merely expressed simple sorrow over the prospect of leaving the United States. Whatever the tone, the remark was the uttermost limit of naïveté. For Dr. Scholz has long been believed to personify those pro-Nazi activities in this country which finally moved the President to send home the entire German consulate corps. Washington long ago decided that if the cruel, ruthless Nazi policy could be pic-

torialized in human form by some inspired artist Dr. Scholz should sit
for the portrait.

Herbert Scholz has the merciless blue eyes, the hard, high-boned face,
the tall, athletic body and the fair complexion of those Germans for
whom the concentration camp, the Jew-baiting, the bombing attacks on
civilians and the tortures of the Gestapo seem to have been especially
contrived as instruments of national policy. He was an early Nazi street-
fighter, in which activity he excelled. His intelligence and certain other
attributes enabled him to escape the consequences of a close association
with the late, lamented Captain Ernst Roehm. And since then the diligence and ability with which he has served the Nazi cause in the United
States should have restored, and they probably have, whatever loss of
confidence he may have suffered about the time of the blood purge.

When Dr. Scholz was in Washington, he was a tremendous social success. "Society," especially its female members, made much of him. His
gay dismissals of the unkind rumors that Nazis are in any way
undesirable, or that they want anything but peace and kindness in the
world, were admiringly quoted, and he was pointed to as proof to the
contrary. When an exasperated male appanage of one of the admiring
females said: "I hope to have the privilege of escorting you personally
to our first concentration camp," the doctor laughed with uproarious
and understanding good nature. But one who looked closely might have
thought he saw in the small, cold blue eyes an expression which suggested that Dr. Scholz was thinking of a possible day when *he* might be
selecting the occupants of that camp in the United States.

If he is, as he sadly contemplates, forced to leave this country and
comes back with the necessary powers, he will have a list of Americans
for internment—or something harsher—which will testify to his ability
and discernment. Some of these Americans Dr. Scholz can choose, if he
will, from the best clubs in New York and Washington, for in the hey-
day of his popularity the submissive male appanages of his lady admirers put him up for many of these.

Washington is quite sure that Dr. Scholz typifies all the reasons why
the American Government today, proceeding *pari passu* with its steps
toward national defense, asked Germany to recall its whole consular
service in this country.

The act is without precedent, so far as the archives disclose, in that it
was taken without a similar request affecting the German diplomatic
corps and, without that request, concerned every consulate. Whether
Germany will retaliate, and if so how, is a matter of speculation here.
Observers who were informed some time ago that the government would

move step by step to make good every pledge in the President's recent fireside address do not doubt that a severance of diplomatic relations will follow.

It will follow, they are certain, unless Germany backs down in its policy of total war, and this is not expected.

Consuls in this country have not the immunity of diplomats, and therefore their correspondence and other activities are subject to police inspection and actions for "high crimes and misdemeanors." It has therefore been simpler to know what the Nazi consuls have been doing than to keep informed concerning the diplomats. But the same condition prevails with respect to the consular officers of Italy and Soviet Russia, many of whom are believed to have been working in concert with the Germans here. Whether, or when, the Italians and Russians will be similarly ordered to leave in a body remains to be seen.

ROOSEVELT'S ORDER TO SHOOT
September 20, 1941

Definite signs are beginning to appear that what may be called the anti-war-involvement group in Congress has lost its solidarity. It is too early to say the group has broken up, and improbable that its stubborn Senate nucleus will be dissipated. But defections have begun to show, more are expected, and the belief here is that the change will be marked in any roll-call that may be taken on repeal of the Neutrality Act and in the sudden silence of some members who have been vocal in opposing the drift toward war.

The reasons are not hard to find for such shifts as have occurred and are forecast.

When the President ordered the Navy to shoot at sight obstructionists to our war-bound commerce in any waters he might deem essential to national defense, a condition supplanted a theory. The foreign policy debate became to a very great degree thunder in the index. Representative Dirksen of Illinois, who voted against the repeal of the arms embargo, the lease-lend bill and the Selective Service Law, expressed the view of many when he suddenly said to a cheering House:

The President has announced a policy of patrolling and clearing the waters which are deemed necessary to our defense and for the mainte-

nance of freedom of the seas. That policy is now known to all the
world. To disavow or oppose that policy now could only weaken the
President's position, impair our prestige and imperil the nation.

He was challenged next day by Representative Thill of Wisconsin,
who declared he and others would not surrender the right and what they
conceived to be the duty of continued policy opposition. But from the
reception of his remarks it was evident that a great change has come
over the House. Things were not as they had been.

The resolutions adopted by the American Legion, which long has
argued against another war adventure abroad, are another factor in the
shift. Among members of Congress the Legion, because of its local activities and the size of its roster, is one of the most influential organizations in the United States. Its endorsement of proposed measures or
policies attracts a large following at once, and its Milwaukee resolutions
were carefully noted by all the members of Congress.

The bad news from the Russian campaign had a similar effect. German successes against the Soviet moved further into the zone of realism
the situation in which this country finds itself. Many who had been
hopeful that Hitler would meet his doom on the steppes and in the
marshes of Russia, and were the more determined to try to keep this
country from war involvement because they believed events would destroy the argument of necessity and inevitability, saw their hope vanish-
ing and with it their expedient reasoning.

As often before in the country's history, when a condition has succeeded a theory, members of Congress suspended an opposition that
could no longer alter the course of policy, particularly when that policy
has entered the sphere of war. But, as often before, an irreducible minimum remained, and there is no doubt the present one will continue to
speak out at intervals and record its opposition in voting form. However, there is also no doubt that this group has been shorn of some of its
most faithful members.

In the main those who have strongly resisted the steps in act or policy
that began with the President's "quarantine" speech in 1937 and grew
longer and longer after the repeal of the arms embargo in 1939, will
turn their critical fire on the rearmament program. The foreign policy
opposition bloc has been almost unanimously in favor of strong defense
measures, their chief objections being to the rate of progress, the confusion of plan and the diversion of so much to Great Britain. On all these
points they may be expected to concentrate again. If the war news grows
worse in Russia, a bad turn comes in the Mediterranean sector and Hit-

ler's all-out attack on Great Britain finally develops, these members may be expected to demand that the bulk of armament production shall be reserved to make more certain the defense of the Western Hemisphere.

But that will await the new alignment which now appears to be forming. That it is forming should not be surprising news. From the time the lease-lend bill was passed, many citizens ceased voicing opposition to the military alliance with Great Britain because the terms of the law made that alliance a fact, and a fact cannot effectively be argued with. They ceased their public resistance to the policy also because, the decision having been made, national unity became vital to the success of the policy, and failure of the policy would expose the nation to great peril.

Hope that somehow the logical consequences of lease-lend would not follow was perhaps also responsible for the continued solidity of the objectors in Congress long after the law was enacted. Germany might crack, Hitler might die, maybe the law was really the non-involvement insurance the Administration spokesmen declared it was, maybe the President would not see to the safe delivery of the goods leased, loaned and given—the hope might have been any of these. But events demolished each in turn, the President gave the Navy its orders, and the shift in Mr. Dirksen's position merely materialized the pondering of many of his colleagues on their courses for the future.

CHURCHILL A CATALYST
December 28, 1941

In the words of one who has participated in the Anglo-American war councils since the arrival here of the British Prime Minister, Mr. Churchill has had the effect of what in chemistry is called a catalyst: he has accelerated a desired reaction.

This was certainly the influence of his three public appearances—at the President's Tuesday press conference, before the White House Christmas tree and in the presence of assembled members of the Senate and the House of Representatives.

But that was oratory, stimulating, inspiring, masterly and reassuring, yet only oratory. The more important contribution (by the agreement of men who have sat in the councils and with whom this correspondent has discussed them) is that Mr. Churchill has made in bringing out a union of ideas, resources and enterprises against the Axis powers.

"The Prime Minister brought enough thinking-caps for us all," said one of the conferees. "He has helped immeasurably to merge two compartments into one in which to pool and wisely allocate everything we have to fight with. One pot is now boiling where two were but simmering."

The reference is, of course, to the common strategy and partition of the anti-Axis struggle, not to the individual war efforts the two nations were making before the Prime Minister came to Washington. The war-kettles were not simmering; they were boiling in the Atlantic and Pacific, in Libya, in China, along the Burma Road and on the frozen battlefields of Russia. But the strategy was uncorrelated, being divided, and to bring it to a boil one common reservoir was required under which the concentrated fire of determination could burn most effectively.

It would have been sufficiently inspiring if the Anglo-American military men had met in Washington with the President. But the arrival and presence of Mr. Churchill invested the meeting with the high tone and color of great and meaningful drama. His participation gave the trait of finality and endurance to the mighty partnership.

Those essential contributions, which only the Prime Minister could have made, or—had the meeting been held in London—could have been made only by the President, would have established Mr. Churchill as the catalyzing element of the assemblage even if he did not possess his unparalleled equipment for such a part. But this equipment made certain that the element would do the work for which it was produced. If present indications do not fail, then nothing in the Prime Minister's extraordinary, and as he says, "not wholly uneventful" life, will surpass in terms of lasting value the influence he has exerted here.

He knows the world and he knows men, of course. He knows war at first-hand and, by virtue of his position, he understands the facts and necessities of the present one better than any other statesman. Mr. Churchill is the leader of a nation which has been in arms against the Axis for more than two years on many fronts. Therefore, he spoke as a veteran, which his American confrères will be soon enough but are not yet.

But in him they recognized more than a veteran: they saw a wise, experienced and realistic war statesman who has always had the gift of putting first things first and has learned in the school of recent adversity what those first things surely are. They were prepared for his flawless ability to go to the heart of a problem and state it, and its proposed solution, in clear and pure English diction. But everyone who talks with Mr. Churchill is freshly impressed with this talent on each recurring occasion.

Outside his work in the conferences, the Prime Minister will leave an achievement that may be as important in the days, both dark and bright, through which the United States and Great Britain must pass. The political community which centers in Congress was left in no doubt that what Mr. Churchill says is true; that he glosses over no hard or dismal fact; that as an ally and a statesman he can be depended on wholly. This impression has swept away a whole fifth column and sent to silence a host of Quislings.

DETROIT'S ACHIEVEMENT
March 31, 1942

This is the forge of Vulcan, and it is roaring with his fires in which the tools of battle are being fashioned. The conversion of the automobile industry into factories of the weapons of total war has been rapid and efficient, the results already overwhelming.

Within a wide circle around Detroit huge prairies have, in a few months, been covered with plants for the production of matériel, and already the means of transporting this to the distant and scattered regions where the Axis must be thrown back has begun to replace conversion as a major problem. The Detroit area is now pouring out the engines of death that are designed to maintain and restore the freedom of human life, and yet it seems but a brief time ago that men were arguing, first over whether swords could be wrought from the tools that had made ploughshares, and second whether the war would not be ended before the tooling changes could be made.

A visit to the great Ford bomber factory, now coming to completion, and to the Chrysler tank arsenal, where the monster wagons of battle have for some time been rolling off the assembly line, dispels much of the concern that besets all observers of the war's direction in Washington. Here are to be seen—in the Chrysler plant—armament production on a scale undreamed of when the plans were made; in the Ford plant —speed-up processes that only American industrial genius could devise; and in both factories a combination of skill, celerity, volume and working space which will assure any spectator that the growth and strength of this country came from no accident, but from the native ability of the people themselves.

What are being and will be produced here are the deadliest and most efficient engines of destruction the world has ever known. Yet, with the ultimate objective in mind, a visitor traveling toward the plants feels he never beheld anything so stimulating and glorious as their huge outlines looming through the snowfall of a belated Spring. And once he has entered the colossal structures—the one clangorous with preparation, the other clamorous with the din of production—he is suffused with the feeling that American industry will triumph over every obstacle that has been set against it—Hitler and the Japanese as well as politics and other forms of internal selfishness.

When the Ford bomber plant is ready—very soon—the war planes, assembled in great numbers on a line, will roll out onto runways more than a mile long, ready to take off for their trial flights. On their way through the assembly line they will undergo speed-up processes; one of these, for example, has already cut from eight hours to thirty minutes a certain operation. While the plant is producing it will be expanding at the same time. When it is even partly completed, a hospital, a hotel and a hangar will be part of it.

Today women are attending classes for instruction in shopwork. There are several parts of the operation available to them already, and if and when a labor shortage appears they will have been made ready to take on more.

In the Chrysler plant production has now exceeded in hundreds of per cents the original capacity design. Very few of the tank parts must be imported—all the rest is done within the factory—and no more importation, perhaps less, will be required for the larger M-4. So vast is the operation that five of the same type of tanks can be lifted and set down further along the assembly line in one operation of the giant cranes.

Workers in the plants appeared to this correspondent to be cheerful and talked that way, and to be giving full concentration to their tasks. In the ranks of management he found ready exchanging of tools and facilities, strong support of proposals that companies with war contracts be limited to a 6 per cent profit, and no disposition to haggle with the government over the fixation of costs to be allowed. "If the cost turns out to have been fixed too low, we can fight that out later," said K. T. Keller, head of the Chrysler Company.

A YEAR AT WAR
December 5, 1942

In the year that has passed since Japan's attacks in the Pacific thrust the United States into war the marked changes that have come over the face, and suffused the body and spirit, of America have been as visible in the capital city as elsewhere throughout the country. But, though the similarities are many, there are certain differences peculiar to Washington.

The similarities include the following:

Uniformed men and women are a wide stream in the street throngs, themselves multiplied many times in volume, that were entirely in civilian dress a year ago.

Public conveyances, in common with hotels, boarding houses, theatres and restaurants, are jammed beyond their capacities and the sharp decrease in the privately driven vehicles has been more than balanced by the darting swarm of government cars and military automobiles.

Atop many public buildings are anti-aircraft gun installations, manned by troops in plain sight of the crowds.

Nearly everywhere the government functions armed guards patrol, and a tedious and exacting inspection system must be passed by those having business with officials. The White House is Washington's own, but its barred gates against a public that was accustomed to roam freely through the grounds, and its circumambient patrol of soldiers with fixed bayonets, are eloquent of the war change that has come upon the face of the country.

The climax of the change, of course, is that from an attitude of defense, in which statecraft guided military assistance against the Axis to keep our position "short of war" if possible, the nation after nearly a year has taken the offensive. Contemporaneous with the long-delayed account of the crushing blows dealt to our battleships and aircraft at Pearl Harbor of Dec. 7, 1941, the dispatches tell of American attacks against the Japanese in the Pacific, and against the Axis in Tunisia, by land, sea and air. The command of last year, "Hold and defend," has been changed to "Attack and advance."

The mood and the activities of Washington, central control room of all this vast machinery of war, have altered in the same fundamental particular. No longer are heard, in Congress and outside it, debates as to whether the Administration's foreign policy could, with any honor or security, have averted the war. Japan's overt act ended much of this, and postponed for later reckoning the rest. Now the accent of criticism in Washington is wholly on the political, economic and military conduct of the war, and very little of that criticism arises from any purpose other than to make the nation's offensive more effective and to bring about the most rapid possible victorious conclusion.

But here the change in the mood of Washington leaves the groove it entered when Pearl Harbor was attacked a year ago and surges into another channel. That channel breaks away sharply from the one through which executive action is flowing and provides a separate course for what has become a coordinate stream of action in the war. This stream is being more and more independently navigated by a Congress which a year ago and for some time afterward was content to be towed along by the executive pilot-ship.

When Japan made war on the United States, one could almost hear in the sunny air of an unusually bland late Autumn day in Washington the click of diverse mechanisms coming together in instantaneous unity. Politics was put aside, and from the White House to the least of the cubicles where Congress does its work the urging came that all personal and party considerations be abandoned for the duration. Everyone publicly subscribed to it. The Commander in Chief had a united government as well as a united people behind him.

But in the ensuing year that part of the unity which concerns methods of management was shattered by acts and omissions of government and by words of individuals which did not conform to the pledge of Dec. 7, 1941. Military communiqués were found lacking in candor and in informative quality, their guiding principle often seeming to be that the people could not be trusted with full knowledge of the events of the war, even when national security was not by any reasonable possibility involved. The President stubbornly resisted reforms in the war management which had been proved in experience and were advocated by most disinterested and able counselors. A discouraging amount of politics as usual entered the sum of Congressional and executive action. The White House personal blacklist, based on disputes preceding Pearl Harbor, shrank very little.

Quarrels over jurisdiction among administrators, which should have been killed in their infancy and could have been by a better executive organization of the war, arose and were allowed to reach acute stages before they were taken up for settlement. Vital situations, such as those affecting the nation's rubber stock pile, raw materials, manpower and the productivity of labor and industry, were tolerated instead of being firmly grasped. Excesses of censorship were permitted, and, having waited much longer than military security required to acquaint the people with the full story of Pearl Harbor, the Administration stretched out the period of waiting until the ill-judged selection of this anniversary for the full account seemed the only way out of a dilemma that stubbornness had created.

Congressional investigating committees, goaded by protests from the people, proliferated in number, and their increasingly sharp probes brought to light much incompetence and lack of foresight among administrators. Government bureaus, heavily overstaffed, and particularly by the academic minds which the New Deal has drawn to it in droves, plagued the people with exacting, often unanswerable, questionnaires that have gone to the Washington scrap heap by the tens of thousands. Confused and conflicting statements on every public subject came out of Washington in a deluge, and the Baruch committee's rubber report revealed a loose and indecisive administrative structure from top to bottom.

These and other manifestations—such as dogged resistance to the call for unified military command, even in separate areas like the Western Pacific—changed the Dec. 7, 1941, mood of Washington from complete unity to questioning, and then, as a result of the November, 1942, elections, to a demand by Congress for administrative reforms that will produce more conflicts with the Executive. The tone of argument is not elevated by the fact that many of those responsible for the war program are very weary in body and mind.

The squirrels and the pigeons in the parks and squares, and many government workers, are the only inhabitants of the capital who seem unchanged after the passage of the fateful year.

THE AFRICAN CAMPAIGN
December 10, 1942

How two storms met headlong in the Atlantic and destroyed each other, calming the sea miraculously for the landings of the Anglo-American forces in North Africa; how the concept and magnitude of the expedition took the Germans by surprise; how work began on that concept as early as last January—these and facts about the expedition can now be told.

Informally, and colorfully, they were related to a group this week by an official who had a large part in the planning: the Assistant Secretary of War, John J. McCloy. The group found the narration as thrilling as it was informing. There follows a brief summary of what to most people will be news:

Obvious considerations made the Mediterranean "the Marne" of this war, the line behind which the Allied armies could re-form and deliver their strength. In January last a code name was given to the North African invasion project and work began: research, discussion of commanders, the tasks involved in making landings. It was agreed that control of the Mediterranean would aid our freedom of choice in picking a European point of entry and that the shipping shortage would be automatically reduced by possession of North Africa.

In June a final decision was reached and timetables were prepared. Almost at once a combined Anglo-American operation, instead of a separate American one, was approved, but with the proviso that it should be American-directed and that the predominant land force should be ours. The next move was to choose a commander, and the selection of Lieut. Gen. Eisenhower was made.

Next on the agenda was the working out in great detail of a tactical plan. The objective had to be fixed, the most rapid way of achieving it plotted, and then a reverse process begun to determine the type of troops, their number, their equipment and their training, and the landings that would be required to cut off Oran, Algiers and Casablanca. This called for infinite detailed information: the characteristics of beaches and tides at each point and the likely obstacles to be encountered. One kind of landing craft would do well in the Straits, but another was required for the Western landings. Engineer equipment and troops had to be supplied against pillboxes and concrete, paratroopers for the capture of airfields and ship-to-shore paraphernalia. Cargoes had to be distributed so that the loss of one or several ships would not cripple the expedition, and loaded so that they would come out in inverse order exactly as needed on the shore. And the whole job had to be coordinated with the British, all their armed services and our own.

The forces that left Britain went 1,000 miles into the Atlantic before turning back toward North Africa, and from America the troops traveled 3,000 miles by sea. At different points the ships separated so that the expedition might appear at fixed points off the coast, as it did, ready to start landing within five minutes of the time selected two months previously. It was the largest military landing expedition in history, greater than that at Gallipoli in the First World War. And it was made through an ocean crowded with submarines.

While Lieut. Gen. Montgomery's offensive from Egypt was timed to coincide with the African landings, these were not dependent on its success. So much was in motion at the time of the El Alamein attack on Rommel that no turning back was possible.

Our convoys were spaced to arrive at intervals after the first landings to support the troops ashore, but the rest carried heavy matériel and had to be unloaded at docks. If they lingered in the open sea they ran the risk of being torpedoed. That made it of paramount importance to get over such fighting with the French as occurred, and, though there were mishaps, Oran, Algiers and Casablanca fell at the hours anticipated, with aid from the arrangements that had previously been made with French leaders and after that with Darlan.

The fortunate meeting of the Eastbound and Westbound storms made the coastal seas calmer than they have been for sixty-eight years.

The Germans, especially after the concentration at Gibraltar, knew that African landings were planned. But they did not know it far enough in advance, or in sufficient details as to the landing places, to take what would appear to have been obvious measures. The Vichy troops also seemed to have been taken by surprise; some were routed out of barracks before they had put their clothes on. Yet at Oran and Casablanca they fought well, immediately, however, fraternizing with our troops when the battle ended. Our own soldiers were overbold at first, but soon they learned the value of caution.

The cessation of fighting with the French came none too soon and our troops moved toward Tunisia not a moment too early. A job of pacification in Algeria and Morocco would have bogged them down for many weeks. But the plan carried in general and in detail, though more than 1,500 persons knew of it last Summer.

AN ESTABLISHED PROPHET'S VISION
January 13, 1943

On the morning of April 3, 1942, the dispatches from and relating to the Russo-German front were far from optimistic concerning the question whether the Soviet armies could survive the Summer intact.

From London to this newspaper came the statement that "what is causing grave concern is the problem * * * of fulfilling the obligations to Russia as the time for the Soviet's supreme test of endurance approaches." A wireless from Stockholm relayed the news from Berlin that the Nazis' great Spring offensive against Russia was under way, "with new weapons, tactics and strategy" which had been evolved during the Winter; the prediction that past errors would not be repeated and that "many isolated blows on different sectors, instead of a simultaneous mass attack along the whole front," would end Russian resistance.

But that day Joseph E. Davies, former Ambassador to Moscow, ventured a written prophecy of another kind which he gave to this correspondent, to be checked for its relation to events June 1 and Dec. 31, 1942. The statement read:

> By the end of the military season of 1942 I predict that the Russian armies will be intact, the Soviet Government will be intact and the morale of the Russian people will be intact—regardless of the territorial belligerents.

On June 1, the time appointed for the first check, Mr. Davies's prophecy was still sound. But there was heavy fighting on the Kalinin front, where the Russians claimed to have taken the initiative but the Germans were doing very well. And this newspaper editorially expressed the prevailing view when it said that "upon the continuance of Russian resistance our immediate hopes depend," and, though the Soviets had fought magnificently, "we do not know how long they can go on."

Mr. Davies continued to have *no* doubts as far as 1942 was concerned. On Dec. 31 of that year, the time appointed for the second check, he was still right. The Soviet armies were on the offensive southwest of Stalingrad, which the Nazis had never been able to take and where one of the most glorious chapters in the annals of human fortitude had been written by the Russians. Today these armies are nearing Smolensk and Rostov, and the frustrated forces of the Reich are also being assailed by the rigors of another Russian Winter.

Since Mr. Davies has proved himself a better expert on Russian military capacity than most of the professional soldiers on whose judgment the United States Government relied for at least the first year of the Soviet-German war, it seemed to this correspondent that a 1943 prophecy from him would be of general interest and have definite value. Therefore he applied for one to Mr. Davies. After some days of reflection, the former Ambassador has offered a preview of 1943, both particular with reference to Russia and general with respect to the fortunes of the United Nations in the field.

He writes that "barring a crack-up internally, which I discount,

Hitler will fall back and dig in in Russia to shorten his line of communication; furiously build a Siegfried Wall along the Mediterranean; fight
a rear-guard action in Africa and in the Ukraine; and use that time for
intensive and effective preparation for a renewed all-out drive this Summer for Baku oil. It is his last, desperate and only hope for victory.
Failing that, he will try to wall himself in for a long siege in order to
obtain a more favorable peace through a dummy government, eliminating himself."

Mr. Davies continues:

His drive for Russian oil will fail.

If the Soviets either have or can obtain, through Murmansk and the
Persian Gulf, sufficient mechanized equipment and air power, they
might smash through the German lines through Rumania and the
Balkans, conjointly with the various pincer movements of an invasion by the United Nations on the south, west, north, or all three.
Such a victory in Russia would not be a Russian pushover. Both desperation and self-preservation will unite the German armies and people into an all-out offensive and an all-out resistance this Summer.

At the end of 1943 I expect to see the Germans still fighting with
shrunken lines, with the United Nations and Russia on the offensive,
holding the initiative on all fronts. Barring an internal collapse, or
the death of Hitler, that is the best we can expect this year.

Those that followed the military analyses and prophecies of some of
the established, or self-proclaimed, experts, who were wrong in the
months when Mr. Davies was right, will probably receive his views with
extra respect founded in that remembrance.

A LITTLE BOOK
IN EISENHOWER'S POCKET
February 22, 1943

The hard going around Kasserine Pass, in Tunisia, has delayed for a bit
the next experience American military commanders will have in governing a zone of occupation. And the distance is still long to the point
where our generals will meet that problem in German-occupied Europe.

But when the forces of the United Nations invest Tunis, and when
they invade the Continent, the American commanders will take out of

their pockets a little book which was an important guide to General Eisenhower in his management of civil affairs in Algeria and French Morocco. Virtually no mention has been made of this book in the many criticisms and defenses of the manner in which the General dealt with the civil and military conditions he found prevailing in North Africa. But if some of the critics had been aware of its existence, they would have had answers to many of the questions that perplexed them.

The book is styled "Basic Field Manual, Military Government," and is issued by the War Department to all commanders. It was prepared in 1940 under the direction of the Judge Advocate General and supplements and amendments have since been published. Officers here who have had the responsibility of command in occupied zones, or those, like North Africa, "taken into protective custody" by American forces, have no doubt that General Eisenhower learned the Manual by heart before he sailed for North Africa and has been dipping in it every day since.

According to the Manual, any plan of military government should be consistent with two basic policies: military necessity and the welfare of the governed. "The first consideration at all times," it reads, "is the prosecution of the war to a successful termination. So long as hostilities continue the question must be asked, with reference to every intended act of the military government, whether it will forward that object or hinder its accomplishment."

This being the preponderant duty which the commander is directed to perform, he is then instructed by the Manual to remember that "military government should be just, humane and as mild as practicable * * * but above all flexible. It must suit the people, the country, the time and the tactical and strategical situation to which it is applied. It must not be drawn up too long in advance or in too much detail and must be capable of change without undue inconvenience if and when experience should show change to be advisable."

That injunction was especially suitable to the political conditions General Eisenhower found in North Africa. And it will be an even safer guide to the administrative solutions American officers must find in Europe. One formula will suit one country of advanced civilization, like Belgium or France. But it will not at all suit certain of the subjugated Balkan States. Those who demand an inflexible and immediate democratic establishment as soon as the Stars and Stripes are raised have not borne this in mind. But the authors of the Manual have.

"The administration of military government," says the official book, "is subordinate to military necessities, involving operations, security, supply, transportation and housing of our troops." But, "since every man engaged in military government is withdrawn either from the combatant forces or from productive labor at home, all plans and practices should be adopted with a view of reducing to the minimum * * * the number of the personnel of our Army employed in that government and the amount of work required of them."

This means, of course, that as much use as possible, in consonance with military necessity and security, should be made of the existing civil personnel, and General Eisenhower followed the book. It informs him and other commanders in similar or more drastic situations that "so far as reliance may be placed on them to do their work loyally and efficiently, subject to the direction and supervision of the military government, the executive and judicial officers and employes of the occupied country * * * should be retained in their respective offices and employments and be held responsible for the proper discharge of their duties. * * * The personnel of the military government should, so far as possible, deal with the inhabitants through the officers and employes of their own government."

This was loftily overlooked, in the rare instances when the existence of the Manual was known, by critics who were asking an American commander to disregard the official instructions of his superiors as expounded in the Manual. And these critics ran counter also to the wise admonition of the book that follows:

"The existing laws, customs and institutions of the occupied country have been created by its people and are probably those best suited to them. They and the officers and employes of their government are familiar with them, and any changes will impose additional burdens on the military government." And the territorial divisions of the military government "should be so organized as to coincide with those previously existing, since the laws and ordinances in one division are often different from those in another and would be unsuitable in the other."

AIR POWER AND BATTLE CASUALTIES
January 31, 1944

To adult civilians, and to veterans of World War I who are not again in uniform, one of the mysteries of the present global conflict is the small number of casualties, actual and in relation to those of 1914–18. Several explanations have been offered by persons with sufficient knowledge and battle experience to make them. But what seems to this correspondent the soundest was given today in answer to the questions so many are asking.

The explanation came from one of the greatest living authorities on modern war, in which he has had almost every variety of service. The following summary of his views, limited by the inadequacy of a layman to grasp the technical phases, appears to be worth passing on to readers among a people with millions of its men under arms.

In World War I a whole male generation from 20 to 40 years old, and large segments of the generations older and younger, were casualties of battle. These were the men of Europe and of the British Empire. The only reason the United States did not suffer proportionate loss is because the war ended so soon after we had begun to fight in force.

Civilization would scarcely survive the taking of a like toll in this war. But, despite the huge expense in dead and wounded that the Russians and the Germans have paid, the fighting generations in World War II will suffer nothing like the subtraction of the previous conflict.

Ask any large-scale commander this question: "What would have been the casualties at El Alamein and in Tunisia if these pitched battles had been fought under the military conditions that prevailed at Passchendaele, in Champagne and Artois and around Neuve Chapelle in the last war?" His answer would be in hundreds of thousands instead of in the tens of thousands that are the fact.

In these World War I battles and campaigns the casualties were in hundreds of thousands. The French alone lost 102,000 men in their offensive between Lens and Arras in 1915. But in the decisive battle of El Alamein British casualties were only 13,600 (85 per cent among troops from the United Kingdom). From the day Italy entered the war, in June, 1940, the British and Empire total is 220,000. The British figure in Italy, from Sept. 3 to Nov. 23, 1943, was 16,074. In Sicily British and Canadian casualties were about 14,000; those of the United States were 7,400.

Remembering the magnitude of the operation at El Alamein, and that some battles in Tunisia were on a major scale, the contrast with World War I is amazing. In those four years Allied casualties were 52.3 per cent in a total of more than 42 millions mobilized; and the Central Powers, with 22 millions under arms, had an over-all casualty percentage of 67.4. These statistics, of course, include wounded, missing and prisoners. But 8½ million men on both sides were killed in battle or died during the war.

This contrast is to be explained by the rise of air power and the terminating effect on battle when one combatant gains control of the air. The superior air force thrusts behind the enemy's lines, breaks up his formations and chokes off his sources of supply. The enemy army then disintegrates, which ends the battle—thus holding down casualties—or becomes demoralized, ending the campaign.

If the enemy is merely disintegrated, he can, under master direction, retreat perhaps and re-form for a later engagement. But if air superiority is maintained against him, the result will be the same. After retreat the next battle can come more quickly, because troops in slit trenches, fox holes and other anti-air cover are not destroyed. At sea, however, air operations are more lasting in effect because victory and superiority in the air mean the destruction of the enemy—ships, men and equipment.

AN OBSERVER AT IWO JIMA
February 26, 1945

Whatever administrative errors may be assigned by history to civilian direction of the American armed forces in this war, it can never be written that those immediately responsible for the War and Navy Departments have failed to acquaint themselves with battle conditions at first hand. The latest sample is that of Secretary Forrestal, who watched the early stages of the desperate fight on Iwo Jima from a ship just offshore, and whose subsequent broadcast from Guam last night thrilled the capital.

Mr. Forrestal is a comparatively young man, but Mr. Stimson's years—twenty-five more than those of his Navy colleague—have not deterred the Secretary of War from visiting the combat lines of the Army, and the late Secretary Knox was active on the same errands. The chief civilian assistants of both present Secretaries have all been in the range of enemy fire on numerous occasions. To inspect the fighting of the war these officials have helped to organize, and for which they are responsible to the President and to Congress, they have taken all the risks of travel in these times.

Mr. Stimson inspected our front lines in both Italy and Normandy in July, 1944, and one year previously he was in North Africa and England. Public opinion and national security would not permit the President to enter the fighting areas, but he has been near them and over them, and he has taken more travel ventures than any man in his position ever did.

The practice of the civilian war leaders to be with their men in time of peril has undoubtedly been good for morale, and it has been valuable administratively. Generals in this war don't "die in bed," and the Secretary of the Navy's trip to Iwo Jima confounds an earlier satirist of the bureaucrats of armed forces. W. S. Gilbert's Sir Joseph Porter advised his hearers to "stick to your desks and never go to sea, and you will be the ruler of the Queen's Navee." Mr. Forrestal, like Mr. Stimson, has not stuck to his desk when he thought it would be helpful to the fighting men to go abroad.

The Navy did not have to drag him to Iwo Jima, but it was almost obliged to drag him to the microphone. His admiration for the Navy forces is such that he dislikes to seem to dramatize them through his personal medium. That is why he balked at the suggestion of yesterday's broadcast until convinced it would help carry out the purpose that took him to the island. Mr. Forrestal's attitude is illustrated by a speech he made on his return from the still-raging battle of Guadalcanal in 1942. Delivered at the Highland Park, Ill., plant of the Chrysler Corporation, it was never published, but these extracts merit the light:

> I don't intend to talk down to this crowd of men and women who have proved by their achievements in production [anti-aircraft guns] that they realize the seriousness and desperate urgency of our national crisis. * * * I speak to you with the same humility I felt in talking to wounded men who had been brought down to the field hospital from the battle area. It's difficult to say anything to a wounded man that doesn't sound flat to your own ears. All I could think of to say was that I was grateful.

Reports from combat areas Mr. Forrestal has visited testify, however, that his presence, and such simple statements as the one above and yesterday's from Guam, are serviceable to the war in many ways. The men have accepted the Secretary's feeling as truly humble and have appreciated the fact he has taken many of their own risks. The feeling again finds expression in Mr. Forrestal's annual report, issued Feb. 20.

> It would be inappropriate [he wrote] for me to try to evaluate in cold analysis the attitude of the men who have fought and who are still fighting our battles on the sea. But no man can stand in the presence of these young men on the eve of battle without a deep humility, nor can he, without being presumptuous, undertake to describe their heroism, their sacrifice and their service.

Mr. Forrestal, Mr. Stimson and their chief civilian aides, however, have "stood in the presence of these young men on the eve of battle" for other reasons than to admire. None of them believes any one service can win the war single-handed, and their journeys have been also for the purpose of assisting in coordination. The Secretary of the Navy has said that no war can be won without seapower or airpower, but that neither nor both is enough. "Wars," he said, "are finally won by the soldier on foot who goes up against the soldiers of the enemy." That is what he saw the Navy's foot, the Marines, do at Iwo Jima.

But basically Mr. Forrestal makes the trips, and so do his colleagues, because they feel that the raison d'être of the Washington military establishment is to support the distant force, and they want to know what the fighting men think of this support. The Secretary of the Navy has gone four times to the combat zones, and he has never stayed aboard ship on any occasion. In the southern France invasion last August he got Lieutenant General Patch's permission to accompany an aide on a night mission to discover what was the actual situation on Levant Island on the night of D-day. That was typical.

THE SUPREME COURT AT ITS PEAK
June 14, 1943

The Supreme Court has often justified Mr. Dooley's statement that it follows the election returns. It still does. Also, justices have managed frequently to find law to cover legislation carrying out their own and their group political philosophies when other justices have said no law exists. But when the court rises to its full height it proves its claim to be regarded as one of the great prides of American democracy, despite the human failings which it shares with all other thinking animals.

Today was one of those when the Supreme Court rose to its full height as champion of the lowly, the laws and those exceptions to the laws which were written in the Bill of Rights. The occasion was the reversal of what is known as the Gobitis case which turned on the penal requirement of West Virginia that all public-school children must offer a uniform salute to the flag. The court's decision, by a majority of 6 to 3, the several concurrences and the one written dissent might well be made required reading for those who want to be learned in the processes of American democracy.

In the decision a former dictum of Justice Frankfurter, in June, 1940, which was then concurred in by every other member of the court but the Chief Justice, was set aside. This was accomplished by a recantation of view by three members—Justices Murphy, Black and Douglas—and by the opposition to the dictum of two others who had not passed on it before—Justices Jackson and Rutledge.

Such circumstances being painful, particularly to Justice Frankfurter, hot and angry exchanges of words among the brethren might have been expected. But what came forth today were earnest, high-minded, reasonable and—except for one passage in Mr. Frankfurter's dissent— impersonal arguments worthy of the highest tradition of the court. That every justice was intent on only one consideration was evident: the extent of protections of minorities by the Bill of Rights in their expressions of freedom of worship.

What was at stake was whether a State—West Virginia—could make a flag salute, and a uniform one, the condition of their right to a free education and could expel and punitively discipline children and their parents who declined the condition on religious grounds. These parents and children belong to the militant and thoroughly unpatriotic, even subversive, sect known as Jehovah's Witnesses, who assert that in their creed a flag is an idol, an image, and therefore impious in their sight.

Justice Frankfurter had held for the court that the State has the right to make the condition which led to the imposition of the penalties. Today, with Justice Jackson as spokesman, the court reversed that holding, making the penalties illegal. Said Mr. Frankfurter in dissent:

I think I appreciate fully the objections to the law before us. But to deny that it presents a question upon which men might reasonably differ appears to me to be intolerance.

Therefore, he said, he felt he had no constitutional power as a Supreme Court judge to assert his own view of the wisdom of the law against the measured judgment of the Legislature of West Virginia. He asserted that the court "has no reason for existence if it merely reflects the pressures of the day." But in the view of many that is what the court did when it followed him in 1940, and what it was resisting when it changed its decision today.

Justice Jackson, in one of the most notable writings in the court's history, pointed out these aspects of the case: The children who declined to

salute the flag made no denial of the rights of others to do so and were
not in conflict with them. The State assumed the right to condition public education, though school attendance "is not optional." The earlier
decision assumed as a major premise that the State has this power. Consideration should begin without that assumption.

The Bill of Rights, he argued, without which he doubted the Constitution could have been ratified, would seem to insure that public education must not be a partisan or an enemy to any class, creed, party or
faction. Congress, in that view, has left flag observance voluntary, and,
even in the critical matter of raising an Army for war, recognizes the
right of conscientious objections to combat duty. The Bill of Rights
withdrew certain subjects from the field of controversial political action,
and this is one of them.

National unity, he said, is not involved. Those who begin "the
coercive elimination of dissenters soon find themselves exterminating
dissenters." The presence of the flag makes the case difficult. But "there
can be village tyrants as well as village Hampdens," and under the Bill
of Rights none may prescribe what may be orthodox in the exempted
areas of human activities.

This is high ground on which to shelter such a group as Jehovah's
Witnesses. But such is the ground that was reserved for the Supreme
Court.

AMERICA'S ELDER STATESMAN
October 31, 1943

He is everywhere in Washington—ubiquitous by unanimous request—a
very tall, lean, eagle-nosed old man, stooping a little now and growing
increasingly hard of hearing. The blue eyes, gentler than in the days
when he pitted his wits against the keenest of those concentrated in the
market place, flash with their old fire when the steel of his viewpoint
strikes the flint of another. And those who steadily meet him in high
council, or seek his advice, testify that his mind is as penetrating as it
was when he read the economic and financial auguries as well as any
man.

He is sought as counselor of every important administrator of the war
program, from the President down, and he is willing to give counsel to
the humblest. His suggestions and his guidance have been often disre-

garded, along with his presence and his vast experience, and time after time, when the event has proved him right, he has been sought out again by those who thrust him aside.

Sometimes when his counsel is not asked, and the issue seems to him sufficiently momentous, he barges in, anyhow, and none has the self-confidence to deem it an intrusion. For always his thought has been of his country and its interests, of the lives of young men on the battle-fronts to be saved, of the international structure to end war, or make it rare and brief, which he sought to erect twenty-five years ago under the leadership of Woodrow Wilson.

Though others have titles, he has none. Yet he is the President's counselor, philosopher and guide, and he serves in the same capacities for innumerable officials, including those military and naval men who are impatient of the views of any other civilian. He is an honored visitor in the Pentagon, the Navy Department, the Department of State, the War Manpower Commission and the office of the Director of War Mobilization, to whom technically he is attached. His rooms at the Carlton and the Shoreham, and the bench in Lafayette Square where he likes to warm his old bones in the sunshine, are the gathering places for all those with problems growing out of the State's business which call for solutions they cannot furnish themselves.

He is the nation's elder statesman. He is Bernard Mannes Baruch.

Much about Mr. Baruch is known: his birth, his breeding, his career in Wall Street and in the chancelleries and conference rooms of the world, his love of and proficiency in riding and shooting, his sociability, his classic good looks, his humor and his odd mixture of hard caution and lavish kindness. It has been much circulated that he is the son of a Confederate surgeon (later a benefactor of the poor as a doctor in New York City) and a lady of pre-Revolutionary stock in South Carolina. The story has often been told how President Wilson, finding the supply front of World War I was not going well, wrote him a letter which gave him full authority over everyone else to make things right, so that, with General Pershing, he was estimated by many as one of the two most responsible for successful American action in the field. Clemenceau once said as much.

The files of the newspapers bear unswerving testimony to these things also: that, like President Roosevelt, he foresaw the coming war, but that Mr. Baruch pressed specific preparations for it that were not made; that one by one, as the shadow of crises impeded, he pointed them out and offered provision to dispel them; that when his counsel was ignored and the crises came, he was called in to solve them and only then his counsel

was adopted; that years before the war came, and again in time to anticipate it, he offered an organizational blueprint to the Administration
against inflation and commodity shortages, and in the direction of close,
non-duplicating cohesion and control of the war program, a blueprint
which was accepted only bit by bit and lost vital efficiency in the
process.

This is an old story, enough to discourage any man. But Mr. Baruch
has never become discouraged, though at times he has felt and said that
everything for which he has labored was in vain. He has carried his
standard unflinchingly and never taken his eyes off what is written
there:

"Win the war. Don't lose the peace again. Don't lose our democracy
in any victory. Don't waste one young life."

This burning zeal, for all his gentle manner, his overpowering reputation, his handsome presence and his unassailable and impersonal
patriotism, has at times made a nuisance of Mr. Baruch. He has not
minded at all when men one-tenth his stature have smiled with vexation
and spoken of him behind his back as "Old Bernie." He has gone ahead
with his errand as steadily when out of White House favor as when in it.
Though no man in the United States could say "I told you so" as often
as Mr. Baruch could, and to persons of equal authority, he avoids the
phrase.

Yet he cannot avoid the fact that his very footsteps in Washington
echo these words—in the White House, in the Pentagon, in the Navy
Department, in the offices of the independent agencies, in Lafayette
Park where once he said to a squirrel which sat up before him ex-
pectantly:

"I have nothing to give you that you want—today!"

EFFECTS OF BETTING ODDS
ON ELECTIONS
October 26, 1944

One of the anomalies of this anomalous Presidential campaign is the
disparity between test-polls, headquarters reports and press surveys on
the one hand and the betting odds on the other. To national, State and

local managements of both party candidates, to directors of the polls and to the newspapers there is a steady flow of reports which add up to the forecast of a very close contest. But the story of the betting odds is that the President's election to a fourth term is a complete certainty.

Roving representatives of the press have never been so cautious in their attempts to assay in advance how the key States will go. Also, many of them have said that almost invariably the expressed confidence of local campaign managers in the victory of their side fades on cross-examination. Except for the latest estimate of Elmo Roper—that the President has a 7 per cent advantage among civilian voters—most polls are nip and tuck. Nevertheless, the betting odds against Mr. Dewey have reached 3 to 1 and those who book them seem to have considerable sums to back up their judgment or information. This information, by the way, if it be such, is based on a private "gamblers' poll," and it has often been proved by the result.

Those who run campaigns for candidates pay very serious attention to the betting odds, and for two reasons. One is, as noted before, that they have frequently anticipated the outcome. The other is that this fact is well-known, and, politicians believe, attracts to the forecast winner many votes which would otherwise be against him. These votes, they think, are cast by citizens who like to be on the victorious side for numerous reasons, some of them material.

Because of this attitude of professional politicians toward the betting odds large sums are sometimes raised to bring them down. This is considered one of the most effective uses of money in a campaign, well worth the risk of loss because of the effect it may have on the psychology of the voters. Only today in Washington the opinion was heard that if, by this means, or because of a change in information coming to the odds-makers, the betting before election day goes down to 2 to 1 on the President his prospects will be adversely affected; and, if they go to 7 to 5, he will lose.

This is the more sordid side of politics, but it is well-established. And this correspondent is in a position to give assurance that the subject of the odds has engaged the attention of some of the most important figures in the campaign and has been discussed in the interested hearing of even more important ones.

By all private and public reports—except those that may be in the "gamblers' poll"—the key States of New York, Pennsylvania, Missouri, Massachusetts and Michigan are listed as very close. If the President should lose New York and Pennsylvania, or New York, Missouri and either Michigan or Massachusetts, few of the so-called experts would be able to make a winning tabulation for him. This is not because no other combination is possible that would give him the 266 electoral votes necessary to a choice. It is because experience and American political history teach that the loss of such States by the White House incumbent would be part of a trend that would engulf others he could not afford to lose. Thus far, however, the odds ignore these listings by the several varieties of pulse-takers. In some books New York has been rated as 2 to 1 for Mr. Roosevelt, Illinois has recently been ruled even (though the Republicans have been claiming it with what appears to be real confidence), and some are willing to wager on Pennsylvania at bettering odds from Mr. Roosevelt's standpoint.

If the professional makers of odds are right, then almost every other analyst is wrong—not in disputing the outcome so much as in the nearly solid front they have made for a close election which still might go either way. Not since 1936, when the great majority of prophets were convinced that the President would have an easy victory, have they been so heavily in his favor for so long, and at a comparable period in the campaign. Yet it would require protracted search to find a Democratic chairman who would with complete honesty express the opinion that Mr. Dewey's chances are as slim as were those of Mr. Landon.

This as well as other campaign aspects will be tested on election day, unless the odds shorten before that. And only then can it be demonstrated whether the odds are sound, are based on poor information or are deliberately artificial.

F.D.R.'S FOURTH TERM
January 20, 1945

Except for the accession of a new Vice President, this Inaugural Day marked no change in the continuity of the nationally elected leadership of the United States, a continuity which will be twelve years old next March. But in almost every other aspect of the Government and its activities there has been great change since March, 1933, and, as the President's third term merged quietly into his fourth, the forecast was for a departure from the past even more momentous.

That departure—unless all signs fail—will be the formal association of this nation for the first time in an international alliance to which the use of the United States Army and Navy will be pledged to keep the peace when it is made. This may even be preceded by temporary military pacts with two sets of the major anti-Axis powers to dismantle the war-making establishments of Germany and Japan by force, and to assume our part of a joint obligation to maintain this situation by force until all peace-keeping nations can share the responsibility.

Four years ago today the President entered upon an unprecedented third term in the midst of an unprecedented situation for the country: the prospect, admitted by the 1940 Republican national candidate as well as by himself, of attack by both Germany and Japan after they had disposed of all other nations strong enough to resist them. Today he begins an unprecedented fourth term in the midst of another unprecedented situation: The prospect that the United States will sign those "entangling alliances" against which American public orators and writers have warned the nation since it was established.

As the President took the oath of office, in a ceremony as simple as those which marked the accession of his earliest predecessors, his mind must have been crowded with meditations on these wholly new phases of our history, and with thoughts of the conference he will soon attend abroad with the British Prime Minister and the Russian dictator, meetings which were also unprecedented in our history until Mr. Roosevelt's third term was more than half over.

But it would have been natural also if, looking at some of the faces around him, the President had let his mind traverse the years of office, now almost twelve in number, and contrasted his previous preoccupations with what they are now and have been since Hitler's ground and air forces struck at Poland in 1939.

Mr. Roosevelt's terms are separable in historical appraisal, even though the thread of one political philosophy has run through them all and the spool is still turning. In his first four years—from March, 1933, to March, 1937—he was wholly nationalist. In his next four years— from March, 1937, to January, 1941—he moved slowly, reluctantly and at times deviously from nationalism to internationalism and the beginnings of armed intervention in the European war. His third term fixed intervention as a deliberate policy (lend-lease, armed convoying of aid to Great Britain before we were at war, etc.) and was less than a year spent when the Japanese attacked at Pearl Harbor and Germany also declared war on us.

The conference abroad which the President will soon attend has for its purpose the planning of final military measures against the Axis, as well as adjusting of political differences which always arise among Allies, particularly when they are governed by systems as diverse as those of Russia and China on the one hand and the United States and Great Britain on the other.

On the home front the thread of the New Deal is still being spun by the Department of Justice (which amid the din of dubious battle files anti-trust and anti-cartel suits against corporations absorbed in war production) and by various Federal agencies that were set up in time of peace to enforce the New Deal ideologies. The colossal costs of war and the total diversion of our industrial economy foreshadow problems of finance and re-employment threatening the near future. But the real present concentration of the Government is on war-making and preparation for enduring peace. How different it was on March 4, 1933.

Mr. Roosevelt had no sooner taken the oath than he began with swift, confident and forceful series of regimented acts which made his first "hundred days" successful as well as historic. The bank holiday, the gold embargo and the economy act came in quick succession. But to the economy act was attached the Thomas (the greenbacks) amendment, as an anchor to leeward if policy was to change from conservative to radical, as it did. And then, with the NRA, the AAA, the gold purchase plan, deficit spending through WPA and other means, and the torpedoing of the London Economic Conference the last vestiges of conservative beginnings disappeared before a year had passed. The New Deal was firmly established, to be retained until many months after the national war peril had given clear signals for its suspension and international necessities had absorbed the President's effort.

The annals suggest two widely spaced eras and a score of Presidents. But they are those of only twelve years and one man.

PRESIDENT ROOSEVELT DIES
April 12, 1945

Franklin Delano Roosevelt, War President of the United States and the only Chief Executive in history who was chosen for more than two terms, died suddenly and unexpectedly at 4:35 P.M. today at Warm Springs, Ga., and the White House announced his death at 5:48 o'clock. He was 63.

The President, stricken by a cerebral hemorrhage, passed from unconsciousness to death on the eighty-third day of his fourth term and in an hour of high triumph. The armies and fleets under his direction as Commander in Chief were at the gates of Berlin and the shores of Japan's home islands as Mr. Roosevelt died, and the cause he represented and led was nearing the conclusive phase of success.

Less than two hours after the official announcement, Harry S. Truman of Missouri, the Vice President, took the oath as the thirty-second President. The oath was administered by the Chief Justice of the United States, Harlan F. Stone, in a one-minute ceremony at the White House. Mr. Truman immediately let it be known that Mr. Roosevelt's Cabinet is remaining in office at his request, and that he had authorized Secretary of State Edward R. Stettinius Jr. to proceed with plans for the United Nations Conference on international organization at San Francisco, scheduled to begin April 25. A report was circulated that he leans somewhat to the idea of a coalition Cabinet, but this is unsubstantiated.

It was disclosed by the White House that funeral services for Mr. Roosevelt would take place at 4 P.M. (E.W.T.) Saturday in the East Room of the Executive Mansion. The Rev. Angus Dun, Episcopal Bishop of Washington; the Rev. Howard S. Wilkinson of St. Thomas's Church in Washington and the Rev. John G. McGee of St. John's in Washington will conduct the services.

The body will be interred at Hyde Park, N.Y., Sunday, with the Rev. George W. Anthony of St. James Church officiating. The time has not yet been fixed.

Jonathan Daniels, White House secretary, said Mr. Roosevelt's body would not lie in state. He added that, in view of the limited size of the East Room, which holds only about 200 persons, the list of those attending the funeral services would be limited to high Government officials, representatives of the membership of both houses of Congress, heads of foreign missions, and friends of the family.

President Truman, in his first official pronouncement, pledged prosecution of the war to a successful conclusion. His statement, issued for him at the White House by press secretary Jonathan Daniels, said:

"The world may be sure that we will prosecute the war on both fronts, East and West, with all the vigor we possess to a successful conclusion."

The impact of the news of the President's death on the capital was tremendous. Although rumor and a marked change in Mr. Roosevelt's appearance and manner had brought anxiety to many regarding his health, and there had been increasing speculation as to the effects his death would have on the national and world situation, the fact stunned the Government and the citizens of the capital.

It was not long, however, before the wheels of Government began once more to turn. Mr. Stettinius, the first of the late President's Ministers to arrive at the White House, summoned the Cabinet to meet at once. Mr. Truman, his face gray and drawn, responded to the first summons given to any outside Mr. Roosevelt's family and official intimates by rushing from the Capitol.

Mrs. Roosevelt had immediately given voice to the spirit that animated the entire Government, once the first shock of the news had passed. She cabled to her four sons, all on active service:

"He did his job to the end as he would want you to do. Bless you all and all our love. Mother."

Those who had served with the late President in peace and in war accepted that as their obligation. The comment of members of Congress unanimously reflected this spirit. Those who supported or opposed Mr. Roosevelt during his long and controversial years as President did not deviate in this. And all hailed him as the greatest leader of his time.

Mr. Roosevelt died also in a position unique insofar as the history of American statesmen reveals. He was regarded by millions as indispensable to winning the war and making a just and lasting peace. On the basis of this opinion, they elected him to a fourth term in 1944. He was regarded by those same millions as the one American qualified to deal successfully and effectively with the leaders of other nations—particularly Prime Minister Winston Churchill and Marshal Joseph Stalin—and this was another reason for his re-election.

Yet the constitutional transition to the Presidency of Mr. Truman was accomplished without a visible sign of anxiety or fear on the part of any of those responsible for waging war and negotiating peace under the Chief Executive. Though the democratic process has never had a greater shock, the human and official machines withstood it, once the first wave of grief had passed for a leader who was crushed by the burdens of war.

President Truman entered upon the duties imposed by destiny with a modest and calm, and yet a resolute, manner. Those who were with him through the late afternoon and evening were deeply impressed with his approach to the task.

"He is conscious of limitations greater than he has," said one. "But for the time being that is not a bad thing for the country."

How unexpected was President Roosevelt's death despite the obvious physical decline of the last few months is attested by the circumstance that no member of his family was with him at Warm Springs, no high-ranking associate or long-time intimate, and that his personal physician, Rear Admiral Ross McIntyre, was in Washington, totally unprepared for the news.

The Admiral, in answer to questions from the press today, said "this came out of a clear sky," that no operations had been performed recently on Mr. Roosevelt and that there had never been the slightest indication of cerebral hemorrhage. His optimistic reports of the late President's health, he declared, had been completely justified by the known tests.

As soon as the news became a certainty the White House flag was lowered to half-staff—the first time marking the death of an occupant since Warren G. Harding died at the Palace Hotel in San Francisco, Aug. 2, 1923, following a heart attack that succeeded pneumonia. The flag over the Capitol was lowered at 6:30 P.M. Between these two manifestations of the blow that had befallen the nation and the world, the news had spread throughout the city and respectful crowds gathered on the Lafayette Square pavement across from the executive mansion. They made no demonstration. But the men's hats were off, and the tears that were shed were not to be seen only on the cheeks of women. Some Presidents have been held in lukewarm esteem here, and some have been disliked by the local population, but Mr. Roosevelt held a high place in the rare affections of the capital.

The spoken tributes paid by members of Congress, a body with which the late President had many encounters, also testified to the extraordinary impression Mr. Roosevelt made on his times and the unparalleled position he had attained in the world. The comment of Senator Robert A. Taft of Ohio, a constant adversary on policy, was typical. "The greatest figure of our time," he called him, who had been removed "at the very climax of his career," who died "a hero of the war, for he literally worked himself to death in the service of the American people." And Senator Arthur H. Vandenberg of Michigan, another Republican and frequent critic, said that the late President had "left an imperishable imprint on the history of America and of the world."

But this tribute paid, this anxiety expressed, they and the late President's political supporters and official aides turned their hearts and minds again to the tasks before the nation. No one said "On to Berlin and Tokyo!" For Americans do not speak dramatically. But that is what everyone meant, and it was the gist of what President Truman said and did after the homely ceremony that made him the head of the State.

He wore a gray suit a white shirt and a polka-dot tie. His face was

grave but his lips were firm and his voice was strong. He said through
Mr. Early that his effort will be "to carry on as he believed the President would have done." * And he arranged to meet with the Army and
Navy chiefs tomorrow to assure them as tonight he did the people that
his purpose is to continue the conduct of the war with the utmost vigor
and to the earliest possible and successful conclusion.

While these simple but dignified processes of democracy were in
motion, preparations were being made to render fit respect to the
memory of the dead President.

* Steve Early was a press secretary to Presidents Franklin D. Roosevelt and Harry S.
Truman.

The Truman Years

When the firmament fell, with all its suns, moons, stars and planets, onto the shoulders of Harry S. Truman, he shared the doubt of the American people of his capacity to bear the burden. This has been the first sensation of most of those citizens who, by constitutional succession, have been elected with and served under the Chief Executives whom history has evaluated as "great" or even "strong." And Franklin D. Roosevelt has impressive claims to both designations.

But Mr. Truman's doubt of his qualifications for the role which fate had thrust upon him was the deeper and more troubling for special reasons. Not only had he dwelt wholly in the shadow of Roosevelt's overpowering personality, but also in the shadow of exclusion from participation in the process by which major decisions of war and peace were made. Not only was Mr. Truman congenitally invested with that "all humility of mind" which Paul spoke of to the elders of Ephesus. His potentialities in government were largely unknown to the American people.

Although his service, as chairman of the Senate committee which kept nonpartisan watch on the conduct of the Second World War, had been a notable achievement, only Mr. Truman's Congressional colleagues, the Roosevelt Administration and newspaper correspondents in Washington were aware of this. So he was the outstanding "Mr. X" among the Vice Presidents who have succeeded to the nation's highest office in times of epochal crisis.

111

But the Presidency is a crucible of which the residue is the measure of the fitness of the occupant for its tasks. And it was not long before the American people were made aware that Mr. Truman was equal to the test. The allies of the United States in the war were slower in recognizing this, misled by the errors of the new President at the Potsdam Conference that were the consequence of his total exclusion from the sources of information on which President Roosevelt had based his vital decisions. But only two years were to pass before London, Paris, Rome and especially Moscow, discovered that one strong President had succeeded another in Washington.

Mr. Truman's first steps were made timid and uncertain by the shock of his sudden transition to the topmost seat of power in the world, his natural humility and his acute consciousness that he was the creature of the Constitution and not of the electorate. Accordingly, when he retreated from his original and instinctive position against rapid demobilization of the civil and military structure of the Second World War, his timing was as faulty politically as his action was internationally. He resisted the removal of wartime controls on the civilian front—particularly the abandonment of the consumers' meat ration—until the Republicans had established the public psychology that the action was forced on the President by their attacks. This was largely instrumental in the election of a Republican Congress in 1946 and a general impression that Mr. Truman was weak in purpose.

Under the same pressure, in which Democratic politicians and voters joined, the President compounded Roosevelt's enormous mistake of anticipating that Soviet postwar foreign policy would be peaceful. He also demobilized the powerful military establishment at a rate which proved to be as inimical to national security as a handful of his official advisers—led by J. V. Forrestal and Averell Harriman—warned Mr. Truman it would be.

In this atmosphere of delusive error, and against his natural instinct, the President at Potsdam formed an impression of Stalin reflected in his comment, "Old Joe; I like him," that was disastrously projected in his ratification of Roosevelt's agreement to the segmentation of Germany that made Berlin an island in the Soviet Zone for ready and continuous use by Moscow as the base of military and diplomatic blackmail.

Among the later decisions by which President Truman reversed the impression of weakness and incapacity these errors had created, his order for the Berlin airlift was outstanding. It exposed Stalin publicly as a maker of threats he would not venture to execute when firmly challenged. And Mr. Truman permanently took his place in history as one of the strongest of American Presidents by subsequent decisions, from which once made (as in his order to drop the first nuclear bomb on Japan) he never wavered. These decisions materialized in the Marshall Plan; the assumption of the military defense of Greece and Turkey when the British became unable to furnish it; and the revolution in the United States foreign policy implicit in the creation of the North Atlantic Alliance and of NATO, its military enforcer.

Before he made up his mind that seven years of the Presidency were as long as any citizen should wield this power, he had also broadened the Greek-Turk aid policy to what became known as "The Truman Doctrine." As Mr. Truman envisaged this, it was a commitment by the United States to "support," but largely by economic and technical aid, any nation or people whose independence was threatened "by external aggression or internal subversion." But under the aegis of the United Nations, he committed the United States to almost the entire military task of repelling the Communist invasion of South Korea from North. And under two of his successors, John F. Kennedy and Lyndon B. Johnson, the United States has expanded this precedent into the doctrine of unilateral obligation to make war in cases of Communist military threats or open aggression where, as in Vietnam but unlike Korea, the writ of the United Nations does not run.

As a founder of the United Nations, Mr. Truman gave it the lavish support of his Government on the shattered concept that it is "the best hope of peace in the world," to which his three successors have clung despite mounting proofs to the contrary.

His domestic programs were first formulated in the middle lane of political philosophy, edging on the conservative side. But by September,

1945, he began to shift them well to the Left. The product became a composite of civil rights enforcement for Negroes that had lapsed since Reconstruction; an expansion of President Roosevelt's legislative and administrative alliance with organized labor; an acceptance of the "absolutist" interpretation of the First Amendment, through which many subversives had filtered into the Government during the Second World War; and a policy of deficit spending for welfare state measures to which the President gave the name of the Fair Deal.

Mr. Truman exploited this program with such political skill that, though it made small headway in the Republican Congress that was elected in 1948, he lured the Republican Presidential candidate of 1948, Thomas E. Dewey, into the position of endorsing its general principles, but promising to shape them to "the Constitution," to economy and to efficient administration. This won Dewey no liberals, alarmed many conservatives; and his plight was capped by the disaffection Mr. Truman created among voters in the normally Republican farm States by bald misrepresentation of Republican agricultural policy.

The war in Korea put the Fair Deal temporarily on the shelf, as the Second World War had shelved the New Deal, both to reappear in the Kennedy Administration and become an attainment under President Johnson far beyond their original and modest concepts. The President was beset by official scandals in his Administration that ranged from peccadillo to serious betrayal of trust; and by well-documented public criticism that he tended to head a "Government by crony." Having decided for the reasons he gave, also perhaps for reasons he withheld, not to run again in 1952, Mr. Truman sought to save the Democratic party from the national defeat he saw impending by suggesting to Dwight D. Eisenhower that, if the General chanced to be available for the Democratic Presidential nomination, Mr. Truman would support him.

I reported the first of these "feelers"—and its dismissal by Eisenhower—which occurred on November 7, 1951, in a dispatch to *The New York Times,* on the authority of a Democrat then and now in "an eminent public position." The President vigorously denied it, and I was attacked as the author of a shocking fabrication. But this approach and several subsequent ones have since been confirmed in detail or substance in several publications—for examples, General Eisenhower's autobiography, and an article in *Diplomat Magazine* by the late Joseph E. Davies, narrating his assignment by Mr. Truman on the same mission of persuasion to the General in Paris. I have in my files the transcript of the account given me by this Democrat "in an eminent public office," then and now, and signed by him.

Despite President Truman's displeasure over my dispatch of November 7, 1951, it did not diminish the generous consideration he had always shown me professionally, or the friendly relation that had existed between us from his early years in the Senate. I have known several Presidents, some quite intimately. But he is the only one who bore no grudges for press critics or the authors of news reports which made difficulties for him, provided he was convinced there was neither malice nor evidence of low professional standards in the product. And this conviction was much more his natural reaction than a judgment to the contrary.

I wrote much that was critical of his Presidency, but he never, so far as I know, indicated regret for having given me, on his own motion, the only exclusive interview he ever granted, and later another which, though not specifically attributed, he authorized to reflect its source unmistakably.

Some years after Mr. Truman left office, he told a Congressional committee he had no recollection of having given me the exclusive interview from which an extract was quoted to him for questioning. But when I refreshed his memory with the details, he instantly made a handsome public acknowledgment. And his hand-written reply to my letter of regret for the incident was extraordinarily magnanimous in the personally painful circumstances.

The following articles, written during the course of the Truman Administration, are commentaries which I trust will reflect the highlights of much of the foregoing history.

TRANSITION AND
THE WAR'S END

TRUMAN ACTS LIKE HIMSELF AGAIN
July 2, 1945

The country, which seems to be immensely pleased with the President, was probably once again favorably impressed by his visit to the Senate today and the simplicity of the attendant circumstances. The occasion was, of course, historic: Mr. Truman's first formal appearance before his former colleagues and the sixth time a President has gone before the Senate alone on official business. And the nature of the business, to help assure prompt ratification of the Charter of the United Nations, is vital to the future of the world.

The President's speech was as simple as the occasion. Also, it was brief, and the only interpolations were good-humored and homely allusions to Mr. Truman's service in this branch of Congress and his knowledge of the tendency of Senators to make speeches. Though the President's errand was of high importance, there were many contrasts to previous visits to the Senate of the Chief Executive, in addition to the significant one that this Senate is ready to do what this President asked and that the atmosphere was saturated with personal good-will.

The first of these historic occasions was Aug. 21, 1789. On the day previous this note was dispatched, addressed to the "Gentlemen of the Senate":

The President of the United States will meet the Senate in the Senate chamber at half past 11 o' clock tomorrow to advise with them on the

117

terms of the treaty to be negotiated with the Southern Indians. *Geo. Washington.*

That was an executive session. The General did not repeat the action, though later he visited the Senate's purlieus to talk with a committee, and departed vowing he would "never go to that place again." This physical separation, so far as President and Senate were concerned, lasted for 128 years, until Jan. 22, 1917, when Woodrow Wilson appeared before the chamber.

His purpose was to discuss his identic notes to the Governments then at war, asking them to state the terms on which they would make peace. He came personally to the Senate again on Sept. 30, 1918, in behalf of woman's suffrage as a "war measure." Mr. Wilson's final visit was on July 10, 1919, when he presented the Treaty of Versailles and urged its ratification.

No other President made the journey until May 31, 1932, nearly 143 years after Washington's mission. On that day Herbert Hoover, after a sleepless night, went up to the north wing of the Capitol. Speaking in a low monotone to an audience that included many severe critics and some downright political enemies, the President said a crisis had developed in which doubts had arisen that the Government would meet its obligations. Twelve hours later, the Senate passed a tax bill of $1,115 millions, reported a measure to save $238 millions and made possible a balanced budget.

No President has come exclusively to the Senate from that visit until today, though a natural retrospective thought is that it is odd Mr. Roosevelt never did. But, like most other Chief Executives who went formally to the Capitol at all, Mr. Roosevelt confined his addresses to joint sessions of the Senate and the House.

But, though the late President never addressed the Senate exclusively on anything, the basis of the friendly reception Mr. Truman received there today for his particular proposal was firmly laid by his predecessor and by the last previous ex-Senator who became Secretary of State— Cordell Hull. Mr. Roosevelt, profiting by a contrary policy by Mr. Wilson, named two Senators to the American delegation that helped to draft the Charter for which Mr. Truman today sought prompt ratification; and that has aided immeasurably in bringing Senate support for the consequent treaty. Mr. Hull, similarly profiting, worked assiduously and cooperatively with Senate as well as House leaders in preparing for the draft of Dumbarton Oaks which at San Francisco was expanded and improved into the Charter of the UN. Had he not done this groundwork so carefully, the President would have faced a much more critical Senate today.

FIRST SEED OF THE UN
July 9, 1945

The Senate Committee on Foreign Relations, which began hearings today on the proposed Charter of the United Nations, considered a document to the same purpose, with many similarities of detail, in 1919—twenty-six years ago—but in an atmosphere of hostility that was wholly absent from today's inspection. Very few persons at the hearing or elsewhere remember, however, that the first important political statement of the central idea of both League Covenant and United Nations Charter was made three years before Woodrow Wilson sent to the Senate the 1919 draft of a world organization to keep the peace.

This statement was written by President Wilson and can be found in the foreign policy plank of the Democratic national platform of 1916, on which he ran for re-election.

But the circumstances of the last two years have revealed necessities of international action which no former generation can have foreseen * * * We believe that * * * the small states of the world have a right to enjoy from other nations the same respect for their sovereignty and for their territorial integrity that great and powerful nations expect and insist upon; and that the world has a right to be free from every disturbance of its peace that has its origin in aggression or disregard of the rights of peoples and nations; and we believe that the time has come when it is the duty of the United States to join with the other nations of the world in any feasible association that will effectively serve these principles, to maintain inviolate the complete security of the highway of the seas for the common and unhindered use of all nations.

The concept of an international league to keep the peace was not new at that time. Many public orators and writers had championed the idea, and in very guarded language it had been mentioned in party platforms. But this was the strongest statement and the clearest outline a major party in the United States had ever been asked to propose, the words "effectively" and "maintain" clearly foreshadowing the use of force to keep world peace. When, however, the use of force was seen to be implicit in two articles of the Covenant which President Wilson brought home from Paris, the successful Senate opposition formed on this ground. Today, twenty-six years later, the instrument of international force is again before the Senate, but now with every prospect of overwhelming approval.

Mr. Wilson did not live to see this flowering of his seed of 1916. President Roosevelt, its latest powerful cultivator, did not live for this day either. Secretary Hull, who approved and directed the new policy of liaison between the Administration and the Senate which is greatly responsible for the present atmosphere, has been ill and could only send a message. And his Assistant Secretary, Breckinridge Long, who pioneered the policy and was its most active executive until he left the State Department, is in retirement. These are among the chief writers of the chapter that began in 1916.

JAPAN SURRENDERS
August 14, 1945

Japan today unconditionally surrendered the hemispheric empire taken by force and held almost intact for more than two years against the rising power of the United States and its Allies in the Pacific war.

The bloody dream of the Japanese military caste vanished in the text of a note to the Four Powers accepting the terms of the Potsdam Declaration of July 26, 1945, which simplified the Cairo Declaration of 1943.

Like the previous items in the surrender correspondence, today's Japanese document was forwarded through the Swiss Foreign Office at Berne and the Swiss Legation in Washington. The note of total capitulation was delivered to the State Department by the Legation Chargé d'Affaires at 6:10 P.M., after the third and most anxious day of waiting on Tokyo, the anxiety intensified by several premature or false reports of the finale of World War II.

President Truman summoned a special press conference in the Executive offices at 7 P.M. He handed to the reporters three texts.

The first—the only one he read aloud—was that he had received the Japanese note and deemed it full acceptance of the Potsdam Declaration, containing no qualification whatsoever; that arrangements for the formal signing of the peace would be made for the "earliest possible moment"; that the Japanese surrender would be made to General MacArthur in his capacity as Supreme Allied Commander in Chief; that Allied military commanders had been instructed to cease hostilities, but that the formal proclamation of V-J Day must await the formal signing.

The text ended with the Japanese note, in which the Four Powers (the United States, Great Britain, China and Russia) were officially informed that the Emperor of Japan had issued an imperial rescript of surrender, was prepared to guarantee the necessary signatures to the terms as prescribed by the Allies, and had instructed all his commanders to cease active operations, to surrender all arms and to disband all forces under their control and within their reach.

The President's second announcement was that he had instructed the Selective Service to reduce the monthly military draft from 80,000 to 50,000 men, permitting a constant flow of replacements for the occupation forces and other necessary military units, with the draft held to low-age groups and first discharges given on the basis of long, arduous and faithful war service. He said he hoped to release 5,000,000 to 5,500,000 men in the subsequent year or eighteen months, the ratio governed in some degree by transportation facilities and the world situation.

The President's final announcement was to decree holidays tomorrow and Thursday for all Federal workers, who, he said, were the "hardest working and perhaps the least appreciated" by the public of all who had helped to wage the war.

After the press conference, while usually bored Washington launched upon a noisy victory demonstration, the President with Mrs. Truman walked out to the fountain in the White House grounds that face on Pennsylvania Avenue and made the V sign to the shouting crowds.

But this did not satisfy the growing assemblage, or probably the President either, for, in response to clamor, he came back and made a speech from the north portico, in which he said that the present emergency was as great as that of Pearl Harbor Day and must and would be met in the same spirit. Later in the evening he appeared to the crowds and spoke again.

He then returned to the executive mansion to begin work at once on problems of peace, including domestic ones affecting reconversion, unemployment, wage-and-hour scales and industrial cut-backs, which are more complex and difficult than any he has faced and call for plans and measures that were necessarily held in abeyance by the exacting fact of war.

But certain immediate steps to deal with these problems and restore peacetime conditions were taken or announced as follows:

1. The War Manpower Commission abolished all controls, effective immediately, creating a free labor market for the first time in three years. The Commission also set up a plan to help displaced workers and veterans find jobs.

2. The Navy canceled nearly $6,000,000,000 of prime contracts.

The Japanese offer to surrender, confirmed by the note received through Switzerland today, came in the week after the United States Air Forces obliterated Hiroshima with the first atomic bomb in history and the Union of Soviet Socialist Republics declared war on Japan. At the time the document was received in Washington Russian armies were pushing back the Japanese armies in Asia and on Sakhalin Island, and the Army and Navy of the United States with their air forces—aided by the British—were relentlessly bombarding the home islands.

When the President made his announcements tonight it was three years and 250 days after the bombing of Pearl Harbor, which put the United States at war with Japan. This was followed immediately by the declarations of war on this country by Germany and Italy, the other Axis partners, which engaged the United States in the global conflict that now, in its military phases, is wholly won.

If the note had not come today the President was ready, though reluctant, to give the order that would have spread throughout Japan the hideous death and destruction that are the toll of the atomic bomb.

Officially the Japanese note was a response to the communication to Tokyo, written on behalf of the Allies Aug. 11 by Secretary Byrnes, which was itself a reply to a Japanese offer on Aug. 10 to surrender on the understanding of the Japanese Government that the Potsdam Declaration did not "prejudice the prerogatives" of the Emperor of Japan as its "sovereign ruler."

Mr. Byrnes wrote, in effect, that the Japanese might keep their Emperor if they chose to do so of their own free-will, but that he would be placed under the authority of the Allied Commander in Chief in Tokyo and would be responsible to that commander for his official and public activities.

The alternative for the Japanese would, of course, have been national suicide. But there are many in Washington, students of this strange race or baffled by the ways of the Orient, who have predicted that such would be the decision of the Japanese military leaders to which the people would submit. The Japanese, they contended, would commit mass suicide before they would yield their god, the Emperor, to an alien enemy as his overlord.

But now this god, in the person of an ordinary human being, representative of other human beings who were vanquished with him, is to take his orders from a mortal man who, above all others, symbolizes the spirit of the alien enemy that was foremost in crushing the myth of divinity and shattering the imperial dream. And the Emperor, with his Ministers and commanders, has been obliged to accept the condition that disproves the fanatical concept used by the militarists of Japan to produce unquestioned obedience to orders issued in the Emperor's name, however much or little he may have had to do with them.

DIRECTIONAL TESTS
September 12, 1945

The President at his press conference today laughed off a reporter's question, whether his fixed policy is to be, in the jargon of the day, "right" or "left." With my acts as a guide, said the President, you must figure that out for yourself.

Congress and the disputing groups that make up the Democratic party, however, are not asking the question any longer. After having read and digested the President's long State-of-the-Union message last week, and noting the effects of it on bellwethers and aggressive members of these groups, Congress accepts it as a fact that Mr. Truman has thrown in his lot with the spenders, the anti-economizers, the New Dealers, the organized labor pressure squads and the social-economists of whom Henry A. Wallace is the appointed spokesman.

The President will have difficulty and meet with reverses in trying to legislate abstract New Deal philosophies into concrete laws. But he has merely to encourage the spenders to assure an increased flow of Federal funds and a continuing majority against the degree of economy in government that could be attained. Presidential leadership is as essential as it has been absent to move toward a balance of the budget and the restoration of production through free enterprise. That same leadership is required to achieve a common-sense base of employment by private means instead of an artificially boosted base shored up by Federal subsidies.

But there was no such leadership in the message which has elated the New Dealers, the spenders and the Henry Wallace school of political philosophers. The President proposed a dozen different ways to disburse the nation's revenues, but he said nothing about balancing the budget. Economy he dismissed in a pious generality, but he offered no suggestions how the goal is to be attained. And he said much to encourage, and nothing to dissuade, those who talk of 60,000,000 jobs as a normal state of employment and refer to a job as a "right."

Because politicians over the last twelve years have found the road to re-election in such a program, and because spending is the easiest habit for Congress to indulge and the hardest to curb, little more affirmative leadership than the President's endorsement is needed to legislate his proposals. Mr. Truman could have let it go at that. But since he delivered his message he has repeated his views to members of Congress who have called to discuss how the bill is to be paid. And he has sent one or two envoys in behalf of bills which those who would move firmly to cut down spending and the national debt have been opposing. One such errand—to the Senate Finance Committee on the $25 per week unemployment compensation bill—was unsuccessful in so far as the committee is concerned. But victories for the spending opposition will be far fewer than defeats. And even the victories may not survive action on the floor.

For these reasons Congress no longer is asking the question which amused the President at his press conference today. If it is "leftist" to call for more spending, more Federal paternalism and new ways of centralization—which Congress and many outside think it is—then the President's direction and position are plain. Proposals are now in the making to provide veterans' bonuses of about $30,000,000,000 and large new costs for social security, and few expect the signer of last week's message to be conservative on either plan.

One cause for the hope that the President's message would be another kind of document were reports of White House conversations with a different trend. Missouri friends represented Mr. Truman as a "middle-of-the-road" man on all current political and economic issues save where party organization and patronage are involved. Others said he spoke the fairest words for unhampered private enterprise and production they had heard for years—as later in his message. But his words crumbled under his proposals. And the "middle of the road" was way off to one side.

'AUDIT' OF MR. TRUMAN
October 13, 1945

The old if not hallowed custom of making periodic audits of a President's leadership is being widely observed in this country as Harry S. Truman completes his first six months in the White House. Washington is probably busier with the task than any other community, being able to see the debits and credits at first-hand, and the general result here is an entry in the black but not a very large one.

The President has revealed himself as a plain man who likes to be direct and candid (witness his offhand statement on the atomic bomb secret), but is too seasoned a politician to permit himself to be so at all times; a citizen of vigorous and definite views on all subjects and men, who expresses these much more often and openly than any Chief Executive of recent times but knows how to temper them to and conceal them from the public; an American very typical of his Southwest Missouri and Confederate background, with a strong penchant to revisit it often, but also inclined to frequent travel elsewhere in the nation; an appointive power who is disposed to put loyalty and personal liking above wiser and better considerations; and an impulsive person who, in his own words, often has to "remember who I am."

As an administrator, the President has made an equally definite and generally favorable impression on those who keep in close touch with government. He decides official issues and disputes rapidly, preferring to be wrong occasionally than to risk worse by indecision and delay. He knows the workings of government intimately, its faults and virtues, by reason of his detailed inspection as chairman of the special Senate committee that bore his name. And he has given a good part of his time to study of the reorganization and consolidation the Federal machine has required for years, but especially so now that it must be reconverted from a war to a peace footing.

If Congress grants to Mr. Truman any considerable portion of the authority to reorganize he has sought, his administration and the entire executive establishment will be smaller and much more efficient in operation than it has been at any time since the early days of the republic.

One example of the kind of Government the President has in mind is to be found in the plan he outlined to his Cabinet at its first business meeting. He said he wanted each member to be responsible for his own domain, to settle all questions that could be settled without recourse to the Chief Executive or the Cabinet as a whole, which he hoped would be infrequent. He said further that he wanted the Cabinet to function as the nation's board of directors, with himself as chairman of the board, making, clarifying and creating policy as a group and seeing as individuals that it was properly executed.

The nature of our constitutional system is such that this plan must be limited in application. Cabinet members, unlike those under a parliamentary form of government, cannot answer at any time for the majority in Congress which at any time may nullify policy. And certain authorities have been so concentrated in the Presidency itself that Mr. Truman will find it impossible to delegate anything like as many as he wishes. But his outline gives an idea of the efficient method that appeals to him and that he would institute if he could.

As a politician he has played a less admirable role. He has followed the old city-machine method of finding berths for his friends, and after that trying to please everybody; of transferring expendables from one job to another instead of dispensing wholly with them; of filling his administration with representatives of every faction and social, racial or economic group to serve as something in the nature of hostages.

If one day the President has sought to satisfy a faction by giving it an appointment, the next day he has given one to the rival faction. And, though in his private talks with conservatives he has left them with the impression he is one of them, he has carefully done nothing that radical adherents can with any definiteness say gives support to such an impression.

As a national leader in time growing more and more troubled the President has also shown little assertiveness. He is both an optimist and a politician, and he wants to be re-elected. Therefore, he has displayed an inclination to let things settle themselves, to avoid Presidential intervention in difficult and delicate situations and to argue that what appear to be bad public sores are not bad at all.

These are some of the debits and credits which this correspondent sees on the Presidential ledger after six months of Mr. Truman in the White House. But it should be added that, while his popularity appears to be shrinking somewhat as acute domestic issues knock at his door without getting an answer, it is still very high. This is undoubtedly because the President continues to mix much and intimately with the people, and as a mixer in all circles, all the while being sincerely himself, he is supremely talented.

THE MIGHTIEST YEAR
December 31, 1945

When the American past is held up for the inspection of the future, however often and however soon the survey is made, current judgment must be that the year now closing will be marked as the high point of achievement thus far in the nation's history and that of any people in the annals of the world. Perhaps there are contemporary historians with the skill and wisdom to subdue the rushing events of 1945 long enough to put them within the covers of a book. But if such there are the assignment would still be terrifying.

The American story of 1945 is thronged with titanic shadows and lethal bursts of unearthly light, too vast and too blinding to be more than suggested on any field of art or page of history:

The rise of a great nation to a peak of military production not even before conceived. The global massing and activity of military forces that destroyed every strategic concept. The great discovery that shattered one of the last locked doors of science, but shattered masses of mankind as well. The development of friendly peace-loving boys into grim, all-conquering armies, and of mere students of the theory of war into commanders who do not suffer by comparison with the greatest of their predecessors.

The Pacific spanned and its furthest shores stormed by amphibious power, refuting the military maxim that the elephant can never turn whale and the whale never turn elephant successively as war requires. The air transformed from an element filled with destruction for ourselves to one black with destruction for our enemies. The dramatic death of the nation's war President on the eve of victory, and the smooth succession of another without a halt in the huge war machine.

The creation of a new world order to make and maintain peace by cessions of political and military power from Congress which, after the rejection of the League of Nations, was not thought to be possible for a hundred years. And then, as the year is ending, a new basis for cooperation with reluctant and suspicious Russia, fragile as yet and somewhat inchoate, but visible just the same.

The first important attempt, again led by the United States, to establish a stable world economy in which restraint of currency punctuations will be included. The progress of public education and mass experience in this country to a stage where politicians, ambitious for the Presidency, venture to discuss, and favorably, the loan to a world government of sovereign powers embedded in the Constitution and in the tradition of our nationalism.

The first full acceptance by the United States of the role of world leadership, despite the fact that this involves long terms of occupational service abroad for American troops and civil servants and responsibility for the internal conditions of strange and distant nations. The transfer of the seat of a world union from Europe to this country, although it was invested and expanded by those who came here to exclude the quarrels and miseries of the old civilizations from their daily lives.

These are but a few of the huge and dynamic events of which the United States was the center in the closing year. And most of them have thrust the nation and the world forward toward the light for which men have longed since they began to realize the evil consequences of unrestrained human nature and the vaunting ambition of races and nations to become masters of the planet.

POLITICS
AND PHILOSOPHY

GOVERNMENT BY CRONY
February 9, 1946

The President's personal relationships and loyalties, and the influences of certain individuals upon his choices for office—not his economic policies and programs—account for the Democratic party disturbance in that limited area where New Dealers and conservatives find themselves on common ground for the first time since the early days of 1933. These two antagonistic groups within the party are split as deeply as ever over Mr. Truman's policies and programs which, with few exceptions, follow the doctrines of Mr. Roosevelt and the New Deal. But they are together in their opposition to what a press gallery wit has called "government by crony."

These Democrats equally disapprove of the influence the President's cronies are reputed to have over him and the designation of several of them to important public office, though their reasons vary. Mr. Truman's critics among the original New Dealers oppose many members of the intimate White House circle because, they say, they are of "county courthouse" caliber and are too receptive to the personal benefits that come from friendly association with men in "big business"—an association which, they further say, is never a one-way street. The New Dealers have carefully made and maintained the opposite affiliation—with organized labor and radical groups—and they point to Mr. Roosevelt's series of electoral victories as proof that this is the most successful politics of Democrats.

129

The conservatives do not object to a sympathetic attitude toward business in the White House circle. But they agree that this should be limited to an expression of political philosophy, if the party is not to lose the House this year and the Presidency in 1948. And they share the criticism of their intra-party foes, the New Dealers, of the caliber of many of the President's favorites and his disposition to shower office on so many members of the Democratic political organization in Missouri.

Both groups want to stay in power if it is posible to do so, because the Democratic conservatives during a period of party majority control much of the procedure of Congress through seniority, which means chairmanships, there; and the more radical wing has dominated the executive and judicial branches of the Government and hopes to continue to do so. Nothing in the President's general approach to economic and social issues gives these latter Democrats any reason to believe that their executive domination of policies and places would not last as long as Mr. Truman can remain in the White House. What they fear is that his personal traits, loyalties and appointments will bring defeat to the party, in which their influence and offices would be lost. And on the ground of this common anxiety the groups have joined hands.

An illustration is to be found in the nature of the opposition to Edwin W. Pauley, nominated by the President to be Under-Secretary of the Navy. This opposition was unorganized until Harold L. Ickes, Secretary of the Interior and an original New Dealer, gave testimony that in his view established Mr. Pauley as disqualified for this office and for any other of public trust. But it is from Democratic conservatives on the Senate Committee and in the Senate that the votes required to reject his appointment must come, if there is to be a showdown in either forum.

"Government by crony" is not new in Washington, and President Roosevelt appointed many persons of doubtful competence or eligibility because of personal relationships. "Raw propositions," such as Mr. Ickes said Mr. Pauley made to him with reference to stopping a Government suit for the Navy's tidal oil, are not unknown to the Democratic conservatives; they are familiar to most politicians and have often been tolerated or condoned. During the recent Administration, for example, the Department of Justice timed certain legal actions with political implications in circumstances that bore every mark of deliberation and none of coincidence.

Mr. Pauley is a citizen and public servant of great and proved ability. The President admires him and feels personally beholden for services to the Administration, and as National Committee treasurer, to the party campaigns. But those who oppose his nomination to be Under-Secretary of the Navy, on the understanding that he was to succeed James Forrestal as Secretary, held that it was selfish of him, and at party expense, to insist on an appointment for which his business connections and his attitude on the Navy tidal oil issue seem generally to disqualify him and were sure to produce a bitter fight over confirmation. And they saw weakness and a cynicism that is politically perilous in the President's decision to give Mr. Pauley what he wants regardless. In lesser degree, and more on the point of incompetence, this feeling exists toward other of Mr. Truman's appointments.

IMAGINARY REFLECTIONS
OF A FORMER PRESIDENT
March 24, 1948

Whenever Harry S. Truman leaves the Presidency his meditations might run something like this:

"My sudden inheritance of the leadership of a party that only war prevented from breaking up in 1940, and of the worst post-bellum situation since the Thirty Years War, soon made it clear I was to deal with continuous conflict. But there were aspects of grim humor. And some of these appeared in March, 1948.

"At first I tried to please everybody. I was told the people were sick of war and its exactions, so when war ended I began to remove them. I was urged to subordinate every policy to recovery and production. Then some of the advisers who had been urging me to do this said I was going too fast and too far.

"I was accused of deserting Franklin Roosevelt and the New Deal. So I tried to maintain a strong OPA in 1946, which was the demand of the New Deal economists and union labor, and the voters that year turned over Congress to the Republicans.

"The Moscow Government made more and more trouble for the world, paralyzed the United Nations and emerged openly as a threat to free institutions everywhere. I was handicapped by the huge concessions Roosevelt made to Stalin, some of which I did not know about until I had been President for some time. They hampered me at the Potsdam conference. And Henry Wallace began to hamper me at home when I tried to reverse the policy of appeasement.

"I should never have approved the speech he made at Madison

Square Garden when he was still in the Cabinet and Byrnes was confronting the Soviets in Paris. But I did, without really reading it, and the result was that to stand by Byrnes and my own policy I had to oust Wallace. From that moment his third-party movement was a certainty.

"The third party soon began to worry the Democratic bosses in the big Eastern and Midwest cities, and they told me I had to do certain things to check it. I must get some solution of the Palestine question through the General Assembly of the U.N., and partition was the minimum that would satisfy those normal Democratic voters whom Wallace was attracting on the issue. I persuaded myself that partition was safe and workable, and, over the strong objections of the State and Defense Departments, I gave the order to support it.

"These bosses also told me that, to hold their Democratic vote without which I could not stay in the White House, I must also demand that Congress pass civil rights laws which were anathema to most Democrats in the South. The South had nowhere to go outside the national party, my advisers said, and nearly all its members of Congress had voted for every New Deal measure except those in the civil rights program. For good measure I was urged to add all the New Deal social security measures Roosevelt had ever endorsed.

"I took this advice. But Wallace's candidate won the New York City by-election, anyhow, on the very issues I was told my message would cancel there. The most serious revolt against the national Democratic party since Al Smith was nominated in 1928 flamed in the South. Said my Northern advisers: 'Just stand firm and count on your Southern friends in the Senate and House'—they named them—'to handle this at the proper time.'

"They handled it all right. First, Virginia passed a bill that would permit the regular Democratic electors to vote against the nominee of the national party convention—if I were he. Then Southern Governors served notice on the national chairman that he could expect more of the same.

"About that time the Communists worked their coup in Czechoslovakia, and I was getting gloomy reports on their chances in the Italian elections. The world menace was now so plain that the American public could doubt it no longer. My duty to trim the ship of state for any conceivable action and danger, throwing re-election politics over the side, was even plainer.

"Accordingly, I declined to hear anything more about the bearing of acts and policies on my election, and I tried to cast the thought from my mind as completely as a human being in my place can. I asked Congress to renew the draft and to support the five-power military alliance in Western Europe. To make John L. Lewis dig coal I resorted to the Taft-Hartley Act, which I fought to the limit for the union leaders. And, this time accepting the warnings of the State and Defense Departments, I abandoned support of the partition plan for Palestine.

"What happened? It seems funnier now than it did then. The big city bosses said I had ruined my chances in their bailiwicks by the reversal on Palestine and must not seek the nomination. My Southern 'friends' —even Lister Hill—joined my Southern enemies to the same purpose because I had taken the advice of these city bosses on civil rights."

Whether or not Mr. Truman ever muses thus, he could.

EVEN GRANT LEFT THEM
THEIR HORSES
July 14, 1948

The South arrived today at its second Appomattox. The non-Southern majority in the Democratic National Convention first rejected its proposed reassertion in the platform of the principle of states' rights and then specifically endorsed the Federal "civil rights" legislative program of President Truman.

This double defeat was followed by surrender on the part of most of the delegations from the states of the old Confederacy in so far as that is represented by not walking out of the convention. But since, unlike General Grant at Appomattox, the Northerners today did not even leave the Southern leaders with their side-arms and their horses, some of the latter are predicting a guerrilla war in the South against the party ticket that will cost it from twenty-five to seventy-five electors in that section.

The "civil rights" plank as presented by the platform committee was an effort to hold in line all the disputing elements on this issue. It generally endorsed the full extension of such rights and "called on Congress" to assure them within "constitutional limits." This was to enable the Northern and Western politicians to go home and claim that the plank ratified the President's ten-point program for Congress on this reasoning: Mr. Truman obviously holds that his program is constitutional for

Congress to legislate; otherwise he would not have "called" on it to do
so.

But the authors of the plank, acting by direction of the President and
the Administration—as the second roll-call plainly revealed—carefully
excluded mention of any of the measures urged by Mr. Truman. This
was to enable the Southern politicians to go home and claim that his
program remained unendorsed.

It was the usual slick political compromise of principle, the usual
expedient of seeming to face both ways. But why urge a "call on Congress," the Southerners demanded, unless Federal legislation was intended in general and the President's program in particular? On their
construction of the rights reserved to the states in the Constitution,
Congress could legally do no more than pass resolutions on the subject,
not laws. Hence they offered their amendment that reasserted the principle of states' rights. And this, as opposing orators truly said, would
wholly nullify the rest of the plank, which would be plain to the most
primitive intellect.

On that ground, the amendment was overwhelmingly beaten, not even
a third of the convention voting in its favor. This imperiled a walkout
by one or two Southern delegations if they carried out their threats. But
it offered hope that the rest would remain regular and could maintain
the strength of their organizations at home.

It was at this point that the Americans for Democratic Action seized
their opportunity. They had been badly beaten in their effort to nominate for President a substitute for Mr. Truman and to get a Vice Presidential candidate of their choice. But by offering a specific plank on
"civil rights" they believed they could force the large delegations in the
East and Middle West to support it.

That happened. It became a question for the New York, New Jersey,
Pennsylvania and Illinois politicians whether, as they thought, to
assure the loss of their organizations as well as of their states by opposing the A.D.A. amendment, which the Administration implored them to
do, or save their local interests at the expense of the national ticket in
the South.

They answered the question by voting for the specific amendment.
The Administration leaders, fleeing from the deep blue sea toward the
devil and then reversing their direction, could muster only a minority
against the amendment, even with the aid of the South.

As the clerk called the roll of states a Confederate flag hung from the
balcony to his right. But this was not the only irony of the occasion. A

sharper barb was supplied when the delegation from the President's home state, Missouri, voted with the Administration against an amendment that began as follows: "We highly commend President Harry Truman for his courageous stand on the issue of civil rights. We call upon Congress to support our President in guaranteeing these basic and fundamental rights." And it named the key legislative items he had urged upon Congress.

With Missouri, the Administration was able only to control the bulk of the votes from these states outside the South: Arizona, Colorado, Delaware, Kentucky, Maine, Maryland, Montana, Nebraska, Nevada, New Hampshire, New Mexico, North Dakota, Oklahoma, Rhode Island, Utah and West Virginia.

Cynical politics was never better served than today. The President's spokesmen tried to reject specific endorsement of him and his program in an effort to prevent total revolt in the South. The spokesmen for the majority of the Southern leaders, by prefacing their amendment with the assurance that they would stay in the party, made it plain their "fight" was only for home consumption, since that pledge obviously doomed their amendment. And Kentucky, where in 1798 Jefferson's famous states' rights resolutions were proclaimed, voted against the assertion of the principle today.

DEMOCRATS GAIN SPIRIT
August 28, 1948

The rooted strength of the two-party system in the United States has never been made more manifest than by developments since the Democratic National Convention last month which have already had these effects:

They have persuaded many Democrats, who a few weeks ago were sure of a crushing defeat for their national ticket, regardless of conceivable campaign incidents, that the President has a chance to win. And they have reduced the confidence of the Republicans to the more prudent state of acknowledging that they must jettison much of their past to gain the victory.

After the Democratic convention, which concluded its business only six weeks ago, few experienced politicians in either party gave Mr.

Truman any chance at all. This attitude was responsible for the demand by powerful state and city bosses that Senator Alben W. Barkley go on the ticket as the Vice Presidential nominee so that he would be in a position to act as "caretaker" of the Democratic organization during four and perhaps eight years out of power. The party left Philadelphia badly split, with the Wallace candidacy forming out of some of its fragments and the "Dixiecrat" ticket forming out of others. Mr. Truman had forced his nomination on an unwilling and discouraged convention after leaders from all sections of the country where voting majorities are essential to Democratic success had openly sought to have him rejected.

Yet since then the psychology has changed in so far as it is reflected by surface evidences. What are the reasons?

First, of course, there is the enduring quality of the two-party system as revealed on the Democratic side. The non-Southerners whose trade is politics, and who must maintain their regularity to command their organizations and realize their personal ambitions, had no alternative but to fall in behind the President. They had nowhere else to go—the labor leaders, who have made an issue for their followers of the Taft-Hartley Act, which Mr. Truman vetoed; the Americans for Democratic Action, who tried to use Gen. Dwight D. Eisenhower for their purposes and failed, and who, as radical New Dealers, are repudiated in the Republican platform, and Southern state leaders, like those in Virginia and North Carolina, who have made party regularity a *sine qua non* for aspiration to local office.

Once a major party has nominated its candidate, and especially if he is President of the United States, these natural forces behind the two-party system begin to operate powerfully. They bring into line bosses—Frank Hague of New Jersey, Jacob L. Arvey of Illinois, and James Roosevelt of California, as examples—who only a short time before were telling the world Mr. Truman could not possibly win. They impel the Democratic chairman of Virginia, faced with the task of re-electing a Senator and nine Representatives, to announce that no use will be made after all of the special law passed there to make it legal for the Democratic candidates for elector to vote for a Democrat other than the party nominee. And these forces in operation soon have the effect of engendering the belief that a campaign deemed lost may now possibly be won.

Some of this is the courage that comes to companions in misery when they find themselves in the same hole. Some is the consequence of Mr. Truman's own stubborn insistence that he was the only available Democrat with whom the party had a chance to win, his proof of this at

Philadelphia and the optimistic belligerence with which he has set out to prove it in November. A fighting candidate, who also is President, can always rouse a party from despondency and energize professionals with the reminder that, if he loses his power and place, they lose theirs too.

PRESIDENT'S NATIONAL TRIUMPH
November 6, 1948

Except on the few occasions in American history when the division of both the popular and electoral vote for President has justified the use of the term "landslide"—as in 1920 and 1936—it is always possible to prove by figures that the result would have been the opposite if a small group of citizens in selected areas had voted the other way. This year the group required for the demonstration is much smaller than usual—a total of 100,000 in Illinois, Ohio, Wisconsin, Iowa and Nevada, which would have elected Gov. Thomas E. Dewey, or a general shift of one voter in every nineteen, which would have given Mr. Dewey a popular but not necessarily an electoral majority.

Therefore, this kind of calculation after last Tuesday's event, though sound in statistics, in no way impairs President Truman's title to the four-year term to which he has been elected. It simply stresses the size of the three voting groups that did not want him, though two of these did not want Mr. Dewey either. And it is very important and useful to government in the general interest if a President, especially in the flush of a dramatic and definitely personal success like Mr. Truman's, bears in mind the amount of the votes against him.

Nevertheless, admitting these statistics, the President won a truly national victory for himself and for his party on the issues as he expounded them to the people. It was multi-sectional, so far as his candidacy was concerned, with a combination of Eastern, Central, Midwestern, Southern, Southwestern and Pacific states. When Massachusetts, Ohio, Illinois, Iowa, Minnesota and California are in the winning column, Indiana, Michigan and Connecticut are very close, and an electoral majority is attained without the votes of New York, Pennsylvania and New Jersey, the victory is set in a national frame.

But there was another and very important decision of Tuesday's voters which intensifies the national aspect. This was the complete overthrow, state by state, of the Republican House and Senate majorities in the Eightieth Congress. That was a personal endorsement of the President's attacks on this Congress and of his plea for Democratic control.

But it was also a victory everywhere except the South for the wing of the party that has supported Mr. Truman and his programs. And nationally it was a party defeat for the Republicans. So definite it was that no evidence supports the theory that, if the distributed group of 100,000 had voted for Mr. Dewey instead of Mr. Truman, they would have given the latter a Republican Congress.

In this campaign Mr. Truman was miraculously able to ignore the fact that the Congressional record of which he complained could not have been made without the aid of large numbers of Democrats from all sections of the country. But he could point to a Republican majority in the Eightieth Congress, and most voters seemed indifferent to the fact that also in the Seventy-ninth, with a Democratic majority, he and his predecessor had lost control. The Seventy-ninth, however, was elected with Mr. Roosevelt, not Mr. Truman, as the party candidate for President. The Eighty-first will come in with Mr. Truman and with a Democratic majority. That assigns all responsiblity for its record to the President and his party.

When all the votes are counted that were cast last Tuesday, it seems probable that Mr. Truman will be President not only by minority choice but by the narrowest of popular margins. Moreover, though no one can hazard the wildest guess how the score of millions who stayed at home would have voted, stay at home they did; hence Mr. Truman may be the actual choice of an even smaller minority of the qualified voters. These factors have been suggested as sources of weakness if the President is obliged to appeal from Congress to the people.

But the suggestion has the usual faults of speculative reasoning. And these counter-points can be made against it:

(1) Mr. Truman went to the polls with a diminished Democratic following because the extreme left and right groups had seceded and entered candidates against him, while the Republicans were united. This made it much more difficult for him to get a popular majority, but it also emphasizes the political miracle he wrought in getting 305 electors and, at the very least, a popular plurality. That is not weakness: it is strength.

(2) The fact that so many millions of the voters stayed at home cannot successfully be explained by the theory that the large majority did so in the assurance Mr. Truman could be defeated without them. It is

more tenable to argue that most of them were sufficiently satisfied with political and economic conditions to take the chance; and again that would be not weakness, but strength, in Mr. Truman.

GOP REFUSES TO WRITE OBITUARY
November 19, 1949

Once again in American history the funeral service is beginning to be read over a political party, this time the Republican. As is usual with political obsequies the knells are unauthorized and are being intoned by outsiders. And, as also is usual in these circumstances, the principal denies that it is dead or even moribund, and the customary reply is being made that the Republican party is dead and doesn't know it.

Political parties have died in this country—the Federalists, the Whigs, the Know-nothings, the Free Soilers, the Populists among them. But in each instance their voting strength had shrunk visibly far below that which the Republicans still can muster, and their position, or the lack of any, had obviously brought about their demise. This has not been true since, in 1908, a major party was last decreed by the opposition to be dead, in that year the Democrats, who went down to their third defeat under the standard of William Jennings Bryan. Mindful of what has happened since, the Republicans are stoutly denying the latest pronouncement, growing out of the elections of Nov. 8, 1949, but are openly perplexed how they can demonstrate that it is greatly exaggerated.

On this problem their counsel are divided because the Republicans are. They are divided on measures to combat President Truman's program for a "welfare state" without opening themselves to the charge that they are indifferent to the economic and social ills of the nation. They are divided on an approach to foreign policy that will not expose them to the charge of promoting American disunity before the world but will still give them an effective and legitimate partisan issue. It is plain that much time and debate will be required before the Republican leaders can reach conclusions which will hold the voting strength they now have and increase it. And meanwhile, these leaders are hoping that something will turn up in the way of events, or that a new national figure will arise in their ranks with the popular appeal that transcends issues.

The Democratic party is deeply divided, too, but, as was most re-

cently established in 1948, not on Election Day. The defection of the
Southern wing, though founded in passion and bitterness, was a minor
incident of the party convention in that year, and President Truman
had an electoral majority despite withholding of thirty-eight electors in
the South. The Democratic split continues to produce a bipartisan
majority in Congress against some of the Administration's measures.
But in Virginia, Georgia and other dissident Southern states that division vanished on Election Day, 1948, while traditional Republican
states were slipping their moorings.

This general situation, which, with the exception of the Congressional
elections of 1946, has endured since 1932, has produced the latest pronouncement that a major party is dead. If that should prove to be true,
in the sense that the Republicans are set in the role of a steadily shrinking minority until they join the deceased political parties of the past, it
would mean that the American people are committed to huge, paternalistic, costly, pro-labor government which is the largest employer in the
nation and the source of widespread bounties. It would mean also that
the people will remain so committed until the Republican party is really
dead and the dire consequences its leaders prophesy from current
Democratic policies have produced a new and more effective opposition.

The frequency of obituary services over parties which declined to die
offers the parallel to which the Republicans are now looking as they
hear them chanted in the camp of the enemy. From 1864 to 1884 the
Democratic party as a national force was pronounced dead every four
years, yet it managed to get a popular majority in 1876, and an electoral majority which was wiped out by disenfranchisement of states still
occupied by the conquering Northern armies. It came alive so powerfully, however, in 1884 that its victory could not be denied, but in 1888
its burial service was said again. Resurrected in 1892, its successive
wounds in 1896, 1900, 1904 and 1908 were said to have ended its career
forever. But a split in the Republican majority in 1910 produced another
Democratic President in 1912 who remained in office until the Republican victories of 1918 and 1920 sounded off the dirges once more.

These were periodically heard until 1932, when Franklin D. Roosevelt swept the country, but in 1936, after the most crushing Republican
defeat since 1912, the funeral music was played over the remnants of
that party. Though unusual events—the war emergency of 1940 and the
state of war in 1944—plainly saved the Democrats from loss of the
Presidency and the majorities in Congress, and the Republicans carried
Congress in 1946, the political wind is again blowing the other way and
the dead march of 1936 is again being played by Democratic musicians.

ON PROCURING TALENT
FOR GOVERNMENT
December 12, 1949

In its searches between wars for qualified citizens to fill high posts that
are vacant the American Government lately has filled the air with
laments that these are becoming increasingly hard to find; and it is
more and more inclined to attribute this largely to the "inadequacy" of
official salaries. No matter how much Congress boosts the payroll, and
the recent boosts have established many high salary brackets even by
comparison with those in private enterprise, this attribution persists.

It even produced an opinion by some sympathetic with this Government theme that a salary of $20,000 a year for an official with a wife
and three daughters, none self-indulgent, was a pittance which imposed
a diet of "roots." The real point was that this official, after long service
on a little more than half of $20,000, had been forced into debt he could
not liquidate with any salary paid by government except the President's
and therefore returned to private enterprise, where he could earn enough
to do so. The impression given, however, was that $20,000 a year, unat-
tainable to all but a small percentage of the population, for a government job was chicken-feed.

The matter of pay is only one of the reasons for the difficulty of getting and keeping Federal officials of the highest caliber, and it is
becoming one of the lesser causes. Here are some of the others:

1. The Government has grown so large, and statutes and "directives"
have become so numerous and conflicting, that it is beset with conflicts
over authority. The widening practice is for an official who feels his domain has been invaded by another, or wants that other's job and cannot
get action from his superiors, to pass on his grievances to gossip columnists and members of Congress under a seal of confidence. The second
official suddenly finds himself the target of "inside stories" which dis-
parage his acts and often his character, and of Congressional heckling
and obstruction which upset his staff and require him to spend at the
Capitol hours he should be devoting to office duties.

This has brought about the disgusted resignations of a number of
good men and unwillingness on the part of those asked to take their
places to undergo this Washington treatment.

2. Like some editors who inherit the prestige and success created by

their predecessors, Government talent scouts concentrate their efforts on recruiting citizens who have already acquired great names. These persons are usually in situations, and have assumed obligations, that make it impossible for them to accept salaries which in fact and in general comparison are adequate for the posts.

If, on the other hand, these posts were offered to eligibles of complete competence to fill them, but who have their names and their fortunes yet to make, they would be promptly filled and well administered. There are any number of such eligibles within reach of the President, as anyone familiar with the staffs of the various departments knows at first-hand. But they have no "names," and names are wanted above everything in this Administration except when a good White House pal and a good vacancy are simultaneously available.

For example, there is a vacancy in the Department of State, an assistant secretary to take charge of information and propaganda, "The Voice of America," etc. A large field of "names" has been canvassed without success. Yet in the department there are several under-officials perfectly competent for the job, and in the American press there are a number of well-qualified reporters and sub-editors. But these as yet have no "names," and the talent scouts are determined to acquire names for the President.

Yet very recently the Department of State revealed a worthy disregard of mere "name-chasing" when it elevated several persons to the second tier of the high command. The public at large knew little if anything of George McGhee, Edward H. Miller and John D. Hickerson, who were appointed assistant secretaries with jurisdiction over great affairs and who could entangle the United States perilously if they made any large mistakes. But these men are serving with competence and distinction, and they furnish a strong argument for the sensible system of promotion they represent.

3. When the Administration seeks manpower for posts requiring "names," in the sense that great and known achievements in industry, finance and statecraft are the essential tests of qualification, it must turn to persons who have attained the pinnacles of private enterprise. Nearly always these disapprove of the headlong rush toward "social reform," regardless and unwitting of cost, which is the program the President calls his "fair deal." And they see a real threat of socialization to the American system in the lavish promises of security and special bounties to many groups of the population. Even in jobs which they are assured will be kept free of partisanship such citizens do not wish to be associated with this Administration.

THE HISS CASE
January 28, 1950

Anyone who doubted that the case of Alger Hiss could become a major political issue would have had his doubts fully resolved if he had been in a position to observe the effects in Washington of two recent developments in the case. These two developments were the conviction of Hiss for perjury at the close of his second trial and the comment thereon by Dean G. Acheson, Secretary of State of the United States.

Anyone who deplored the expansion of a question of the guilt or innocence of a citizen, charged with making untrue statements to a grand jury, involving a breach of public trust, into a political issue of any degree would, by the same observation, have discovered that the circumstances of the case made this inevitable long ago. The circumstances are briefly these:

(1) Alger Hiss first came to the notice of Washington as a vigorous supporter of the domestic programs of the New Deal and as an exponent of an international theory very popular in the Thirties with some New Dealers. This was that great industrialists and global bankers recognize that war gives them their best chance to profiteer, and do so, even at the delay of essential war production. For hours one day, as assistant counsel of the Nye Committee, Hiss vainly endeavored to induce Bernard M. Baruch to concede World War I facts in support of this theory as applied to the steel industry.

(2) In the Thirties also, as the domestic New Deal met widening opposition, Hiss was prominently associated in the political mind with those Harvard Law School protégés of Felix Frankfurter to whom were attributed most of the acts and doctrines to which the anti-New Dealers chiefly objected.

(3) When there followed the threat of American involvement in World War II, and then the actuality, Hiss was utilized by the Roosevelt Administration for diplomatic work of varying importance, accompanied that President to Yalta as an adviser and was made Secretary General of the United Nations Organization Conference at San Francisco early in President Truman's Administration. At all times in this period Mr. Acheson made evident his trust in Hiss and his belief in his high capacity.

(4) With his election as director of the Carnegie Foundation for

Peace, Hiss passed out of government service and the zone of political interest until the events in the Un-American Activities Committee of the House of Representatives that led up to his libel suit against Whittaker Chambers and the trials for perjury. When Chambers' charges became public the political community divided along the lines of the Thirties. Those who disliked and distrusted New Dealers and accused the Roosevelt Administration of enthusiastically harboring Communists and fellow-travelers were sure Hiss was guilty as charged. But the people who believed in him were numerous, and many were respected and powerful.

(5) These, however, were steadily confronted with the challenge that, if Hiss was innocent, a libel suit against Chambers was an effective means to assert it. After a period of hesitation Hiss brought the action.

(6) The consequence of this was that Chambers produced the "pumpkin" documents in his defense, having previously withheld them from the committee. Also, he stressed that he had attempted to warn the State Department of Hiss' connection with him as a Soviet courier and was informed that the warning had been hotly rejected without investigation by Mr. Acheson, then an Assistant Secretary of State.

(7) The case was now spotlighted on the stage of politics. The "pumpkin papers" created public pressure on the Department of Justice that resulted in grand jury proceedings in New York against Hiss, out of which came the two indictments for perjury.

(8) The issue was then predominantly political, but it might have occupied a larger place in the public mind as an issue of one man's personal guilt or innocence if President Truman and Mr. Acheson had not made their contributions. On more than one occasion, though his own Department of Justice had brought the action against Hiss and was prosecuting it, Mr. Truman referred to the actions of the Un-American Activities Committee in this matter as merely an attempt to "draw a red herring" to divert attention from the record of the Eightieth Congress. And Mr. Acheson, asked about his relations with Hiss by the Senate committee to which his nomination to be Secretary of State was referred, stood by the indicted man. He said his friendship was not "easily" given nor "easily" withdrawn, emphasizing the provocative adverb.

(9) During Hiss's first trial before a judge appointed by the President, the judge was openly criticized as favoring the defendant. Mrs. Roosevelt made a sympathetic reference to Hiss in her syndicated column, and two justices of the Supreme Court of the United States, appointed by her husband, shattered all precedents but one (Chief Justice

Fuller similarly appeared) by testifying as character witnesses for the defense.

(10) The case, however it might terminate, was now in politics to stay. The division was not entirely along partisan lines because a few Democrats joined most Republicans in viewing the outcome of the charges against him as criteria of the Roosevelt and Truman administrations.

(11) When Hiss was convicted for perjury Republican critics were jubilant and Democratic strategists fearful that the political ammunition it furnished might be very powerful. At this juncture their fears were intensified by an utterance of the Secretary of State about the case.

(12) Having plainly deliberated on his answer to a request for comment he obviously expected, Mr. Acheson refused to limit himself to noting that the case was still before the court, the customary reply in the circumstances, especially of a lawyer. With visible emotion he said he would not "turn my back on Alger Hiss"; it was an issue between every man and his conscience; as for him, the matter was resolved by Jesus in His Last Judgment when He stated the doctrine of compassion for all in trouble, whatever the cause.

The courage and the Christian spirit of this utterance were widely admired in Mr. Acheson the man. But, since the case was pending, and the verdict accepted by critics as proof of their charges against the last two Administrations and Mr. Acheson in particular, many Democratic politicians were aghast at the comment by the Secretary of State, in his public office at a formal press conference. It was noted that two days later the President, who is quick to defend friends in any kind of trouble, vehemently refused to say anything on the subject.

These inflammable materials have made the Hiss case a burning political issue in which may be consumed the influence of important officials and vital national policies.

AN INTERVIEW WITH TRUMAN
February 14, 1950

In the age of atomic energy, transmuted into a weapon which can destroy great cities and the best works of civilization, and in the shadow of a hydrogen detonant which could multiply many times that agent of destruction, a serene President of the United States sits in the White House with undiminished confidence in the triumph of humanity's better nature and the progress of his own efforts to achieve abiding peace.

This President, Harry S. Truman, is a controversial figure in the world and in domestic politics. But to those who talk with him intimately about the problem of global life and death, his faith that these good things will happen, and probably in his time, shines out with a luminous and simple quality which no event or misadventure of policy can diminish.

The following is an account of the President's current views on the international and domestic issues of his time which I can vouch for as to accuracy. It may serve further to reveal to doubters and critics what manner of man he really is; and crystallize in the minds of those who instinctively supported him in the campaign of 1948 what were the personal qualities they sensed but did not always comprehend.

He sits in the center of the troubled and frightened world, not a world he ever made; but the penumbra of doubt and fear in which the American nation pursues its greatest and most perilous adventure—the mission to gain world peace and security while preserving the strength of the native experiment in democracy—stops short of him. Visitors find him undaunted and sure that, whether in his time or thereafter, a way will be discovered to preserve the world from the destruction which to many seems unavoidable, as moral force is steadily weakened by the conflict of two great rival systems and by new skills in forging weapons of destruction that make the discovery of gunpowder seem like the first ignition of the parlor match.

His reasons for this serenity and this sureness emerge from current conversations with the President on the issues of the time. For Mr. Truman is the kind of American who must be observed at first-hand, free to speak with the candor and natural piety of his makeup, to be wholly understood.

In such meetings he answers questions that bear directly on the problems before him. And these questions and his answers that follow (the latter put mostly in the indirect discourse which is due to a President for his own protection and that of the country) reveal the man and what he conceived to be his mission and his methods of accomplishing it better than the formal record can do.

Q.—You recall the hopeful prospect of peace that surrounded you, and you expressed, at San Francisco in 1945 when the United Nations was organized. What has happened since to bring about deterioration to the point where a member of your Cabinet can say of it: "The cold fact is that we are still in a hot war"? When did you conclude that normal negotiation with the Kremlin was hopeless?

A.—The President said he remembered that time well, and with what good-will toward the Russian people and their rulers he went to Potsdam shortly thereafter. There he planned to offer help for reconstruction, of Russia as well as the rest of the world, on a very large scale. He remembered with pride and sympathy how Russians had smashed the German armies in the East, and he believed their assistance was necessary to win the war against Japan. But he found that all Stalin wanted to talk about was the abrupt cessation of lend-lease; hence the atmosphere was unfavorable to what Mr. Truman had in mind.

"To abolish lend-lease at the time was a mistake." But he was "new" then; the papers had been prepared for Roosevelt, and represented a Government decision. He felt there was nothing else he could do but sign. He had no staff and no Cabinet of his own. Now he has both.

The agreement the Russians made at Yalta to enter the war against Japan was the only one they ever kept out of nearly forty. He has no hope they will keep any which now it would be good policy to seek. But he remains hopeful of the outcome.

When the Russians, after the Potsdam agreements, blocked East-West trade he began to lose the last vestige of hope that what seemed so good a peace prospect at San Francisco had survived. Gen. George C. Marshall, he recalls, came back from Moscow deeply discouraged. And when Ambassador Bedell Smith reported to the President from Moscow that the Russians were carefully concealing from the people all facts about the war assistance we had given them, and what our proposals had been for joint reconstruction of the world, that last vestige disappeared.

It would have been the same in Japan as in Germany if the President had not demanded an American as the Allied generalissimo there at the signing of the surrender on the Missouri. Otherwise the Russians would have divided that country as they have Germany; and the situation in the Far East would have been so much worse than it is that one can take comfort from it.

The real trouble with the Russians is that they are still suffering from a complex of fear and inferiority where we are concerned. If a campaign had not been in progress in 1948 he would have sent Chief Justice Fred M. Vinson to try to straighten out Stalin and the other Russian leaders on this and on our real intentions. Maybe that will be the thing to do some time. But in nothing must we show any sign of weakness, because there is none in our attitude.

He is reliably informed that the Russians have 16,000,000 people in concentration camps. This is the way of the police state, which he finds utterly abhorrent.

Q.—In view of your background, training and dislike of debt, how do you reconcile these with your toleration of deficit spending and your advocacy of new spending programs? Critics of the Fair Deal program say it proposes permanently to burden the more able, diligent and successful with the cost of "insuring all others against the results of their own improvidence, ill-luck or defective behavior"; that this is very nearly the Marxian doctrine "to each according to his need, from each according to his ability."

A.—In no sense does the President tolerate deficit spending. There wouldn't be any now if the Republicans had not cut the income taxes in the Eightieth Congress. Tax changes should not have been made piecemeal at any time, but conformed to a general and revised plan. This was equally true when he approved the repeal of the excess profits tax. He wishes he had not done this, because it was piecemeal also. But then again he was new at the job.

His object is steadily to expand the economy so as to provide jobs and careers for the million and a half young people who come annually into the stream of commerce. This cannot be done without the measures outlined in the Fair Deal. From a peak of 59.6 millions of persons employed in civilian activities last September, the number has gone down to 56 millions, with 4.8 millions unemployed. A certain amount of unemployment, say from three to five millions, is supportable. It is a good thing that job-seeking should go on at all times; this is healthy for the economic body. But the main thing is to keep the economy rising to absorb the new entrants into the stream of commerce. There are now 62 millions employed in the labor force in the United States, including the military. Ten years ago whoever had suggested that this could happen would have been written down a fool or a dreamer.

He has no policy which contemplates permanently burdening the more able, diligent and successful with the cost of insuring all others against the results of their own improvidence, ill-luck or defective behavior. This charge—also that the Fair Deal approximates the Marxian doctrine—is absolutely untrue. The President's aim is to preserve life and property and expand opportunity and the standards of living. "There isn't a drop of Marxist or Socialist blood" in him.

The globe shows vast areas inhabited by hundreds of millions of people who want to improve their lot, and this can be done with our American surpluses and with a moderate amount of our assistance, financial and technical. When that is done, the chief threat of international communism will pass, and this is the primary objective of his policy.

Q.—Your views on party obligation: that all elected as Democrats must abide by platform pledges. Suppose (1) you construe a pledge in detail differently from a member of Congress; or (2) he has made a commitment to the contrary prior to the adoption of the platform. Is he recreant as a party man?

A.—The President does not expect 100 percent support from those elected to Congress on the same platform with him. He recognizes that local situations may require some members to refuse to follow a President on certain matters. As a Senator, he reserved the right of independence at times for himself. But he does believe that, after a platform has been duly adopted by a convention, all those who have participated or run on that platform should generally abide by its detailed construction by the national candidate.

Only that national candidate, the President, can translate a platform into actionable terms. There are few chairmen of Congressional committees who follow the platform and the President's construction of it more than 50 percent of the time, and this is very bad. These chairmen should be the right arm of the Administration in orderly government by party. If there is any other way to have a responsible government, he does not know what it is.

Q.—You favor the Fair Employment Practices Commission legislation providing Federal powers in the states to correct employment discriminations, some of which are implicit in the present condition of racial minorities. You know intimately the condition of the Negro race and the limitations of its capacity to fill certain kinds of employment. Many believe that education will be required before an FEPC could operate even on a voluntary basis. Why then is it desirable in mandatory form, requiring that the burden of proof be on the employer?

A.—The President would not support or continue to support any legislation which deprived a citizen of the right to run his own business, for which that citizen was responsible, as he thought best. The President does not agree that the Administration's FEPC legislation would have any such result. If he thought so, he would not be for it, and under him it will not be so administered.

But opportunities to get jobs for which applicants are fitted by every fair test must not be denied in this country on grounds of race, color or any similar discrimination. The value of the FEPC bill will be to give this position the dignity, strength and clarity of a national policy, not just political, but social and economic as well. For that reason he wants the bill passed, even if it were only to serve as a club in the closet.

Q.—When you became President you expressed a sense of inadequacy which many thought was far too humble for your abilities. Now and for some time you seem to have dropped that feeling overboard, where it belongs. How did this change come about?

A.—When Mr. Truman became President he did not intend to convey the sense of inadequacy which many people thought he did. He came into office without a single member of the Cabinet who was devoted to him personally, without having been briefed on the processes or current problems of government, without knowing who the people were to whom he should apply for the counsel and facts a President must have to serve the best interests of the country. Often some member of that Cabinet tried to see him privately to complain about another one. He stopped that: first, by recounting the incident at the Cabinet meeting and asking the two or three involved to work it out; second, by getting his own Cabinet. Now he is served by the best personal staff he could find and by a loyal and able Cabinet. The problem remains how to find the very best qualified persons outside for counsel and for collecting the facts in special matters. That is an unending task, as well as a vital one. But the inadequacy of the position he was in to do that has disappeared, and that was all he meant at the time.

Q.—It is true that chairmen in Congress get these places through seniority, and it is a bad system. Have you any idea of a better one, or any other that would be operable?

A.—The seniority system by which chairmen of committees in Congress are selected is a defective one because the best qualified men do not always get the jobs. But any substitute that has been proposed is unworkable, and the present system has the merit of keeping order in the legislative process. If the Administration were allowed to pick the chairmen, which is one substitute that has been proposed, the Executive would dominate Congress, and this is not only undesirable but contrary to the intent of the Constitution.

Q.—Will you explain your use of "red herring" and "hysteria" in the context of the spy trials and hunts since you are charged (1) with not comprehending the gravity of this situation or (2) playing for votes of groups under suspicion?

A.—When Mr. Truman on several occasions spoke of "hysteria" and "red herrings" in connection with revelations about espionage, etc., he was criticizing the *methods* employed by the Un-American Activities Committee and by individuals in Congress and out of it. The objective of having only loyal citizens in Government service and in positions of importance and responsibility has been his fundamentally, too.

His loyalty board (Chairman, Seth W. Richardson) has done much more effective screening of this kind without headlines and personal publicity than the Congressional spy-hunts, which have been animated chiefly by quests for headlines and personal publicity. These produced the "hysteria" he was talking about, reminding him of the public excitement in the days of the Alien and Sedition Acts, the Know-Nothing Movement, the Ku Klux Klan and the Red scares of 1920. And he has never changed his opinion that the way the Un-American Activities Committee handled the Hiss and other cases was a red herring to distract public attention from the blunders and crimes of the Eightieth Congress.

When the President was chairman of the special Senate committee during the war, he followed a method which he sought to endorse by contrast when he made the above comments about hysteria and red herrings. Whenever he found something wrong or some indication of potential wrong in the war program, he privately communicated the facts to the departments concerned, and usually it was corrected or averted without the kind of publicity that unfairly shakes public confidence, and spreads through the more than two millions in Government employ a feeling of insecurity in their jobs which hampers and damages their work.

The result was that no major scandal occurred in the war. This is the responsible method which, because it was not followed in these other matters, impelled him to say what he did. The Government service is 99 per cent plus loyal and secure.

If the facts about a Government employe show the contrary, out the man will go at no expense to public stability—though, it is true, without a headline for a politician who has that chiefly in his mind.

* * *

Such are the President's statements of his views.

Those who have the privilege, necessarily a limited one, of searching in this way the mind and purpose of Harry S. Truman usually come away with faith in his honesty and courage. They usually come away also with the conviction that, whether or not he has the greatness which the times require—a question that must be left to the verdict of history —he means to preserve the basic system by which this nation attained its greatness, and to achieve and maintain that peace which has been its highest aspiration since 1783.

LABOR RELATIONS

LABOR AND THE PRESIDENT
November 27, 1946

The President was asked to "do something" to end and prevent the recurrence of nation-wide strikes and give the country a chance to produce again. No louder calls were sounded than by Republicans, particularly the Presidential aspirants of that party. Mr. Truman waited until he and the government had been patronized and defied by two leaders of railway labor unions and until it was obvious that the raising of the flag over the struck coal mines meant nothing to John L. Lewis' miners. Then he responded vigorously.

He forced an end to the railway strike of the two holdout unions by pillorying their leaders at the bar of public opinion and announcing he would run the trains with the Army unless the men returned to work at an hour specified by him. Then he went before Congress with a drastic temporary program calculated to make it impossible, until the country gets into production again, for any union or their leaders to paralyze essential industry and create menaces to public health and safety, and to national security. Borrowing from Governor Tuck of Virginia, who headed off a strike of this nature by drafting public utility employes into the National Guard, the President proposed that he be given similar Federal authority to put men to work who are striking against the government.

The cheers died away on the Republican side of the aisles in Congress. Labor leaders saw a chance to raise the standard of "democracy" against a President who had fought all their battles when he was in the Senate. They thrust it into the trembling hands of politicians who, in
152

exchange for votes, resist the imposition of any curb on the proved power of the unions to subject government as well as the national economy and welfare to their purposes. Thoughtful citizens who hold that such a draft of labor will not work, and others who oppose it in principle whether or not the immediate emergency can be effectively handled by any substitute, joined the resistance to the proposal of a draft.

The first President in thirteen years who has really employed the authority and prestige of government to assert its responsibility for the general welfare when labor was threatening that welfare began to experience the consequences. Senator Morse, Republican, of Oregon, called him a ham actor because he had interrupted his joint session address to inform Congress that the railway strike had just been officially settled on Mr. Truman's terms. Mr. Whitney, leader of one of the brotherhoods that crippled the nation, assailed the President as a political accident and said his union would spend the $47 millions in its treasury to defeat him for re-election. Senator Taft, generally credited to aspire to the Republican nomination for the Presidency, organized his colleagues to defeat a proposal he termed "unconstitutional" and a plan to set up "involuntary servitude." Mr. Stassen, another Republican candidate for the White House, declared the President's whole temporary program is "totalitarian in its nature."

The C.I.O. and the A.F. of L., together as always when any effort is made to balance the industrial equation, cried "fascism" at the President's proposals and also denounced the Senate's draft of the Case bill. Some of their leaders said they will turn their political support away from the Democrats if any strong curbs are imposed, and these statements were imparted to ambitious Republicans, who quickly saw the point.

One of the most important effects of the uproar was to stiffen Mr. Lewis in his refusal to call back his own strikers against the government until he has taken every possible advantage of the fact that none can mine coal but his followers. The least consequence to good government was Senator Pepper's threat that he will resign his seat if Mr. Truman's legislation is passed. Yet it belongs in a recital of what happens to a President who, assailed by industry and workers for his first move to revise labor laws (fact-finding), lectured by arrogant union chiefs in his own office, bombarded by the country to do something to save the nation's economy and the dignity of its government, does what he believes the emergency requires, temporarily as in war.

* Claude Pepper now serves in the House of Representatives, from Florida.

The angry chorus against the President, composed of such a strange assortment of voices, has torn up the prelude in which Mr. Truman tried to shelve the Case bill and all permanent labor restraints by substituting his temporary program, and that is labor's position also. When a Senator he did the unprecedented thing of trying to legislate a wage increase (for railway labor) over the denial of a statutory board—unique in Congressional history. But if a politician seeks to befriend the unions he must do all they ask and nothing they oppose, as the President has discovered.

THE PROSE STYLES
OF JOHN L. LEWIS
March 31, 1948

The seasonally embattled leader of the United Mine Workers of America, John L. Lewis, has displayed more than one prose style in the letters, articles, speeches and offhand remarks with which he has enriched the record of industrial controversy in the United States. He is adept in employing what Bret Harte called "the saber-cuts of Saxon speech," as when he assailed John Nance Garner as a "card-playing, whisky-drinking, evil old man." He can be arch. But his preference is for the ponderous turgidity beloved by Dr. Samuel Johnson.

It is possible that Mr. Lewis, treated to the rough edge of a fishwife's tongue, would retort as Johnson did: "Madam, you are a parallelepipedon." The word, its length and its derivation from a dead language should have for him an irresistible attraction. But thus far public officials and representatives of business management, not fishwives, have been the targets of his sesquipedalian prose.

A recent example of his pachydermatous style is Mr. Lewis' letter to the board that was appointed by the President to investigate the work stoppage in the soft-coal fields. To illustrate the pains taken by the author to be downright rude in the Johnsonian manner, this correspondent ventures to translate it into the simple diction others would have used in the same circumstances. It follows:

> *Lewis:* My disinclination to attend falls substantially into two categories.
> *Translation:* I have decided not to attend for two reasons.

Lewis: 1. The law.

Translation: (Same.)

Lewis: No action has been taken by this writer or the United Mine Workers of America, as such, which would fall within the purview of the oppressive statute under which you seek to function.

Translation: Neither this writer nor the United Mine Workers of America, as such, has done anything prohibited by the tyrannical Taft-Hartley Act, the source of the authority you claim.

Lewis: Without indulging in analysis, it is a logical assumption that the cavilings of the bar and bench in their attempts to explicate this infamous enactment will consume a tedious time.

Translation: Your hearing will be tedious and a waste of time, during which judges and lawyers will mouth about what this infamous law means.

Lewis: 2. Prejudice.

Translation: (Same.)

Lewis: Two members of your board are biased and prejudiced and in honor should not serve. They are Ethridge and Taylor. Since the inception of this imbroglio Ethridge has published biased and prejudicial editorials and special articles deleterious to this union and this writer in a newspaper controlled by him.

Taylor for five years has been an administrative hanger-on in Washington, and he has never lost an opportunity to harass and persecute this union and this writer. He is inherently incapable of determining the distinction between a fact and a scruple.

In attendance is Ching, a truly remarkable man, who sees through the eyes of United States Rubber.

Translation: Two of your board members, Ethridge and Taylor, are so biased against this union and me that they cannot honorably serve. Ethridge has filled the newspaper he publishes with prejudiced editorials and articles ever since this controversy began.

Taylor, in the five years he has clung to government jobs, showed his bias against me and the union whenever and in any way he could. Also he is fundamentally unable to tell a fact from an allegation.

Ching, the odd character who attends your meetings, still sees labor problems from the viewpoint of an executive of the United States Rubber Company.

The form to which Mr. Lewis' orotund and often opaque rhetoric has been brashly reduced in this translation would not, however, appeal to him. The bulk of his written prose so testifies. Sometimes it seems that two maxims guide his pen: "Never fail to write a paragraph when a sentence would do," and "If there is a long word for a short one, be sure to use it." For certain literary effects this is a valuable formula; Dr. Johnson, for example, was ever aware that an elephant on a tight-rope attracts more attention than an acrobat.

The great doctor and the dictator of mine labor resemble each other at another point of style. Both are bad etymologists and more often than not miss the exact polysyllable for the desired meaning. But the former's syntax and parsing are those of the classical scholar. The same cannot be said of Mr. Lewis', though his grammar is impeccable.

Either might have written the description in "Rasselas" of "The Common Process of Marriage": "A youth and maiden, meeting by chance, or brought together by artifice, reciprocate civilities, go home and dream of each other." If that language wasn't Johnson's it would be widely identified as pure Lewisese.

The dictator's show of archness is rare and impromptu. He revealed it yesterday to the Truman Board when, like a bishop frolicking in the vernacular, he replied to a question with "Oh, but yes."

THE STEEL SEIZURE
April 21, 1952

If the courts ever squarely face the broad constitutional issue posed by President Truman's seizure of the steel industry, instead of narrowing the question to whether it can be seized by a subordinate on an executive order, the probability is that the final opinion will produce dissents in the Supreme Court, and that dissents will also appear in the court below. This is because the Constitution can be construed both to forbid and not to forbid the President's action.

Certainly Mr. Truman has subjected Article II and the Fifth Amendment of the Constitution to one of the greatest strains in the record of the republic. He was not required to do this at the time he did because at his disposal was a specific statute whereby the impending strike could have been delayed. The reason he gave for not invoking the Taft-Hartley Act—that it would not have prevented at least the temporary shutdown of an industry in which any loss of production would have endangered national security—is challenged by the fact that the President's delay in invoking the law was responsible for this effect. The steel dispute indicated the need of statutory intervention in plenty of time for him to have used the Taft-Hartley Law without this consequence. And there is good basis for the viewpoint that if the President had employed the law when that became plain, and refrained from encouraging the unions to hold an uncompromising attitude, the strike could have been averted without straining the Constitution.

But, just as Mr. Truman in his speech on the air quoted statistics of steel industry "profits" as if these sums remained in the treasuries of the companies, so he failed to justify his delay in resorting to the statute until it could not have prevented a shutdown.

Instead, he seized the industry and raised once more the issue of the scope of Executive power within the Constitution that has never been specifically resolved and, by its nature, probably will not be without an amendment to the national charter. For even if the Supreme Court should take a clear-cut and unanimous stand on this recent and acute manifestation of the old dispute, the President might hold it to be within his obligation to the people to disregard it.

President Truman, in his letter to Vice President Barkley today, made plain that in seizing the steel industry without definite statutory warrant he was proceeding on what is known in history as the "stewardship theory." He wrote:

I have regarded it as imperative, for the sake of our national security, to keep the steel mills in operation. I should not, I think, be forced to a public disclosure of information that would be of value to the enemy. However, I will say this: A shutdown in steel production for any substantial length of time whatever would immediately reduce the ability of our troops in Korea to defend themselves against attack.

If the Communists stage another offensive this spring, the success or failure of that offensive may well depend on whether or not we have kept our steel mills in operation.

One of the strong foundations of this view of Executive power when the President regards its employment to be "imperative for the sake of our national security" was supplied by Theodore Roosevelt. In his "Autobiography" he spoke of his "insistence upon the theory that the Executive power was limited only by specific restrictions and prohibitions appearing in the Constitution or imposed by the Congress under its constitutional powers."

It is true T.R. made the reservation that Executives could do any but those things that are forbidden by the Constitution and the laws. And against Mr. Truman's seizure one of the legal arguments is that the Fifth Amendment forbids taking private property for public use without just compensation. But in its favor are cited the obligations assumed for the general welfare and national security by the President in Article II as Chief Executive and Commander in Chief. Once again a President has found all the law he needed there.

A CONSTITUTIONAL DISPUTE
June 2, 1952

The President announced in advance of the Supreme Court's decision on the legality of his seizure of the steel industry that he would abide by its finding; therefore, once more the irresistible force and the immovable object created by the language of the Constitution will not collide. But to read today's dissent, by three members of the Court, to the broadest limitation on executive power ever defined by this tribunal, and to remember that it was written by the Chief Justice of the United States, is to realize that circumstances in which this collison can occur are sure to arise again.

For the majority Justice Black held that: "The Constitution did not subject the law-making power of Congress to Presidential or military supervision or control"; Mr. Truman's seizure order to the Secretary of Commerce was "law-making" because it was done without the authority of any statute, actual or claimed; Congress specifically refused to grant this statutory power when it was proposed; hence District Judge Pine correctly enjoined its exercise, and the industry must be restored to its private owners.

But, retorted the Chief Justice for himself and Justices Reed and Minton, this is a "messenger-boy concept of the [Presidential] Office" whereby the Chief Executive cannot even act to preserve legislative programs (for national defense, carrying out Treaty obligations and supplying our troops engaged in Korea) from destruction "so that Congress will have something left to act upon." He grimly predicted that "Presidents have been in the past, and any man worthy of the Office should be in the future, free to take at least interim action necessary to execute legislative programs essential to survival of the nation." "There is no question," he said, "that the possession [of the industry] was other than temporary in character and subject to Congressional approval, disapproval" or regulation of "the manner in which the mills were to be administered and returned to the owners."

But to most of those here who commented the Supreme Court had reasserted, against a dire threat, the basic principle of the American system that no man is above the law. To many the Court also had reasserted the fundamental protection to private property from public power that is stated in the Fifth Amendment. And many also rejoiced to reread these words of Justice Brandeis, approvingly quoted and expanded in the separate concurring opinion of Justice Frankfurter:

> The doctrine of the separation of powers was adopted by the Convention of 1787, not to promote efficiency but to preclude the exercise of arbitrary power. The purpose was, not to avoid friction, but, by means of the inevitable friction incident to the distribution of the governmental powers among three departments, to save the people from autocracy.

Better, said these commentators (and so in effect said the court majority), to have a strike, to risk all the grave consequences to the free world of non-production of steel, to pay "the price" the designers of our Government "deemed not too high in view of the safeguards these restrictions afford" (Justice Frankfurter), than to expand the "Commander in Chief" theory to domestic affairs in peacetime and lay down the rule that the President has and can use legislative powers "that the Founders of this nation * * * entrusted to Congress alone in both good and bad times" (Justice Black).

However, it is significant of the force and future potential of the dissent that each of the five justices who agreed with the basic reasoning of Justice Black found it necessary to write concurring opinions. Justice Jackson, as Attorney General, concluded that President Roosevelt had "an aggregate of powers derived from the Constitution and from statutes enacted by Congress," and thus justified seizure of the North American Aviation Company six months before Pearl Harbor. Today, taunted with this by the dissenters, he said that similarities of this action with Mr. Truman's were "superficial, and upon analysis yield to distinctions [which he cited] so decisive that it cannot be regarded as even a precedent, much less an authority for the present seizure." But he warned Congress that, while the courts may say today that emergency legislative power belongs to it, "only Congress itself can prevent power from slipping through its fingers." Justice Clark, who as Attorney General held that the President in emergencies affecting national health and safety had inherent power to seek injunctions, wrote that, though

Mr. Truman invoked the procedures of a statute, the Defense Production Act of 1950, it did not grant him the power "to seize real property except through ordinary condemnation proceedings, which he did not use."

Justice Burton noted that "Congress has reserved to itself the right to determine where and when to authorize the seizure of property in meeting such an emergency": therefore this seizure "invaded its jurisdiction." Justice Douglas said some future emergency may bring an amendment to the Constitution giving the President lawmaking power, but he hasn't it now and his seizure was legislation.

And though in effect the Supreme Court enjoined the President, which by the legal fiction "cannot be done," even the dissenters agreed that subordinates to whom he gives unconstitutional executive orders are "not immune from judicial restraint."

CONGRESSIONAL OPPOSITION

THE POWER OF CONGRESS
TO "DECLARE WAR"
February 14, 1949

When Senator Vandenberg, supported by Senator Connally, told the Senate and the people today he would assent to nothing in the proposed North Atlantic pact that would constitute "a moral obligation" for the United States to go to war under that treaty, he was dealing with an ancient and perplexing relationship between Congress and the Chief Executive. This turns on the words in Section 8 (11) of the Constitution which reserve to Congress the exclusive and absolute power "to declare war."

The Senators were giving assurance, as often before in American history, that no international compact submitted by the Executive would be approved which in any way invades this exclusive Congressional power. Having previously and privately prevailed on the Department of State to eliminate the word "military" in the draft of the North Atlantic pact as a description of any form of assistance this country pledged itself to contribute to an associate nation subjected to aggression, Mr. Vandenberg and Mr. Connally decided to make the reservation of aid stronger and do it publicly. If or when the North Atlantic pact is ratified and invoked, they promised, in effect, no other member of the alliance would be able to point to a word or passage on which a claim could be founded that the United States had "morally obligated" itself to go to war.

161

The model phrasing, of course, is in Article 20 of the Pan-American Treaty of Rio de Janeiro. In this, though the treaty asserts that a community of interest exists among all the nations of the Western Hemisphere and a threat to the security or independence of one is a threat to all, each nation reserves the right to make its own decision how to deal with such a situation if it arises.

But the Constitution also imposes on the President the duty to "take care that the laws be faithfully executed," and treaties are "the supreme law of the land." Furthermore, the Constitution makes the President the Commander in Chief of the armed forces, entrusted with the national security. More and more, as this twilight zone of legislative-executive authority and responsibility has been illuminated by the fires of conflict between these two arms of government, it has been made clear that the President can bring the country to the verge of war, and enter undeclared war, within a concept of his constitutional responsibilities. And after that the declaration of war by Congress has been an inevitable formality.

But, throughout this period, except when the nation twice was brought to this point by Congress itself—the War of 1812 and the Spanish-American War of 1898—Congress has endeavored to check the warmaking trend of executive acts by such advance notices as Senators Vandenberg and Connally gave today and by treaty reservations to the same purpose.

It was very early in the chapter that Hamilton, using the *nom de plume* "Pacificus," championed executive powers over international relations which can have the effect of making Section 8 (11) a scrap of paper. Washington in 1793 committed the United States by proclamation to "impartiality" between France and Great Britain, then engaged in war. The pro-French party attacked this as outside the President's authority. Hamilton inspected this protest, and dealing with treaties, wrote:

> While treaties can only be made by the President and Senate jointly * * * their activity may be continued or suspended by the President alone. This serves as an example of the right of the executive, in certain cases, to determine the condition of the nation, though it may, in its consequences, affect the exercise of the power of the legislature to declare war. Nevertheless, the executive cannot thereby control the exercise of that power. The legislature is still free to perform its duties, according to its own sense of them; though the

executive, in the exercise of its constitutional powers, may establish an antecedent state of things, which ought to weigh in the legislative decision. The vision of the executive power in the constitution creates a concurrent authority in the cases to which it relates.

This theory, though Madison, answering "Pacificus" under the pen name of "Helvidius," opposed it, has grown steadily in practice. In bringing the nation to a point of hostilities where the declaration of war became an inescapable formality, Congress on four occasions has dragged its feet as the follower of the executive. These, the greatest conflicts in which Americans have engaged, were the Mexican War, the War Between the States, World War I and World War II. It may be argued that Capitol prodding of Woodrow Wilson for "preparedness" and fiery orations when the Lusitania was sunk remove World War I from the above category. But it was the President, after Congress in 1917 declined to pass the "armed ship" bill, who put the guards on American vessels in the submarine lanes.

In full realization of this history the Senators served their notice on the executive today. The Senate, they in substance asserted, will approve nothing in the proposed North Atlantic pact which, *standing alone,* could create what "Pacificus" termed "an antecedent state of things" that would present Congress and the nation with no honorable or safe alternative to a declaration of war. That is the most Congress can do, and the same is true of public opinion.

LOYALTY TRIALS SHAPE POLITICAL ISSUE FOR 1950
June 18, 1949

The political issue between the two major parties which is being shaped out of the current loyalty trials and investigations arose from these circumstances:

(1) The fact that members of the Democratic party, except for the period (1947–1949) in which there were Republican majorities in Congress, have controlled the legislative and executive arms of the Government for sixteen years and also occupy most of the Federal judicial seats.

(2) The fact that during a large part of this tenure, the exception being the lifetime of the Stalin-Hitler alliance (1939–1941), most Communists, fellow-travelers, thinkers on the far left and labor leaders of the radical stripe affiliated with the party in power and gave it their support at the polls.

(3) The further fact that, while Democratic candidates in this period, including the late President Franklin Delano Roosevelt and President Truman, regularly disavowed Communist support when charged by their opponents with inviting it, inner offices of the executive government became accessible to subversive agents, and the Administration steadily resisted Congressional inquiries into the degree of this accessibility.

(4) The further fact that the post-war policies of Soviet Russia have aroused public opinion in this country against American Communists and their fellow-travelers that has extended to the advanced group of "liberals" who were the core of New Deal officialdom until Mr. Truman began to replace them, though retaining their ideas in his "Fair Deal."

Because the Democrats were in executive power in all this period, this Administration, like its predecessor, is acutely sensitive to the mounting charges of coddling Communists and fellow-travelers and taking no measures to prevent their infiltration into Government until Mr. Truman issued his "loyalty" regulations. President Roosevelt did what he could to discredit and obstruct the first Un-American Committee of the House, headed by Representative Martin Dies of Texas, greatly aided by the extravagant and reckless capers of that regime. President Truman, after issuing his "loyalty" order and setting up an enforcement board—the result of revelations of subversives in the Government by the second Un-American Committee—has steadily denounced these inquiries.

He said of the House committee's hearing of Whittaker Chambers, which brought about the current trial of Alger Hiss, that it was a "red herring" to distract attention from what he terms his progressive policies and from the character of his opposition. He repeated the term to cover related inquiries. At his press conference last week the President implied that all the loyalty trials and investigations were "headline-hunting." This could have been taken to include the Congressional inquiry into the management of the Atomic Energy Commission by David E. Lilienthal, and the trials of Hiss and Judith Coplon, which were initiated by Mr. Truman's Attorney General. At this week's press conference the President said the whole business was typical post-war hysteria, which was not manifest in the executive department, however. But, in evading a question whether he thought the FBI had grown "hysterical," he left room for the impression that he is displeased with the methods of J. Edgar Hoover.

The ideal solution from the standpoint of Truman's political strategists would be: (1) the acquittal of Hiss from the perjury charge in such a way as to clear him also of the underlying charge of serving Soviet agents while an official of the State Department; (2) a finding by the Joint Congressional Committee on Atomic Energy that Lilienthal has been a good manager and has not allowed "liberal" or cosmic views to weaken national security in the slightest degree; (3) repudiation by public opinion of the more sensational testimony before the third Un-American Committee; (4) at least one substantial trial victory for the Department of Justice.

This is a large order. But the deep-thinking Democratic politicos think there is a good chance for it. Both the presentation made by Senator Bourke B. Hickenlooper of his case against Mr. Lilienthal, and the curbs of secrecy imposed on that presentation by the committee, make them confident of the outcome. The background of Chambers makes them at least hopeful that a damaging link between Moscow agents and trusted aides of the Roosevelt Administration will not be established. These politicians feel also that they can always count on the Un-American Committee discrediting itself and its inquiry at some point. And, while they don't want the Attorney General injured, they would not mind the loss of all his cases in this area.

Certainly these immediate trials and inquiries will be concluded and the verdicts rendered some time before the Congressional elections of 1950. If the event shall disclose the solution of the political issue which these Administration politicians hope for, they think the present cloud will vanish from the prospects of 1950 and 1952. If enough of the verdicts go the other way to form the issue, then these strategists trust this will occur long enough before the Congressional elections to give them a chance to dispel it. In either case, of course, new and startling revelations of subversive activity in the Government could upset all their calculations and make it even more difficult than now for the President to get "Fair Deal" legislation through this Congress.

Because of these possibilities his strategists, despite their rising hopes, wish the President would refrain at this juncture from all-inclusive disparagements. But he has made them anxious before and proved his political judgment to be better than theirs. It may happen again.

SENATORS AND ACHESON DUEL
ON AID PROGRAM
July 30, 1949

One of the greatest acts Washington has ever seen is now playing a return engagement. The star is Dean G. Acheson, Secretary of State, and the business is that of persuading doubtful or flatly opposed members of Congress to support, in detail as well as in substance, foreign-policy legislation proposed by the Administration. For skill, daring and the dramatic element of suspense this performance has been fitly compared to sword-swallowing.

The routine is always about the same. Mr. Acheson, after a lavish show of deference to the President as his chief in foreign policy, announces a program and adds that a bill to carry it out is under preparation. Loud outcries of protest arise in Congress against the proposed program. Mr. Acheson summons a press conference to which, with infinite proficiency and persuasiveness, he explains away most of the protests. At once the opposition begins to slacken at the Capitol, and by the time the Secretary takes the stand in the Foreign Affairs Committees of the House and the Senate the general atmosphere he encounters is only "show me."

After engorging the first sword with what appears to be the greatest of ease, the Secretary sends to the Capitol a draft of legislation to execute the program. Even louder protests arise, because the bill goes far beyond Mr. Acheson's statement of the objectives. At another press conference he reconciles the alleged disparities in a masterly statement. Then he is ready for the Foreign Affairs Committees again, where few venture or are able to dispute the premises or challenge the legal interpretations of one of the most accomplished statesmen of our times.

This latter phase of the famous sword-swallowing act is now in progress, the opening set having been the House Committee hearing on the proposed measure to rearm Western Europe, Greece, Korea, the Philippines and any other areas the President may wish to rearm. At this hearing the Secretary was received with awe by the chairman, Representative John Kee of West Virginia, who is 75 years of age and a life member of the Moose and the Elks. Nor were other members far behind the chairman in their reception of the brilliant, handsome, lean and reasonably young Mr. Acheson.

It seems likely, as so often before, that the Secretary will get most of what he wants, and all essentials, from the House committee and the House itself, and that, as so often before, the skill of the celebrated act will have its real test in the Senate Committee on Foreign Relations and the Senate. Senator Tom Connally, the committee chairman, has a habit of yielding to Mr. Acheson's persuasions after frightful thunders in the preface—much as Byron's "Julia," who, vowing she would ne'er consent, consented. But the swords of Senators Arthur H. Vandenberg and Henry Cabot Lodge Jr. will be harder to swallow. And if Senator John Foster Dulles is permitted to sit with the committee, the Secretary will meet a colleague in law and diplomacy at least as skilled as he, and more experienced.

The issue will be joined over three revisions in the Administration's arms bill which are urged by these Republican leaders and are supported by other Republicans and a number of Democrats. These revisions are designed to bring the legislative draft into exact line with Mr. Acheson's prior statements of what the Administration intends to achieve with it. The position of the revisionists is that the bill goes far beyond these professed objectives with which they find themselves in no substantial disagreement. The changes they propose are as follows:

(1) Limit the rearmament powers of the President to Western Europe, Greece, Turkey, Iran, Korea, the Philippines, and perhaps add something for China, instead of giving Mr. Truman blanket authority to rearm everybody equally if he chooses, including Latin-American states, India and Indonesia as examples. The proposed bill gives this broad authority to the President, though no advance statement foreshadowed that.

(2) Instead of giving Mr. Truman indefinite authority as to the time, the amount and the value of the rearmament program, put limits on all three. The Administration bill does set a monetary limit of $1.45 billion, but this is its estimate for one year's operation only, with no estimate for future operations or the length of the enterprise.

(3) Telescope the arms program into the North Atlantic pact's functional machinery instead of starting it as a separate enterprise. The design of the pact is for unified defense, and Senator Dulles contends that, if the rearmament program doesn't begin as a part of this, there will be no unified defense, but, on the contrary, a buildup of separate national military establishments. "If you don't make the mold," he said, "before pouring in the molten metal, you will be confronted with a dozen molds to pour it in when the stuff is ready."

Acheson's opening strategy is familiar: Not a bullet, not a dollar must be subtracted from the amounts proposed by the Administration; not a substantial line in its legislative draft must be altered. If either is done the consequences may be grave, though some of the reasons cannot be imparted except in super-secret executive session and some cannot be stated at all. And when he says such things, Mr. Acheson is unbelievably impressive, the more so because he actually has superior sources of information and is accepted as a man of honor.

Nevertheless, he has used this strategy before, and changes have been made, and the heavens have not fallen. The revisionists will press their proposals as planned, and their prospects seem good. But Mr. Acheson's sword-swallowing may one day engulf the Senatorial blades also, and this reservation should accompany any prediction that involves him.

THE ADMINISTRATION
VERSUS SENATOR McCARTHY
March 27, 1950

At the end of what might be compared to the seventh inning in baseball the Administration's score against Senator McCarthy of Wisconsin is nine to nothing. The rules by which the scoring was done were fixed by the Senator himself, notably when he said he would base his entire case of Communist infiltration in the State Department on his charges against Prof. Owen Lattimore Jr.

Unless, therefore, under these same rules Mr. McCarthy manages to score ten runs in the next two innings and to hold the Administration's team—the home team—where it is, this game will go down in the records as the emphatic victory which at this juncture it is rated by most political statisticians.

But, as the schedule reads in this year of Congressional elections, other games will be played before the season ends and the final scoring is done by the voters in November. The letters and telegrams which continue to pour into the Capitol indicate that the spectators want still more assurance that the contest is as one-sided as it has been thus far. That (dropping the metaphor) can be, and is, deplored by eminent and just ordinary citizens who are alarmed over the consequences to patriotic public servants and to the prestige of the country abroad. But such evidences of public opinion are discernible; and the following events are probably responsible:

1. The conviction of Alger Hiss for perjury in the attendant circumstances of that charge; the testimony of Julian Wadleigh and the undisproved citations made by Whittaker Chambers against others, some of whom have fled the country and at least one of whom is dead.

2. The record which shows erroneous bases on which our post-war diplomacy was laid, among them (a) the theory that the Chinese Communists are not Russian Communists but agrarian reformers and (b) that the United States could soon restore world peace and order in harmonious negotiation with the Kremlin. Any current accusation, however irresponsible, against officials who once made policy on these bases feeds the fires of public doubt.

3. The repeated proofs that persons who once had been more or less lured by the Soviet system and its propaganda abound on the public payrolls, their recantations fully accepted by their superiors.

It was significant that today Senator Smith of New Jersey, a legislator and citizen of great repute, who, incidentally, has no election this year to color his thinking, defended Mr. McCarthy from some of the attacks made against him, said his colleague was doing "his obvious duty" and urged him not to be deflected from it. Senator Taft also has come to the defense of his fellow-Republican and, though Mr. Taft is a candidate for re-election in 1950, his record does not justify any charge that he employs or condones the assassination of character for political or other reasons.

But Mr. McCarthy would have many more party defenders if he had not discredited whatever case he may have by trying to stretch his indictments to dimensions they emphatically have failed to reach, and by filling in the names of persons who have offered refutations he has been unable to counter. Among these Professor Lattimore and Ambassador Jessup have been most conspicuous.

If Mr. McCarthy expects to return effectively to his charges against Mr. Jessup there is no sign. But he promised to give the Senate tomorrow new "evidence" against Professor Lattimore, though the latter's cable to The Associated Press contained this confident sentence: "Delighted his whole case rests on me, as this means he will fall flat on face."

Those Democrats who are defending the Administration from accusations that its sensitive units tolerate the presence of Communists and their sympathizers in the midst of a desperate struggle with Moscow are about ready to conclude that this sentence anticipated the popular verdict, not only with respect to the charges Mr. McCarthy made against Professor Lattimore personally but with respect to his basic charge. The full arrival of this conclusion will be marked by a change from silence or timid defense to attack, in which, at long last, Secretary of State Acheson will get vigorous championship on the Democratic side at the Capitol, both personally and as the President's chief deputy in carrying out foreign policy.

The Democratic leaders at the Capitol are still feeling their way. But last week's development and Professor Lattimore's confident second sentence have served as a push from behind.

BUDENZ TESTIMONY
April 22, 1950

Senator Ralph E. Flanders of Vermont, a progressive Republican who is rated by his colleagues as a fair man of decent instincts, spoke what appears to be the general verdict of the political community at this point in the investigation of the charges of Communist infiltration in government made by Senator Joseph R. McCarthy, Republican of Wisconsin. Referring to the testimony of Louis F. Budenz on Thursday before the Senate subcommittee of inquiry, Mr. Flanders said: "I find it disturbing."

Many fair-minded persons here have been hostile to the manner in which Mr. McCarthy has presented his charges and up to now have been persuaded—by his inaccurate arraignment of the State Department which he repeatedly was obliged to revise downward—that the Senator had little basis for it. Yet there is evidence that these persons are beginning to lose confidence in their appraisal. There are even more tangible signs that Administration Democrats, fearful of the political effects of the uproar, are becoming confirmed in their fears.

The reasons for this change, reflected in the words of Senator Flanders, are obvious:

(1) Mr. Budenz, who on Thursday told the committee he had been "officially informed" by the highest American Communists that Owen Lattimore was a member of their underground, engaged in undermining the Chinese Nationalist Government, though he had never seen Mr. Lattimore at a Communist meeting and did not know him, was for years deep in the councils of the party.

(2) The American Government, since he recanted and returned to his early Catholic faith, has used his evidence to convict persons charged with subversive activities, or, failing, has found this evidence sustained by later events.

(3) He exposed Gerhard Eisler as the No. 1 Communist operator in the United States, a fact until then generally unsuspected; was the key witness in the Government's successful trial of eleven Communists in New York City; rated Alger Hiss as a known Communist in August, 1948; and flushed out Sam Carr, convicted of assisting the Communist spy ring in Canada.

(4) He is now a member of the faculty of Fordham University, with good standing in a most respected institution of learning.

When, therefore, Mr. Budenz made the sworn statements he did, and reiterated they could be corroborated by the committee if diligently pursued, many more than Mr. Flanders, who had been highly skeptical of Mr. McCarthy's information and incensed at his words and tactics, found this developing situation "disturbing."

The Wisconsin Senator is well aware of the support these circumstances give him in embedding public suspicion that there is much fire beneath the sulphurous smoke he has emitted. In a question-and-answer period which followed his dramatic appearance Thursday night before the American Society of Newspaper Editors, in convention here,* he demonstrated this most effectively. He was asked why he did not waive his immunity as a Senator and why, when he spoke on the subject outside his Senate area of immunity, he protected himself by modifications designed to avert suits for libel. He answered he would waive immunity in all places if the Executive would make public the pertinent files. And he added that, if these files could prove him a liar, the Executive "would open them tomorrow."

Observers of that evening at the A.S.N.E. reported an effect created by the Senator's speech and answers to questions which reflects the comment made by Senator Flanders. The audience at first seemed hostile, and Mr. McCarthy got only the perfunctory applause at the outset which courtesy required. But at the end of the question-and-answer period the applause was noticeably great. "His hearers apparently concluded," said one reporter of the proceedings, "that though he is a barroom fighter who pays no attention to the rules designed to make fighting fair, he has something."

It was startling to this audience to hear Mr. McCarthy calmly describe the Secretary of State, Dean G. Acheson, as "incompetent." And doubtless more than the many who do not agree with him on that estimate resented his further statement that it was "pathetic" to put George C. Marshall, "a great general," in the difficult post of Secretary of

* Washington, D.C.

State—an act "little short of a crime." But in this audience were editors who constantly are assailing the pussy-footing of politicians and constantly are complaining that the Washington reporters who serve them gloss over official deficiencies for reasons of personal friendship and so on. So they listened with mixed feelings which Mr. McCarthy's confident manner and unhesitating answers created among them.

But Mr. Lattimore is proving himself a fighter, too, and continues to show as much confidence that the charges are baseless as Mr. McCarthy displays on the opposite tack. In his Friday press conference the distinguished director of the Johns Hopkins University School of Public Affairs carried on the battle in full force and stung his assailants with barbs of satire and humor, which have been noticeably lacking in Mr. McCarthy's equipment. He said the Senator was trying to put him in the position of proving himself a Communist both by suing for libel—which Mr. Budenz said was a concerted fifth-column tactic to scare off revelations of its activities—and by not suing for libel—which would be hailed by the Senator as a confession of guilt. He said the "Chinese Nationalist lobby" in Washington is a "cesspool" which the Government should investigate, expose and destroy. And he urged that the Government not permit "this campaign of intimidation" to keep it from "clearing up the 'mess.' " As for Mr. Budenz, said Mr. Lattimore, he had lived long "in a fantastic, conspiratorial atmosphere" which inclined him to gain the impressions he gave to the subcommittee.

Thus the violent but serious and troubling quarrel proceeds toward a final judgment which probably will be disputed or may never be reached at all.

FOREIGN AFFAIRS

A NEW FOREIGN POLICY
March 22, 1947

For better or for worse, the global anti-Communist policy which the President asked Congress to inaugurate with loans and grants to Greece and Turkey is the "Truman Doctrine" far more than a famous predecessor's was the "Monroe Doctrine." This, despite what seems to be a growing impression, spreading even to Moscow, that Mr. Truman merely adopted the view of counselors, of which Secretary of State George C. Marshall was the principal, is the conclusion reached by this correspondent after inquiry.

The point is important for more than historic and currently political reasons, and it is especially important to Soviet Russia. Executive counselors, including a Secretary of State, serve at the will of a President and he can terminate their connection with the government at any time.

Mr. Truman will be the chief magistrate of the nation, entrusted by the Constitution with the "conduct" of foreign policy, and senior partner of Congress in formulating it, until January, 1949, and possibly four years longer. But by January, 1949, the "Truman Doctrine," if activated by Congress, will have become a position from which the nation could only retreat at tremendous risk and loss of world influence. Therefore, it would be a good idea for Moscow not to view it as something which might disappear with the advent of new and conceivably transient executive counselors.

There is good reason to believe that as long ago as the London Conference of Foreign Ministers the President began to abandon real hope of the effectiveness for enduring peace and security of a continued policy of appeasement and official treatment of Russia as a government friendly to the United States. He made up his mind then that, when a fitting opportunity arose and one which Congress and the people would recognize as such, he would proclaim the new doctrine. On several occasions he thought the time had come, but some of his important advisers talked him out of it.

The British note of economic and military withdrawal from Greece, culminating a situation of which Washington had been wholly aware as it developed, pointed to a vacuum which the President found suited to the long-held purpose. In conferences with the British that followed, they argued what Secretary of the Navy Forrestal had accepted and acted on months ago—that Turkey, from which a request for aid was pending, was part of the same strategic package. Turkey was then included.

A memorandum was prepared for the President after the British note had been considered by the Secretaries of State, Navy and War, their Under-Secretaries and their chiefs of military staff. Though it fit into the framework of Mr. Truman's now-matured policy, the question that remained was how to inform Congress, the American people and the world adequately, with sufficient candor and with assurance of success.

It was agreed that communism, inspired by Russia in its political form, was a continuous subterranean movement, exploding to the surface one day here, one day there and another place next week. It was agreed that the spread and effectiveness of these explosions was the greatest possible menace to the security of the United States and its system, and to enduring peace. The issue was whether to make a global statement of policy to cover the perambulating threat, proposing that it begin with Greece and Turkey, or whether to limit the doctrine textually to the immediate purpose and broaden it in words as well as in actions as new threats arose.

An alternative proposed—and some military commanders still believe in it—was that the anti-Communist doctrine be applied to Western Europe (determined by a line running roughly from the Oder to the mouth of the Adriatic), the Western Hemisphere and areas of obvious strategic importance in the Far East. For the present, others urged, we should merely announce we would by request assist Greece to retain its political, and attain its economic, independence, and omit any mention of the fact that this enterprise would include the dispatch of any advisory military personnel.

General Marshall opposed the limitation, and so did the President. Mr. Truman also insisted that, since it was the intention to send military personnel, the fact should be openly stated. The speech was then put in the works in the usual way. Doubtless Clark Clifford, the President's legal counsel, who must at first hand have heard the doctrine in its long period of oral formulation, had a large share in preparing the actual draft. Doubtless also it is in part a composition by the Under-Secretary of State, Dean G. Acheson. But it was written to suit Mr. Truman, and he rehearsed its delivery several times with apparently growing satisfaction.

Hence it seems definite that the central idea was Mr. Truman's, and that the important word "must" (instead of "should"), which appeared in the master-key to the doctrine in the message, was inserted at the President's express direction as follows:

I believe that it must be the policy of the United States to support free peoples who are resisting attempted subjugation by armed minorities or by outside pressure.

That is the sentence which makes the new policy a global one, sets no reservation on the type or scope of the proposed "support," leaves open to dispute what are "free peoples" and, if Congress does not write in definite reservations, commits the United States to unlimited expenditure for an unlimited future and to whatever economic and military consequences may accrue. Therefore that is the sentence which has made many members of Congress and other citizens uneasy.

On the other hand, a sentence which did *not* appear and seems *not* to have occurred to anyone is the center of another disturbance. This might have been: "I have today instructed the United States delegate to the Security Council of the United Nations and the Assembly to advise the United Nations of the steps and policy I am proposing to Congress," etc. Then the charges of by-passing and ignoring the U.N. would have rested on slighter foundations.

The Monroe Doctrine has been mentioned in comparisons. The burden of this, however, was, as Jefferson said, that we "would not suffer Europe to meddle in cis-Atlantic affairs" and would not ourselves ever "entangle" in its "broils," while the Truman Doctrine excludes no world area from our "entanglement." But both are founded on the fear that our freedom is threatened by ambitious European powers, and both were precipitated by Russian policy.

BURDENS ON TRUMAN
WITHOUT PARALLEL
October 11, 1947

Citizens who have administered the executive offices of the United States in time of war have generally cast for posterity a longer and more admired shadow than those who served in time of peace. The sobriquet of "War President" or "War Governor" is usually employed by historians and others as a term of gratitude and implicit praise. But the problems facing President Truman, and the difficulties they pose, are reminders that Executives of post-war eras carry the heaviest Presidential burdens.

These are staggering enough when they are undertaken in the atmosphere of a general will toward peace and recovery. But when, as in this instance, they must be dealt with during a "cold" war, the burdens equal and perhaps exceed any that an American President has borne.

The words "cold war" were first used by Bernard M. Baruch in an address last winter to the Legislature of his native State of South Carolina. But they have been so universally accepted as the best descriptive of the current struggle between Soviet Russia and the United States to shape the post-war world that they are now often used without credit to the author—like a passage from the Scriptures or from Shakespeare.

No word combination, however, can adequately suggest the complexities which the present situation between the two great global powers has added to the problems of post-war administration of this Government. World War II was the most destructive activity in which mankind ever engaged, and it was certain in any event to have brought in its wake national ruin, famine, pestilence and moral disintegration. It was probable also that, for the United States, it would be followed by such partisan political upheavals as that of 1946, in which the opposition was given control of Congress by the voters and two pilots instead of one were commissioned to operate the Federal craft.

This condition, though not in equal degree, has confronted other Presidents—Andrew Johnson, particularly. But, though internal political battle was the consequence, the post-war and reconstruction problems of the past did not have to be considered in an international atmosphere charged with menace to the security and the institutions of the United States.

No power of vast strength, openly inimical to the foreign policies of this nation, was challenging them fiercely when the Presidents of the

Reconstructoin Era were dealing with the aftermath of the War Between the States. No great, opposing power, the recent ally in a struggle against one form of world totalitarianism, was working through another form of autocracy to achieve the economic collapse of the United States when Harding and Coolidge were engaged in the recovery effort that followed World War I.

President Truman, however, not only has larger aspects of all these Presidents' problems to contend with. He must labor in the dangerous and difficult situation created by Soviet policy. Every Executive move or plan is complicated by it. The proceedings of Congress are overshadowed by it. The effects of it on the stricken areas of Western Europe and Asia require the American Government, while seeking a high level of domestic economy and recovery from war, to withdraw from that economy enough raw materials and goods to enable free peoples elsewhere to remain free.

The state of "cold" war also obliges the United States to pursue a paradoxical course. Its industries for more than four years were successfully mobilized to destroy the cities and works of other nations. Now they are being utilized to rebuild and expand what their products destroyed. But, because of the threat in Soviet policy, the United States is at the same time compelled to devote a large share of its industry and resources to maintain the machines of potential destruction—in the Army, the Navy, the Air Force and the manufacture of atomic weapons.

The problems intensified by Soviet policy have been complicated further by divisions of opinion among the American people. These have arisen from the sincere belief of some that the economy of Europe cannot be restored by economic and political assistance from this country because of the incompetence of some of its governments and the slackness of labor in the essential industries of some countries. While partisan politics has not yet exploited this opinion to get votes, regardless of the consequences, the oncoming Presidential election furnishes a temptation to do so.

The dispute over food conservation in the United States is another indirect result of the Soviet policy. If Russia would distribute its wheat surpluses as the United States proposes to do it, requirements from this country would be far less. In that event a dispute over methods of conservation would not occur because the diversion would be a simple matter. But the Soviets, thus far at least, have shown no disposition to feed the hungry without some assurance that the repayment will be adherence to the Communist ideology. The United States, on the other hand, wants only to assure that men and women everywhere will have the physical stamina on which the will to make free decisions is most apt to depend. It has no international ideology or military end to serve in its relief program.

Thus far the evidence is strong that Soviet Russia has. And that has put on the United States the major responsibility to provide the food and fuel, without which millions in the world will go cold and hungry. This imposes an exaction on the people of this country, and on the means of its fulfillment Americans very naturally differ. They differ also on the Marshall Plan, and these divisions, too, arise from the magnitude of the European recovery problem for which Soviet policy is greatly responsible.

If the two great Allies in World War II were acting in concert for the reconstruction of a peaceful world, the problems of the United States would not be so staggering. Therefore they would be simpler of solution and less provocative of strong divisions of public opinion.

This is the situation which a "cold" war imposes, far more difficult for a President than the one he must deal with in a "shooting" war when the Nation is united and the path to the principal objective—to destroy the enemy—is plain.

BACKGROUND TO
THE BERLIN BLOCKADE
July 7, 1948

The notes to Russia from the United States, Great Britain and France protesting against the Soviet blockade of their sectors in Berlin were written in forceful language. Morally and practically, and as a statement of the relations that should exist among victorious allies, the case they present is strong. But legally they are deficient for the simple reason that the Western Powers failed specifically to reserve in all cases a corridor into Berlin through the Soviet zone which surrounds it.

This reservation was omitted from the agreement on the control of occupied Germany that was entered into by the four Powers in June, 1945. And the omission was certified permanently in the Potsdam protocols of July and August in the same year by the following language in the second pact—carried over from the first:

* * * Supreme authority in Germany * * * is excercised by the commanders in chief of the armed forces of the United States of

America, the United Kingdom, the Union of Soviet Socialist Republics and the French Republic, *each in his own zone of occupation,* and also jointly, in matters affecting Germany as a whole. * * *

Hence, when the joint control prescribed is broken, as the Soviets broke it recently, each commander in chief has supreme authority in his own territory. The Soviet zone wholly envelops Berlin, and consequently the British, French and American sectors therein. The Soviet commander, supreme in his own territory by the terms of two compacts, was instructed by Moscow to exercise that supremacy by barring the shipment of supplies to Berlin through it from the other zones, and has done so. Like the man who painted the floor of a room toward himself from the walls, each of the Western Powers is trapped in the center, which is its sector of Berlin. There must be an Aesop fable which describes a similar lack of prevision.

Yet when the June and July–August pacts were made the United States, Great Britain and France already had learned that the Kremlin takes advantage of every loophole in a compact, or finds them in Russian when they do not exist in other languages. They had learned it from the Soviet's "interpretation" of the Yalta agreement respecting free elections and other democratic processes in Poland. Nevertheless, the Western military commanders, and then the civil statesmen of these nations, signed papers which gave to the Soviets textual grounds for their current blockade of Berlin.

We have asserted the existence of an "understanding" which precludes such action. But it is not on any paper signed by all concerned, and is therefore a matter of dispute as to who said what.

And without a scrap of paper, commonly accepted and signed, this is only an argument over what was said and by whom and what he meant when he said it. The Soviets may lift the blockade and return their regulations to "normal" for other reasons which they think compelling in practical terms. But we can't throw the book at them, because there is no book.

This time not only the Americans but the British and French also—long experienced in Continental diplomacy and the convolutions of the Asiatic mind—played sandlot baseball in the big league. Perhaps in the joyous relief of victory over the Nazis, and admiration for the fortitude displayed by the Russian people, they abandoned their efforts for precision.

And imprecision led straight to the blockade of Berlin.

INTERCEPTED CABLE
FROM A FOREIGN DIPLOMAT
January 20, 1949

Comrade: Pursuant to your instructions I hasten to give you my impressions of the celebration here today of the inaugural of President Truman and Vice President Barkley. I am weary with the turmoil and movement of the day and could do with a glass of strong tea. But the samovar must wait on duty.

In everything that has been printed and said here with reference to this occasion the stress has been on the strength they claim for their democracy versus ours. It was the President's central theme, and I assume it was the intended effect of the curious pageant that followed Truman and Barkley to the reviewing stand. I am informed that this mélange of the circus and the military review is in the tradition of American inaugurals. But if I may relate the impressions made upon me by this political snake-dance up Pennsylvania Avenue perhaps I shall be able, within the limits of this brief preliminary report, to convey why I think this democracy is careless, foolish and weak.

The rulers took the oath of office on the steps of the Capitol, which faces on a wide esplanade suited to such a display of military power as we would have used to put down any thought of opposition in the minds of members of the parliament who were in attendance. But evidently the caliber of official intelligence here is too limited to have grasped the opportunity. There was no show of power, and only a few detectives were on hand to guard the persons of the President, the Vice President and the justices who administered the oath.

The political effect of this oversight was immediate. In his inaugural address the President announced that his Government would foster loans of private American capital to what he called "areas needing development" and implied that his Government would underwrite these loans if private capital in turn guaranteed it would divide its profits with these serfs of colonial imperialism. Not ten minutes after Truman had finished speaking, members of Congress, emboldened by the absence of the Army, Navy and Air Force in the Capitol portico and at the doors of their chambers, publicly criticized the idea as neither wise nor practical. Imagine the utterance of such treason after one of your reports to our free but loyal legislature! Yet not one of these members of

Congress will be taken from his home for questioning in the middle of the night or at any other time.

From the Capitol, where this feebleness of the American "democracy" was made so plain, I went to inspect the pageant. Knowing as you do the grim and mighty processions of armed men and women who pass to do you honor on comparable occasions, I fear you will not believe this truthful account of part of what I saw.

From West Point, Annapolis, other military schools, and from the armed services there were detachments in the parade. Though I suspect that the qualities they displayed when they assisted us to win the late war against the Nazis and the Japanese have been sapped by soft living and mental resistance to true political philosophy, I must confess there was no evidence of this as they marched. But these land, air and naval units were only an insignificant part of the procession—and this in the nation which is out to conquer and exploit the world.

The greater part of the pageant was made up of revelers, led by bare-legged females in fancy costumes who are known in this western jargon of English as "drum majorettes." Most of the states had what are called "floats" on which were placed symbols of their history and production. I remarked with interest and pleasure that the accent in nearly all of these state displays was on their colonial and ante-bellum past. Nothing could more completely demonstrate how insulated Americans are from the social and economic revolution which we in time will bring to them. Their successful politicians prate of "civil rights" for the oppressed masses and say that profits must be better distributed. But when Americans, including these politicians, celebrate, they show their instinctive nostalgia for the historical periods in which physical and economic slavery were the prevailing system. This adds to my assurance that the chains of their masses will never be sundered until we come to do that ourselves.

The floats of Missouri and Kentucky—the home states of Truman and Barkley—were typical. They featured mules, which in the animal kingdom are oppression incarnate; fair women, who run the men in this country; whisky, that poor imitation of our spirits and, unlike them, very inebriating; colonial mansions, which white and black slaves still toil to maintain for the masters; bluegrass, which our scientists have denounced as a fascist hybrid; and so forth. And the music of the bands was definitely bourgeois, typified by a favorite number known as "Buttons and Bows."

The crowds were permitted to cheer or not as they pleased: thus no ovation having been decreed for Eisenhower, he got only what here is called "a good hand." A coach dog which did tricks for the California unit got as good a one. I shall send more details by pouch.

With homage. I am your greatly encouraged—

ASTIGMATOFF.

KOREA: TRUMAN'S LEADERSHIP
July 1, 1950

Just after the President had broadened the scale of the military intervention in Korea of the United States, on behalf of the United Nations, he made a remark in the homely colloquial phrasing of this country which helps to explain his prompt exercise of vigorous, daring leadership when he was informed of the Communist invasion from the North.

He would not, said Mr. Truman to persons within hearing, let the United States and its President be pushed around. And he would not let the United Nations be pushed around.

From the moment of his first discussion of the North Korean attack, which was by long-distance telephone between Independence, Mo., and Washington, the President made two things very clear to his associates in the Government. One was the determination reported above. The other was that Mr. Truman was aware that the risks in carrying out his determination involved the following:

(1) Direct counter-measures by Moscow of a nature that would immediately precipitate World War III.

(2) Indirect counter-measures by Moscow which would bring the Communist Government of China into the conflict and precipitate World War III at a time the Kremlin deemed more favorable.

(3) A protracted campaign before the North Korean invaders could be beaten in which the United States would be obliged to put in a quantity of armed force that would weaken its ability to deal with sudden aggressions in Western Europe, the Middle East, Greece, Malaya and even Japan.

(4) The maintenance of Russia's full military strength meanwhile, because the Soviets can use satellite forces for the early stages of such engagements while the United States, except for very limited help from other members of the United Nations, is forced to use its own.

Before flying back to Washington last Sunday, the President had been briefed often and thoroughly on all these possible consequences, in event of sudden aggression. He had listened to and participated in many discussions of this nature among his military and diplomatic counselors. When, therefore, he made up his mind in Missouri that there would be no more "pushing around," he had calculated the risks. And at the Sunday night meeting in Blair House these were exhaustively detailed before the President gave his first order—that our naval forces in Philippine waters, and their aircraft, proceed toward the troubled coasts of China and Korea.

From that time on, the decision of Monday night—to defend Formosa and give sea and air cover up to the Thirty-eighth Parallel to the South Koreans—was foreshadowed. And the decision later in the week—to employ ground troops, blockade the entire coast of Korea and strike at North Korean invasion sources beyond the Thirty-eighth Parallel—was anticipated as a probability by the President. Hence, as the time came to give each order, Mr. Truman was ready, and he acted without hesitation.

The leadership he displayed, after full calculation, unified his civilian and military advisers who as late as Monday morning still revealed a difference of opinion about the defense of Formosa. It also unified Congress and the country. Thus it became historic, not only for its promptness and courage, but for the unity it produced out of division. Whatever the outcome, whether a "ten days' war or a thirty years' war" (as Herbert Elliston, the editor of The Washington Post, summoned up the prospect), the course of the President from last Sunday morning forward will be the topic of contemporary chroniclers and those still hundreds of years unborn.

Once the mood of the President was established, and this, as has been said, was at the outset of the crisis, the Government of the United States moved with unusual smoothness and efficiency. The State Department directed with great skill and prescience the vitally important association of the United Nations, which moved promptly, too. The fortunate timing of the visit to the Far East, just before, of Secretary Johnson, General Bradley and John Foster Dulles, which equipped the first two with the latest reports and counsels of General MacArthur, enabled the Department of Defense to act as rapidly and surely in its own area of the problem.

These moves under the stimulus of the President's leadership contributed to the action an element which Mr. Truman believes would have stopped Hitler's aggressions before they culminated in World War II. He was resolved, he said to visitors, that the year 1950 should not see another Munich, followed inevitably by the collapse of such guarantees as Neville Chamberlain gave to Poland in the late Thirties. If the European statesmen of that period had started in time to check Hitler, the President has been heard to say, their guarantees of the integrity of nations in his path would have been made good.

In Mr. Truman's words, they let themselves be pushed around. And as long ago as the closing of Berlin to Allied traffic by the Russians, he apparently made up his mind that the Government of the United States and the peace mechanisms of the United Nations would not be so used. Though obviously neither he, Government intelligence units nor other executives in Washington expected the North Korean invasion to come when it did, Mr. Truman was prepared for it.

By all visible indications popular opinion agrees with the President's estimate of the prospect and with the measures he adopted to avert it if possible. In the body of agreement are many who saw the prospect much earlier and struggled vainly, even before Yalta, to change policies of the last two Presidents that they insisted would lead to the present situation.

They will eventually call for a reckoning by the transfer of office and power. But few among them are disturbing the indispensable unity of the moment, or contending that in the circumstances the President could have done otherwise.

MacARTHUR AND TRUMAN
April 21, 1951

The first oratorical phase has ended in the political-military dispute between the Administration and Gen. Douglas MacArthur over Far East policy, and the Battle of the Documents has begun. Though the General's spoken words after he laid down his command (especially his utterances at the joint session of Congress and the convention of the Daughters of the American Revolution) inflicted heavy blows on the policy-makers in Washington, the deeper wounds, possibly to be quickly followed by curative surgery, will come with the laying bare of the secret records of Washington and Tokyo.

As this is written and only publications from this file have originated with the Administration, their purport being (1) to prove that General MacArthur deliberately disobeyed Mr. Truman's directive against pub-

lic controversial statements on policy, and (2) to prove, by an aide-
memoire of the conference on Wake Island last October, serious inconsistency and bad military judgment on the part of the General. But soon
it will be MacArthur's turn, and few doubt that he, too, will be able to
produce textual support for some parts of his version of what really
happened.

In the grave and acute debate which the General's summary dismissal
and its immediate consequences have evoked, and in determining what
the national verdict will be, this contrast would give him an advantage.
It would more deeply imbue in the national consciousness the impression of dignity, restraint and other forms of high-mindedness which he
made when he addressed the joint session. Since the dispute is in American politics to stay a long time, and candidates will be elected and defeated on the issues it has raised unless, meanwhile, the larger one of
actual war sweeps them aside, this factor can be influential in the political solution.

But, though politics must necessarily play a large part in that solution, the military factor serves to diminish it and to require all concerned to proceed with great care in the political arena. The security of
the United States and the fate of the free world may well hinge on
whether our military program in the Far East is recast, whatever the
degree, in the form advocated by General MacArthur, assuming that
events will not themselves compose a new program. The President has
said that the MacArthur proposals will fruitlessly expand the present
conflict in Korea and make it much more difficult to prevent a third
world war. The General is as confident that only by adopting them can
either Asia or Europe be saved from Bolshevism and the United States
avert the direct threat in its history. In such a conflict of opinion, aware
of what a wrong or partisan judgment could mean, would the American
people tolerate politics as compulsory arbitrator?

A strong conviction that they will not has encouraged many to see
eventual good in the opening of the dispute to the public and in the
emergence of the President and General MacArthur as the principals.
The prestige of the Presidency is tremendous, even when an Administration is on the defensive and the popularity of the White House incumbent is in the low percentage brackets. Moreover, the Presidency
controls agencies of information and propaganda which no citizen or
opposition group can match, and the silencing power of the President
over military as well as civil authority is not elsewhere possessed. An
effective challenge to this power, its effectiveness depending in large

measure on the presence of the whole people in the jury box, can be made only by a public figure of great stature. Such a leader is General MacArthur.

In joining battle with this adversary, as the President is now obliged to do, Mr. Truman and his supporters must exert constant vigilance lest they forget the aphorism which applies both to politics and to war: "When you strike a king you must kill him." They may think they can do it with secret documents, including ex parte versions which they can have sworn to by any number of impressive witnesses, in uniform and in mufti. They may be able to do it in the exhaustive re-examination of Far East policy which Congress and the people are about to undertake. They may even rely on the touch of stock-company tragedian in General MacArthur. But they cannot afford to make any blunders in dealing with him.

The temper of the crowds and of the letters pouring in to newspapers and officeholders suggests, however, that in the present phase of the controversy, before the contenders become fully engaged with their documentary weapons, General MacArthur is in a more privileged status. The basic American principle of government is that the civil authority, not the military, is paramount; that the President is Commander in Chief of the armed forces, and officers on active duty may not undermine his authority in any way. This basic principle General MacArthur disregarded with increasing openness, but it certainly does not seem to be disapproved by millions of Americans. The President, though he tolerated this disregard too long, supported the basic principle in relieving General MacArthur. But seemingly this did not serve to prevent General MacArthur from being established with millions of Americans as a martyr to patriotism. It is not insignificant that among the people of Washington, who greeted the General as the hero of the episode, are some who twice booed the President next day at the ball park.

MacARTHUR'S TESTIMONY
May 5, 1951

In hours of questioning by Senators this week General MacArthur challenged the President personally and Mr. Truman's foreign policy as expressed in the limitations on military action in the Far East; also the validity of all the reasons given for these limitations. The specific challenges were too numerous even to list here, but some important items were:

(1) The President and General MacArthur differ fundamentally on how to end Communist aggression against the Republic of (South) Korea, the core of the dispute centering on what military measures to take against the Communist Government of China.

(2) Under prodding by Senator Kefauver, General MacArthur took the extreme position of declaring that officers on active service, including those in his own command, who feel that "the full truth" is vital to the public interest and is not being given by their civil or military superiors, should have free freedom to assert it publicly.

(3) When armed force is employed in a situation the area commander's exercise of authority in the political and economic as well as the military field should not be limited in any way by the superior civil power except by relieving him.

(4) The Chinese Communists would not find it to their advantage to take Hong Kong from the British now because of the "flow of strategic materials" that come to them through that port. If or when the Peiping Government attains its ends in Asia, however, it will promptly seize Hong Kong.

(5) We do not need Formosa for occupation, for bases or much of anything else. But if we permit it to fall into unfriendly hands the Pacific will be "lost" and Alaska and the Pacific Coast will be actively threatened.

(6) In trying to "buy time" with the limitations imposed on United Nations military action in the Far East we are not buying time; we are "sacrificing our youth" to no effective purpose (and presumably Soviet Russia can make as good use of time as we can).

(7) This is "inertia * * * there is no policy—there is nothing. I tell you, no plan, or anything."

(8) Soviet Russia is in no position to provide the supply line it would need to intervene in a war in the Far East; also the stakes are not large enough for Soviet Russia to become engaged there. The General agreed he may be "wrong," as he was in his belief that the Chinese Communists would not intervene in Korea. But our own intervention there exposed us to risks which, against the world threat of "communism," must be taken.

(9) We are in war in Korea; and, when you are in a war, "you can't just say, 'let that war go on indefinitely while I prepare for some other war,' unless you pay for it by the thousands and thousands and thousands of American boys."

(10) The method used by the President in dismissing General Mac-Arthur was without precedent; and undoubtedly "the interest of the United States was jeopardized by such a summary mode of turning over great responsibilities which involve the security of our country."

(11) In saying that "no segment of American society should be so gagged that the truth and the full truth shall not be brought out," General MacArthur said he was not—as Senator McMahon suggested—proposing that there be a "national referendum" on how to "conduct the strategy of defending America." But he said it remains a fact in this country that the voters hold a referendum on an Administration every four years.

(12) He would not bomb Soviet sources of supply to the Chinese Red armies because that is not a *casus belli* under international law. Also, the general has no evidence that Russians have entered the Korean war directly in any way.

General MacArthur. . . presented a positive policy in sharp contrast to the Administration's negative one, though he espoused a much more militant, global version of the "Truman Doctrine" than its author ever has.

For example, the General testified:
The general definition which for many decades has been accepted was that war was the ultimate process of politics; that, when all other political means failed, you then go to force; and, when you do that, the balance of control, the balance of concept, the main interest involved, the minute you reach the killing stage, is the control of the military. A theatre commander, in any campaign, is not merely limited to the handling of his troops; he commands that whole area politically, economically and militarily. You have got to trust [him] at that stage of the game when politics fail and the military takes over; you must trust the military, or otherwise you will have the system that the Soviet once employed of the political commissar who would run the military as well as the politics of the country.

As far as the United Nations in Korea is concerned, it is limited to Korea. They are trying to clear Korea. I don't understand that in any decisions or discussions that have arisen we are trying to do more than stop the Chinese from aggression in Korea. I believe when we do that we have to put sufficient military force upon them to do it. I do not believe we can put that sufficient military force upon them if we limit ourselves to the inhibitions we do now, just in the area of Korea. I believe the minute that we put those pressures on them that the Red

Chinese, if they have any sensibilities of discretion at all, would enter into a cease-fire parley.

It is manifestly impossible in this space to do more than deal with the highlights of a lengthy examination in which General MacArthur asserted that at least one statement by the President was "tommyrot," and called for no United Nations' dealings with Communist China and an ultimatum to Peiping—the consequences of which, if necessary, the United States should be willing to face alone, and could successfully, without landing ground troops in China or bringing Russia into what would then be a global war.

PROBES BY CONGRESS
July 16, 1951

The Senate joint committee inquiry into the dismissal of General MacArthur seems to have faded away; and no demand has yet been made for an investigation why great rivers stubbornly continue to inundate contiguous lands and cities. But at any moment something may happen that will produce another probe by Congress in which all the errors and injustices of the system (notably absent from Senator Russell's direction of the MacArthur hearings) will reappear.

Nevertheless, these abuses are being studied with increasing intelligence and care in an effort to put an end to them. Three suggestions have been especially discussed as pointing the way to public inquiries which will be not only fair and orderly but will not divert as many members of Congress from their primary duty to legislate. The suggestions follow in the order of their publication.

The first was made by Senator Lodge of Massachusetts in a Senate speech delivered April 3, 1950. He said in part:

> The repercussions from the present investigation into disloyalty charges are such that it would not be right for me to disregard the mounting damage which is being inflicted on the position of the United States abroad and on the respect here at home for the justice and efficacy of our institutions.
>
> I suggest that confidential investigations be made by a trained commission of twelve members, four to be appointed by the President, four by the Senate, four by the House, and that the whole membership be equally divided between the two parties. * * * This method

* * * received the unanimous support of Congress three years ago and has since proved itself workable and nonpolitical.

(The reference was to the Hoover Commission, of which Mr. Lodge was a legislative parent.)

The second suggestion was made in the 1951 Spring number of the University of Chicago Law Review by Prof. Lindsay Rogers of Columbia. After reviewing the tribunals of inquiry in Great Britain, and the history of public probes in New York under the Moreland Act, Dr. Rogers wrote:

> If Congress wishes to make its investigations more efficient and conclusive it need only pass a statute modeled on the British Tribunals of Inquiry Act. * * * Three members [of each commission] are ample. Nor should a commission include members of Congress. They would be amateurs and would, as they do now, wish to publicize themselves. One important advantage of the Moreland Commissionership or the British Tribunal is that it frees legislators from tasks that reduce the amount of time available for their legislative work which is always in arrears.

The third and most recent suggestion came from Eli E. Nobleman, a member of the professional staff of the Senate Committee on Expenditures in the Executive Departments, and is included in a committee study of the subject issued July 10 and titled Senate Document No. 51. Mr. Nobleman would have Congress continue to exercise the function of inquiry. But he proposed that all investigations "not related directly to pending legislation" should be "performed by a permanent investigating body." He continued:

> Such a body is already in existence in the Senate as a standing subcommittee [of the Executive Expenditures group]—the Senate Investigations Subcommittee. Its staff, both clerical and professional, is composed of persons who are trained not only in investigative techniques but also in the operation of the executive branch * * * at all levels. During the past few years [it] has conducted investigations into virtually every phase of governmental activities with notable success, many of which were referred to it at the request of other committees. In addition [it] has performed a large number of preliminary investigations for standing committees. * * * In an effort to insure that its proceedings are conducted fairly and judiciously the subcommittee has adopted rules of procedure to govern the conduct of its investigations. * * *

It is staffed and equipped to handle all general investigations in the Senate. * * * Participation by Senators who are not members, when they have a particular interest, can be achieved by permitting them to serve as *ex officio* members.

The same machinery could be established in the House and often be joined with the Senate's. There is no estimating the time, labor, overlapping and duplicating that would be saved for other duties. And members of the standing committees would be enabled to concentrate on pending legislation.

The rules to which Mr. Nobleman referred are designed to protect individual rights of a witness from current abuses. A unanimous subcommittee or a full committee majority is prerequisite to public hearings; witnesses may be assisted by legal advisers and have the privilege of cross-examination in certain circumstances; and "no photographs, moving pictures, television or radio broadcasts" are permitted against the wish of a witness while he is on the stand.

The subject is one of great importance; the reform is overdue. It is timely also in view of the fact that, as hundreds of cases touching the loyalty and security of Government employes are being reopened, certain hunters in Congress are on the alert for a new bag of headlines, and perhaps thereafter serial articles and a book "revealing the inside story."

TRUMAN'S HISTORIC WARNING TO STALIN
January 10, 1953

The President's solemn reminder to Stalin, in his last message to Congress on the "State of the Union," that war in the atomic age meant the devastation of the Soviet lands and hegemony was the most portentous warning the head of one nation has given to the head of another in a long historical series. And it was a final act of statecraft for which Harry S. Truman will be remembered when much else in his record has been forgotten.

It belongs in a historical series, because the heads of states often before have warned their opposite numbers of the consequences of making or provoking war. And it is the latest in a great moral series which runs from Hosea and Revelation to Shelley, Wilson and Franklin Roosevelt, admonishing those who would sow the wind that they will reap the whirlwind.

But the authors of the Old Testament, the poets and the Presidents before Mr. Truman never knew the fury of the atomic whirlwind that war would lose upon the world. Even President Roosevelt died without proof that the bomb which he authorized to be made and which was dropped on Hiroshima and Nagasaki would be the devastating weapon it became. President Truman's warning was uttered, not only with this proof, but with the terrifying implication that the new weapon called the H-bomb is available for war.

Hence this reminder to Stalin dwarfs all those of the past by its horrid potentialities and will occupy a page of its own in human history, to be followed by the preservation of modern civilization, or its destruction amid scenes of agonizing and widespread death. If preservation is the sequel, Mr. Truman's act of tremendous statecraft must be credited with a large share of the cause. If the sequel is to be destruction, he will have done as much as any one man in the world could have done in 1953 to avert it.

There has been no higher point in the last official phase of a President of the United States. And the words in which Mr. Truman addressed his warning directly to Stalin were on the same level.

> You claim belief in Lenin's prophecy that one stage in the development of Communist society would be war between your world and ours. But Lenin was a pre-atomic man, who viewed society and history with pre-atomic eyes. Something profound has happened since he wrote. War has changed its shape and its dimensions. It cannot now be a "stage" in the development of anything save ruin for your regime and your homeland.

The President said that war would also bring calamity to the United States and to other peoples and other regimes. But certain Soviet policies suggest this is not a deterrent. The deterrent, if there is to be one, is in Mr. Truman's final sentence above. And that adds to the statecraft of the utterance.

It is appropriate that the development of atomic weapons should have been the subject of these momentous paragraphs in Mr. Truman's last message to Congress on the "State of the Union." For in his Presidency the atomic age arrived; he has had to bear the heaviest of the burdens it imposed on Government policies of war and peace; and he has not shirked any of them. It devolved on the President alone to decide whether the atom bomb of 1945 should be dropped on the cities and civilian population of Japan. And when, several years later, the Atomic Energy Commission divided on a proposal to try to manufacture the tritium weapon—with its power to crush man and all his works in whole counties and wreak hardly lesser destruction in the areas surrounding them—Mr. Truman again made the decision to proceed.

He gave the order of 1945 for the purpose, which was attained, of bringing to an end the war with Japan and saving countless lives. He directed that work begin on the tritium weapon in an effort to keep our atomic armament paramount over that of our potential enemies, so that our aggressors would fear to resort to war and eventually would be forced by that fear to agree to international control that would exclude such weapons from war if it came. And when the successful work of foreign spies clearly hastened the time when enemies could match our atomic weapons, even though not in numbers (a time that scientists never doubted would arrive in due course), the President gave the warning to Stalin that if he sowed the wind he would reap a whirlwind never dreamed of in Lenin's philosophy.

The President took hard advice in all these decisions, though the thought that his endeavors for peace on earth might be successfully aspersed among friendly nations must have greatly disturbed him.

His atomic policy may prove to have prevented World War III, and that has been his ardent mission.

THE EISENHOWER-
STEVENSON CAMPAIGN

TRUMAN'S BID TO EISENHOWER
November 8, 1951

The effort of Democrats to induce General of the Army Dwight D.
Eisenhower to become the Presidential nominee of their party in 1952
instead of confining his availability to a "draft" by the Republican National Convention has been a much more active and organized campaign
than has been generally known.

On the authority of a person whose public position can be correctly
described as "eminent," this correspondent reported in a dispatch published today that President Truman, during the General's visit here this
week, had offered to support him for the Democratic nomination, which
amounted to assuring it, and that General Eisenhower had strongly implied rejection by citing his opposition to some of the President's major
policies and programs—toward union labor, for example.

This account Mr. Truman vehemently denied, on leaving the airport
here this morning for Key West, Fla.; and in France members of the
General's staff at Supreme Headquarters, Allied Powers in Europe, described it on his behalf as wholly "fictional."

But the source of the information repeated his account today after the
denials. And evidence is growing that the President's proposal was the
culminating point in a major enterprise by important Democrats that
seems to have failed.

The principal item in the new evidence that came to this correspondent today was this:
194

Within the last five weeks a Democrat, described as very influential in the party and not associated with the Southern opponents of the President—and later a group of similar type—called on General Eisenhower in France. Only one was particularly close to Mr. Truman, but all were on very friendly terms with him. On each occasion—by the unaccompanied visitor and by the group spokesman—the same statement was made to the General.

It was that if, at any time before the Democratic National Convention, he would say he would accept its Presidential nomination his visitors were convinced they could get it for him unanimously; in any event they could "guarantee" it and he could count on the support of President Truman.

General Eisenhower's reported reply was:

"You can't join a party just to run for office. What reason have you to think I have ever been a Democrat?"

And, in relating this incident to a friend while on his recent visit here, the General said:

"You know I have been a Republican all my life and that my family have always been Republicans."

This account, like the one published today, comes from a person of great importance in one of the major political parties.

In view of the vehemence of the President's denial, and the use of the sweeping word "fictional" used by reputed spokesmen for General Eisenhower at his headquarters, something of the background in the preparation of the dispatch about the President's offer has a direct bearing.

After the information published today had been obtained from the source whose qualifications alone justified its publication, a check was made with the White House. It was explained to Joseph Short, the President's press secretary, that the information was of such importance that Mr. Truman should know about it in advance and have an opportunity to comment if he desired; that he might feel publication could adversely affect General Eisenhower's mission and therefore not be in the national interest; and if the account was to be denied, this should be established prior to any publication.

Mr. Short courteously agreed to relay this suggestion to the President. Several hours later he replied that Mr. Truman did not wish either to be advised of or questioned about the information, and that this correspondent must be the judge of its accuracy without any assistance from the President.

The press secretary also declined to hear what the information was, saying he knew nothing of what had passed privately between the President and General Eisenhower and did not wish to know.

Since the source of the account has the qualifications described in the foregoing, since it could only add to General Eisenhower's prestige in Europe if it were realized that both major parties want him to be President, and since Mr. Truman and his press secretary declined to hear the information or offer any reasons for or against making it known, the dispatch was written and published.

A MEDITATION BY HAMLET
AT KEY WEST
December 3, 1951

A reader suggests that "it has been a very long time since the Gridiron Club or anybody dusted off that Hamlet routine of a politician trying to make up his mind." The following attempt will probably demonstrate that it hasn't been long enough, but, as too many people like to say, "This is a challenge."

(Act first and last. Scene one and only. A room in the Little White House at Key West. Enter Joseph Short and Major General Vaughan.* Mr. Short speaks):

And can you, by no japes and anecdotes
Get from him why he puts on this confusion;
Grating so harshly all his days of quiet
With turbulent outcry that "It just ain't so"?

(The Major General replies):

He does confess he feels himself distracted
But from what cause he will by no means speak,
And with evasions he doth keep aloof
When I would rib him into some confession
Of his intent. . . . But hark, he's coming.
Leave us beat it, Joe.

(Exeunt S. and V. Enter the President):

To run or not to run, that is the question:
Whether my grand designs—foreign and domestic—
Can safely be entrusted to Another,

* Respectively, the President's press secretary and military aide.

And whether he will fight the Special Interests,
Endlessly plotting 'gainst them, I'm unsure.
Nor am I sure whether my bounden duty,
And my necessity it be as well,
To hold the helm against this sea of troubles
And, as in '48, to end them.
To quit, to go back home to Jackson County
And leave the heartaches, and the thousand daily shocks
That shake the White House, to a new incumbent?
Ay, there's the rub. For how can I be certain
That in my rustic ease nightmares won't come,
As when I had to shuffle off Bill Boyle?
How can I know that Fred or someone else
On whom I might bestow my accolade
Will keep things right with Murray and with Green,
Will shut his ears to Byrnes and Harry Byrd,
Or—grimmest thought—will fail to get elected,
Yes, even if the G. O. P. names Taft?
That is what gives me pause. The gimmick's that.
And yet there is calamity in tenure
That lasts o'erlong beyond its early vigor.
For who would bear the whips and scorns of Congress,
The lying press, the proud South's contumely,
The pangs of solitude, mobilization's delay,
The insolence of MacArthur and the spurns
That patient merit of the unworthy take
When he himself might his quietus make
With a straight Sherman? Who would Caudles bear,
And stifle under clutches of mink coats,
But that the dread of him who might succeed,
That yet unchosen Someone from whose bourn
Fair Deals may ne'er return, strengthens the will
Rather to bear the ills heavy upon us
Than fly to others that we know not of.
Thus politics makes wobblers of us all,
And the Missourian hue of resolution
Is sicklied o'er with the pale cast of thought;
And plans to abdicate that we would publish
With this regard their currents turn away
And lose the name of action. . . . Soft you now!
Is that Kefauver? Or Douglas, who, as eke the young Victoria,
Might weep on getting crowned? Avaunt such visions!

(Re-enter his Press Secretary):

Short, in thy matins with the scurrilous press
Be all its sins remembered.

(Mr. Short):

Aye, Aye, Sweet Prince,
And I will mention some it hasn't got.

There is more reason than the poetic poverty of this paraphrase supplies why the whole effort should be confined to one scene. For instance, Hamlet determined to stick it out and did so until he willed the royal succession to young Fortinbras. And any resemblance between young Fortinbras, Mr. Taft, Chief Justice Vinson or General Eisenhower is not even coincidental. It just isn't there at all.

CAMPAIGN PROMISES DEBATE
ON HIGH LEVEL
August 16, 1952

As the Presidential candidates maneuver toward their most favorable positions for the active campaign their common problem comes more clearly into view. Governor Stevenson already has given strong indications that his political philosophy is nearer to the Jefferson-Wilson than the Roosevelt-Truman school. General Eisenhower has indicated that his doctrine somewhat resembles his rival's. Therefore, each must take care he does not find himself too close ideologically to the other to foreclose a popular choice on plain issues.

There is little likelihood, however, that this will happen. To begin with, Stevenson and Eisenhower are very different—the one deft, intellectual and at the same time politically acute; the other impulsive, intelligent as contrasted with intellectual, and a man who requires constant schooling in practical politics. Second, to come very near to Stevenson's middle-of-the-road position on the economic-social issues raised by the New Deal and the Fair Deal, Eisenhower would be obliged to eat thousands of his own words, and in public—something that by character and conviction he would not do. Third, on many aspects of the foreign and domestic record of the Roosevelt-Truman Administrations which he disapproves with a varying degree of intensity, Stevenson must tread very softly, while Eisenhower can jump on them with both feet. Fourth, each must keep silence on, or defend, party members who handicap them electorally.

Nevertheless, both the candidates are moderates, as thus far revealed. This presents both with the problem aforesaid. It involves the risk—ever to be guarded against—that extremist Democrats or Republicans may stay home on Election Day. And no political expert can say for sure what percentage of the eligible vote that is cast in November will be more helpful to Stevenson than to Eisenhower. Consequently, President Truman, the two candidates, their national chairmen and others in both parties have called on the people to register and vote to the peak of eligibility.

To assure a sharp line of demarcation with Eisenhower some have counseled Stevenson to this effect:

The South is now pretty well nailed down for the national ticket. You can now go stronger on "civil rights" legislation, etc. With a couple of speeches in that area, in which, without making the President mad, you can show the South you are your own man, you can remove the last vestiges of a Republican threat in Texas, Virginia and Louisiana. So your strategy from here out is to move a visible distance to the left of where you have been standing. This will preserve for you enough of the racial and economic group-combination Roosevelt made to add the big populous states of the Northeast and West to the South, and you can hold Truman's 1948 capture of the Midwest farm states with a reasonable price-support policy.

With different details, counsel to move leftward has also been directed toward Eisenhower:

Please don't ever again compare "security" to prison. Tell labor it won the war, or almost. Denounce segregation and racial and religious prejudice every day. Say some more about how governmental relief payments to old folks should be raised. Maintain a more popular position on ownership of submerged coastal lands than any Stevenson takes—it might assure the electors of Texas and Louisiana and clinch California's. If you will do these things, then you can go after Federal spending, corruption, foreign policies and acts, favoritism for certain groups, the need for a complete change in Washington, and so forth, without having to pull punches for strategy's sake.

Naturally, these counsels have not been offered to the candidates in so many words or even in face-to-face meetings. None in the groups that surround the two highminded men whom the major parties have nominated for the Presidency is obtuse, cynical or reckless enough to propose such bold and corrupt expediency. But broad hints of this kind have been sent in the candidates' direction through channels. And as each nominee clarifies and consolidates his position on the various campaign issues some changes and expansions of strategy are bound to be made by both.

The prospect for a campaign on a high level is better than usual, not only because of the characters of the candidates but because they incurred no obligation to any person or group for their nominations. They were chosen because the delegates to their party conventions considered them the best vote-getters, and the Democratic nomination was actually forced on Stevenson by a majority that shoved union labor and other special groups aside in so doing.

THE 'LIBERAL' PROFESSOR
HOLDS A PRESS CONFERENCE
October 27, 1952

"I have summoned you representatives of the press," the "liberal" Professor began, "for a fuller exegesis—or perhaps for this audience I should say explanation—why the group of college educators of which I have the honor to be chairman feels that, by any test of morals, ethics, logic or intelligence, no citizen or newspaper can justify being for General Eisenhower for President and must switch at once.

"First, by not asking the voters of Wisconsin, Indiana, Missouri and Nevada to reject the Republican nominees for the Senate and return Democrats, Eisenhower has embraced politicians who have spread the smear of communism on innocent persons, including his military creator, General Marshall.

"Second, by not mentioning the name of General Marshall in Senator McCarthy's presence at the Milwaukee rally, and by saying he didn't think it was 'the right place,' Eisenhower showed himself spiritually unfit to be President.

"Third, by not concentrating his campaign on his differences over foreign policy with Senator Taft, and instead seeking to find policy areas in which he and Taft agree, Eisenhower betrayed the cause that took him twice to Europe.

"Fourth, by stressing concern (a) over the cost of the Administration's social uplift programs; (b) over a few instances of petty corruption; (c) over a few lapses from patriotism by sad young people who were victims of the blunders of the capitalist system, and (d) over our loss of China and the arrival of the war in Korea during this Administration, Eisenhower has run as an opposition candidate instead of cooperating with Truman and Stevenson to have past errors forgotten and unify the country behind a new Democratic Administration."

Q. "Professor, you mentioned the 'smear of communism,' for which your group has demanded that Eisenhower repudiate these four Republican Senators. Do you believe that, if a Democrat as prominent as a Senator, or more so, puts a 'smear of nazism' on an equally prominent Republican, Governor Stevenson should denounce it and its author?"

A. "I do."

Q. "But you and your group have made no such call on Stevenson since the President said that Eisenhower, by not repudiating Republicans who voted to override the veto of the McCarran immigration bill, had 'accepted' the Nazi 'concept of the master race.' Why is that?"

A. "The President is not a candidate for re-election. These Republican Senators are. Also, 'accepting,' used in the sense Mr. Truman used it, is not tantamount to 'assenting to.' But as a general proposition Stevenson would split his following if he criticized the President, and that might prevent his election."

Q. "But, Professor, is it not a fact that both the President and Stevenson agree that the President's record is a candidate for election? And, according to the dictionary on your desk there, to 'accept' is to 'receive (a thing offered to or thrust upon someone) with a consenting mind.' Also, you oppose Eisenhower because he declined to split his following by asking the people of several states to return Democrats to Congress in place of Republicans or by attacking Senator Taft, who will be the Senate Republican leader, regardless of who is elected President."

A. "All that is impertinent, irrelevant and incompetent."

Q. "Why, sir?"

A. "Because, in my judgment and that of my distinguished associates, the President and the Governor are good men needed by the country, and our function is to promote, not injure, their cause by stretching mere logic to the point of political impracticability."

Q. "Then it is as political tactics, to serve the interest of the candidates you favor, Professor, that you and your group have not criticized Stevenson as you have Eisenhower on similar grounds?"

A. "Don't put words into my mouth, sir. I have told you that in this instance we, among us eminent Protagorasians and philologists, have decreed that 'accepting' does not mean what the dictionary says; therefore, there was no slur of Eisenhower by the President; therefore, no repudiation from Stevenson is called for. I have also pointed out that McCarthy is a candidate for election and Truman is not; that the country needs Stevenson; and that hence any who obstruct this consummation in any way do the country a disservice. As liberals my group and I will not sacrifice the hope of mankind to mere consistency."

Q. "Back there a bit you denounced Eisenhower for failing to mention Marshall at Milwaukee and for saying he didn't think it was 'the right place.' Did you notice that at Cleveland Thursday night Stevenson kept mentioning McCarthy in denouncing 'reckless defamers of character' but that, Saturday night, taking the same line at Boston, he never mentioned McCarthy once? Was that because Stevenson didn't think Boston was 'the right place'?"

A. "That is a tortured parallel."

Q. "Like, maybe, the Thirty-eighth?"

The Professor said that would be all for the day.

WIT AND HUMOR
DURING A CAMPAIGN
September 15, 1952

General Eisenhower and his advisers have come to the deliberate conclusion that the witty gibes and humorous anecdotes with which Governor Stevenson is wont to lighten the necessarily serious business of discussing grave issues may be turned against him. They hope the American people can be brought to resent these as a wisecracking approach to weighty affairs and the mark of an essentially frivolous man.

The General launched on this strategy today when he said at Fort Wayne: "As we face the issues of the campaign I see nothing funny about them and no way to make them amusing." And he implied this was especially true of any discussion of the Korean war, which certainly is nothing to laugh about.

Of course, Stevenson did not laugh about the Korean war. But he did say a couple of witty things in the speech in which that war was a large topic. It will be interesting to try to discover whether, for example, the people of the United States believe, or can be brought to believe, that when a Presidential candidate discusses such a topic, as Stevenson did at San Francisco Sept. 9, he establishes himself as light of mind by preceding it as follows:

> I want to share with you, if I may, a letter from a California lady who knew my parents when they lived here fifty years ago. She writes that after Grover Cleveland was nominated for the Presidency in 1892, and my own grandfather was nominated for Vice President, she named her two kittens Grover Cleveland and Adlai Stevenson. Grover, she writes me, couldn't stand the excitement of the campaign and died before the election. But Adlai lived to be a very old cat. And this, my friends, is obviously for me the most comforting incident of the campaign so far.

It seems improbable the Republicans can establish, from the method used by Stevenson to get his audience "with him" at the outset, that he is congenitally frivolous and light-minded and finds everything funny, including the deadly serious. True, people who are opposed to a Presidential candidate for any reason, or are looking for reasons to be, can readily be persuaded of almost anything by his critics. And it is also true that, if the impression can be created a candidate is "too light to be President," this constitutes a real danger to his chances of election. Some of the political strategists who are circulating the sobriquet of "The Little Joker" for Stevenson understand that very well, and the favorable contrast for Eisenhower that might be effected thereby.

But it would seem that, to make this impression stick with enough voters throughout the nation, who otherwise would support Stevenson, to affect the result of the election, the masterly prose and the excellent delivery to which the witticisms and anecdotes are but narrow fringes must first vanish from the Governor's oratory. Or he must grow so fond of gags and stories that he will subordinate the issues to them.

This is always a danger for a man with a strong sense of the mirthful and the ridiculous. And in the case of Stevenson the danger is increased by the fact that, through the channel of some bright young men around him who are adept at saying and writing clever things, the gag-writers of Broadway and Hollywood are deluging his headquarters with japes and quips that go fine at "21" and the Brown Derby but on the Presidential stump are not so good. It seems probable that the other day, when Stevenson facetiously offered to quit telling the truth about the Republicans if they would quit telling lies about the Democrats, he had become unwisely infatuated with one from the professional gag factory.

Except for that, however, and a couple of impulsive remarks at his press conferences, Stevenson has furnished his opponents with little substantial hope that they can prove him to be but a postprandial wit at the core. His two speeches at the Chicago convention where he was nominated restored the level of political oratory in this country to that which Woodrow Wilson occupied. Throughout the campaign thus far he has kept on this level. He has been urbane at times and humorous, but not flippant. And not only is his prose style facile in presenting the complex and the profound; it is his own.

Stevenson may be trapped by his wit into saying something disastrous in the context, or something where the offensiveness kills the humor. The eminence of his opponent makes that a constant hazard. But the skill in composition and the political sagacity he has shown so far make this improbable. "Were it not for this occasional vent [of humor]," said Lincoln in 1864, "I should die." And that has always been a vent for the American people, too.

It is when Stevenson's wit and anecdotes are employed to cover a weakness of position that the Republicans have their opportunity. But Eisenhower has yet to strike hard at these. The Labor Day speech at Detroit, when the Governor swallowed the C.I.O. program on labor relations while asserting his independence of all groups, is one example of a shining target for courageous attack.

G.O.P. TURNS NIXON CASE TO ITS ADVANTAGE
September 27, 1952

Thus far the Democrats have got the worst of it by cutting in on a problem that was greatly embarrassing the Republican candidate for President and the party organization. When it was revealed that the political activities of Senator Nixon, General Eisenhower's running-mate, were being paid out of a fund contributed by constituents in California, Democratic campaign spokesmen, instead of being content with the public spectacle of Eisenhower in political travail and indecision, peremptorily admonished the General to drop Nixon from the ticket. And Governor Stevenson, though he did not go so far, listed three questions about Nixon's fund which he said would have to be answered before judgment could be passed on the legality or ethics of the arrangement.

The immediate result was to put Nixon in a spotlight where his combative nature and a theatrical technique reminiscent of "East Lynne" enabled him to put on a performance that drenched the soil of the United States with tears. When Nixon, on television, with his wife also on the screen, had completed the most extraordinary political oration in long memory—in which he gave a moving account of a financial status far more modest than his station and of the struggles of an attractive young couple to get along—the vast audience responded overwhelmingly and affirmatively to his request to say to the Republican National Committee whether he should remain as the party candidate for Vice President. So, unanimously, did all members of the committee who could be reached; and so, with evidence of deep emotion, at last did General Eisenhower.

As if to fill the bitter Democratic cup to overflowing, the nation in the same period learned through Chicago dispatches that Governor Stevenson also had collected one or more private funds so that he could supplement the public pay of aides of the high caliber he required, but who were financially unable to serve him otherwise. Though it was argued that the fund or funds were no secret, they were to the people of the country as a whole. Though it was argued that the donors could not influence the Governor's aides because their identities were unknown to the recipients, the obvious and effective answer was that Stevenson knew them; and that it was as fair to assume he might be influenced by the contributors to his fund or funds as it was to assume that Nixon might be by his.

The final Democratic mishap came when Stevenson said he could not possibly give a breakdown of his funds because that would be a "breach of faith." Since the Democrats had filled the air with demands that Nixon do this very thing, the Governor's position was untenable politically and he was obliged to abandon it; but the Republicans will be sure to attack his listing of some large contributions as "anonymous." He also announced that he and his running-mate, Senator Sparkman, would make public their income tax returns for the last ten years.

In the wave of emotion that Nixon's telecast loosed across the country a number of points he did not meet were lost sight of. His financial tabulation did not explain, for instance, where and how he got the $20,000 he said he paid on the purchase price of a $41,000 house in Washington. In the swift succession of dramatic incidents after Eisenhower heard the news the nation's attention was so fixed on Nixon that the General's uncertainty what to do, and the hot dispute on that subject between his chief adviser on the train, Governor Adams, and Arthur Summerfield, the Chairman of the Republican National Committee, got little notice. The Democrats, whose plain strategy it was to emphasize this situation, were apparently too groggy for the time being to do so.

It looked then as if the triumphant Republicans might say of the Democrats in the words of Hosea: "For they have sown the wind and they shall reap the whirlwind; it hath no stalk; the bud shall yield no meal; if so be it yields, the strangers shall swallow it up."

For their part, the Democrats are not through with Nixon. In the words of one Democrat, "We are out to knock off the Senator's halo."

But the Democratic campaign managers will run a serious risk if they pursue this objective. For if they make the purpose plain and fail to achieve it, the kickback will be more stunning than the recoil of Mitchell's prompt demand that Nixon be dropped from the Republican ticket. And there will be no recovery from this particular injury by Nov. 4.

There are several reasons to support this opinion. The wave of sympathy for and approval of Nixon as a candidate for Vice President is probably beginning to subside somewhat, as emotional manifestations always do. But there are no signs it will disappear. And it can be renewed in greater force by a comparable disturbance. Among the forces that evoked the wave is Nixon's record as the principal producer of the evidence that sent Alger Hiss to prison as a traitor, and as the determined delver into other facts about Communist infiltration in Government to whom the Administration lent no aid and whom it sometimes obstructed.

The Democrats will have to be sure of their ground in further attacks on Nixon, or they will be very sorry, indeed.

THE CANDIDATE'S DREAM
THAT IS SELDOM FULFILLED
October 2, 1952

The intensive campaigning through the country by the rival candidates for the Presidency, in which Mr. Truman has now joyously joined, is a strategy of electioneering that many aspirants to the White House have sought vainly to reject. Ever since William McKinley spent the campaign of 1896 rocking sedately in his porch chair at Canton, Ohio, while William Jennings Bryan, his unsuccessful opponent, was covering every whistle stop, other candidates have dreamed they could pursue the same tactics and get elected. But since 1896 only Harding and Coolidge came anywhere near fulfilling the dream.

Maybe it vanished indefinitely from the hopes of Presidential candidates in 1948 when Mr. Truman took to the road and retrieved what almost all politicians but himself believed to be his lost cause. At any rate, years may pass before a Presidential nominee, including any future incumbent of the White House, ventures to imitate the McKinley-Harding-Coolidge strategy.

Governor Stevenson's reported new plan to forgo several political excursions among the voters, in order to prepare and deliver more "fireside talks" like that of last Monday night, suggests that the advent of television may presage a swing back toward McKinley's stationary campaign method of 1896. Talking to the people from a quiet room, free of the noise and other distractions of crowds and exploding flash bulbs, a candidate can concentrate on his message and experience no interruption. But the experiment will be made cautiously, with 1948 in mind. And, if Stevenson is elected, the President's undoubted conclusion that the Truman whistle-stop tours were essential to the event will probably prolong the successful pressure of political managers on national candidates to spend most of their time speaking to the people at first-hand.

The record contains many entries since 1896 of Presidential nominees who wanted to take McKinley for their model and were argued out of it.

In 1904 the Democrats nominated the dignified and eminent jurist of Esopus, N.Y., Alton B. Parker. He had warned the party convention before it balloted on the Presidency that, whatever the monetary plank of the platform might say about the parity rate of silver to gold, he would advocate the maintenance of the gold standard. The idea of what was then called a "swing around the circle" was repugnant to Parker.

And, if anyone had suggested the modern expansion that Senator Taft in 1948 derisively named "whistle stopping," he would have risked banishment from Esopus for himself and apoplexy for the judge.

Parker announced that, like McKinley in 1896 and 1900, he would stay at home and receive delegations with whom he would discuss the issues. He would permit certain of these discussions to be made public. But there would be no speaking tour. Before the campaign was in its final phase, however, the Democratic nominee was making speeches in New York and states near-by on industrial "trusts" and finance. They got him into trouble because the Republicans assailed them as ignorant. But the point is that, against his will, he went campaigning.

In 1908, after his third nomination by the Democrats, Bryan decided on a total change in his tactics. McKinley had rocked on his front porch throughout two contests with Bryan and been elected. Well, Bryan would do the same. But by Aug. 20 he was engaged in what Mr. Truman would concede to have been a classic whistle-stop tour.

In this same year the Republican nominee, William H. Taft, informed all concerned he would not stump the country. He did not think it seemly. His resolution lived longer than Bryan's, but on Sept. 23 he started traveling and speaking and kept it up until the returns disclosed his election.

"My private judgment," said Woodrow Wilson to his political advisers, after the Democrats named him for President in 1912, "is that extended speaking tours are not the most impressive method of conducting a campaign." He would make a few addresses at strategic points. There would be no rear-platform oratory (at whistle stops). The split in the Republican party made Wilson's election almost a mathematical certainty, yet it was not long before he totally abandoned his "private judgment" and went on the road.

Four years later, when President Wilson's opponent was Charles Evans Hughes, he returned to his resolution of 1912. He had, he said, no intention of making a campaign tour. He would accept a few invitations to discuss public questions, but only if they came from nonpartisan organizations. But in October he changed his mind and spoke under partisan auspices in several cities, concluding the series at Buffalo and Madison Square Garden. When the President discovered that Tammany sponsored the latter engagement he talked of refusing to appear because he had not been fully consulted before it was made. But he kept it and delivered one of the most notable addresses of his career.

After that, except for Harding and Coolidge, Presidential candidates have bowed to the inevitable.

The Eisenhower Years

The quadriennial campaign chant of the party out of power is "It's time for a change." But seldom has this evoked a more sympathetic response from the voters than in 1952. For seldom had any party out of power produced the Presidential candidate who more precisely exemplified change, and at a time when change had a broader appeal to the electorate.

The Democratic party, with the exception of one Congress, had controlled the political branches of the Federal government and many State capitols and legislatures for twenty years. The Administration of President Truman was beleaguered with charges of official malfeasance, petty and great, and by evidences of the presence of crypto-Communist fellow-travelers in the Executive branch that were being successfully exploited by Senator McCarthy of Wisconsin.

The Korean War was vastly unpopular—partly because the American people were weary of military involvements abroad; particularly because, having been proposed and undertaken by President Truman as a "police action" of the United Nations, the United States for the first time in its history was restrained by this alliance from pressing the war to a military conclusion.

The Republican Presidential candidate, Dwight D. Eisenhower, had been the victorious Commander of the Allied forces against the Nazi hegemony in Europe, a professional soldier who practiced war as the only solvent in the current circumstances from which world peace could emerge; and, in political philosophy, was a firm believer in the tenets of what he viewed as "progressive conservatism."

Against this combination of popular appeals effectively dramatized by Eisenhower's pledge, if elected, to "go to Korea" and bring that war to an honorable conclusion, the Democratic party ticket headed by Governor Adlai E. Stevenson of Illinois was doomed to defeat from the start. The majority of the delegates to the Republican National Convention had been swung from Senator Robert A. Taft, as the ideal and proved exemplar of the principles which offered the sharpest contrast with those of the party in power, by convention strategies of the pro-Eisenhower leaders that lured the Taft forces into errors which the Democrats could effectively exploit in the campaign. And the nomination of an untarnished national hero was the logical and inevitable consequence.

However, this was not accomplished without incurring commitments to "favorite son" delegations, the most important of which, in shaping the future American society, led eventually to the choice by President Eisenhower of Governor Earl Warren, California's candidate, for Chief Justice of the United States. As in most of these political trades, this one was made without the knowledge of the beneficiary, an exclusion the more necessary in this instance because Eisenhower, before and since, has rejected political deals with deep repugnance. When he redeemed the commitment he did so on persuasions from which it was carefully omitted. And some of his private comments thereafter on Supreme Court decisions written or influenced by the Chief Justice created the strong impression that this was an appointment he particularly regretted.

The articles which follow deal with some of the major events during the General's incumbency of the Presidential office. They reflect my principal conclusions as to the wisdom and necessity of his choice and the quality of his Administration, among them that:

The national interest needed, and was well served by, the uprooting of the party which had been 20 years in power. One of the most important and salutary disciplines in this democracy is the casting from office of a long-entrenched political regime. For after a protracted period it tends to view office as its rightful possession, an attitude which readily develops toward tyranny.

President Eisenhower was unable to make good his pledges, which expressed his true determination to reverse the movement of the American governing system toward the Welfare State that was initiated by Franklin D. Roosevelt and Harry S. Truman. He also was unable to maintain a balanced Federal budget after he restored it to this condition; to prevent cyclical recessions; or to attract to the candidates of the Republican party the popular majorities twice cast for him, and that would have been cast three times if he had been eligible to and sought another term.

But he liberated the nation from the war it was indecisively waging when he was elected, and he kept it free from involvement in another. He successfully sustained the military fabric of the North Atlantic Alliance by promptly responding to the call of the Government of Lebanon for American troops to assist in repelling the "foreign intervention" of the United Arab Republic in behalf of the Lebanese rebels. This was a narrowing of the global commitment of the Truman Doctrine into the Eisenhower Doctrine, which, in this instance, operated to confine to the non-Communist states of the Middle East positive United States guarantees of military assistance against exterior aggression. The President applied in the Congo this same policy by which American military intervention was selectively limited.

In cooperating with the United Nations to suppress Tshombe's effort to make a separate state of Katanga, Eisenhower restricted the United States Air Force to the delivery of United Nations troops and munitions at Leopoldville, instead of conveying these to the battlefront. The result was that not until his successor removed this limitation did the Air Force incur the resentment and enmity of African noncombatants caught in the United Nations line of fire.

An unusually clear paradox in history invests the issue over the degree of the responsibility of General Eisenhower, while in the White House, for the fact that the United States eventually became deeply and flounderingly caught in the morass of a land war against Asians in Asia. But there is one blot on his record of policies designed to keep the

United States out of that kind of involvement. The United States Government was only an "observer" at the Geneva Conference in 1954. But it officially stated it would not stand in the way of the Geneva Contract, which included the provision that the stipulated "free elections" in Vietnam were to be supervised by the International Control Commission of Poland, India and Canada.

By substituting the requirement of United Nations supervision, after it became evident that the Communists would win the 1956 elections, the Eisenhower Administration at least provided Ho Chi Minh with grounds for resorting to armed aggression.

In his personal account of his policies toward Vietnam, from the time in 1953 when the shadow of doom lay dark over the French armed forces in Indo-China to his retirement from the Presidency, General Eisenhower thoroughly documented that his policy rested on the following bases:

(1) He was against a combat role for the United States, on the ground or in the air, under any policy "limiting" the steps essential to winning a war, whether self-imposed or by the French. (2) There would be no intervention unilaterally (the British had refused to make a military commitment), for that "would drain off our resources and weaken our over-all defensive position." (3) Experience in India, Indo-China and Algeria prior to the founding of the United Nations had "demonstrated that the use of occupying troops in foreign territory to sustain policy was a costly and difficult business unless the occupying powers were ready to employ the brutalities of dictatorship," etc. Otherwise, there would be "local unrest which would soon grow into guerilla, resistance, then open revolt and possibly wide-scale combat."

For all these reasons he would not commit the U.S. armed forces to more than the supply of "material and technicians" in Vietnam.

This policy of restraint in the circumstances grew out of the fact that Eisenhower had been a General and knew the art of war. But, also because he had been a General, Eisenhower automatically thereafter acted on the principle of lifelong duty to support whatever military decision was made by the current Commander-in-Chief. Accordingly, he responded favorably to all the calls made by both his successors in that capacity for comment on such decisions.

To the American public, therefore, he became paradoxically the champion of the very policies in Vietnam which as President he had both specifically and broadly rejected. But he refused to involve this Government, beyond training the anti-Castro rebels, in the active phase of a similar operation in Cuba that, when unleashed and then abandoned by President Kennedy, ended in the shaming episode of the Bay of Pigs.

General Eisenhower left the formulation as well as the conduct of foreign policy to his Secretary of State, John Foster Dulles. And he delegated great administrative decisions to his principal White House assistant, Sherman Adams—applications of the military staff system to civilian government that he had several occasions to regret, and which exposed him to charges of indolence and incapacity for his high office. Yet his public support remained strong enough to enable him, by veto or the threat of veto, to hold Democratic Congresses in the middle way. And the sum total of his public record greatly overbalances these debits, both the real and those which were tactical partisan exercises.

Nevertheless, the criticisms were effective in dimming the glory which enveloped Eisenhower when he became President and for some years thereafter. One reason is that glory withers in the controversial fires of politics. Others were supplied by the General himself: his frequent revelations at news conferences that he had not done his homework, his often blind and always labyrinthian syntax when extemporizing. These were gleefully seized on by the articulate "liberals" who were his principal critics to lampoon him as an old fogey, and caricature him as something resembling a duck that was an unusually dim-witted member of the species.

But, in my judgment and close, sometimes intimate, observation, the American people will be deeply indebted to Dwight D. Eisenhower for whatever may be the duration of the historical span in which the United States continues to hold its present place as a world power and the locus of a free, privileged society.

POLITICS, PERSONALITIES AND PHILOSOPHIES

NO REGIME CAN ENTRENCH ITSELF INDEFINITELY
January 20, 1953

As darkness descended on the District of Columbia, and the streets and the windows of the capital blossomed with electric lights, the mightiest pageant ever to pass before a President on the afternoon of his Inaugural was still in motion, its length testifying, as did its splendor, to the enormous significance of the election of Nov. 4, 1952.

Because on that day a large majority of the voters of this country decreed that the Democratic party should turn over to the Republicans the executive power it had held for twenty years, and that the Republicans once again should have majorities in Congress, the nation united to give visual form to the historic decision by the mammoth jubilee which was today's parade.

Because Gen. Dwight D. Eisenhower carried every state outside the South, four within it and two of the border states as well, the rejoicing marchers represented popular majorities on a national scale never attained by a Republican before.

These are perhaps the principal reasons why the spontaneous desire arose in all parts of the country to outdo every previous Inaugural procession in size and length and trappings. In the usual sense of the word, the movement was unorganized. That was not necessary: when plans for today were first discussed the committee heard from every state of elaborate arrangements already in preparation.

The unmatched impressiveness of the parade was the product of an-

217

other reason—the fact that Americans were fighting a bitter war in
Korea against one thrust of the Soviet aggression, which this nation and
the others in the non-Soviet world were arming to confine to the embattled peninsula and shatter there.

Spaced regularly among the marchers, with brief civilian intervals,
were more groups in the uniforms of the armed services, equipped with
more of their weapons, than have ever been seen on such an occasion.

And the silence, though brief, that came upon the celebration when a
great atomic gun appeared on its block-long carriage showed that the
people were conscious they lived in a dangerous world where deterrent
force was the only argument a powerful enemy understood.

But to this onlooker it seemed that there was another meaning to the
magnitude of the gesture of political victory. This was, that the spontaneous enthusiasm that put the paraders in Washington to pass in review before the new President and his aides, and with which the parade
was hailed today, sprang from the reminder it stressed that no political
regime could indefinitely entrench itself in the United States.

The ability of the American majority to have the Government and
the public servants it wanted, and the inability of any political combination to fragment that majority any longer than it desired, was proved
once more. And also was proved the vitality of an old American sentiment against allowing one party to remain in office after it had revealed
the flaws that go with long tenure.

That meaning and cause of the overturn at last November's polls
seemed to this observer to account in great part for the extraordinary
number and elation of the marchers, and for the joy that radiated from
those who watched them give physical form to a momentous fact that
was implicit in General Eisenhower's electoral victory.

The American people had registered a truth of transcendent importance and were not wholly aware of it until it materialized in the Inaugural pageant today.

'BUTTON YOUR LIPS'
January 26, 1953

Ever since 8:02 o'clock last Wednesday morning, when President Eisenhower began his first full day in office, those visitors who have not arrived
and left by the side door, and hence eluded the White House reporters

entirely, have been notably uncommunicative to the representatives of the press. It is customary for responsible persons who talk privately in the inner sanctum to refer questioning reporters in the White House lobby to the President for the answers. But some of these visitors to the new Chief Executive gave the impression of looking apprehensively over their shoulders when they said even that.

The explanation of their timidity seems to be that President Eisenhower has been greatly annoyed by publications of some of his decisions before he announced them formally and has taken steps toward the difficult goal of achieving a "no leak" Administration. The first of these steps, according to a member of Congress today, was the President's notice to whom it may concern that anyone (within the purview of his authority or range of his confidence) who gives information about matters reserved for White House release—so far virtually everything— may consider this tantamount to submitting his resignation, or being excluded from further confidential relationship, as the case may be.

The fact that this report of the President's attitude is in itself a leak suggests how difficult of attainment the goal will be. For some members of Congress will continue to keep newspaper reporters posted when this suits their purposes; others will do so out of personal amiability or a belief that such information provides one of the checks and balances on official action that is basic in the philosophy of the Constitution; and the reporters themselves will intensify their already intense effort to break through a curtain of secrecy between the people and the progressive stages of newsmaking.

Presidents have tried and failed before to prevent these penetrations of the curtain, though the warning represented as coming from General Eisenhower suggests a more drastic enforcement method. And on numerous occasions when reporters have published accounts of important matters that an Administration wanted to announce later in its own words Presidents and their top subordinates have given orders to trace the source of the leaks. But seldom have the Executive bloodhounds tracked down the real offender. And the actual dismissal by a President of any important official as the source of leaking is an occurrence that is extremely rare.

The disclosures that appear to have annoyed the President have largely been of appointments decided on, including some that have run into snags on Capitol Hill. They could not conceivably have affected national security, even in the catch all definition that is standard among the military. Perhaps General Eisenhower's long training in a service where an officer's sense of responsibility is heavily judged by the tightness of his lips has led him to rate this quality higher than it is or needs to be in the process of democratic, civilian government. Perhaps the fact that his Administration is new and he wants to set the opening scenes himself—a wish easy to comprehend with sympathy—has helped to produce the attitude described to this correspondent by a member of Congress today. But if it is maintained the President has a long prospect of similar annoyance, and, much as individuals in the press may not wish to vex him, their common duty is to procure and publish at all stages the accurate and legitimate news of government.

If every Executive plan and decision could be excluded from public knowledge until a President was ready to announce it, the principle of the free press would disappear in the United States and the newspapers would become mere official gazettes. That is the arrangement in autocracies, logically attended by the regulation that the press not only publish the announcement as officially issued but also accept it fully at its face value. President Eisenhower, of course, has no thought of trying to move the press in any degree toward such a consummation. But his early visitors, even including today's group of Congressional leaders, reflect an unusual determination on his part to prevent publication of anything he may deem premature. And that, if true, would mean in effect that the President would at all times establish himself over the press as the judge of what among his activities is news and when its publication is legitimate and responsible.

In matters affecting national security, and in the course of negotiations calculated—if revealed—to give aid and comfort to the enemy, a President can act as a voluntary and effective censor with whom the overwhelming proportion of the American press fully cooperates. If he is not entirely successful the fault, as has repeatedly been proved, is with his subordinates. Often in recent years Presidents have complained about publications that were authorized by their own appointees, with Presidential directives to issue such information. If General Eisenhower can prevent this in such instances, if that is the extent of the effort attributed to him, a responsible press and the public it serves will approve and applaud it.

But until a President can do all his planning and deciding by himself certain kinds of leaks will continue. They are usually harmless; and the intolerable alternative is total secrecy.

IMAGINARY CONVERSATION
AT GETTYSBURG
November 24 1955

"Mr. Hagerty said Mr. Hall would come to Gettysburg 'at the President's invitation' for a 'political discussion of Republican party matters' " (from a Gettysburg dispatch in today's issue of this newspaper).

In view of an all-important and unresolved "Republican party matter" on which every other depends (selecting a Presidential candidate), the conversation next Monday between the Party Leader and the Party National Chairman could be imagined to go like this:

Party Leader. By golly, Len, I'm glad to see you. You're looking well.

Party Chairman. Sir, I don't look as well as you do, and in fact I don't think you ever did yourself. That will be the most wonderful news I can take to the boys.

P.L. By golly, I feel as good as I look, Len . . . Now, what I wanted you up here for was to talk over the situation of the party, and about plans to take it into this '56 campaign raring to go and able to win.

P.C. That won't be any problem at all if a certain thing happens.

P.L. My concept of the Republican party, Len, is that no one thing and no one—as I was saying, no one thing can be of that importance if we know how to tell our story to the people with a unified voice. We have stabilized the dollar. We put an end to the bloodshed of the military stalemate in Korea. We have cut more waste out of the budget than seemed possible to find. Our foreign policy is based on a single-minded determination for world peace, and no setbacks from the Russians will alter that. Meanwhile, we are providing the country with military defense adequate against any threat to our security, and at the same time lifting the burden of excessive taxes and an unbalanced budget from the back of the free enterprise system. Just ram those things into the public consciousness, and we're in again.

P.C. It makes a big difference who does the ramming, boss. We're a little understocked in rammers. Now, if you——

P.L. Why, I brought the best business brains in the United States into the Government, Len. And the most effective publicity techniques are at our disposal. With these you ought to be able to increase the normal

Republican registration by about 15 per cent, make sure they vote the way they register and victory in 1956 will be certain. It's as simple as that.

P.C. I admit, boss, we couldn't lose with that formula. But formulas don't prove out by themselves. I didn't take as much math in college as you did, but I remember something called a coefficient, you know—a joint agent. Our Republican workers in the field tell me the folks seem to think we've got, at the most, only two of those joint agents we could count on to do the job, and you put one of them in that marble mausoleum where the sign over his door says "Politicians—Do Not Enter." That leaves only one coefficient we can positively rely on. If he would just say—no hurry, of course, for a few weeks—that he——

P.L. Let's see now. There are the accomplishments I listed of the Republican party in office. There are peace and prosperity. There is the extra 15 per cent we are bound to get if we go after it properly. I haven't seen the political boys lately, but I have the feeling that the party management is moving like it has lead in its pants.

P.C. Feels more like hayseed.

P.L. It won't after the farmers hear our story. I understand you've bought a lot of television time and started a party newspaper and made the most, in so far as public statements are concerned, of the big Democratic row over their Presidential nomination. But, by golly, I feel there's something lacking.

P.C. I couldn't have said it better, boss. There sure is. I'm not a military man, as you well know, but maybe I can illustrate what I mean by what happened at Lookout Mountain.

P.L. You know, of course, Grant's victory there made him Commander in Chief of the Union armies.

P.C. All I know about it, boss, is what an old G.A.R. in Suffolk County told me. He said the outcome of the battle was in doubt until a few privates climbed up the mountain and broke out the flag, and when the troops in the valley saw it there nothing could stop them. What is lacking in the Republican party, boss, is that right now they don't see the flag moving ahead on the upward path. When they see it you won't find anything lacking.

P.L. I notice you said privates climbed up and broke out the flag. It wasn't a general.

P.C. But in politics, boss, the general has to take the flag to the pinnacle if it's going to get there. And the Republican party has only one gent—

P.L. Well, Len, I've sure enjoyed this political discussion of Republican party matters. You must come again soon.

P.C. About the first of the year, boss?

P.L. I'll let you know when *I* do.

EISENHOWER'S POSITION UNIQUE
December 24, 1955

The President will attend the Christmas services at the National Presbyterian Church, and his usual prayer for divine guidance will be only one of scores of millions that will be said for him on the same day. The supplication of all these is that he may be clearly shown the path of duty, and that he may find the strength to tread this path if it leads to continued public service.

The President's recent heart attack doubtless has intensified the worldwide sense of the need for him. But even before illness this evaluation had become a modern phenomenon that required no personal sympathy to increase. The magnitude of this estimate of a national hero, and its unabatement even after his embroilment in politics, are tributes to a public man almost unique in troubled and controversial times.

Never was there a more winning personality projected to the American people, and to millions beyond their borders, and television has magnified its effect. Never did a winning personality more thoroughly radiate what may be called the inner goodness of a man. Never was there a more engaging smile and grin in politics. "With a face like that," the late James Forrestal, Secretary of Defense, used to say to the then Chief of Staff, "you can be President whenever you want to." And nature threw in a graceful bearing and a strong physique for good measure.

The President also is enveloped in the aura of military command and victory in the field. Conquerors in the past often became awkward and arrogant figures in the give-and-take of democratic civilian life, stamped forever with the rigidity of high command, pompous or impatient of question. But though the general in Eisenhower plainly appears when he makes up his mind to some act or policy others would still debate, he has an almost infallible instinct to know when tolerance is the key to attainment. It is this gift for diplomacy that impelled Harry S. Truman, in the happier days of their relationship, to refer to Eisenhower as "the statesman of the Army."

The President also and effortlessly reveals the simple faith, the clean mind, the temperate and courteous parts of speech in controversy, that especially appeal to the American people in their first magistrate. His few rebukes are restrained; he calls no names; he shuns personalities in his public utterances; but there is nothing soft about him. His candor in answering questions at his news conferences often amazes an audience used to official evasion.

In opening these tough sessions to television without limiting the scope of inquiry he invited a most hazardous test of his mental capacity and of his familiarity with the details and philosophy of public affairs. At times he has shown surprising ignorance of subjects and details. But he took this risk knowingly; his boldness has added to the goodwill he enjoys; and the quality of popular condonation when the President reveals he has slighted some of his homework appears never to have been strained.

By this special public consideration the Republican party is criticized for many acts and policies, but its leader and fervent eulogist (even Mr. Truman never made greater claims for the virtue of a political label) is excluded from the attacks. His Administration is assailed for a number of official shortcomings, but the public disposition seems to be that the President is not responsible for them.

Destiny wrought for Eisenhower, too, when, vowing he would ne'er consent, he consented to accept the Republican nomination in 1952 if it were freely tendered and, when it was not, won the nomination by a fight he vowed he would not make. It was his destiny that the managers of his only formidable rival, the late Senator Robert A. Taft, would virtually hand Eisenhower the nomination by presenting him with the gift of the Texas delegate issue at a time when the outcome of the convention was in great doubt.

This need was supplied by destiny with the sense of timing that only destiny has. When Eisenhower became President, and began cautiously to reverse the trend of government in dealing with free enterprise, a growing Democratic chorus prophesied a crippling economic recession. But the industrial and financial boom continued to expand, and in an orderly manner under the light but watchful supervision of the President's happy choice for Secretary of the Treasury, George M. Humphrey.

Presidents traditionally have made "peace" the aim of their foreign policy and never lost an opportunity to commend it to the world. But often as they spoke war was an unhappy fact of existence. When Eisenhower took office the foundations of free world defense that were laid by his predecessor had reached the status of deterrent power; so that it fell to him, at Geneva, publicly to persuade the Soviets that atomic war between two such forces was unthinkable since the United States had the capacity to destroy the Soviet Union, whatever the devastation wreaked on this and other nations.

The President could not end the cold war any more than Mr. Truman could, and some of its new aspects are more menacing than the old ones. His Administration is on the defensive in phases of foreign policy; and the falling income of the American farmers threatens the tenure of his party in power.

But, this despite, no public figure has the firm appeal to the human race that is the strength for good of the President who will join the nation in a prayer on the Nativity of the Prince of Peace.

A SENATOR SMOTHERED
WITH APPROBATION
February 13, 1956

Once again it has been demonstrated that the thing a "business" Administration has most to fear is business itself. In latest proof of this is the $2,500 donation to a Republican Senator's campaign fund that was made by the lobbyist for an oil and gas company at a time when the company's economic interest was centered on legislation before the Senate, and made for motives as yet unclarified.

Corporations these days have public relations experts as well as lawyers and lawyer-lobbyists. Officers of corporations who, as individuals, are generous with campaign contributions usually have warm friends in the professional political community where these officers have displayed so welcome an interest. If the public relations experts don't know any better than to let their officers get involved in such a backfiring incident as the contribution to Senator Case of South Dakota, the grateful political friend can be depended on to stifle the plan or impulse. So it must be assumed either that competent advice was not sought in this matter or it was not heeded.

The consequences of the campaign fund donation in the circumstances are as serious as anyone with ordinary common sense—not to mention ordinary conscience—could have foreseen. The merits which a large majority of the Senate saw in the natural gas bill—and in that majority were Senators who have earned the high respect in which they are held—are obscured in the unpleasant atmosphere created by the incident.

The President is confronted with a tainted bill. If he signs it, on the conviction that it is a proper and equitable service to free enterprise, his political opponents will not let the taint be forgotten by the people. If he vetoes the bill on the ground that it does not sufficiently protect consumers to whom no other fuel is available, its supporters will feel that the Case incident made his mind more receptive to this criticism that they spent hours trying to disprove in long Senate debate.

It does not require a vivid imagination to forecast what will be said about the bill, if the President signs it, by former President Truman and all the Democratic candidates for that party's nomination. And if he vetoes the measure he will put on the defensive many of the Senators who voted for it after Case made his revelation. Among these were such dependable supporters of the Administration as Allott of Colorado, Bridges of New Hampshire, Flanders of Vermont, Hickenlooper of Iowa, Payne of Maine, Saltonstall of Massachusetts and Watkins of Utah; also the Republican leader, Knowland of California. Among them were such "liberal" Democrats as Anderson of New Mexico, Fulbright of Arkansas, Mansfield of Montana, Monroney of Oklahoma and O'Mahoney of Wyoming.

Some of these and Senators who voted with them were largely influenced by regional interests, exactly as were many of those who were registered in opposition. But some who voted "aye" did so as an expression of a public philosophy: that the Supreme Court's decision to put the natural gas producers under Federal price regulation was a "legislative act"; that this is a denial of the rights of free enterprise and discriminatory to one group of fuel producers; and that the bill is needed to encourage essential production of natural gas.

Now all these motivations have been subordinated to yet another disclosure that many business men will never learn what to do and what not to do, or how to do it, when they engage in politics. That has been proved in this "business" Administration by recruits from business who simply could not comprehend the special and rigid standards required in office by the public interest, particularly from "crusaders." And now this occupational flaw has appeared in the sensitive matter of campaign contributions.

The facts as developed make no sense at all. According to the testimony, the contribution was not made to Case until the donor was assured that Case was favorable to the bill in which his company was interested. Whether or not the contribution was in response to a suggestion by a friend of the Senator that campaign funds for his re-election were a problem—a point still unresolved—the background of prior inquiry about his stand on the gas bill, the timing and the form of the donation—in cash and from "the personal fund" of the oil company's president—all are unsavory. If the contribution was, as contended, merely a pat on the back for a Senator who was "thinking along the right lines," the kind who the donor decided should be kept in the Senate, it is still another instance of "business" promoting its interests in a clumsy and vulnerable manner.

A CLEAR ISSUE
September 27, 1956

An issue on which voters can pass with understanding—thus assuring a decisive election—at last has been clearly and fully presented to them. As stated last night by Adlai E. Stevenson, it is that the President has "consistently rejected the positive responsibilities of leadership"—of the country, of his Administration and of his party. On this fundamental proposition Stevenson asks the people to replace the President with himself.

It is a simple issue, and historically it has been raised by the opposition against a President with a large popular following that criticisms of acts by his Administration and his party do not seem materially to reduce. The opposition tactic in that situation is to put the blame for everything on the President as a "dictator," or to charge that he has permitted wrong things to be done by abdication of, or incapacity for, "positive leadership." His is a "one-man government," and hence he is responsible for everything, and everything, of course, is very bad. Or: he let the bad men he selected run the Government he was under oath to run, and everything he let them do was, of course, very bad.

Stevenson has now firmly seized the second horn of the dilemma in which President Eisenhower's vast and abiding popularity has placed the opposition in this campaign. By the general charge that the President is the kind of leader who "means well feebly" Stevenson can logically assert that he is not talking about temporary or permanent effects of Eisenhower's illness, but about a congenital fault which a lifetime of perfect health could not eradicate. And by taking this position he obviously seeks to prod many, who otherwise might stay at home from a showdown on an argument about an Excecutive and party record, into going to the polls to vote against an individual.

A major political theory is that the vote in the United States is heavier, and the opposition has a better chance of victory, when the people are impelled to vote *against* somebody. There is danger in testing this theory with a President who also impels so many to vote *for* him, as Eisenhower unquestionably does, as F. D. Roosevelt did on the several occasions when the Republicans offered him as the paramount issue of the campaign and large majorities were cast in his favor. But Stevenson, after a number of speeches that merely offered an unlimited expansion of the New-Fair Deal and repeated the classic Democratic charges of innate Republican callousness toward the welfare of the masses, apparently decided that this technique was not adequate for victory.

The details of Stevenson's adverse finding against the President as a leader were smoothly assembled to support the finding; also the corollary conclusion that "if the President * * * does not lead, our system cannot work effectively and every American citizen will suffer":

¶ Eisenhower offered Congress programs that "looked good on paper" but he "did little to get them enacted. * * * When a Republican Congress tore his State of the Union message into little bits and pieces and scattered them to the winds * * * the President watched in [at least public] silence."

¶ While he declined to exert "Presidential leadership," the party Senate leader, Knowland, "carried on [a] personal and belligerent foreign policy"; McCarthy, unchecked, pursued his "career as national bully"; Senator Bricker "pressed his amendment to cripple the Republican President's control over foreign policy," and so on. And the President continued to suffer "Republican irresponsibility" after a Democratic Congress was elected and "got things done" for him.

¶ The "typical scene" of the last four years has been that of the President trying "to repair the damage done by his own lieutenants * * * but the more trouble they cause him the more they evidently grow in [his] admiration and affection."

¶ "Many people have wondered how much President Eisenhower has to do with the Eisenhower Administration * * * sometimes the President seemed to wonder himself."

¶ "There is only one question to be asked * * * 'Who's in charge here anyway?' Who, in this business man's administration, keeps the store?"

There is the charge and there are the specifications, comprehensible to everyone. In effect, Stevenson sees the President as Dolliver saw W. H. Taft: "A large, good-natured body surrounded by people who know exactly what they want." And now he has offered this as the over-all reason why Eisenhower should be defeated for re-election.

THE DEMOCRATIC LEADERSHIP
IN CONGRESS
November 12, 1956

The simultaneous re-election last week of a Congressional majority of one party and a President of the other, for only the second time in American history has been attributed to several reasons: local issues, the greater popularity of many Democratic candidates than their Republican rivals, an over-all national preference for the Democratic party label and so forth.

But the leadership in Congress, which will also be the national leadership of the Democratic party until a new national ticket is chosen, views the political phenomenon of Nov. 6, 1956, as an affirmation of its guiding principles in the Eighty-third and Eighty-fourth Congresses. As defined by Lyndon B. Johnson, the Senate majority leader of these and the incoming Congress, the principles were:

¶ Partisan politics stops "at the water's edge." The only test of all legislation is whether "it is good for the country."

When Senator Johnson saw the President last week, at the White House meeting with Congressional leaders, he told the President that these two simple standards would continue to be his guide in the Eighty-fifth Congress, in which Senator Fulbright said today he expects to colorate in "a watery kind of bipartisanship." And, as in the past, he counts on Speaker Rayburn to follow the same principles in the House of Representatives.

After the election of Johnson to the Senate leadership in the Eighty-third Congress he set up and maintained these standards. He was criticized for doing this by some Democrats in the Capitol and more outside, their argument being that (1) he was blurring the line of demarcation that should distinguish an opposition from the party in power if the opposition was to dislodge it, and (2) Johnson is congenitally "pro-Eisenhower." But in general he pursued the same course in the Eighty-fourth Congress, and the return of Democratic majorities in both branches while the President was being re-elected by a margin of more than nine millions has persuaded him that the country believes the opposition leadership acted on these two tests, and approves them.

He will be deprived of the services as party whip of Senator Clements of Kentucky, whose unexpected defeat by Thruston B. Morton is a Democratic casualty of Nov. 6 that is especially deplored by all his fellow-partisans in Congress. But in Senator Mansfield of Montana the Texas Senator will have the best available replacement. And the popular personality and rich experience of Clements will not be lost to the leadership if he is amenable to a plan being made for him by his party colleagues. It is to appoint him executive director of the Senatorial campaign committee, to which is entrusted (a) the search for good, new candidate timber in the states and (b) assistance to the party nominees for the Senate.

After the national convention at Chicago last August, Johnson was the object of another line of party criticism that the results of Nov. 6 have revived. This was that he used his influence, with calamitous consequences, to induce the convention to "appease" the South in the party platform plank on "civil rights" by omitting a specific endorsement of the Supreme Court's school desegregation decision. But the critics have the burden of proving that this face-saving for the Democrats in several Southern states was not the reason why one or two of them failed to follow the five that gave their electors to Eisenhower; also that a platform plank outweighed in the minds of Northern Democratic voters the repeated support of the desegregation decision by the Democratic national candidates throughout the campaign.

Johnson has expressed the opinion to friends that, in addition to other bases of appeal, the President has the backing of the country because it believes he is not "partisan for the sake of partisanship and is more interested in where he is going than where he has been." And that describes Johnson's concept of his own role.

WHERE THE TALK
IS OF MANY THINGS
April 4, 1957

"Little drops of water, little grains of sand," sang the poetess, "make the mighty ocean and the pleasant land." The truth of this observation invades the mind behind the eye that scans the pages of one of the Government's most popular publications.

The popularity of this publication is largely confined to its contributors. But since they are exclusively members of the Congress, and the writers of articles that appeal to these statesmen, the product must be accepted as a mirror of the interests of those who legislate for the American people. And that assumes greater significance because most members of Congress strive ever to reflect what interests their constituents.

If most legislators are mirrors of popular concerns, then this publication of unspoken words also demonstrates that the American people are not thinking very much of some great matters which dominate the front pages of the newspapers and the minds of commentators. Except for one or two of these subjects, the Appendix of the Congressional Record—for this is the Government product referred to—deals instead with a multitude of little things. For instance, today's edition.

Forty-five insertions by members of the House of Representatives appeared in this Appendix, and there would have been many more if the Senate had been in session. One member contributed four, another three and another two. (The House gave its unanimous consent for the insertion of others, which will appear in a subsequent Appendix.) And what were the topics that members sought to bring to the attention of the country at large?

Representative Mumma of Pennsylvania proudly called to the nation's notice the fact that nearly 400,000 reserves will train at Indiantown Gap Military Reservation. The outrage implicit in the question "Why Tax Us for England?" was put in print by Representative Belcher of Oklahoma. The typical lack of a decent schoolhouse (in this instance "at the mouth of Hurricane, on Knox Creek," in Pike County, Ky.) was spread on the record by Representative Perkins of that state. The "tremendous national service of the American Legion" was the subject of Representative Henderson of Ohio. And Representative Saylor of Pennsylvania, in National Wildlife Week, stressed that the destruction of "proper living places * * * has left our wildlife in a critical state."

Secrecy of Government agencies, which he finds "excesssive," was the topic of Representative Macdonald of Massachusetts, a former Harvard football captain. The "absence of adequate statistics" for appraisal of "the current economic situation" claimed the pen of Representative Bolling of Missouri. Urban redevelopment had a champion in Representative Holland of Pennsylvania; a postal rate increase in Representative Harden of Indiana; the Iranian murders of Americans in Representative Dorn of South Carolina; and Representative Younger of California extolled the morality of Arthur Larson's direction of the United States Information Agency.

Let not the United States Steel Corporation succeed in making its employes the "scapegoat for price increases," thundered the typewriter of Representative Price of Illinois. The Department of Labor must not suffer "ill-advised" cuts in its appropriation, wrote Representative Shelley of California. How King Cotton "went international" was the subject of an anxious insertion by Representative Smith of Mississippi. And proposed limits on taxation, replenishment of the roster of scientists, the passion of the New Republicans for peace, the leadership of Senator Byrd, New England flood control, social security abuses, the Twenty-second Amendment and the statehood claims of Alaska evoked essays from respectively: Representative Brooks of Louisiana, Representative Durham of North Carolina, Representative Vorys of Ohio, Representative Abbitt of Virginia, Representative Rogers of Massachusetts, Representative Rabaut of Michigan, Representative Udall of Arizona and Representative Pelly of Washington. To all America Representative Hillings of California proclaimed that the United States has "short-changed Los Angeles in the smog fight."

Of the repeaters Representative Lane of Massachusetts fought freight rates, urged Spain in NATO, excommunicated the Chinese Communists and cried "hold the fort" against the Eisenhower budget. Representative Multer of New York called for the independence of national banks, asked with Walter Lippmann if "we can muddle through" our foreign problems, and gloomed over the economic effects of a large cut in the arms budget.

There were insertions by other members, even former Speaker Martin not scorning to use the Appendix to laud the statesmanship of President Garcia of the Philippines. A collection mostly of trifles? But if that, also a reminder that political action often has its source in durable trifles only temporarily displaced by violent events.

'COMES A PAUSE . . .'
April 7, 1958

When John Newbery, in 1765, published a collection of nursery rhymes since known as "Mother Goose," the London coffee-house gossips decided they were satires on persons and events in British politics. George III, who was lucid at the time, shared this opinion. If there is any excuse at all for the following perversion of some of these children's classics to current American politics and politicians, the author, but not very hopefully, pleads the precedent.

A Partisan Outer Space Note

Hey, diddle, diddle,
Faddle and fiddle,
Ike better orbit soon.
The Democrats laughed
At Johnson's craft
When Lyndon ran off with the moon.

Incident of the Golden West

Knowland was a leader,
Knowland was a chief,
He went to Goody's house and took away his fief.
Goody went to Bill's house,
Bill was in bed . . .
Goody dropped his blunderbuss and headed East instead.

Early Bird-Watching

Sing a song of Boston,
A pocket full of dough,
Sixteen Bay State delegates
Lined up in a row.
When convention opens
They'll vote back to back.
Won't that be a lovely gift
For bonnie young Prince Jack?

It's a Sort of Secret

Governor Ad is hopping mad
At what Ike's brought the Nation to.
But, though to please Ad we'd be glad,
We can't quite tell what *he* would do.

A One-Way Proposition

Sherm the Firm hailed Sherman Cooper
At the Senate door.
Said Sherm the Firm to Sherman Cooper:
"Vote with Ike much more."
Said the Southern to the Yankee Sherman:
"That should work two ways."
Said Sherm the Firm to Sherman Cooper:
"That ain't how we plays."

The Wyatt Earp of Phoenix

Six-gun Goldwater
Vowed no quarter
To Reuther when cameth the Day.
But he dropped Colt and halter,
Outshouted by Walter,
Who frightened big Six-Gun away.

Wisdom of a House Freshman

I love Speaker Rayburn,
His heart is so warm,
And if I obey him
He'll do me no harm.
So I shan't sass the Speaker
One least little bitty
And then I'll wind up
On a major committee.

The Farm Bloc Planned It That Way

Sing, sing, what shall I sing?
Ike has vetoed the farm-bill thing.
Do, do, what shall I do?
Holler, that's all you intended to.

Hazards of a Senatorial Economist

Paul, Paul, from Illinois,
Studied economics when a boy,
Whene'er recession comes our way
He calls for a tax cut, night and day.
"Next month will be too late," said he
In '49 and in '53.
In '58 the same advice.
Will Paul turn out to have been wrong thrice?

A Fall Between Two Schools

There once was a Republican
And he was wondrous wise.
He joined up with the Old Guard
And lost at the next assize.
And when he saw he'd lost his seat,

With all his might and main
He'd joined up with Ike's Modern wing
And lost his seat again.

It Could Be W——e M——e

There was a wrathful Senator
From Portland, O.R.E.
He sang a dirge from morn to night,
No merry note sang he.
And this the burden of his song,
Or so it seems to me:
"I don't like nobody, no, not I,
"Since nobody cares for me."

Another Chance—the Last, Maybe

Harold sat on the White House wall.
Foster caused Harold to have a great fall.
And only the State of William Penn
Can put poor Harold together again.

Isn't That the Truth!

"Where did you come from, Richard dear?"
"Up from the ranks, from the very rear."
"Where are you going, Richard dear?"
"Into the everywhere out of the here."
"That plan some Republicans aim to spike."
"They can't unless one of them is Ike."

Another plea to the reader for clemency, and a seasonal one, is: Why
should the Easter bunny be practically the only mammal allowed to lay
an egg?

THE ADAMS CASE
June 21, 1958

"The White House," next to the flag, is the symbol of the power, the
glory and the honor of the United States. And never before, not even
when E. M. House and Harry L. Hopkins spoke and acted under its

aegis as with the authority of the President, has this national symbol been more closely associated in the public mind with a Presidential aide than with Sherman Adams.

Moreover, as The Assistant to the President, Adams has projected to the public the image of a man of flinty official integrity and ascetic private life who was born and reared in and lived up to the New England copy-book of simple virtues. To him have been generally imputed the recommendations for the hard Presidential decisions that separated from the public service Administration subordinates who had infringed, even moderately, the strict code of official standards to which, in two successful campaigns, the Republican spokesmen pledged scrupulous practice and enforcement. And these pledges, voiced with particular stress by President Eisenhower and Adams himself, were offered as a means by which the voters of 1952 and 1956 could register their repudiation of the standards of official conduct during the Truman Administration.

These are the principal reasons for the crisis in public confidence in the official ethics of the Administration produced by testimony before the Harris subcommittee of the House that Adams had accepted gifts of value, as mere ordinary tokens of old friendship, from Bernard Goldfine of Boston, an industrialist whose affairs have been subjected to the critical surveillance of Government agencies. These, and the further knowledge that the President has largely delegated to Adams the choice of Executive appointees, including those to the agencies, are also the reasons why the episode has:

(1) Pervaded the Republican party with fear of grave political consequences to its candidates in the next two elections, an emotion that is being increasingly revealed by Republican calls on Adams to resign or on the President to dismiss him.

(2) Revived an ancient and cynical public attitude toward the ethical standards of both parties when in office.

(3) Obscured the back-breaking labor Adams has expended in the performance of his onerous duties, and his many excellent personal qualities, in which selfless loyalty to the President is foremost.

(4) Added a new threat to the programs of President Eisenhower and injured his prestige.

This final consequence, augmented by the President's announcement that Adams is indispensable at his post—"I need him"—is at this writing the gravest of those evoked by what in many respects is one of the most regrettable official and personal tragedies of recent times. It is the more tragic because all who know Adams also know his influence could not consciously be "bought" by anyone. And they can attribute his errors of conduct only to an inexplicable insensitiveness, where he is concerned, to the stern ethical requirements he has made of others in government.

Psychiatrists, if and when all the facts become available, may conclude that the answer is to be found in the donation to Adams by the President of unusual powers and the privilege to exercise these with total immunity from question—by Congress, by the press and by the public. But, whatever the rounded explanation may be, the record already affords ample basis for the alarm of Republican candidates for office.

The word "already" is an allowance for the possibility, for which hints have come from the Harris subcommittee, that more testimony will add to the damage to the public interest wrought by and to the Assistant to the President. The subcommittee wants to know much more about Goldfine, his industrial operations and his profession of collecting important political friends and dropping their names where these might have influence. If this should add to the apparent incongruity of Adams' choice of an intimate to whom he allowed himself to be so materially beholden, the Republican pressure on the President and his principal assistant that Adams vacate his office will be even stronger and more directly applied.

But even if the record of the episode is now complete, and certainly if it is expanded by new evidence, the indications are growing that the party leaders will not hold to this attitude of consideration of the President's feelings and helpless acceptance of his announcement that, because he likes, admires, respects and above all "needs" Adams, this principal White House assistant will remain indefinitely at his post. For the moment they seem to share a prevailing opinion that, when the campaign gets hot, Adams will be an unavoidable sacrifice to the party's and to the President's political necessities. But if the President adheres to his position, that his and the general belief in Adams' integrity sufficiently cancel the episode, these leaders will move firmly to persuade the President and Adams otherwise.

The immediate strategy of the Democrats is to let the President and the Republican party suffer, with just enough prods at the sensitive areas to make sure the suffering is not abated. Conceivably, the Democratic campaign strategists now prefer that Adams remain at his post in the circumstances. But President Truman, Adlai E. Stevenson and others still burn with the wounds inflicted by Republican charges of "corruption" and "shielding of traitors and fellow-travelers" in 1952, 1954

and 1956. And in the next campaign this burning sensation will impel
them to make sure the voters will remember its sources. Such as these
passages in the Republican platforms of those years:

> Dishonesty and corruption * * * have shamed the moral standards
> of the American people * * *. We pledge unimpeachable ethical
> standards and irreproachable personal conduct by all people in gov-
> ernment.

As for Adams, though his spirit must surely be burdened by the
knowledge he has injured the President, to whom he has given deep and
self-abnegating devotion, his icy remoteness and his supreme confidence
that it is enough he and the President know his heart is pure appear
unchanged and unshaken. He has coldly rebuffed associates expressing
sympathy. "Imprudence" is the limit of the concession this human phenomenon grudgingly has made, or ever will.

EISENHOWER'S PHILOSOPHY
January 15, 1958

It was more than eight years ago, at St. Louis before the American Bar
Association, that President Dwight D. Eisenhower of Columbia University expounded a political philosophy which President Eisenhower of the
United States told his news conference today "I have lived by" ever
since, "still believe in * * * and try to practice * * * ." This was the
"middle-of-the-road" speech during which his audience interrupted him
nine times with heavy applause and three standing ovations.

A political philosopher differs from an expedient politician in that the
former never deviates from the basic principles of his belief, though,
with the assumption of public office and changing social-economic and
international conditions, he may feel or be obliged to apply them with
the tolerances official responsibility and new conditions impose. This has
been the record and the experience of every President who had and practiced a basic political philosophy. And it is pertinent to an examination
of Eisenhower's administrative record in parallel with the speech of
Sept. 5, 1949 (Labor Day). In that speech he stated "three fundamental
principles of American life":

1. "Individual freedom * * * our most precious possession * * *
is to be guarded as the chief heritage of our people, the wellspring of our
spiritual and material greatness, and the central target of our enemies

—internal and external—who seek to weaken or destroy the American Republic."

2. "* * * All our freedoms—personal, economic, political and social —to buy, to work, to hire, to bargain, to save, to vote, to worship, to gather—are a single bundle. * * * Destruction of any inevitably leads to destruction of all."

3. "* * * Freedom to compete vigorously among ourselves, [with] a readiness to cooperate wholeheartedly for the performance of community and national functions * * * , make our system the most productive on earth."

"The path," he went on to say, "to America's future * * * lies down the middle of the road between the unfettered power of concentrated wealth * * * and the unbridled power of statism or partisan interests. * * *"

¶ "* * * If Marx were right, this day should be * * * an annual provocation to riot, physical strife and civil disorder. [Yet] some among us seem to accept the shibboleth of an unbridgeable gap between those who hire and those who are employed. We miserably fail to challenge the lie that what is good for management is necessarily bad for labor."

¶ "The clear-minded are determined that we shall not lose our freedoms, either to the unbearable selfishness of vested interests, or through the blindness of those who * * * falsely declare that only government can bring us happiness, security and opportunity. [However] in all cases we expect the government to be fore-handed in establishing the rules."

¶ But "we in turn carefully watch the government—especially the ever-expanding Federal Government—to see that, in performing the functions obviously falling within governmental responsibility, it does not interfere more than is necessary in our daily lives. * * * Extremists * * * use the cloying effect of subsidy as well as the illusory prospect of an unearned and indolent existence to win our acceptance of their direction over our lives."

¶ "We will not accord to the central government unlimited authority any more than we will bow our necks to the uninhibited seekers after personal power in finance, labor or any other field."

¶ "The purpose of [management-labor] unity will be—without subordination of one group to the other—the increased productivity that alone can better the position of labor, of management, of all America. No arbitrary or imposed device will work."

¶ "By opening the sciences and professions to all our people, our colleges and universities have destroyed the curse of inherited caste and made our society the most fluid yet attained by man. * * * Each year education does a little more to promote the efficiency of our system, and thereby the opportunities, security and prosperity of our people."

The President said today that he believes the "majority" of the Republican party shares this philosophy, and it is these Republicans "whom I will do my best to help elect." This estimate of the Republican support of his creed as a generality is probably correct, and it could be expanded to take in the overwhelming majority of the American people. The argument, the popular and political divisions, have arisen from the acts and policies by which this philosophy has been pursued. Former President Truman, for example, is as sure he has enforced it as he is certain President Eisenhower has not. On the latter contention right-wing Republicans, on different grounds, agree with Truman.

This is the kind of argument that elections in this republic periodically dispose of but never settle.

THE STRAUSS NOMINATION
June 6, 1959

If the President's nomination of Lewis L. Strauss to be Secretary of Commerce is rejected by the Senate, that will be only the eighth exercise of this constitutional power since the establishment of the republic. Partisan war between a President and the Senate fought on the high level of opposing political philosophy has been the reason for several of the rejections; less intellectual partisan considerations explain others. But in the battle now raging over Strauss's confirmation these causes have been clearly subordinate.

The main bases of opposition have been these:

(1) The social-economic issue over the public vs. private use of natural power that arose in the Nineteen Thirties between New Deal Democrats on the one hand, other brands of Democrats and most Republicans on the other. Strauss's policies as chairman of the Atomic Energy Commission in making the Dixon-Yates contract and contracts promoting the peaceful use of atomic power convinced many influential Democrats that he has the type of capitalist mind they oppose in high Government office. And this has conditioned them for the sympathetic reception of the charges of other Democrats against his mental integrity that they felt they required to justify rejection of a Presidential appointment, and to a post not administratively connected with power policy decisions.

(2) The stated conclusion that Strauss's testimony before the Senate Commerce Committee, in answer to questions dealing with his previous official record, demonstrated habitual evasion, distortion, misrepresentation or downright falsifying of facts—sometimes to protect himself from merited censure, sometimes to claim credit for popular achievements made solely, or shared, by others.

(3) The estimate that his concept of executive privilege and over-all Government responsibility is that these justify and require a Presidential appointee to deny Congress information to which it is constitutionally entitled, or to deceive it as to the facts by the evasions, misrepresentations or downright falsifications he is charged with before the Senate Commerce Committee.

(4) The personality of the Secretary—involving adverse reactions by some to such imponderables as his manner, his "style" of oral and written communications, an air these critics describe as self-satisfied, complacent, anointed (or, as the Scots say, "unco guid"), and what they complain of as an over-sensitive tendency to see slights where none is intended.

(5) The development of what began as policy differences between Strauss and Senator Clinton Anderson of New Mexico into a personal feud which the Senator has waged bitterly against the Secretary; and has moved him to use his great influence among Democratic colleagues to induce them to vote against confirming Strauss as a personal vindication of Anderson.

All these charges against Strauss made by his opponents, except with respect to his leanings in the issue over public vs. private power, are as emphatically denied by his supporters. The findings of the committee minority against his confirmation are specifically rejected in the findings on the same points by the committee majority of one that recommended it. The conflict in the reports to the Senate, between the judgments of one group and the other respecting Strauss's character, his willingness to cooperate fully with Congress and the moral aspects of his committee testimony, was never more fundamental in such documents.

This is the unusual quality of the controversy that has so confused a number of Senators that neither supporters nor opponents of Strauss have been able to make a conclusive estimate of what the vote on confirmation is likely to be. At least twelve Senators either have not made up their minds or are keeping their intentions from the poll-takers.

Three other pressures, all generated by the prestige of the Presidency, should be listed, and these are favorable to confirmation. One is the political comfort for doubters supplied by the President's full backing of his nominee against every point that has been made against him. A second, expressed by Senator Albert Gore of Tennessee, is that the President's influence in current international negotiations may be weakened by Senate rejection of a nominee to his Cabinet. The third is the record of history in which only seven Cabinet rejections have been listed since 1789, only two in the last 100 years.

Frankly in the open is intense concern over how the Senate majority leader, Lyndon B. Johnson of Texas, will vote. He is indignant about the reason, though it merely is recognition of the practical political potential that, in so confused a battle, enough fence-sitting Democrats to determine the issue of confirmation may climb down into the massive shadow of his protection. This calculation has evoked from Johnson a series of statements in which he has urged all Senators to make their independent judgments on the highest level to which the moral promptings of duty can carry any citizen.

Among the extraordinary aspects of this controversy, one is most inexplicable to Strauss's supporters, especially the President. This is that the Secretary's integrity in thought or act can be denied or even called into question—that he can be pictured as, in effect, a pious hypocrite. It is the antithesis of the estimate they have made on the basis of long association of various degrees of official and personal intimacy. And it is these aspersions which have transformed the ordinary Senate process of weighing confirmation into a shattering ordeal for Lewis Strauss.

STRAUSS CASE AN ELECTION ISSUE
June 20, 1959

The Senate's rejection of the President's appointment of Lewis L. Strauss to be Secretary of Commerce had its roots in personal and atomic policy differences between Strauss and a few Senate Democrats. But certain aspects of the events leading up to the rejection assure that the action will be nourished by the Republican leadership of the 1960 Presidential campaign for development into an inter-party issue. Because, however, two Republican Senators could have effected the Secretary's confirmation by voting for instead of against it, and fifteen of the sixty-four Senate Democrats supported the President's appointment, the party vs. party issue will not be as clear-cut by the process of arithmetic as it was made by the following circumstances:

(1) Whether or not it can ever be proved that, as Vice President Nixon put it, Lyndon B. Johnson, the Democratic leader, "engineered" the Senate action in a way to justify criticism, at any rate Johnson and the other Democratic Senators viewed as Presidential aspirants were solidly aligned against the nominee. These were Humphrey (Minn.), Kennedy (Mass.), and Symington (Mo.).

(2) Democratic Senators whom Johnson has found dependable on tests of his leadership, but a number of whom would have surprised no qualified observer by voting for Strauss, all opposed the appointment.

(3) Five or six Republican Senators had left Washington for outside engagements after the majority leader made this statement to the Senate Wednesday: "If I can, I should like to assure any members * * * who desire to be away on Thursday, Friday and Saturday—so far as I know, I will say, they are not members of my own party—that we shall have a definite agreement as to when to vote, so that no one will be taken advantage of." But this was conditioned before and afterward by repeated notice from Johnson that Republicans were leaving at their own risk, so that it is only an argument that they had good reason to be surprised by Johnson's decision to hold the Senate in session until a ballot was taken.

By filibustering, the Republican leaders were able to stave off a vote until all their absentees but Milton R. Young had been brought back to the Capitol. But the filibuster was determined enough to force the Democratic leadership to agree at that point to a "pair" of Young who was pro-Strauss and the assistant majority leader, Mansfield (Mont.), who was present, and anti-Strauss. This prevented the Democrats from taking advantage of that situation. But bad feeling was engendered on both sides of the party aisle by charges and counter charges of leadership sharp practice.

(4) The real leader of the fight against confirmation, Clinton P. Anderson (N. Mex.), was a very influential Senate Democrat to whom many of his party colleagues are indebted for help in both personal and legislative situations. His individual war against Strauss, beginning over differences between them with respect to the latter's activities as chairman of the Atomic Energy Commission, grew on his side into one of the most implacable vendettas ever waged on Capitol Hill. In pursuance of this Anderson made every possible type of appeal to his fellow Democrats for support in the controversy. He argued that in a personal contest between a loyal Democrat (himself) and a "reactionary Republican" (Strauss) there was a party obligation to be considered.

The success of these arguments, which the final line-up suggests was much more effective than Anderson's attack on Strauss's personal and official integrity, offers further material for a Republican 1960 campaign charge that Democrats were basically responsible for the rejection of the Secretary of Commerce.

Bitter consequences are sure to emerge from all this background of intrigue, of personal and leadership pressures, of attacks on character, of suspicion or proof of unworthy motives, of accusations of broken promises.

The prestige of the Presidency has been challenged, and/or General Eisenhower's official and personal moral standards have been aspersed, by the Senators who voted to reject the eminent public servant he chose to associate with himself in the intimate relations of the Cabinet.

Not only is this the eighth rejection of a Cabinet appointment in the history of the republic. It marks a Senate repudiation of the type of highly talented, self-sacrificing citizen that it has become increasingly difficult for Presidents to recruit for Government service except in time of war. Furthermore, this particular citizen who became the eighth of his species had served and been commended by four Presidents, awarded five of the highest national decorations, was an officer in the Naval Reserve who rose to rear admiral, and who, as he vastly understated it in his comment on his rejection, had "done the best I knew how to do to protect and defend the national security when that was not the recognized, nor easy, nor popular course of action at the time" (the decision to produce the H-bomb).

PROBLEMS IN
THE MODERN
WELFARE STATE

DEMOCRATS SEE ISSUE
IN G.O.P. FARM POLICY
February 14, 1953

The month-old Administration of President Eisenhower has run into potentially serious political trouble by choosing a period of falling farm markets to expound the thesis that, while Government price supports "should provide insurance against disaster," they should not be used to "encourage uneconomic production and result in continuing heavy surpluses and subsidies."

These were the words of Ezra T. Benson, Secretary of Agriculture, in a speech to a farm audience Wednesday night at St. Paul, and they were intended as an invitation to agrarian producers to endorse the general plan of the Administration to include farmers, with industry and organized labor, in taking all possible restraints off "the free-enterprise system." But, though the Secretary assured his glum audience that support programs "now in effect or previously announced will be continued," Democrats conjured up the spectre of a sink-or-swim agrarian economy in a population group long accustomed to an artifically sustained high level of prosperity, when artifice was required to sustain it, by bounties from Washington.

Granting that the Democratic critics fear that the farm economy is threatened with a recession, they made their attack with the enthusiasm of politicians who see a forming issue that may restore their party to power in Congress and the White House. Party factionalism was tempo-

245

rarily forgotten in the remembrance that the Republican farm states turned to President Roosevelt, saved President Truman from defeat in 1948, and could be the means of electing a Democratic Congress in 1954 and a Democratic President in 1956.

The storm raised by Democrats, who wish farm economy well but want farmers to worry about the Republican program, alarmed that party's leaders. For the Congressional farm bloc is bipartisan, and it usually has the votes to give the rural areas what it thinks they want or need, or can persuade them they want or need. Even the influences of organized labor and veterans' groups are subordinate to that of the real and self-appointed spokesmen of the farmers in Congress. And if they can arouse the agrarian producers to believe that the program of the Eisenhower Administration is designed to take away the special economic privilege of agriculture, and to repudiate the plea that farmers should cooperate in the general public interest, the President may suffer a stunning defeat in this quarter and serious damage to his goal of a national return to "free enterprise."

Secretary Benson was bewildered by the tumult, but the vegetable and cattle producers rallied to him and his aides were quick to point out that he is pledged to carry out all the price-support programs of the Truman Administration. But the history of farm legislation, and its politics, should have prepared him.

The original concept was that the farmer was disadvantaged by the artificially high costs of what he must buy, that these in turn reduce the "real" prices he received and therefore his income, and that his purchasing costs are in consequence of the protective tariff and other industrial subsidies. On this concept the "parity" system was devised.

First, there were parity payments to farmers cooperating in acreage control. Then when World War II required more food production, the emphasis was shifted to "production goals" and payments were made for that. After this the idea of price supports took hold (the farmer was to be paid the difference between parity and the prevailing market); and added were facilties for Government guaranteed loans from banks at stated percentage of parity on crops classified as "basic commodities."

The Eightieth (Republican) Congress then required the Government to make commodity loans ranging from 60 to 90 per cent of parity on wheat, cotton, corn, tobacco, rice and peanuts. The Eighty-first (Democratic) Congress upped the range to 75–90 per cent. The Eighty-second (also Democratic) removed the range and fixed minimum parity at 90 per cent until the end of the 1954 crop year. Dairy products were added to the loanable commodities with 75–90 per cent parity, and the Secretary of Agriculture was authorized to decide whether commodity loans should be made, up to 90 per cent, on oats, barley, rye, flax, soybeans and certain other products. Many farmers now think of these protections as their right.

Benson, however, proposed in substance that farm prices, on which the parity percentages are based, should be fixed in the market place instead of being assured by the Federal Government. And in this he echoed the economic philosophy of the President's message on the State of Union.

But he made his speech at a time when the farmer has been caught in a price-cost squeeze. Realized farm income in 1952 was $14.3 billions, compared with a volume of farm products marketed totaling $33 billions. No effective way has been found for price protection of the nonbasic commodities from which more than half of farm income is derived: Livestock, dairy products, poultry, fresh fruit and vegetables. Corn and wheat prices are slipping below their loan figures, and in some areas even cattle breeding stock is being sold.

The incident may prove to have been only a case of bad timing.

PROBLEMS OF THE ATOMIC AGE
October 17, 1953

President Eisenhower has entered upon his sixty-fourth year, burdened with more fateful and complex problems and heavier responsibilities than ever have beset the incumbent of his great office. The testimony of qualified scientists and military men that man now possesses atomic weapons able to obliterate himself and his works, and the truculent world policies of one of the two Nations with that power or close to its attainment give unparalleled weight to the problems and responsibilities of the President of the United States.

The basic task of General Eisenhower is to give adequate protection to the lives, the territory and the installations of this people, and at the same time preserve their economy and construct a military force in being that will dissuade an enemy from attack for fear of retaliation more dire than any injury it can inflict on the United States. The preservation of the national economy is essential because a bankrupt country is feeble both in war and defense unless its Government can and will abolish all the civil liberties and rights of its citizens, including property rights, and make everyone the slave of the State. That is not yet a tolerable idea in America, even as a temporary emergency measure, and only some inconceivable disaster could give it lodging.

As General Eisenhower begins his sixty-fourth year it may well be that, like Shakespeare in the sonnet, he "summons up remembrance of things past . . . in the sessions of sweet, silent thought." The portraits of his predecessors on the walls of the White House may stimulate reflection on what troubles beset those who lived there at his time of life. They were not comparable to his for obvious reasons, principally created by the atomic age. But the burdens of the Presidency were onerous in their day, and the fact that they were solved or evaporated is implicit in the steady and remarkable growth of the United States to its present stature among the nations.

In 1795, when Washington turned 63, he was under an attack by critics of the Jay Treaty with Great Britain who, Washington said, hunted him as if he were a mad dog, "with exaggerated and indecent terms that scarcely could be applied to a Nero . . . or a common pickpocket." The next year he announced his total retirement from public affairs, but the Jay Treaty had justified itself among the people.

John Adams, at the verge of his sixty-fourth year, was deeply plunged in his effort to avert war with France and preserve the neutrality of the United States in the conflicts of Europe. His policy antagonized Hamilton and cost Adams' renomination. But he attained his great objective.

In 1806, at Eisenhower's present age, Jefferson was engaged in the last and legal phase of his resolve to prove Burr a traitor, and, though he did not carry that point, he succeeded in removing his great rival from public life. Just past sixty-three, Madison was directing his negotiators of the treaty that ended the war of 1812, which left the President, in the eyes of one observer, "miserably shattered, woe-begone and heartbroken." At the same age Jackson was bitterly fighting the famous battle with Nicholas Biddle over the Bank of the United States and uttering, at a dinner in memory of Jefferson, his immortal line: "Our union, it must be preserved."

In 1919 Woodrow Wilson fought with the Senate for our adherence to the League of Nations and lost his hardest battle and his health as well. Franklin Roosevelt reached sixty-three on the threshold of the Yalta Conference, with death to come three months later, just before victory in the war he had directed. Lincoln died before he attained General Eisenhower's present age. Theodore Roosevelt was out of office and dead at 61.

Some of these Presidents "borrowed time"—as Samuel Lubell said of Harry S. Truman in his epochal book, "The Future of American Politics," observing that "deadlock is the essence of the man, stalemate is his Midas touch. Is this deadlock to be broken or are we to continue to drift in irresolution?" Certainly, in his nine months in the White House President Eisenhower also has borrowed time and, in submitting pressing issues to study groups, he, too, has given to many an impression of irresolution.

But he has common sense on his side in holding that problems of long standing for which his predecessors found no solutions, only nostrums that temporarily relieved their symptoms, cannot be disposed of quickly. If the studies and re-examinations the President has ordered are to produce programs that will prove their effectiveness, he can repay in overflowing measure the time he is borrowing.

The President seems confident of this consummation. The outward man is unusually hearty-looking for his years and incredibly serene when his crushing imposts are remembered. Faith has moved mountains, and good fortune wields a mighty lever. General Eisenhower has an abundant store of the one. His share of the other is as yet to be finally computed.

THE CAPSTONE OF
AN EXTRAORDINARY CAREER
June 30, 1955

At midnight tonight an official group with a long name ends its appointed tenure, and soon thereafter its chairman and in every other respect its outstanding member will be 81 years old. The group under him, like its predecessor, is known by his name, despite its formal title of Commission on Organization of the Executive Branch of the Government. And its passing and the Aug. 10 birthday of its chief are merely incidents in the extraordinary public service record of Herbert Hoover, former President of the United States.

The reports of the Commission to Congress carry 350 recommendations for the greater efficiency of the Executive establishment that, in the group's opinion, would if adopted balance the Federal budget and decrease taxes also. The first Hoover Commission made 275 recommendations to Congress, of which 72 per cent have been put into effect, and the chairman is hopeful of an even higher percentage this time. The 350 recommendations are almost equally divided between those which can be effected by administrative acts and those which will require legislation.

The President has already taken steps to set up a unit in the Bureau of the Budget to deal with the proposed administrative reforms. The Hoover Commission, at the request of members of Congress, has drafted fifty or sixty bills to enact the other recommendations. Of these forty-three have already been introduced, ten by Senator Kennedy of Massachusetts.

Many of the legislative proposals are controversial, those in this week's report on water resources being good examples. But that was inevitable. Between the commission majority and a large Congressional bloc there is a basic conflict in political philosophy. The Federal concept represented by the New-Fair Deal programs in the social-economic area is directly challenged by the concept which the President has called "moderate progressivism." The latter, with its emphasis on leaving to state and local governments and private enterprise many functions which the New-Fair Dealers believe only the Federal Government can do effectively, and equitably for all the people, is the guiding principle of the Hoover Commission reports.

Their high quality, and the low rate of dissents—even when the fact of a middle-of-the-road majority on the commission is remembered—are the results of the unusual equipment of the chairman. No one has a wider acquaintance with Americans of great capacity in all the commission's appointed fields of inquiry. No leader in this country has been served with more devotion by persons of that caliber. Of 300 prominent citizens drafted for the commission's task forces by the chairman only two declined—one by reason of ill health, one because he was sailing next day on a mission that could not be deferred.

The task force method was Herbert Hoover's own device for the initial reports to be put before the Commissioners for consideration and action. Its success in the work of both Hoover Commissions has demonstrated the skill and wisdom of the method. The members of the task forces have worked for long periods, usually a year and sometime a year and a half. And theirs are real examples of "sacrifice" to perform a public duty.

In assembling the task forces Chairman Hoover followed the formula of fitting the experience of the individual to the job he was to do. Preferably he selected people who had served the Government to investigate the departments and agencies where they had served. This was especially valuable in the inquiry into the Department of Defense that produced an outstanding report of the commission. The principle was well illustrated by the choice of Maj. Gen. Robert E. Wood, U.S.A., retired, to head the task force on the disposition of surplus property owned by Government agencies.

General Wood was acting Quartermaster General of the Army (1918–1919) and afterward the head of Sears, Roebuck. He is therefore an expert in buying, selling, storing and making inventory of supplies. This facility he brought, with notable results, to the work assigned to him by Chairman Hoover.

The former President himself built the first multiple-purpose dam (it bears his name), and this pioneer experience was reflected in the commission's momentous report on water resources.

"As chairman," said an associate today, "Mr. Hoover set and maintained objectivity as the commission's foremost rule. Though he was its dominant force, intellectually and morally, he protected to the utmost the right of dissent and its fullest expression. No one worked longer or harder—from ten to fifteen hours a day throughout the life of this commission."

Some of the products of these labors will not withstand the fires of political controversy. But they are the capstone of an enduring tower of public service that is unique in American history.

THE LAWYER PROSECUTED HIS CLIENT
February 12, 1958

The discharge of Bernard Schwartz by the House subcommittee whose commission he held as counsel was inevitable after he became its prosecutor. In the course of his reactions to the obstacles he encountered in his effort to center the inquiry on the personal conduct of Federal Communications Commissioners, Schwartz managed to transgress every obligation which a Congressional committee counsel assumes.

He culminated this by turning over to Senator Morse documents containing information about the acts of certain commissioners which Schwartz obtained, and could only have obtained, by the authority derived from his employment by the House group. As such, of course, this material belonged only to this group, and to the House which gave its subcommittee this basic power.

Schwartz' goal is the admirable one of exposing to the people any improprieties or worse that have been committed by public servants. This is, moreover, a service to the President, who took office sworn to appoint only officials who would make the Government "as clean as a hound's tooth" and to dismiss any shown to have sullied it. But Schwartz was hired for a different type of investigation, which he never would have been if either the House or the subcommittee had faintly conceived he would do any of the following:

1. Release to the press, on his own responsibility, a staff report which was the property of the subcommittee.

2. Retain his brief as counsel after the time, "some months" ago, when "I have known that this subcommittee was not interested in a real investigation but was instead engaged in an attempt at a bipartisan whitewash."

3. Publicly characterize as official misconduct what is only evidence of this, however well documented, before the accused could offer their defense or the subcommittee could weigh the evidence and make the finding the House assigned it, and it only, to make.

4. Furnish a Senator with information and allegations that are the property of the other branch of Congress and were gathered by means of the power delegated to the counsel.

Several examples appeared in Schwartz' statement published today of his assumption of the simultaneous roles of investigator, subcommittee lawyer, prosecutor and judge, not only of subcommittee members but of claimants before the F.C.C. One is this: "I accuse the majority of this subcommittee, in order to further their own partisan interests, of joining an unholy alliance between business and the White House to obtain a whitewash." Another is: "The notorious grant of a multimillion dollar television channel to a leading Republican newspaper" (this is under judicial review).

These are only opinions. But they are stated as incontrovertible facts. The same is true of the names Schwartz, without furnishing proof, put on the public record as engaging in "White House machinations": Sherman Adams, Gerald Morgan, Secretary Weeks, Colonel Moore (Mrs. Eisenhower's brother-in-law) and Thomas E. Dewey. And on one occasion Schwartz similarly tossed in the name of Vice President Nixon as having "possibly" shown an interest in certain cases.

The forthcoming inquiries—for Senator Morse kept the House subcommittee documents long enough to base a demand for a Senate investigation also—will produce conclusions as to these and other of Schwartz' charges. But this will be done in the proper way, after the defense record has been fully made. And the proper function of a committee counsel is to see to this (as Robert F. Kennedy has done notably in the Senate McClellan committee), or to resign when he "knows" (Schwartz' word) that a whitewash is the sole committee objective, and take his case to the public as a private citizen.

In his excellent book, "The Supreme Court" (Ronald, 1957), which this correspondent did what he could to commend to general readership, Schwartz had something to say about Congressional inquiries that exceed their warrant. "It is a basic principle," he wrote, "that a Congressional committee is wholly the creature of the resolution setting it up and cannot act *ultra vires* that instrument." In setting up the current investigation last February, the language of the resolution and Speaker Rayburn's endorsing speech were then construed to mean that instances of submission to Executive pressures by the "independent" agencies was the material sought, and that other personal exposures were the day-by-day business of a special House committee.

These exposures are rightfully in the public domain, and supporters of Schwartz' procedure can impressively argue that, beginning with a series of leaks to the press, he disposed of any possibility that they will not be aired. But no committee of Congress could or should tolerate this concept of the relationship between itself and its counsel, who meanwhile holds on to the job.

TO MR. TRUMAN IT MUST SEEM
LIKE YESTERDAY
January 6, 1960

Since neither the Eisenhower Administration nor a visible majority of Congress is prepared to challenge the basic monopoly power of an industry-wide trade union, it is obvious that any Government-impelled strike settlement accepted by industry and labor must inevitably be a capitulation to most of the striking union's demands. Therefore, if the judgment is sound that the steel-strike settlement longer deferred would have been even more costly for the industry, then the compliments for their successful intervention now being lavished on Vice President Nixon and Secretary of Labor Mitchell are merited chiefly on the consideration that "it might have been worse."

But, if and when the new inflationary prod of the settlement is registered in subsequent labor contracts and in the higher price-level usually incident to increases in the cost of steel, American consumers may see more plainly that they are being constantly exploited by the politicians and the labor leaders who combine to maintain the laws by which big unions control the labor supply of nationwide industry. And, so long as this power, which no other economic group possesses, continues to have the sanction of law, "settlements" of nationwide strikes will always be political and pro-union.

This fact has often been demonstrated since organized labor was uniquely exempted from the antitrust laws. But apparently the population at large, which is the victim of this arrangement, doesn't know how to engender the pressure on both major parties that would produce an equitable system. Or the American people require the shock of currency inflation of the post-war European disaster type and the rising unemployment that would be the consequence of successful foreign competition in the world markets, before they will move effectively to protect themselves from the alliance of politics and big labor.

The Eisenhower Administration has been as one with its Democratic predecessor in declining to attack the root of the union labor monopoly —the immunity from the antitrust laws by which the steelworkers, for example, were able to shut down a nationwide industry by withdrawing its labor force. No sooner had their strike "settlement" been reached than Secretary Mitchell announced the Administration would seek no new power over strikes that paralyze the economy. And this is the second time (the first occasion was in 1956) in President Eisenhower's tenure that Government pressure has been applied to the steel industry for capitulation to the union.

"In the current settlement," commented Iron Age, "the union won about everything it wanted except a complete carbon copy of the 1956 package. * * * The steel firms * * * settled for about one-half that cost. * * * [Hence], if there is a price increase, as expected, it will be a moderate one. * * * The thing that hurts most is that twice Government pressure has come from a strong [sic] Republican Administration. And most painful of all: the steel industry could have had a cheaper settlement last July when Mr. Nixon offered to lend a helping hand to both sides."

The Vice President has this justification to cite for the compliments he is receiving. And also according to Iron Age, Nixon's first effort to settle the strike "early last July" only "missed by an eyelash." But the odds against the industry were insuperable: the union's legalized control of its labor supply, subject only to the temporary restraint of a Taft-

Hartley injunction; and the prospect, which finally materialized, that the Administration would follow the pattern of intervention, bound in existing circumstances to be pro-union, which the Republicans assailed President Truman for applying.

Suppose, after a long abstinence from effective action and instead of intervening himself, Mr. Truman had turned the job over to his political heir-apparent and to a Cabinet member who wanted to be Vice President. And suppose, after these officials had ended a strike, the latter had immediately announced the Administration would abandon all its huffing and puffing about new laws to strengthen public power to sustain the economy. Republican shouts of "a political deal" would have shaken the heavens.

What's the big difference?

AN OBSCURE DIFFERENCE
February 11, 1960

The recent Administration comments on proposals for free hospital and nursing care of elderly citizens, to be paid for out of Federal revenues, marks another unwilling step by the Republican party toward the "welfare state" they long arraigned and opposed. This is another indication that, when the national platforms and candidates of 1960 have been chosen, the American voters will find it difficult to detect a basic ideological distinction between the two major parties.

The voters will see two paths, one marked "Democrat," the other "Republican," between which the only apparent difference will be the rival assertions of the signposts that each is pointing out the only sure route to a prosperous and secure future. But whichever path is chosen, it will lead in the direction of a welfare state, and the price tag will be about the same. The Republicans, however, make a good case of the claims that, under their management of this system, the dollar will buy more and its spending will be directed locally.

They also contend that, since they resist growing federalization and put public welfare responsibilities on local governments to the highest possible degree, in contrast to the policies of the Democrats, their kind of America will remain a republic, as provided in the Constitution. But when the chief exponent of this general philosophy, President Eisenhower, states he is giving "consideration" to proposals to expand free services to the elderly by the central government, this blurs the fundamental distinction between the parties he urges voters to discern.

The Democrats welcome this situation. They are the certified, Grade A, Number One shakers, and movers of the welfare state, centrally financed and administered in Washington. It is the natural product of the New Deal and the Fair Deal. Therefore, they reason, and very sensibly, that the people will put them, the eager—instead of the Republicans, the foot-dragging—in charge if they want the Federal Government to increase the services which traditionally were the responsibilities of localities and families: public education, teachers' pay, housing, hospitalization and nursing for elderly citizens, etc. Also the Democrats are becoming daily more certain they can persuade the voters of November that the President has risked the nation's survival because of incompetent military judgment; and that he has checked its natural progress by obsessive concentration on a balanced budget.

The inflation he is trying to combat through budgetary policy, the Democrats argue, will be halted by the force engendered by extra billions Federally expended for armament and human welfare projects. In this way, they assure, the defenses of the nation can be made "adequate," and the productive capacity of the United States in all respects, including cultural, will rise beyond challenge anywhere.

Taxes? Don't worry about them. The increase in the Gross National Product will either bring about their reduction, or shrink their present percentage take from income by circulating more wages for everybody.

That the Republican Administration is examining the newest version of the Townsend plan—Federal financing of hospitalization and nursing for what its advocates refer to as "our senior citizens"—became known in statements by the President and Secretary Flemming. At his news conference, Feb. 3, the President answered as follows a question whether the Administration was planning to "recommend changes in the Social Security Act": "There is under consideration a possible change to run up the taxes by a quarter of a per cent to * * * make greater provision for the care of the aged. * * * No conclusion [has been] reached [and] I have not yet made any recommendation."

Next day Secretary Flemming announced he was "at work on proposals for the Federal financing of [only the] 'catastrophic' illnesses of the aged." Among the alternatives being studied were (1) a larger payroll tax, in which employers and workers would provide these funds for elderly and disabled citizens who are already paid up on Social Security and are now its recipients; (2) larger assistance by direct Federal-state appropriations; and (3) "some supplement" to voluntary insurance plans.

Thus, a Federal legislative concept which was once to Republicans and a good many New-Fair Deal Democrats "a monster of so frightful mien," etc., is now becoming a fellow-traveler of both parties on their way to the centralized welfare state.

THE SECURITY ISSUE

THE ROSENBERGS
June 20, 1953

The great dispute over the legality of the death sentence for Julius and Ethel Rosenberg, convicted of conspiracy to commit atomic espionage, which at the end embroiled the Supreme Court of the United States to a degree rare in its annals, has now entered the small file of those controversies that will be debated indefinitely by partisans of the opposing viewpoints throughout the world. The issue, finally decided by a Supreme Court vote of 6 to 3 that the President accepted as the fullest exercise of due process in refusing a last appeal for commutation of the death sentence, was made historic by many unusual elements, among them:

(1) After the Supreme Court had thrice refused to review the conviction of the Rosenbergs in Judge Irving R. Kaufman's trial court in New York City that was as steadily upheld by the Court of Appeals, Associate Justice Douglas of the nation's highest tribunal granted a stay of execution, set for Thursday night in Sing Sing Prison.

(2) The grant was in acknowledgment of a legal point made by volunteer attorneys for the Rosenbergs that, because its makers were barred from intervening by Judge Kaufman, was never posed to the appellate courts. It did not appear in the record that went up on appeal. Therefore, in granting a stay and ordering the trial court to hear argument on this point, Justice Douglas acted within powers fully acknowl-
258

edged by his colleagues and invested in any Supreme Court justice by a statute of 1925.

(3) He did not, as critics of his course in the matter contended he was bound by "good practice" to do, ask his Supreme Court brethren for advice before granting the stay or for a review of it en banc. Instead, this review was made by the full Supreme Court in an extra session, its current term having ended, that Chief Justice Vinson summoned at the request of the Attorney General of the United States, Herbert Brownell Jr., who commented that Justice Douglas' action was "unprecedented."

(4) Six members of the Supreme Court, including the Chief Justice, held that the point accepted as substantial by Justice Douglas was unsubstantial. Of the three dissenters only two—Douglas and Hugo Black—differed fundamentally from this conclusion. The third—Justice Felix Frankfurter—thought the magnitude of the issue called for prolonged consideration by the Supreme Court that could not be given in the limited extra session.

(5) In dissolving the Douglas order, the court majority made more history, because this is the first time a stay by a single justice has been overridden; and Justice Black questioned there was power in the majority to do so. But the circumstances were without parallel because the stay was granted by Justice Douglas on a legal argument that had never been presented in court; and its affirmation by the Supreme Court majority might also have quashed the indictment and set the Rosenbergs free.

(6) The point at issue was briefly this: Since some of the acts of atomic espionage, for which the Rosenbergs were indicted and found guilty, occurred after the Atomic Energy Bill became law in 1946, the penalty visited on them must conform to the procedures of that law instead of the Espionage Act of 1917 on which they were arraigned. The latter did not prescribe that a death sentence could be imposed only on recommendation of a jury, or that the crime charged must be proved to have been committed with intent to injure the United States. The act of 1946 did. Therefore, since neither of these prescriptions was met in the trial and the Government's presentation of the Rosenbergs' guilt, the death sentence was illegally imposed and could not lawfully be carried out.

(7) Though this contention was not made by accredited attorneys for the Rosenbergs, though the "intruders and interlopers" who tried to make it before Judge Kaufman were, with their argument, denied trial court recognition, and it was never argued before the appellate courts, its recognition by Justice Douglas as the basis for his stay and order to

the trial court started a train of events that finally put this very issue before the Supreme Court of the United States, whose majority then found it unsubstantial.

For these reasons the Rosenberg case entered the legal category of "celebrated." But its lengthy history was also invested with elements of international politics, Soviet propaganda against the United States and organized pressures for retrial or clemency. Foreign statesmen, lawyers and clerics in nations friendly to this country urged Presidential clemency, if not retrial on a revised indictment, as essential to the good name of United States jurisprudence.

But the imposition of the death sentence and the Government's determination to see it carried out were powerfully and broadly supported in all parts of the United States and among numerous groups, including lawyers and politicians. Some of these expressed the view that the long delays in the case, and the protracted period in which appeals were allowed and made, not only were achieving the obvious—mounting organized pressure and anti-American propaganda from the Communist world—but were making a joke of American jurisprudence. So when Justice Douglas, after it was generally supposed that the Supreme Court had finally banned intervention and the court had adjourned, granted another stay and left Washington, a Democratic Representative from Georgia instantly demanded his impeachment by the House.

This would have come to nothing, anyhow, because Douglas exercised the undoubted power assigned him by Congress itself and simply acted on his judgment as a lawyer and according to the promptings of his conscience. But when the entire Supreme Court acknowledged his authority to do what he did, and two other justices supported the end in view of the stay he issued, the impeachment demand passed from the status of an irresponsible legislative threat against judicial independence into something grotesque.

When the high legal drama ended this correspondent asked Justice Douglas these questions relating to circumstances which brought sharp criticism from friends as well as others and greatly disturbed his supporters in the "liberal" movement: Why had he not, before acting, asked his brethren to reassemble for advice? Why did he term "new" the legal point on which he granted the stay when it had been rejected by Judge Kaufman?

He replied: (1) He knew Justices Minton and Reed had already left town; and since he was in no doubt about the legal point there was no purpose in recalling them. (2) The point was "new" because it is nowhere in the record of the case; it was never raised before any appellate judge by the Rosenberg attorneys; and its existence was "entirely un-known" to him and to the other members of the Supreme Court until it was presented to Douglas in chambers.

THE WHITE CASE
November 15, 1953

When the story of the Harry Dexter White case is reduced to its factual essentials, and the bludgeonings of partisan politics have produced the final casualty, the lesson of the episode may be a very ancient one. This is, that the careless use of words in the course of any human action inflicts more wounds than the facts that evoked their use.

As these facts begin to show in their true proportions, they appear to say that both Attorney General Herbert Brownell Jr. and former President Truman had a good case which each damaged at the outset by failing to bear in mind the Old Testament apothegm that words fitly spoken are like apples of gold in pictures of silver. To witness:

The Attorney General, conning the files of the Department of Justice in President Truman's regime, came upon an extraordinary set of circumstances which strongly supported one of the 1952 campaign accusations against the regime. This charge was stressed by General Eisenhower and is accepted as an important contributory factor to his overwhelming choice over Adlai E. Stevenson last November to be President of the United States.

A report of the circumstances belonged in the public domain. They were that President Truman, after the F.B.I. on two occasions sent to him impressive testimony that White was a member of a Soviet espionage apparatus, had nevertheless appointed White to be Executive Director for the United States of the International Monetary Fund and, on White's retirement from this post fourteen months later, had written him a letter of effusive praise for his Government service, concluding with an expression of hope that the President could call on White for more in the future.

These stark facts powerfully supported the Republican campaign accusation that, whatever the reason, President Truman and his Administration had harbored known traitors and cried down as partisan politics or "red herrings" every revelation by Congressional committees that this was the situation. Though the F.B.I. and its director, J. Edgar

Hoover, were by then subordinates of the new Attorney General, and presumably would have an explanation of Mr. Truman's remarkable attitude toward White, in contrast to the fact that this President bitterly opposed treason and everything for which Russian communism stood, the present record implies either that no good explanation was forthcoming or that the Attorney General did not seek it.

This theory may be exploded by Director Hoover before the strange case has run its length, but, at any rate, Brownell evidently was supplied by his department with no data to shake the conclusion he then dramatically stated in a speech at Chicago on Nov. 6. This was that President Truman, twice put on notice that White was established to the satisfaction of the F.B.I. as a Russian spy, had promoted him from a powerful position in the Treasury to a more powerful one where he could be of even more value as a spy to the rulers of Soviet Russia.

"Harry Dexter White," said the Attorney General to his Chicago audience, "was known to be a Communist spy to the very people [the President] who appointed him to the most sensitive position he ever held in Government service. * * * The Senate Banking and Currency Committee was permitted to recommend White's appointment in ignorance of the report [by the F.B.I., delivered to the White House, of Feb. 4, 1946]. * * * The Senate itself was allowed to confirm White on Feb. 6 without the Senate being informed that White was a spy."

This was the case offered to the American people by the Attorney General in the Eisenhower Administration. And all over the United States headlines, accurately summarizing what Brownell said, attributed to him the charge that President Truman had appointed a man known to him as a spy to a place in which he could more effectively betray his country.

But a few days later, after President Eisenhower told a press conference that the implication of disloyalty in these words was inconceivable as directed to his predecessor, the Attorney General was in full flight from this intimation. He meant, he said, to impute to Mr. Truman only that "blindness" or laxity toward Communist infiltration in Government which the Republicans had charged and which other evidence has amply supported.

But before the Attorney General had retreated from the most serious implication that the manner of his statement conveyed, the former President had fallen into the same slovenly use of semantics. Mr. Truman said he knew nothing about "any F.B.I. report" on White's alleged spying activities—a declaimer that was promptly refuted by precise testimony to the contrary from his Secretary of State at the time—Gov. James F. Byrnes of South Carolina.

Mr. Truman, reverting to his old fault of shooting from the hip, said also that he had "fired" White as soon as he discovered White was "disloyal." But White's retirement occurred fourteen months after Secretary Byrnes, on the basis of a second F.B.I. report, urged Mr. Truman to remove White from public service; it was a resignation and not a "firing"; and Mr. Truman had signalized it by signing a letter to White, which someone—possibly White—had composed in which he loaded White with praise for his services to the United States and expressed the hope he could one day call for more.

At this point both the Attorney General and the former President were entangled in the tentacles of words unfitly spoken. If it proves true that, in commissioning White after reading the second F.B.I. report and celebrating White's retirement fourteen months later by a letter of fulsome praise, Mr. Truman was abetting a complicated scheme of the F.B.I. to get evidence that would establish White as a Russian spy, Mr. Truman still has to eat the impulsive words he spoke that were, at the least, misleading. And if the explanation is established that, in commissioning and praising White, Mr. Truman was assisting a scheme to prevent White from being alerted about the F.B.I. surveillance that was designed to prove him to be a Russian spy, Mr. Brownell will be obliged to withdraw several key words of his Chicago speech that led to the impression he was bringing charges of misfeasance against a former President of the United States.

Had both principals exercised the care in semantics that their training and experience prompted, the controversy would have been free of some of the bitterness that has made it so regrettable and created so bad an impression abroad.

On a much higher plane Woodrow Wilson discovered the perils of the phrases in which he called for "peace without victory" and asserted that the people of the United States, in the face of unendurable provocation from the Kaiserist Government of Germany, were "too proud to fight."

THE STEVENS-McCARTHY
CONTROVERSY
May 16, 1954

Viewed as a drama of political life, the hearings of the Stevens-Mc-Carthy controversy by the Senate subcommittee have everything elemental to drama, including the "unities" of Time, Place and Action which Aristotle prescribed as its fundamental law. This has become increasingly apparent as new characters and new conflicts have come onto the stage of the Senate Caucus Room. And the vivid consciousness of the principals that, by means of television, the audience is one of the largest ever assembled and its seats are all in the front row has given additional spirit to the performance.

For these and other reasons this drama is much more exciting than the simulation of life in the theatre, however sensational, well written and well acted. The stakes of the battle alone are so tremendous that the dramatic art, or its lack, possessed by each of the principals is a minor factor in the effect of the hearings on that public opinion which, as also in the theatrical realm of make-believe, will pass final judgment.

Careers and reputations are at stake—of men long prominent, of men newly prominent, of lawyers, ambitious politicians and civil servants. The clashing functions of two branches of the American Government, a strife implicit in the constitutional system of separated powers, fan the fires of the controversy. Also involved are the future relations between the Executive departments and Congress. And interwoven in all this are a potential struggle for the control of the Republican party and the ultimate national evaluation of President Eisenhower as a leader of the people.

The proceedings—a combination of the courtroom, the Congressional inquiry and the New England town meeting—have on many occasions risen above the basic defects of such a mélange by providing color that is rarely to be seen in the annexes of parliaments.

Thus the personalities, the manners and the facial expressions of the actors in this drama have entered into the awareness of the audience as never before in related circumstances. And much of the basis of the final public adjudication will be supplied by this visual testimony, since it is already clear that a flat judgment for either side is unlikely on who is right and who is wrong, who is lying and who is telling the truth, who is forthright and who is evasive. There may be casualties in the subcommittee verdict. But probably they will be confined to minor principals —not minor in the controversy but minor in public stature.

It may be that, when the testimony has been completed, Senator Joseph R. McCarthy's national influence will have suffered the heavy injury which is the hope of many. But if that is dependent on proof that his investigation of security risks in the Army was unusually ruthless, was the direct consequence of the Army's refusal of certain favors for Private G. David Schine, and was pursued for the purpose of discrediting the Army's former commander, now in the White House—whatever the cost to national security—the testimony so far has not supplied it.

It may be that, in consequence of the hearings, the President will openly bring his prestige and that of his office into direct conflict with McCarthy, as many within and without the Administration have been urging him to do. But nothing he has said or done since the hearings opened gives solid basis for that belief.

His chief assistant, Sherman Adams, has been disclosed as the official who proposed that the Army's counsel, John G. Adams, compile a formal list of the pressures he has charged to McCarthy and the subcommittee staff. His roving political counselor, Ambassador Henry Cabot Lodge, has been disclosed as present and approving when that proposal was made. The issue has been brought close to the President's person by the revelation that John G. Adams is under high Executive instruction to withhold certain facts that the entire subcommittee considers to be relevant. But as yet the President is aloof, confining himself to vague references to "unworthy scenes" in Washington, but refraining carefully from saying what is "unworthy" and who is responsible.

The reputation of Secretary of the Army R. T. Stevens for maintaining the dignity of his office and that of the Army throughout a lengthy period of accepted humiliations has been damaged by the testimony— how badly only the future can manifest. Roy Cohn, McCarthy's chief subcommittee counsel, has been put heavily on the defensive, as has the Army counsel, too. And, much more importantly, the issue has been joined of how far the restrictions of the Executive on making information available to Congress can go with Congressional acceptance when it deems this information relevant to inquiries within its long-established scope.

The one clear product of the hearings thus far is overwhelming assent to the proposition that violation of his oath by a member of the military personnel is indefensible, however patriotic may be his asserted ground; and that no Congressional investigator should abet the crime. This relates to McCarthy's testimony that he was tendered, accepted, and made use of an essentially secret F.B.I. report to the Army that was furnished him by an Army intelligence officer.

The cast of characters could not be supplied in any theatre or on any movie screen, and this is one of the fundamental contributions to the elements of the high drama. No playwright could create more realistic trial lawyers than Ray H. Jenkins, the committee counsel, and Joseph Welch, the attorney for the Department of the Army. The Senators act more like Senators are supposed to act than simulators could on the stage. To those in the audience who long ago estimated them to be the villains of the piece, McCarthy and Cohn ideally fill the bill in the lenses of television. Stevens has been perfectly cast as the good and honest man floundering beyond his depth, John G. Adams the man at bay.

The drama of human conflict has always been absorbing. And when stakes like these are involved, the fact, however deplorable in a world on fire, is made plainer.

OPPENHEIMER
June 30, 1954

In upholding the 2-to-1 conclusion of the board headed by Dr. Gordon Gray, that Dr. J. Robert Oppenheimer is a security risk, the Atomic Energy Commission accepted, 4 to 1, the board's basis of his "trustworthiness" as the governing criterion. On this test the commission, like the board, decided that the requirements of national security as set forth in the McMahon Act, the commission's regulations and President Eisenhower's April, 1953, directive were disregarded by the famous scientist in acts, "associations" and a nonconforming attitude toward his sworn official obligations that amounted to "fundamental defects of character." Only Commissioner Murray, however, assessed these as, in effect, "disloyalty."

Thus the two groups joined with the A.E.C. general manager in the finding that, though Oppenheimer preserved the nation's atomic secrets, and despite the great role he played in furnishing the nation with atomic war power, he represents a security hazard.

Oppenheimer's suspended "Q" clearance for access to top-secret material will, therefore, not be renewed. Because of the explosive nature of the case, and the indignation it has evoked among Oppenheimer's fellow-scientists, it is far better from the standpoint of the national interest that the Gray board's recommendation of nonclearance was ratified by a larger percentage of the commission. But this will not end the emotional protests, dispel the practical fear—which Oppenheimer is seeking to allay—that in a critical hour many scientists will be disaffected from Government service, or gain acceptance in the large and influential group which considers the findings an expression of what its members call "negative security" in a national emergency so acute they think all criteria should be "positive."

This group's views with respect to that distinction were reflected in

the lone dissent of Commissioner Smyth, but they have been more ex-
plicitly stated by John J. McCloy, chairman of the Chase National
Bank. In his testimony before the Gray Board he was greatly concerned
with the official admission that the technological gap is narrowing between the United States and the Soviet Union. And McCloy took the
opportunity to emphasize what he called "positive" or "affirmative," as
contrasted with "negative," security. On that reasoning in part he said
to the board:

> In the light of his [Oppenheimer's] other record, as I know it, I
> would [take a chance on a man that has great value]. I can't divorce
> myself from my own impression of Dr. Oppenheimer and what ap-
> peals to me as his frankness, integrity and his scientific background.
> I would accept a considerable amount of political immaturity in return
> for this rather esoteric, this rather indefinite, theoretical thinking that
> I believe we are going to be dependent on for the next generation.
>
> It seems to me there are two security aspects. One is the negative
> aspect. How do you gauge an individual in terms of his likelihood of
> being careless with respect to the use of documents or [verbal] ex-
> pressions, if he is not animated by something more sinister? There is
> also, for want of a better expression, a positive security.

Recalling the occasion during the Second World War when the scientist Niels Bohr informed President Roosevelt that the uranium atom
had been split and German possession of an atomic weapon must be envisaged, McCloy continued:

> I think we [the Roosevelt Administration] would have taken pretty
> much anybody who had certainly the combination of * * * qual-
> ities * * * to deal with this concept and reduce it to reality * * *
> the theoretical ability, plus the practical sense, to advance our defense
> position in that field.

His point was that, in consideration of the menace of the Soviet
Union to our survival, the country needs all those with "great imagination" in the atomic field that it can recruit; if anything is done "to
dampen their fervor * * * to that extent the security of the United
States is impaired"; to do so is "a security risk in reverse." On that
balance of national interest alone, he said, Oppenheimer's intimate service should not be terminated in the lack of proof or assertion that he was
insecure with defense secrets.

This was McCloy's stated conclusion after he had agreed, under cross-
questioning by Roger Robb, the Gray Board counsel, that if a hypothet-

ical Chase branch manager had lied and covered up about a projected robbery as Oppenheimer had done in his on-again, off-again tale of attempted espionage, the witness would be "disturbed" and "puzzled." McCloy added, though, that if such a branch manager knew more about "the intricacies of time locks" than anybody else he would "think twice" before firing him, "because I would balance the risks."

This viewpoint has now been impressively rejected after three fair and painstaking examinations of Oppenheimer as "the man himself," and as an official from whom the nation, having entrusted him with its deepest confidence, had a right to expect very different conduct.

THE VOTES FOR CENSURE
December 1, 1954

If a Senate majority that Senator Joseph R. McCarthy and his defenders expect to be emphatic in favor of censure is disclosed when the voting on the Watkins committee report has been concluded, it will reflect agreement with the over-all opinion of this special group that McCarthy has generally done violence to the dignity and repute of the Senate as a whole rather than with all the specifications cited in support by the committee. The debate, now ending, has encouraged this analysis from the beginning.

Other Senators have exchanged insults. Other Senators have browbeaten and abused witnesses, some of whom furnished less provocation than Brig. Gen. Ralph Zwicker did to McCarthy by evasive testimony. Other Senators have declined invitations to appear from committees they deemed to be animated by personal hostility. But not in modern records has a member of the Senate impressed so many of his colleagues as heaping obloquy on the body as a whole. And not in that period has a member evoked such personal distaste and distrust and persuaded so many of his colleagues to give the widest latitude to the constitutional permission that "each house shall be the judge of the * * * qualifications of its own members."

Whatever may be the defects in the political perception of the Senator from Wisconsin, it is obvious that the situation has been perfectly plain to him since the appointment of the Watkins committee. Therefore, it must be assumed that his aggravation of it since that time—by the nature of his attacks on Watkins and other committee men—was deliberately designed to put the situation beyond substantial change in his own favor. What benefit to himself he envisaged by this strategy is a matter of speculation. But this theory was advanced today by a Senator who said the vote he will cast against the Watkins committee resolution was made politically more hazardous for him by McCarthy's latest tactic:

¶ The Senator from Wisconsin accepted the creation of the special committee by the Senate as making certain that, if it recommended censure, the finding would be supported by a Senate majority.

¶ In the early stages of the hearings he thought he could split the group on its findings (a belief which, by the way, did materialize after the unanimous report went to the Senate), and for several days he sought to assure this by his quiet and respectful behavior before the committee.

¶ But when Chairman Watkins, without protest from his colleagues, refused to take jurisdiction of McCarthy's complaint that committeemen had shown prejudice against him, and made the public comment that every Senator had a bias one way or the other, McCarthy abandoned his hope of a split, accepted the prospect of a censure recommendation and took the offensive against the committee in a way certain to make a group of Republican Senators more unhappy over the decision about to confront them.

¶ To this end he made the harsh comments that angered Watkins and put fresh obstacles in the path of those Republican colleagues who were trying to work out some kind of "compromise."

¶ Certain by now that he could expect no Democratic aid, even from the fundamentalists on Senate precedents, he determined to intensify himself as a future as well as a present problem of the Republicans in Congress and the Administration.

¶ When the returns from the Congressional elections showed that the Democrats, by the vote of Wayne Morse, the Oregon independent, would organize the Senate in January, and the loss of his chairmanship was beyond recall, the last restraint from that determination was removed for McCarthy.

This speculation, as noted above, is the theory of a friendly Republican colleague who thinks the censure concept is all wrong and that its political effects will be much more severe on others than on McCarthy. But it is at least an explanation why McCarthy seemed to be resorting to the precise measures that would further embarrass his own party and increase the majority he expects to be registered against him. . . . Ap-

parently he is persuaded that he can best take his case to the country
in the posture of an exposer of communism who invited conviction instead of a suspended sentence when he concluded he was being tried before a packed jury.

SENATE LEADER
AS POLITICAL STRATEGIST
June 23, 1955

Lyndon Baines Johnson of Johnson City, Tex., today as usual was the
busiest man in the Senate, of which he is the majority leader. He was
staging one of his parliamentary spectacles, and presenting it effectively
as a political morality play.

The moral of the dramatic performance was: the Senate is a responsible partner of the President in foreign affairs; the country owes the
proof of this to the Democrats, and the locus of irresponsibility is the
Republican side of the chamber.

Senator Johnson was made a present of this plot by Senator Joseph
R. McCarthy of Wisconsin. The gift was in the form of a resolution recording the Senate as opposed to the forthcoming Big Four conference
at Geneva unless discussion of the status of the Soviet satellite nations
was accepted by the Kremlin as a topic and in advance. In effect, the
Senate was to advise the President not to attend the "meeting at the
summit" set for July.

The Republican as well as the Democratic spokesmen in the Senate,
and those of the Administration also, recognized this proposal as a register of distrust in the President, an attempt to limit his freedom of action
at the meeting and an assertion by the Senate of the role of the President's senior partner in foreign affairs. Therefore, when the McCarthy
resolution came before the Committee on Foreign Relations it was unanimously opposed.

The ordinary procedure was to kill the proposal in committee, not
even dignifying it by an unfavorable report. By voting solidly against
reporting the resolution at all, the committee Republicans would have
made plain the party opposition. But incidentally this would have
spared them a vote on the floor, in which they had reason to believe that

several of their number would shatter their committee record of unity by voting with McCarthy for his project.

Senator Johnson, however, advised the committee Democrats that here was an opportunity to dispel any belief the McCarthy resolution might have evoked in other nations that the Senate would not support the President in any course he might choose to pursue. No room for doubt of this, he insisted, must be left for Soviet exploitation at Geneva. In the nature of politics he viewed it as a minor circumstance that whatever partisan embarrassment ensued from the course he recommended would be visited on the Republican party. And a minor circumstance it proved, even to that party, only their "Four Mule Men" voting aye.

Under his influence, therefore, the committee Democrats voted down a motion by the Republican leader, Senator Knowland, to "table" the McCarthy resolution. And when that motion failed the inevitable sequel was that the resolution was unfavorably reported by a unanimous committee vote.

But in executing this strategy Johnson conceded one vulnerable point —that the procedure could be distorted as abandonment by the United States of its long-maintained position that independence must be restored to the captive peoples in the Soviet hegemony. So he said on the floor today he would support an "appropriate" resolution reiterating that position, "appropriateness" to be a matter of consultation with the State Department.

Once again the Democrats without exception approved a tactic supplied by the leader who has brought about a remarkable show of unity among them at this session. Nor was this approval shaken by Republican statements in the debate that the President would have preferred to have the McCarthy resolution killed by tabling in committee. Senator Knowland reported that the President indicated "satisfaction" with this procedure when the Republican leader talked it over with him beforehand. This, at least, certainly implied no Presidential enthusiasm for Johnson's strategy.

But it also implied no resistance by the President, with whom Johnson told the Senate he, too, had conferred. Clearly the majority leader concluded that, since that was the situation, it was a matter for the Senate to resolve according to its concept of the most effective course in the premises as the constitutional partner of the Executive in foreign affairs.

There will be two opinions as to this. The ultimate wisdom of strategy like Johnson's, involving as it did complex international problems and partisan considerations, must inevitably be a subject for dispute. But viewed as an example of his leadership methods it is an enlightening instance of how he dramatizes the Democratic championship of the President in foreign policy as contrasted with the division among the Republicans in that area. It is an instance also of how he handles the general Senate problem of McCarthy—with an axe.

INTEGRATION AND
THE SUPREME COURT

A MILESTONE
IN MORE WAYS THAN ONE
May 18, 1954

The most diligent search of the records of the Supreme Court will probably not disclose more than a couple of instances, perhaps not those, in which the high tribunal disposed so simply and briefly of an issue of such magnitude as racial segregation in the public schools. Probably also this search will not reveal the same unanimity in the Supreme Court in anything like comparable circumstances.

These attributes of today's decision that racial school segregation is unconstitutional are not, however, the only ones which make it remarkable as it becomes a milestone in the history of the United States. It is remarkable also because the fundamental divisions on political philosophy and legal interpretation that have manifested themselves among the present Justices were submerged by agreement on one basic proposition. This is that, in education, discrimination based on origins tends to retard the ability of the segregated to acquire equal opportunities in life with those from whom they are segregated, and in the public schools that violates the guarantees of the Constitution. On this proposition the upholders of states' rights on the Supreme Court joined with those who are the champions of Federal supremacy—Stanley Reed and William O. Douglas as examples of this historic union.

The reasoning of the Supreme Court and its unanimity were further remarkable because dissents on this basic proposition were generally expected, a familiar prophecy having been that there would be nine opinions written and a close division among the Justices on the central finding. This was indicated in the complexity of the legal questions presented and exhaustively argued in the briefs and oral statements of the opposing attorneys. It was also indicated by the fact that the "separate and equal" doctrine sanctioned for public transportation by the Supreme Court in 1896 (Plessy v. Ferguson) has long been protected by the majority from direct constitutional review in the field of public education.

But this Court, through the voice of the Chief Justice, confounded the prophets and swept away, in a very few words, everything standing in the way of nonsegregation in the public schools except a modus operandi. The equal protection clause of the Fourteenth Amendment is violated by a segregated school system in the states, said the unanimous Court; and the due process clause of the Fifth Amendment (which has no equal protection clause) is violated by a similar school system under the federal power in the District of Columbia. But implicit in the decision is a general interpretation of the Constitution as a whole—that, even if these amendments did not specifically apply to the issue, the national Charter would outlaw public school segregation because it is "not reasonably related to any proper government objective" (local or national) and "education is the most important function" of both state and local governments.

That is the over-all meaning of the Constitution, said the nine Justices; we will no longer keep "the clock turned back to 1896" and Plessy v. Ferguson, and will meet the direct issue here presented. But we realize that this interpretation of the fundamental law of the United States, as we see it, strikes down deeply embedded social and political systems and affects the economic aspect of regional civilization as well.

Accordingly, the detailed application of our findings must be deferred until through further examination we can reach conclusions on the means to apply it that will be effective and yet not produce public disobedience or disorder. So we shall ask further advice on this modus operandi from those chiefly affected by the ruling: a violent social change like this, a new statement of the supremacy of the Constitution, as we see it, over local education, locally paid for, can well await a little more delay before materialization.

In view of the gravity of the decision it was vastly important, next to unanimity, that it should be delivered by the Chief Justice of the United States. The prestige of his office is second only to that of the President. But within the Court it is likely that Earl Warren's influence was great in producing the finding that insured unanimity: the coupling of a new and sweeping interpretation of the Constitution with the order for reargument at the next term on how to apply it. If that order had not accompanied the decisions, this correspondent feels sure the prophets of dissent would have been justified by the product.

There was another virtue in the factor of gradualism in the decisions. The states where the public school segregation system is entrenched in the law, and in the benevolent social consciousness as well as in the prejudices of the people, are given an opportunity of many months to survey the acute problem which the Supreme Court has imposed on them and to decide how to resolve it. In many localities that problem is not reduced in gravity by the fact that American citizens elsewhere do not comprehend it, or think it should disappear instantly because the Supreme Court now declares unconstitutional a practice it has sanctioned for fifty-eight years.

The problem will not instantly disappear. And those who have been pressing for the decision that came today should be foremost in cooperating with those who are confronted with its incalculable consequences at first-hand.

THE SCHOOL VOTE IN MISSISSIPPI
December 23, 1954

The analysts of political action in this country occupy safer ground than the prophets because their deductions are after the fact and can't be proved or disproved, whereas the soundness of prophecy must undergo the test of the event. But the American people, who steadily confound predictions of what they will do at the polls, also have the fixed habit of making trouble for the analysts. And that was demonstrated again this week in Mississippi.

The question before the people was whether to change the Mississippi Constitution to permit the Legislature to abolish the public school system and subsidize private, segregated schools throughout the state or in selected communities as it might elect. The issue grew out of the unanimous decision of the Supreme Court of the United States that racial segregation in the public schools violates the Federal charter. Ever since then the politicians of Mississippi, Georgia, Louisiana and South Carolina have been busy with plans to prevent the enforcement of this decision. All these states have now changed their Constitutions, without waiting to discover whether the Supreme Court, in issuing its decree of enforcement, will also prescribe a gradual rather than an instant compliance with the ruling.

In Mississippi particularly, where the Negroes outnumber the whites and emotional attacks on the decision were made by nearly all the leading politicians, these circumstances were expected to bring out a heavy vote for the amendment. But the stay-at-homes amounted to many more than half of those qualified to vote, and the turnout of Negro citizens was light. This poses an unusually interesting "Question Why."

The answer most favored in Mississippi is that adoption of the amendment was a foregone conclusion—so certain that odds of 1,000 to 1 would not have been excessive. But in the belief that closer examination was due to the sparsity of the vote on an issue represented as the most emotional one that could have arisen in Mississippi, this correspondent sought it by telephone from local sources. The analyst who seemed most objective was the leading opponent of the amendment— Hodding Carter, the distinguished editor of The Delta Democrat-Times, published at Greenville. These are his answers to the question "Why?":

¶ The "foregone conclusion" point is sound as far as it goes. But an organized attempt was made to evoke a pitch of high emotion, and it succeeded in only eighteen counties (of a total of eighty-two) where the preponderance of Negroes, two-thirds of the qualified voters, creates an acute social and economic problem. In this area the amendment carried 10 to 1, but the large majority of those who went to the polls was white.

¶ Elsewhere in the state the vote was close, and "nobody seemed excited." In Washington County, where Carter's newspaper opposed the amendment, the vote was only 2 to 1 in favor. And though a bond issue proposal to modernize the port of Greenville was up for decision, and a 60 per cent affirmation was required for its adoption, the city vote was light and the proposal barely won. This was strange for the further reason that the county interest was arrayed against that of the city, and the modernizing of the port is of vital concern to Greenville.

¶ The impulse to neglect chores which is engendered by the spirit of Christmas played a part in this public attitude, but how much no analyst would attempt to estimate.

¶ The most active organization in the eighteen-county area was the new, aggressive and pro-amendment white supremacy group known as Citizens' Councils. One of its leaflets was particularly effective. On one side was listed virtually every white leader in the state as supporting the constitutional change. On the other was a meager roster of opponents carefully selected for their provocative qualities—two editors, of whom Carter was one, the National Association for the Advancement of Colored People, the Congress of Industrial Organizations and the American Federation of Labor ("Northern Branch.").

¶ Without this activity the voting turnout would probably have been even smaller, and—though Carter did not say this—perhaps the effort influenced many Negroes to stay at home.

"The Delta Democrat-Times opposed the amendment," said Carter, "on these grounds: a surrender of the basic right to a public school education, an irrational method to meet a grave problem, a threat to the rating by out-state colleges of Mississippi high school diplomas, an invitation to a ban of the State University by national educators and an invitation also to a taxpayer's suit against the use of his money for private schools—a suit the Supreme Court might well sustain."

In this framework it seems very sensible for the state to proceed as indicated—apply the amendment locally, which is the least sweeping of the alternate authorities newly vested in the Legislature.

A 1955 REMINDER
OF THE RECONSTRUCTION
April 6, 1955

The Fourteenth Amendment is the law in Maryland as in the rest of the Union, but it still lacks the formal approval of the "Free State." At the legislative session in Annapolis, just concluded, a proposal that Maryland formally approve the amendment, which it declined to do in 1867, was rejected by the State Senate.

Henry L. Mencken designated Maryland as the "Free State" in tribute to the open refusal of its citizens to obey the national prohibition laws enacted under the Eighteenth Amendment. This latest instance of Maryland independence of mind differs from the other in that there is no official or mass rebellion against the Fourteenth as now construed by the courts. But specifically Maryland still withholds its approval of a section of the Constitution which has a shady past.

That is because the ratifying votes of ten Southern states, particularly those of North Carolina and South Carolina which provided the final units of the three-fourths required, were obtained under the duress of the Union armies of occupation in the post-bellum South, and from the

Reconstruction Legislatures put in office by the Federal military power. New Jersey and New York, though vainly, tried to withdraw their approvals of the Fourteenth Amendment after giving them. Maryland, with Kentucky and California, also withheld approval. And Delaware, which rejected the amendment in 1867, did not accept it until 1901.

At the recent session of the Maryland Legislature, State Senator Harry A. Cole of Baltimore offered a resolution to put Maryland on the historic record as favoring the intent and purposes of the amendment. On a voice vote in the Senate Judicial Proceedings Committee the resolution was rejected and reported unfavorably on the floor. There Cole successfully moved to substitute his resolution for the unfavorable report. But on final passage it got only thirteen of the fifteen votes which are the required constitutional majority, and twelve Senators voted "no."

There was no floor debate. And in the committee the reason advanced for reporting the resolution unfavorably was that it represented a futile gesture, since the amendment was already the law in Maryland. But, though unvoiced, the old opposition on the old ground figured in the action.

The Supreme Court has been of two minds about the intent and effects of the Fourteenth Amendment. Its most recent expression was made through Chief Justice Warren in the school segregation cases. For a unanimous court he held that the "equal protection" clause of the amendment was denied by racial segregation in the public schools of the states. But this clause, and the clause forbidding the abridgment of the privileges and immunities of any "citizen of the United States," were not always construed so liberally, or on the sociological thesis advanced by Chief Justice Warren.

In 1873 the Supreme Court upheld a Louisiana law which was attacked on the plea that the Fourteenth Amendment placed all civil rights under Federal protection. The state had given to one firm the privilege of operating slaughter houses and banned all others. This was upheld in the state courts as a legitimate exercise of state police powers. For a divided Supreme Court, Justice Miller held for Louisiana. He also advanced the principle of "dual citizenship"—Federal and state. He decreed that the reference to "privileges and immunities" in the amendment, though it admitted Negroes to citizenship, with all its rights and privileges, meant only those conferred by the Constitution, laws and treaties of the United States, not the "fundamental rights" which adhered exclusively to state citizenship.

There were four dissents to this reasoning and conclusion, and later the Supreme Court rejected both. But in 1875 the tribunal decided that the amendment did not confer the right of suffrage on women though no sex discrimination was made in its definitions of "citizens." A constitutional amendment, much later, was required to give females equal suffrage privileges with males. And the use of the word "person" instead of "citizen" in the guarantee against deprivation of "property without due process of law" was long contended, with Supreme Court assent, to have reflected a deliberate intent by the drafters of the amendment to include corporations as persons.

The changing and broadening interpretations of the Fourteenth make it, in Maryland and elsewhere in the United States, the law which the Supreme Court successively says it is. And, despite the cloud on its title, the amendment is as firmly in the Constitution as any other. But with Maryland's formal approval? Not in 1867. And not in 1955.

It should be noted, however, that the Fourteenth made mincemeat of the Dred Scott decision. And in 1954 the Supreme Court agreed with the dissenters of 1873 as to its guiding principle.

AN INDISPENSABLE ELEMENT
IN NEGOTIATION
October 3, 1957

The net of the President's comments on the Governor of Arkansas at his news conference today could be summed up briefly as this: "You can't do business with Faubus." This conclusion by the President was implicit in these statements:

> I certainly thought [after the Newport conference with Faubus] that, at the very least, the orders to the [Arkansas National] Guard to prevent the carrying out of the court's orders were going to be modified. I thought we [the President and the Governor] had an understanding. I know that the four [Southern] Governors thought that they had an understanding.

The implication of these comments is that Faubus is unreliable in negotiation, and in negotiation the reliability of all participating is indispensable to achievement. This estimate of the Governor's character would appear to cancel the value of another conference between him and the President at which the impasse over the circumstances in which the

Federal troops will be removed from Little Rock could be broken. And though Governor Hodges of North Carolina today said his group will "stand by" for the same purpose, he seemed to confirm the President's estimate of Faubus by saying that the Governor had "agreed" (over the telephone) to the text of a statement required by the President and proposed by the Southern Governors' group, to which Faubus later added or interpolated words the President rejected.

Faubus interpolated, in the sentence narrating what "the President was informed at my request," these words: "that it has never been my intention to obstruct the orders of the Federal courts." In the proffered statement, "I am prepared to assume full responsibility for maintaining law and order in Little Rock," Faubus interpolated: "as I have always been." And in two places he added "by me" to the pledge that "the orders of the Federal court will not be obstructed."

The more these changes are studied, the more curious it seems that Faubus ever "agreed," as Hodges says he did without the slightest alteration, to a text that in effect was his unconditional surrender, and that he must have known his multitude of critics would proclaim it to be. That promise, from a politician in a hot corner, should have astonished the other Governors, all politicians themselves. Until the President's comments today it also seemed curious to many that, in view of the importance of the negotiation, the President rejected these moderate face-saving semantics.

After all, the signer of the text was to be Faubus, not the President and not the Southern Governors' group. And since the President said today that he "never tries to interpret the motives of a person who does something I believe to be a mistaken action," it has been asked why he rejected a settlement simply because Faubus, whose motive has been widely represented as among the lowest, sought to enter a disclaimer to that assumption in a text for his own signature.

And as for the addition in two places of the words "by me," this, as pointed out here yesterday, was direct compliance with the requirement in the President's text that "he [Faubus] will not obstruct," etc.

The explanation seemed to emerge in the President's comments today. In sum, he does not take Faubus' words at their face value, this attitude beginning after the conference at Newport. Even though in saying he "thought we had an understanding," and that the Southern Governors "thought" they also had one, the President put the case in the most parliamentary terms, this factor was apparent. And though the President said that his impression at the Newport conference—that Faubus would "modify" his orders to the National Guard—was the result of a conversation of which "a great deal was private, with no one present but himself and myself," he knows as well as anyone that he has a clear mind, a good memory and an integrity that forbids the deliberate misrepresentation of anyone.

So the matter stands at the present, with negotiations at a standstill for the most basic reasons. They have impelled the President to keep Federal troops in a state, when he thought he would never post them in any; he said a while ago he could not conceive of circumstances that would seem to him to make this action mandatory on his oath of office. These reasons have impelled him to abandon a maxim he stated not long ago to another news conference: "Always give the enemy a line of retreat." And they have confronted an ambitious politician with terms of settlement that politicians view as the death sentence of ambition: unconditional surrender.

After the Newport conference a high Administration official who was closely involved said to this correspondent: "Faubus promised in my hearing that he would 'work it out.' " Whatever that may have meant to Faubus, and to those he may have said it to, grows more obscure with every event and every statement in the dismal record.

A 'CONDITION' REFUTES A 'THEORY'
September 26, 1957

On a peaceful occasion, in happy contrast with the civil crisis in which the President acted yesterday, one of his predecessors aptly stated the reason for a stiffening of Executive procedure. "It is a condition that confronts us—not a theory," wrote President Cleveland to Congress in 1887 in support of his proposal to modify the protective tariff. And in ordering Federal troops to Little Rock to enforce integration of the high school President Eisenhower forsook a theory to grapple with a condition he steadfastly refused to anticipate.

In numerous comments, and with increasing vigor and confidence, the President had affirmed this theory. Typical was his news conference statement of July 17: "I can't imagine any set of circumstances that would ever induce me to send Federal troops into a Federal court and into any area to enforce the orders of a Federal court. * * *" "American common sense," he was sure, "would never require it." And months ago when, in a National Security Council discussion of school integration enforcement, it was suggested that Federal troops might have to be sent South for this very purpose, the President, with flushed face, exclaimed: "Over my dead body!"

Possibly the theory that inspired the President with confidence to make these repeated statements originated in his own training as a soldier—whose unconditional duty is to carry out the orders of constituted authority, however repugnant or unwise. Or perhaps he accepted the assurances of non-Southern advisers that, after all orderly resistance to school desegregation through legal process had been exhausted by Southern officials, these and the people they represented would peaceably accept the orders of the Federal judiciary, on the hours fixed, as integral parts of the Constitution.

Whichever the source of the President's confidence, there is no doubt it was real and deep. Yet ever since the 1954 decree of the Supreme Court that ordered racial integration in the public schools "with all deliberate speed," any of the following "circumstances" he found himself unable to "imagine" not only was plainly imaginable, but some were anxiously prophesied by distinguished Southerners who, too, revere "the Constitution":

1. Spontaneous physical resistance, sparked by the very real fear of racial amalgamation, to the visible fact of Negro children of both sexes joining Caucasian children in the lower schools.

2. Physical resistance subtly encouraged by ambitious politicians, or the consequence of community resentment arising from the belief that competition for the Negro vote by the Democratic and Republican national majorities was mainly responsible for pressure for quicker action to effect the drastic social change.

3. The more rigid construction by some lower Federal courts than others of "all deliberate speed."

4. Increased Southern resistance because of the fact that the drastic social change being enforced was not imposed by a Congressional statute or a constitutional amendment, but by a Supreme Court decision that what it long had held to be valid under the Constitution was now invalid under that same Constitution.

5. The encouragement to resistance, particularly among certain elements of the population that exist in the South as elsewhere, that would surely be given by any show of indecision by Federal authorities.

But once the President pledged himself to enforce the orders of all Federal courts, and classified these as part of the fiber of the Constitution, he was bound by his oath of office to use national force to effect school racial integration where local force, as in Little Rock, resisted a Federal judge's "do it now" command. In conceding that the Constitution is what the Supreme Court says it is at any time, the President followed a historic White House line from which there have been few deviations. President Jackson declined to enforce at least one Supreme Court decision that overrode a claim of state sovereignty. President F. D. Roosevelt had ready a statement, in the event the Supreme Court held that the gold payment clause in contracts was inviolable, that in a superior and emergent public interest he would not enforce it.

But otherwise, except when the Supreme Court modifies or reverses its own decrees, or Congress uses its power to restrict the court's jurisdiction, its rulings for many years, steadily expanding in jurisdictional scope, have been officially accepted and enforced as the law of the land. The only alternative is a breakdown of the Federal system.

Now that a series of events has occurred, some foreseen by those who understood the problem that the 1954 Supreme Court decree and its enforcement created in the South, the Federal pattern of that enforcement finally is made clear by the President's military order. Once given, it must now be applied in all areas of physical resistance, with consequences to race relations and respect for the National Government that one can only hope will not be as grave as their portent. One of the worst of these possible consequences is that a number of politicians are sure to exploit them for personal preferment and power.

INTEGRATION STRUGGLE
ENTERS A NEW PHASE
September 13, 1958

The Supreme Court's order that there shall be no interruption in the racially desegregated status of the Central High School in Little Rock, Ark., not only reiterated the court's ancient principle that public opposition, violent or otherwise, to its interpretation of the Constitution shall not impede enforcement of that interpretation. It also marked the end of the positive period of state legal obstruction to the 1954 Supreme Court decision that compulsory racial segregation in the public schools, by statute or otherwise, violates the "equal protection clause" of the Fourteenth Amendment.

But the negative period of state and local resistance will now begin. And this will present enforcement difficulties to the Federal power that will require new approaches during which the public school systems in several states may be closed down entirely. The following, divided into categories, is a forecast of what this negative period may disclose:

What the Supreme Court, backed by the full Executive power, can do:

(1) It can, and has, required the local authorities of existing public schools to disregard state laws and local ordinances compelling racial segregation, and to open them on an integrated basis when a Federal court so orders. And the Little Rock decision has generally been taken to mean the beginning of the end of the period of community "adjustment" since 1954.

(2) The Supreme Court can, has and successively will strike down state laws that amount to evasion of its 1955 decree.

(3) The Executive can, has and will interpose Federal force adequate to put down violent resistance, and will interpose this force against that of Governors who, like Faubus of Arkansas, employ state military units to prevent desegregation.

What the Supreme Court, even when backed by the Executive, cannot do:

(1) It cannot require white or Negro parents to send their children to integrated schools in the public school system.

(2) Neither the Court nor the Executive can compel state legislatures to finance integrated schools, except by such Federal laws and methods as were passed by Congress during Reconstruction and enforced by Federal troops in the legislative halls.

(3) Certain Supreme Court decisions have persuaded some lawyers that under the "general welfare" clause of the National Charter, it can and would hold unconstitutional state legislation providing tuition for private education outside the public school system, even if this fund is made equally available to white and Negro children. This may be so. But nothing in the Constitution specifically requires a system of public education or authorizes the Federal Government to take it over if the states refuse to provide it.

What local school authorities can do:

(1) They can request Governors, who have invoked state laws requiring that integrated public schools be closed, to return these schools to the local boards. If or when the Governors agree, the schools can be financed by local taxes. But if the Governors refuse, and the boards

apply to the Federal courts to compel them to accede, that will create a new and untested body of litigation.

This, as revealed by the injunction sought to force Gov. Faubus to open the high schools he had closed, will seek to make defendants of Southern governors personally, with their jailing for contempt among the legal penalties.

What Congress can do:

(1) The Fourteenth Amendment specifies that Congress shall have power to enforce its "provisions by appropriate legislation." It does not mention the Executive or the Federal judiciary as original agents of this implementation. Congress, therefore, can (a) legislate the Supreme Court decision of 1954, (b) positively reject or modify it, or (c) by a vote of two-thirds submit to the States, subject to approval by three-fourths, a constitutional amendment embodying the decision or invalidating it. The political situation is such, however, that Congress is not expected to legislate in any of these ways.

(2) Public education did not come into existence nationally until the nineteenth century was well along, and much later in the South—a proposal in the constitutional convention that it be established by the Federal Government having been rejected—and Congress has left its establishment and administration to the state.

It will be noted in the above categories that the negative factor predominates, and there is every indication that the Southern States and communities where the 1954 decision is anathema to the great majority will employ this factor to the fullest degree. But that in itself will be an acknowledgment that, when the Supreme Court totally rejected the ground on which the Little Rock school board sought to interrupt the school integration plan it initiated last year, and moreover ignored the brief proffered by Senator J. W. Fulbright of Arkansas as "a friend of the court," resistance by positive legal devices was nearing the end.

Fulbright, taking note that the Supreme Court had based on a tenet of sociology its ruling that "separate" could never be "equal" because it implants a sense of inferiority in those pupils compulsorily separated, sought to equate this with a sociological argument of his own. "We must observe," he pleaded, "a constant in the affairs of men. When their ancient social convictions are profoundly violated, or when sudden change is attempted to be imposed upon attitudes or principles deeply embedded within them by inheritance, tradition or environment, they are likely to react almost as by involuntary reflex, and often violently. * * * I suggest that the Circuit Court * * * was unduly preoccupied by the violent and unlawful acts of individual citizens * * * and failed to give proper weight * * * to the further fact that there was involved 'a conflict between the two sovereignties' [State and Federal Governments]."

But that conflict, as members of the court remarked during the hearings, was "settled long ago" in rulings which for decades have been accepted by the American people as a governing principle. And public "reaction," by positive resistance, will not be recognized by the court as a reason why the Constitution, as it interprets that, shall not be enforced.

Now its problem and that of the Federal Executive is how to overcome negative resistance.

'RIGHTS'
IN THE SOUTHERN SIT-INS
March 21, 1960

In his televised discussion yesterday of the Negro demonstrations against denial of service to them at privately owned Southern lunch counters, during which he furnished a model example of high intelligence, tone and temper, Roy E. Wilkins of the N.A.A.C.P. spoke of this service as among Negro "rights," and of local police protection of the discrimination as illegal.

In view of the basis of the Supreme Court's 1954 decision that state enforcement of racial segregation in the public schools violates the Fourteenth Amendment, because the very principle of Negro segregation generates "a feeling of inferiority" among them and thereby breaches the amendment's "equal protection" clause, it is conceivable the court would sustain Wilkins' interpretation. The grounds of the 1954 ruling are so broad that the court might find room for a decision that, regardless of damaged private-property values, police protection could not be given the discriminatory lunch rooms when the sit-in protests were peacefully registered. In this event they would have the choice of serving all well-conducted patrons or closing down.

To make this ruling, however, the Supreme Court would be obliged to hold that implicit in the Fourteenth Amendment's ban against "state" laws compelling racial segregation are local ordinances protecting its voluntary private exercise. This would overrule a number of state court findings, and particularly a 1959 decision by the Fourth Circuit Court of Appeals that only "some positive *provision* of state law" for racial segregation violates the Fourteenth Amendment. The issue of the legality of local police protection of voluntary discrimination by private enterprise was not raised in this case. Judge Soper's decision exclusively accented the words "state law."

The plea was that the refusal of the Howard Johnson Restaurant in Alexandria, Va., to serve Negroes violated the Civil Rights Act of 1873 (held invalid by the Supreme Court in 1883); and also violated the interstate commerce clause of the Constitution because the tavern served patrons passing from state to state. After rejecting these points, the High Court firmly rejected also the legal right of Negroes for service in privately owned restaurants.

"This argument," wrote Judge Soper, "fails to observe the important distinction between activities that are required by the state and those which are carried out by voluntary choice and without compulsion by the people of the state in accordance with their own desires and social practices. Unless these actions are performed in obedience to some positive provision of state law they do not furnish a basis for the pending complaint. * * * The customs of the people of a state do not constitute state action within the prohibition of the Fourteenth Amendment." This would appear to sustain the full, constitutional right of private eating establishments to make the service discriminations, the target of the Negro sit-ins, when no "state" law requires them to do so.

To those who approach the Southern restaurant sit-ins from what they consider the only "moral" values, citations like this of the laws and judicial opinions upholding the private rights involved are spurned as "legalistic." Yet there are "moral" values in private rights, too, and they derive from a Constitution in which these rights are rigidly protected as vital to a moral system of democratic self-government. The Bill of Rights, which is the heart of this protection, would remain only as a pious statement of the ideals of this Republic if Jefferson had not taken the "legalistic" course of ramming them into the Constitution. And the method by which the Bill of Rights has been made a live force is the "legalistic" one of its assertion by the courts and its protection by the Executive.

There are "moral" values aplenty in the protest expressed by the Negroes in the South. Governor Collins of Florida thrust one of them into a withering spotlight when he denounced department stores which will sell anything they can to Negroes except the facility of eating with whites at their lunch counters.

But however much may be deplored the local custom which enforces racial discrimination as an economic necessity, or the personal bias which impels a private restaurant owner to turn away Negro patrons, Government protection of rights affirmed as constitutional is a "moral" value also.

FOREIGN AFFAIRS

PRESIDENT CUTS CONSTITUTIONAL DEBATE ON FORMOSA
January 29, 1955

There was no constitutional issue before Congress over the powers of the President as Commander in Chief of the armed forces to protect Formosa and the Pescadores, and the reason is to be found in the President's very act in sending to Congress a message on the subject.

No precise line has been drawn, or ever can be, between the limits of Executive and legislative authority when the President concludes that the national security is imperiled, whether or not in time of formal peace. General Eisenhower asked Congress for advance support of what he might find it necessary to do in the Formosan Strait partly to avert a revival of this ancient controversy in time of national peril. But this was an objective corollary to his overall purpose—that the Government of the United States should present an unbroken front to the world in the danger area.

If the President had proceeded without consulting Congress, and not a scrap in the Constitution or the statutes required him to consult Congress in the circumstances, he would have invited the kind of legal debate which often in the past has split the Executive and Congress and also Congress itself. If the President had told Congress that he would, and had the authority to, defend national security in this instance according to his own judgment, and was merely notifying the legislature of this as a matter of information, the same unsettling result would have followed. And the invaluable unity he sought between the policy-activating arms of the Government would have been impaired.

That is why, though the President and his advisers had no doubt of his unilateral power to make whatever he might consider to be an effective defense of Formosa and the Pescadores, he employed this language in his message:

> Authority for *some* of the actions which might be required would be inherent in the authority of the Commander-in-Chief.

If he had written *"all,"* which he could have so far as the laws and precedents are concerned, the debate in Congress would have taken a different, violent and much more divisive line. But in order to make it clear that he reserved the right to substitute "all" for "some" if this became necessary "to protect the rights and security of the United States," the President carefully added: "Until Congress can act I would not hesitate * * * to take whatever emergency action might be forced upon us." However, still pursuing the objective of forestalling a debate on this point, the President inserted, after "hesitate," "so far as my constitutional powers extend."

As a consequence of this tactic the debate on the message and the accompanying resolution to effectuate the President's request was political and military, and the Constitution was spared another search for the clear line of demarcation its drafters wisely, and thereafter the courts prudently, declined to draw.

The principal critics of the resolution objected that, in approving it, Congress might be giving its advance sanction to "preventive war," to military actions which might bring on a third world war, to interference with the Chinese Reds in what the United Nations conceivably might hold to be their right to the traditionally Chinese islands in the shadow of the mainland that are occupied by Nationalist China in the framework of a civil war. These theories, and the contention that our active military intervention should wait on the efforts of the United Nations to arrange a cease-fire in the Strait, were the principal criticisms advanced in the Senate, and to a lesser degree in the House.

In the latter body, the debate included the surprising complaint that the President was asking Congress to approve authority he already has, and therefore this might be cited as a precedent obstructive to that authority in a time when the President would be obliged to use it without resort to Congress. Although the President made plain in his message that he would act unilaterally now or later, in the presence of a sudden emergency, this anticipation and refutation of the argument was not even mentioned by Speaker Rayburn, who led in voicing the complaint.

The law books and treatises on the Constitution are full of the controversy which the President avoided by the word "some," and avoided also by the resort to Congress that troubled Speaker Rayburn. In time of war or the clear imminence of war those who have questioned the President's powers as Commander in Chief have got nowhere, ever since Lincoln expanded them after Fort Sumter to undreamed-of limits, including his right to suspend the writ of habeas corpus. And both Wilson and F. D. Roosevelt, the latter particularly, adopted the Lincolnian precept before Congress supplied them with War Powers Acts.

But in time of peace, even the technical peace that now exists, it has always been easy for a President to touch off a violent dispute on the subject by unilateral actions. Dr. Edward S. Corwin, a leading authority on the subject, wrote in the New Republic in 1951 of "the shadowy line that separates Congressional power when raising an Army and creating a Navy or Air Force to specify the purposes for which they may be employed, and the President's right to dispose the forces thus called into existence." And he added:

> What then is the answer? Futile and embittered debate between the holders of powers that must be exercised in close cooperation, if at all, or a decent consultation and accommodation of views between the two departments of Government concerned?

He was referring to the constitutional dispute over the disparate authorities of President Truman and Congress with respect to sending ground troops to Europe in the North Atlantic Treaty Organization. But it was Congress he was urging the Executive to respect by "decent consultation and accommodation of views." And while, in this instance, President Eisenhower left no doubt that he would be obliged under his oath and responsibility to proceed if his views and those of Congress were not "accommodated," the Corwin point as to "consultation" was fully met. And Congress itself furnished the "accommodation."

But the President's message was more than a show of wisdom and skill for a special occasion. He was redeeming his frequent public pledge to seek a combination of the often conflicting Executive and legislative powers to protect the vital interests of the United States.

LEADERSHIP OF A WORLD WE NEVER MADE
November 14, 1956

Ever since the United States accepted the responsibility of a world power, and then became the mightiest industrial-military nation in history, its foreign policy has been the target of heavy criticism at home and abroad. This has not merely been the consequence of the grave errors made in the formulation and conduct of that foreign policy by every Administration since Taft's. The criticism is rooted in an unhappy fact of modern history.

This fact is that, beginning with 1914 and except for short breathing-periods, world peace has constantly been threatened and war has been initiated by aggressor nations and their dictators in Europe and Asia. And the United States, after rising to world leadership, has been obliged to contend with these totalitarian aggressors under the limitations of a democratic system.

Analysts of the First and Second World Wars have argued that, if the United States had used ultimatum diplomacy to warn the Kaiser in 1914 and Hitler in 1939 that war against Britain and France would at once involve the military forces of this country on their side, neither dictator would have undertaken his adventure. And because they agreed that the theory, though not conceivable in the isolationist psychology of the United States in 1914, carried considerable persuasion as to Hitler's war, Presidents Truman and Eisenhower conformed our foreign policy to it.

They did so by general notice to all potential aggressors in Europe and Asia that the United States would regard an attack on its allies and other nations in a wide zone of our security as an attack on this country. Advancing from the indirect form of warning to Hitler that President Roosevelt employed in the Lend-Lease Bill after the Second World War had started, President Truman sponsored the Greek-Turkish military-economic assistance program and the North Atlantic alliance. After he took office President Eisenhower made advance and direct warning to aggressors the cornerstone of his foreign policy.

These moves have been effective deterrents thus far of the Third World War. And the Soviet Union was again reminded of their grim reality by General Gruenther in Paris yesterday. He warned Moscow that if the West is attacked the Soviet bloc of nations will be "destroyed * * * as sure as day follows night." But though the truth behind this establishes the strength of a foreign policy that could have averted the First and Second World Wars, the critics of that policy concentrate on its failures and attribute their source to Washington.

The failures are real enough. The Soviet Union has gained its centuries-old ambition for a foothold in the Middle East. Nations we have assisted to independence stand either uncommitted or "neutral" in the tactical conflict between the United States and its associates on the one hand and the Soviet Union, its allies and its satellites on the other. Hungarian revolutionists against Soviet domination and communism are massacred, and no rescue party comes from the free world. Nassar seizes the water lifeline of Western Europe and rallies the Arab world for the extinction of Israel, and the United Nations Charter becomes his unwilling shield of protection. The Western alliance is broken, at least temporarily, under the strain.

At home and abroad, the United States Administration gets the blame for these Soviet successes, and even the martyrs of Hungary in their anguish ask why the United States does not come to their aid. But, unless this Government and this people go to war with Russia, what means of quick rescue have they for the oppressed inhabitants of the satellites? And who of the critics at home advocates that?

Israel precipitated the Middle East crisis by a desperate resort to preventive war; France and Great Britain followed with military force to protect the Suez Canal and overthrow the Egyptian dictator; and Soviet Russia seized an opportunity its foreign policy had cunningly fostered. The United States probably could have prevented the military expeditions of Israel, Great Britain and France by sending an ultimatum to Nasser when he seized the canal and, if this was disregarded, attacking Egypt with its Air Force and Navy and destroying the United Nations with the same attack. Has any responsible domestic critic of our foreign policy urged that course? If not, it is merely another theory that the Russian plot in the Middle East and Nasser's cooperation in its professed rewards for him could have been frustrated by a different brand of United States diplomacy.

This country, bound by its constitutional processes and sworn against preventive war, is confronted in the world by an autocratic, bolshevist, ruthless dictatorship over an aggressor nation almost as powerful as our own, a situation unique in American history and, because of atomic weapons, more perilous than any in world history. This is the source of the Western failures. This is the yardstick on which all criticisms of policy should be measured.

EFFECTS OF THE SUEZ CRISIS
May 9, 1957

Marco Polo spent almost twenty years in thirteenth-century Cathay, and he waited four years after that to write his impressions of the country and its people—a disturbing reflection for the authors of quick commentaries like this one. But this report is admittedly confined to mere surface indications of what may or may not run deep in the structure of the North Atlantic alliance.

For what they are worth as traces of what lies beneath, these surface impressions that certain Allied differences on policy, both revealed and assumed, have not yet been adjusted. They appear in conversations with the nationals of Allied countries to almost the same degree they appeared last December at the height of the Suez crisis. Perhaps the conference just concluded at Bonn may have reduced these differences on the official level and moved to restore the confidence in the Eisenhower Administration that Western Europe felt for the first few years of the new American regime. But if that healing process has occurred at the top it has failed thus far to remove some fundamental doubts and fears that exist in the press and among the people represented by the statesmen.

These, as expressed in the form of questions to a visitor from Washington, are not wholly unfamiliar to Americans. The same doubts and fears have circulated in sections of the United States press and have been voiced by American politicians.

None of these questions was asked or implied by officers of the NATO Defense College here. But it is startling to discover at first hand how much credence they have gained in this part of the world, among them that:

¶ The President is isolating himself more and more from the problems of foreign policy and leaving to Secretary of State Dulles the ultimate responsibility for their formulation and direction.

¶ "The Radford Plan"—for a sharp reduction of American ground forces in Western Europe—represents at least an Administration "tendency" that is disturbing.

¶ The British "White Paper" was commented on sympathetically by the President at a recent news conference because he is exploring a substitute for the military concept of the North Atlantic alliance which was to defend Western Europe on the ground.

¶ There is fear that the Administration will not ultimately bring President Nasser of Egypt to book for the provocations to Israel and the treaty violations that led the Israelis, the British and the French to send their troops into Egypt. United States "acceptance" of Nasser's terms for Suez may reflect a permanent course of conduct toward Nasser, not a temporary policy to be succeeded by the stern measures that could have "cut him down to size" months ago.

¶ The dispatch of the Sixth Fleet to the Eastern Mediterranean was an effective stroke of United States policy. But, "as often with the

Eisenhower Administration," it was critically belated. And the effect may be dissipated by "another shift to a lead from weakness."

¶ Secretary Dulles is long on promises, though now and then he reduces their value by ill-chosen language. But he is notably short of performance in carrying out his promises.

These are samples of the criticisms, doubts, fears, complaints, etc., with respect to the Administration's foreign policy that are voiced by some nationals of our associates in the North Atlantic alliance. And their tenor—that United States courses are wholly ad hoc and likely to bear no general relation to one another—is echoed in some American circles also. There one hears that the State Department will not give guidance to the military as to what policy will be in the event X, Y or Z comes to pass—all reasonable possibilities. There also the Department of Defense bears its share of criticism as a labyrinth through which ordinary enlightenment must often be sought in vain.

It is a time of inter-Allied complaints which a transient, who thinks he knows that some of these lack any foundation in Washington, hopes may be a dying phase. And a transient necessarily cannot report them as other than superficial. But it is surprising to discover that the inter-Allied griefs of last December have such vitality, if only in words heard in passing.

Not so surprising, but at least discouraging, is the infrequency of comment on the great balance of credit to the United States for its immense service to the free world. But that is an old story in alliances where the other members are obliged by circumstances to depend so heavily on the resources of one.

PROCEDURE AS
A SUBSTITUTE FOR POLICY
July 16, 1958

The President spoke with the candor required by the gravity of his order which dispatched the marines to Lebanon when he conceded that "grave consequences" could come from this action. The American people had the right to expect this from their leader. And their interest also has been served by the press forecasts of what these "grave consequences" could be.

But despite such of the forecasts as were employed to demonstrate that the military intervention should never have been made, there is more weight in the opinion, generally expressed in this country, that the President adopted the only course for salvage left open to him by the massive errors of politics and diplomacy that preceded the present crisis in the Mideast. The errors that can be traced to competitive partisan politics in the United States were committed by both Republicans and Democrats. The diplomatic errors are attributable to poor statecraft, in the record of both the Truman and the Eisenhower Administrations.

The present chapter begins with the activities in 1947 of the Special Committee on Palestine of the United Nations. On Nov. 29 of that year the General Assembly of the U.N. approved a recommendation of this committee that the British mandate in Palestine be ended and the area be divided into a Jewish and a Moslem state, to be linked by an economic union of which the internationalized city of Jerusalem would be the third member.

In March, 1948, Senator Austin, the United States delegate to the U.N., who had been executing State Department policy to support the Palestine partition, suddenly asked that action on this be halted by the Security Council and that a special Assembly session be called to substitute a temporary trusteeship for the area. The Truman Administration had changed its mind on evidence of an unexpected degree of Arab hostility that it now concluded might shut off Western Europe from the oil required for industry and defense.

Thomas E. Dewey and other Republican leaders immediately attacked the Administration for fumbling and vacillation. This put the Jew-Moslem issue in the Mideast squarely into the Presidential election of 1948, and politics took over diplomacy. When the British mandate for Palestine expired May 14, the Security Council was still discussing the United States proposal for a temporary trusteeship. But at midnight Ben-Gurion and his Government proclaimed the new State of Israel, and instantly—to anticipate the demand of Dewey or another Republican for the action—the Truman Administration recognized Israel de facto.

In the mounting Arab nationalism which followed these actions the United States became its principal target. And resentment against the Western pro-Israel powers was aggravated by the sustained misery of the displaced Palestine Arab migrants. This situation was ripe for the rise of Colonel Nasser in Egypt as the symbol of Arab nationalism which, as opponents of Secretary Dulles' diplomacy had predicted, he adroitly used the "Eisenhower Doctrine" and the Baghdad Pact to inflame. And with his rise the Eisenhower Administration continued the series of errors in the Mideast. First it wooed Nasser with tangible encouragement of financial assistance in the building of the great Aswan Dam. Then, most abruptly, the State Department announced that there would be no such participation by the United States. To Nasser's anger and humiliation over this incident some good authorities on the Mideast ascribe:

Nasser's seizure of the Suez Canal Company and the closure of the waterway to Israeli shipping. The Israeli-British-French Suez expedition that was aborted by the United States through the United Nations. The closer entente, if not more, between Nasser and Moscow. The pan-Arab plots which fomented the revolts in Jordan, Syria and Lebanon that, culminating in Iraq, produced the appeal to the United States from Lebanon and the landing of the marines.

This catalogue, though inadequate, demonstrates that in the Mideast the United States has been following expedient procedures and not a policy at all. That applies both to the Truman and the Eisenhower Administrations. And even viewed alone it justifies the critical reassessment of foreign policy now undertaken by the Senate Committee on Foreign Relations.

A SOUNDER STANCE IN THE FAR EAST
October 2, 1958

With their restatements this week of the Far East policy of the United States, the President and Secretary of State Dulles have outlined a position to which the American people and our allies should be able to give general support.

The American people would have closed ranks behind the Government if what seemed to be its previous—and clearly unpopular— position had led to involvement in war with Communist China. This is a confirmed native trait which cannot be too often impressed on Governments like those of Peiping and Moscow that readily might make the fatal error of mistaking criticism for basic disunion. But a policy the large majority intrinsically favors has the extra strength of greatly narrowing the chance for this fatal error abroad.

This policy as restated is:

1. The United States will maintain its supply of the Nationalist troops and people on the offshore islands of the Chinese mainland, and its pro-

tective patrol of the international waters of the Taiwan Strait, so long as the Communists attempt to take these islands by force.

2. But if the Chinese Communists will agree to cease their military attacks on the islands in exchange for the end of Nationalist Chinese military overconcentration on these islands, the United States will use its powerful influence, as the Nationalists' only armed ally, to effect the exchange. The arrangement can be de facto so far as the United States is concerned—that is, facesaving by being informal, and even publicly un-acknowledged by either side. The principal which blocks such an agree-ment, though it be the Nationalists, can expect arraignment by the United States before the world opinion of the United Nations.

3. The United States, neither as a military nor a diplomatic-political proposition, approves Chiang Kai-shek's deployment of "approximately one-third of his best troops on these islands—roughly 120,000, of whom some 85,000 are on Quemoy." (The quoted words are from Under Sec-retary of State Herter's Atlantic City speech, Sept. 29.) Obviously, therefore, in any negotiation with Peiping toward peace in the Taiwan Strait, the United States would view the withdrawal of most of these troops to Taiwan as a prudent and sensible concession to make in return for a Communist Chinese agreement to accept negotiation of the future sovereignty of Taiwan.

4. But in no circumstances, present or conceivable, will the United States leave Taiwan to be taken by Communist Chinese force. As a corollary, the United States not only will give the Nationalists no assist-ance in any design to overthrow the Government on the mainland; it also states in advance the opinion that, even in the "hypothetical" event that a "Hungarian-type" revolution overthrows the Communist regime, it is "problematical" that a Chiang Kai-shek Government would be its successor.

According to official custom, which in this instance is justified by the situation, the Administration rejects the interpretation that the above represents a fundamental or even very important "change of position." By the laws of the same diplomatic game of make-believe it has so in-formed Chiang Kai-shek. But he has only to contrast two statements made by the President—Sept. 11 and Oct. 1—and Secretary Dulles' latest with those preceding, to realize that there have been at least two fundamental changes. Quemoy, which some days ago was so vital to the security of Taiwan and our security in the Western Pacific generally that the Chinese Communists must never be allowed to occupy it in any circumstances, is such no longer. Chiang Kai-shek's troop build-up on the offshore islands, which some days ago was vital to these two securities, is now unwise and the United States never approved it.

These moves to a sounder position satisfy some of the fundamental criticisms here and abroad of the position the Government appeared to be rooted in. They do not remove the risks faced by any Government pledged to meet force with force anywhere in the world. They do not eliminate the just complaint that the United States stood by inactively when Chiang Kai-shek took the military steps which imposed on us the unnecessary and exaggerated risk implicit in Quemoy.

But in that region this kind of inaction and these heavy consequences are not new in American diplomacy. The Truman Administration decided to "let the dust settle" in China, and when the dust cleared away the Communists had the country.

HUMPHREY AND KHRUSHCHEV
December 8, 1958

There follows the public record of certain sequels to the launching of the first American Presidential campaign from the steps of the Kremlin: the gradual easing of Senator Humphrey's self-imposed vow of silence on any aspect of his eight-hour-long interview with Soviet Premier Khrushchev until he had consulted the President and the Department of State; how the Senator did this with his own "crowbar"; and how he got more publicity mileage out of a span of eight hours than Lincoln did out of weeks of debate with Douglas:

Moscow, Dec. 1 (AP): Members of Senator Humphrey's party said he had held a long conversation with Mr. Khrushchev and then stayed on at the Kremlin for dinner. No details of the conversation were announced.

(The first detail is wrung from the Senator):

Moscow, Dec. 2 (Special to The New York Times): Mr. Humphrey said the situation was so delicate that he did not want to reveal the substance of his conversation with the Premier before he could report to Washington and obtain some guidance in evaluating his extensive notes.

(He drops a wee hint, the kind known as a "teaser"):

Oslo, Dec. 4 (AP): "Make no mistake about it," said Humphrey on arrival from Moscow today after his long talks with Premier Khrushchev, "the Russians have declared economic war on us. They may call it competition, but it is plain war."

(A psychiatric evaluation pops out):

London, Dec. 5 (AP): Senator Humphrey said tonight he believed that Premier Khrushchev's plan to make West Berlin a demilitarized free city was "phony."

(A crowbar, anyone?):

London, Dec. 6 (AP): Senator Humphrey said today that he was taking a personal message from * * * Khrushchev to President Eisenhower. "And it is significant." He said Khrushchev told him, "Now I'm going to tell you a secret. * * * And now I'm going to tell you another." Asked to reveal them the Senator told reporters: "You couldn't pry them out of me with a crowbar."

(The Senator makes a little use of his own crowbar):

New York, Dec. 8 (UPI): Senator Humphrey will report to the State Department today and President Eisenhower tomorrow on two "secrets" told him by Soviet Premier Khrushchev "relating to items of our security." He will also give the President a private message from * * * the Premier. * * * Humphrey said he was "convinced Khrushchev would like nothing better than a high-level summit meeting."

Washington, Dec. 8 (UPI): Senator Humphrey returned today. * * * He told reporters at the National Airport the information he will give the President tomorrow does not necessarily "bode ill" for the United States. * * * He declined details but may talk more * * * at his news conference scheduled for 3 P.M.

(The Senator then "talks more"):

Washington, (later) Dec. 8 (from the notebook of a reporter at the news conference): H. believes no political progress in our Soviet relations for long time. No great political decisions in the offing on what divides U.S. and Soviet Russia. No war for seven years anyhow, while Kremlin works on its [Seven-Year] Plan, but he doesn't mean to imply would be war then. As for "secrets" for President and State Department, these are "military atomic" and H. can't believe they don't know all about one of them. But our Moscow Embassy told him they don't.

(So a crowbar, probably the Senator's, did some successful prying at the embassy.)

And in today's section of this itinerant build-up of an interview with the Soviet Premier, which was unique in its eight-hour length unless one understands that the Minnesota Senator can easily out-talk, and has, the most durable Southern filibusterer among his colleagues, the crowbar of the Washington press was able to "pry" out that the "personal message" he is taking from Khrushchev to the President concerns "Germany and nuclear problems." But, according to a Soviet personage who expressed mystification here over Khrushchev's apparent choice of a messenger to Eisenhower, the message is unlikely to be one of historic nature.

He remarked privately that he didn't know his boss, as he thought he did, if the Premier would send an important communication to the President through one of his foremost foreign policy critics in the political opposition.

DULLES RETIRES
April 25, 1959

The President returned from his stay in Georgia with an acute consciousness of the void in his official household created by the retirement of John Foster Dulles as Secretary of State, and this sense of heavy loss he continues to convey. It was as implicit in his public welcome here to the new Secretary, Christian A. Herter, as it was in the Augusta news conferences at which the President announced Dulles' resignation and Herter's succession.

By commissioning his long-time principal guide in the making of foreign policy as his consultant on these problems the President has done what he could to retain what can be retained of the intimate official relation between them on which he utterly relied for the execution of this vital part of a President's responsibilities. But he is well aware of the administrative principle that there can be no man or influence between the President and his Secretary of State in the conduct of foreign policy if this Cabinet officer is to have the authority and prestige he requires at home and abroad.

Also, the President has subscribed to Dulles' rigid concept of this principle on every occasion when the Secretary believed that another executive department, a new assignment for a White House assistant or for Vice President Nixon infringed the province of the State Department in the area of foreign affairs; and when Dulles interpreted an activity by some unit of Congress as an attempt at infringement. Yet the President conceivably might have relaxed this formula by putting Dulles, as his consultant, between himself and Secretary Herter as his habitual practice.

But the President had barely left the room at Walter Reed Hospital after the swearing-in of his former Secretary in the new role when Dulles made a move to forestall this possibility. He urged Herter to stand by the principle as firmly as he had, out of his "reverence for the office of Secretary of State." And with high-mindedness rare in those who have wielded great powers, he made the all-important application to himself by adding that he had never wanted to be an "interloper," and did not intend to become one.

So the President must fill as best he can the void he so evidently and so sorrowfully perceives in the complex of his crushing responsibilities. And since the President returned from Augusta, some of his close associates think they have detected certain evidences of changes in his administrative attitude to deal with the new situation before him.

These changes were defined to this correspondent by one of these associates as follows:

"The President is digging into problems more deeply. He is making more decisions, and more that are wholly his own. He shows he is troubled by the potentials of his loss, and now and then his temper appears to be a little shorter.

"He dealt with his old Cabinet, before George Humphrey left the Treasury, and especially before the retirement of Dulles, as an equal with equals. Now I have the impression that his attitude is much more that of Lincoln's—of the boss to subordinates, though trusted, respected and still greatly relied on for act and judgment. Only with Anderson, the Secretary of the Treasury, does he seem to have the old air of intimacy in the high policy meetings.

"As soon as Herter can establish a positive identity as Secretary of State, I am confident he will have as much of the President's trust and attain as much intimacy with him as any successor of Dulles possibly could. Herter will, of course, need to impress the President with his performance at international conferences and in the public appearances he is capable of making effectively in this country. Within a year he should be able to attain the close relations with the President that necessarily must be the closest in the Administration. They must be so because the President is the kind of man who requires this emotionally as well as administratively, and Herter requires it to do his job at the top of his ability."

The President's Moscow assignment to the Vice President, just before his announcements of the retirement of Secretary Dulles and the succession of Herter, has created some speculation in this highly speculative community that he might be thinking of Nixon as someone vaguely "between" himself and the new Secretary of State. But the timing was fortuitous. The assignment was decided on well before the President had faced the inevitability of Dulles' retirement; it was made at the urging of the then Secretary of State "to feel out the water" in the Soviet Union and put to the best use whatever facilities of television the Soviet authorities may make available.

The assignment, it is also said on good authority, is merely another logical move in pursuance of the President's wish to give the Vice President every opportunity to observe world conditions at first hand in preparation for great new responsibilities he may have before or at the end of this Administration. Therefore, according to this same authority, the mission to Moscow has neither the purpose, nor can it have the result, envisaged in the speculations which followed the news that Nixon is to undertake it. And it was also pointed out that Nixon led in the effort to increase Herter's public stature as Under Secretary and make him eligible for succession.

In the new evaluations of the President's Cabinet and his relations with its members, that have been evoked by the retirement of Secretary Dulles, it is frequently being suggested that the Eisenhower Cabinet already had lost strength by previous changes and with the resignation of its Premier now must be rated as "weak," not only by comparison with its membership during the President's first term but with the average Cabinets in American history. On the basis of this estimate the argument follows that the President must change his whole concept of governing through his ministers if the severest critics of his Administration are not to be justified by the over-all record.

A MODEL OF TREATY NEGOTIATION
December 10, 1959

The importance of the international agreement on Antarctica and the value of the treaty provisions to the objectives of world peace and scientific progress were so obvious that the contributions of the American citizens who led in the negotiation have generally been overlooked. But a large share of the credit for the achievement represented by the treaty can be attributed to their work in preparing for the conference and then directing the proceedings.

The chief of the American delegation, who dealt skillfully to remove the obstacles to agreement that arose during the negotiation, was Herman Phleger of San Francisco. As legal adviser to the Secretary of State, in which capacity he effectively participated in several international conferences before he returned to his law practice, Phleger had established the reputation for distinguished public service that he justified again in presiding over the making of the Antarctica treaty. Phleger's special talent in this difficult field was on the occasions when Soviet Russian, Argentine, Chilean and French misgivings were adjusted without damage to the main objectives of the compact.

His deputy, Paul C. Daniels of the Department of State, spent more than a year in preparing for the conference and all its eventualities. He also was Phleger's working partner in eliminating the snags that appeared on the path to agreement from time to time. And in the long period of preparation Daniels was most ably assisted by George Owen, also of the department.

The product of their labors was the first treaty the United States has initiated, and successfully negotiated, since President Eisenhower's "Atoms for Peace" proposal to the United Nations Assembly Dec. 1, 1953, took form in an international compact. On June 18, 1957, the Senate voted 67 to 19 to approve United States membership in the International Atomic Energy Agency, to which seventy members of the U.N. belong.

In the course of the Washington negotiations on Antarctica, over which Phleger presided, Argentina expressed special concern lest the treaty provision for freedom of scientific research invade its national sovereignty. On the point whether nuclear explosions should be permanently banned in the Antarctic area, Soviet Russia's reservations were dispelled by the agreement to leave the permanent regulations to the action of a subsequent international conference on nuclear disarmament. The issue of what the treaty would provide as to current national claims in Antarctica, which disturbed the French, was resolved by the agreement that no present or potential claimant need renounce his claims, but no new ones will be recognized or old ones furthered. It was also agreed that military personnel and equipment already in Antarctica could remain and be employed—a matter of great importance to the United States because Navy personnel and equipment are there.

These and other snags disposed of, the treaty excluded use of the polar continent for any but peaceful purposes; bound all signatories to enforce this against non-signatory intruders—Russia, for instance, if Communist China makes the attempt; assured freedom of scientific research and administration in a system of international cooperation; set aside all political issues; and totally prohibited nuclear explosions but not atomic reactors, such as the United States operates in the area.

To observe that all these were American objectives is not meant to imply they were not also the objectives of other signatories. A notable aspect of the treaty, and what reflects further credit on Phleger's management of the proceedings, is that each of its provisions represents an objective asserted by all the participating nations. On that basis there were no "losers." But none was a larger "winner" than the United States, whose representatives designed, and supervised the manufacture of, this instrument for peace as they did the creation of the International Atomic Energy Agency two years ago.

This record does not take the humor out of Will Rogers' famous remark that "the United States never lost a war or won a conference." But it does spoil the implication that the United States always is the patsy in international negotiation.

THE KENNEDY-NIXON CAMPAIGN

NIXON LEADS
FOR NOMINATION IN '60
January 26, 1957

There are several reasons why Vice President Richard M. Nixon was somewhat less of a secondary figure to the President on Inaugural Day, 1957, than successful candidates for his office—even re-elected ones—usually have been. As a matter of commonly agreed-on fact, he is the outstanding Republican prospect for the Presidential nomination in 1960, and the Twenty-second Amendment, which limits a President to two terms, automatically assures that Dwight D. Eisenhower will not be available for renomination.

But the Vice President emerged more importantly in the inaugural by initiating a news conference—a step without historic parallel—before he went to the Capitol to take the oath of office. And in consequence the first pages of the newspapers that reported the events of the President's second inaugural also carried an account of a press interview with the Vice President in which he predicted an even wider and more important government role for himself in the next four years than during his first term.

Late Saturday afternoon, January 19, news bureaus here were notified by the Vice President's office that a car would be waiting at the Statler Hotel at 9:30 A.M. Monday to take the reporters assigned to him that day to his residence in suburban Washington. When they got there the

Vice President was ready to be interviewed. The reporters, in the words of a dispatch to this newspaper, found in the living room "a relaxed, quietly spoken and unharried man whose manner was much at variance from the youthful and somewhat flustered impression that he had left on a similar January day in 1953."

He spoke at first of small, intimate things. Then he came to the point of the interview. "In the past four years I have had a chance for a more liberal education in what goes on in the world than perhaps any other man in recent American history * * * . This increases my ability to make a worth-while contribution in the high councils of state."

When the politicians gathered here from all parts of the country heard of the interview and what the Vice President had said their general and instant comment was, "He wanted to be the first to stake his claim for the Presidency next time." But the claim already had been staked so plainly that perhaps it would have been more accurate to say that Nixon was putting the claim on the news and video record to fix its priority in the public mind.

This priority among those Republicans who will, or hope to be, his rivals for the Presidential nomination was acquired by natural and available means:

(1) In his first term the President turned to the Vice President for more types of assistance than a President ever had before: help with the Administration's legislative program, formal and informal counsel in meetings with the President and his principal aides, foreign missions, major speeches as General Eisenhower's substitute and so on. All these assignments Nixon performed well, and to the satisfaction of the President as frequently and publicly expressed.

(2) The Vice President easily overcame the effort of Harold E. Stassen, a high Administration official, to displace him for renomination with Governor Herter of Massachusetts. On Stassen's challenge the Republican leaders and the party rank-and-file overwhelmingly rallied to Nixon, despite a series of comments by the President that at times seemed to be encouragement to Stassen's attempt. And the Vice President's renomination was formally proposed and made unanimous at San Francisco amid scenes of authentic party enthusiasm.

(3) Nixon bore the brunt of the 1956 campaign for the party, and, though a number of the candidates he endorsed on their home grounds were defeated, the President had the same experience. Also the popular plurality of nearly ten million for the party ticket was a stunning refutation of Stassen's principal argument for displacing Nixon—that he would cost it "several million votes."

(4) During the campaign and after re-election the President gave additional demonstrations of his approval of Nixon.

All these events had the obvious effect of making the Vice President the leading Republican prospect for succession to Eisenhower. But the calendar lag of four years before the next party convention is equivalent to an epoch in politics. Many kinds of hazards are in Nixon's path, and it is conceivable he could not surmount all of them. But he has shown the skill and endurance necessary to do that. And, of course, if the President did not serve out his second term, the Republican choice of Nixon, then in the White House, to run for election in 1960 would be as nearly a certainty as anything in human life.

Yet there is opposition to Nixon as President, in the party and among the roving unpartisan voters who lately have been contributing the winning margins for national party tickets.

In the Republican party are elements inimical to his White House succession: other members who want the Presidential nomination for themselves; conservatives who have no such ambition but who want a nominee closer to their own political philosophy; reactionaries against the crypto "New-Fair Dealism" they impute both to Nixon and the President in domestic and foreign programs. Embedded in this opposition is a powerful Republican faction in California, anti-Nixon personally, politically and just in general, that Senator Knowland or Governor Knight might aspire to lead in his own Presidential interest.

Among the roving unpartisan voters also there are anti-Nixon elements. And, while the opposition of some may be retrogressive from the last ditch, there are others who will make their stand against the Vice President there.

At this distant point from 1960, across a time span in which coming events are necessarily obscure, the current fact seems to be not only that Nixon is foremost among Republican Presidential aspirants but that he is unlikely to make the errors which would displace him from that position. This prospect would not in itself, however, exclude the possibility that the delegation of his home state will come to the national convention in support of a rival. In that case, even if Nixon had highly commended himself to the country in his second term as Vice President, he could lose the grand prize that he covets and is seeking.

THE ISSUE OF
A CATHOLIC PRESIDENT
September 8, 1960

Three comments issued yesterday on the "religious issue" in the 1960 Presidential campaign have in common the value of clarifying what the argument is all about. And, since the nomination of Senator John F. Kennedy by the Democratic party was certain to make the issue a voting consideration in November, it is far better to have the discussion brought into the open and on a high level.

The issue was certain to become a voting consideration because of its historic link with the separation of church and state, which is a political doctrine that sparked the Reformation among the peoples from which most Americans are descended. This doctrine, with the growth of religious tolerance, was a principal result of the Reformation. The dispute over church ritual long since was reduced to a clerical from a popular concern in this country.

In the United States the two religious communities whose numbers encounter serious prejudice are those of the Roman Catholics and the Jews. But, as yesterday's three statements make plain, the ritual of Senator Kennedy's faith is not the cause of the disturbance raised by his candidacy: that springs from the international form of the Roman Catholic Church and the supreme Papal authority over the positions of its members on matters which include some that come within the area of political action. And the prejudice against Jews, which differs from the other in that it is registered more in the area of social association, arises from the common concept that regardless of whether they subscribe to any version of the ancient faith they constitute a distinct race. As with the Roman Catholics, the ritual of the synagogue is not a factor in their exclusions.

How largely the three statements coincide in their presentation of the so-called religious issue in this campaign is apparent from the following extracts:

(*By Robert F. Kennedy, the candidate's brother*)—The overriding and only question is whether Senator Kennedy believes in the separation of church and state. He has said unequivocally that he certainly does.

For the National Conference of Citizens for Religious Freedom, even though its statement concedes that Kennedy has opposed Government financial aid to parochial schools and other recommendations of his clergy, the question is evoked by the form and canon laws of the Roman Catholic Church, and is this:

> Is it reasonable to assume that a Roman Catholic President would be able to withstand altogether the determined efforts of the hierarchy of his church to gain further funds and favors for its schools and institutions, and otherwise breach the wall of separation of church and state?

The Protestants and Other Americans United for Separation of Church and State accept as final the Democratic candidate's opposition to certain activities by his Church in the public sector. But, finding him "equivocal" as to whether he would sign and/or "administer" the Federal birth control legislation condemned by the Catholic hierarchy they still depose that:

> [It is] an elementary fact that one church in the United States has for centuries pursued a policy of partial union of church and state. * * * It is not bigotry or prejudice to examine * * * credentials [of a Presidential candidate who is a member of this church] with the utmost care and frankness and to ask how far his commitment goes [against any governmental junction of church and state].

However, the P.O.A.U. slants the so-called religious issue to be "whether the election of a Roman Catholic President would promote or hinder the historic American principle of church-state separation." But the actual, fair question is whether the mere fact of being a Roman Catholic would impel any such citizen as President to "hinder" the principle, and only bigotry could direct an affirmative answer.

If a personal appraisal may be permitted, this correspondent, who has known Senator Kennedy since boyhood, has no doubt at all he would as President firmly and faithfully support the principle. Moreover, the history of religious conflict amply demonstrates that Protestants have shared with Catholics the responsibility for "hindering" it.

TV AND THE CAMPAIGN
October 15, 1960

The joint appearance of Vice President Nixon and Senator Kennedy on the same video screen, to state their views on current public issues, has produced several effects new to national political campaigns. It has projected the personalities of the candidates for President for appraisal by more millions of people than ever had this opportunity. It has provided a basis, not previously available, for simultaneous comparison of their personalities, physical and mental, and of the capacity of each to expound his views under the immediate and constant challenge of the other.

The size of the public audiences these programs have attracted, and the nation-wide discussion of the leadership qualities the candidates may have revealed, support the general opinion that the public will demand these joint appearances in all future Presidential campaigns. If this is a sound forecast, then even an incumbent President of the future will find it difficult, if not impossible, to refuse to meet his challenger in person.

The new form of campaigning, therefore, may become an institution in contests for the Presidency. But the defects in the format of the Nixon-Kennedy programs have been so widely noted, and commented on so unfavorably, that in 1964 and thereafter the arrangements perhaps will more nearly resemble the formula which assures a true and responsible debate. Under those rules, which especially demonstrated their soundness and informative value in the exchanges between Abraham Lincoln and Stephen A. Douglas in 1858, the candidates:

Agree on the issues they will discuss. Decide by lot the order in which they will speak. Ask each other questions pertinent to the discussion. And allow sufficient time for orderly and comprehensive rebuttal and surrebuttal.

In the Nixon-Kennedy discussions the topics discussed have been decided by questions that have occurred to members of panels composed of newspaper and television reporters. Since the panelists must share the programs equitably, and there are time limits on each candidate for his answers and for comments on the answers of his rival, most of the responses are fragmentary. Under this arrangement when an answer requires more time than the format allows, or a principal wants to evade a specific response, the question is left hanging in the air.

The result has been a Q. and A. series that roves from the important to the trivial, depending entirely on what subject interests the member of the panel who has the floor. That is why Vice President Nixon and Senator Kennedy became embroiled on a subject which has no proper place in a political campaign because it concerns a most delicate matter of United States foreign-military policy in the most dangerous of the areas where international communism threatens the free world—the Taiwan Strait.

The intrusion of this subject, and the decision of the candidates to discuss it, are excellent illustrations of the irresponsibility generated by the panel format and the lure of television's gift of widespread and photographic publicity. The deplorable incident began on the night of Oct. 1 when the following question occurred to Chet Huntley of N.B.C. during a two-man panel interview with Kennedy:

Do you agree * * * with the present policy with which it seems to me we are committed now to the defense of the tiny islands off the coast of China, Quemoy and Matsu?

Kennedy quickly substituted for these words an accurate statement of U.S. policy toward these possessions of Nationalist China. Our commitment, he pointed out, is conditional: "We would defend Quemoy and Matsu if it [an attack on the islands] was part of an attack on Formosa." But then he added comments which amounted to public notice that in his judgment the islands are not a necessary part of the defenses of Taiwan (Formosa). And he made it plain that if elected President his policy will be to eliminate the islands from the defense pattern in the strait.

Nixon was quick to challenge Kennedy on this comment as the kind of "woolly" thinking that, he said, had brought on the Communist attack on South Korea and the terrible war into which this drew the United States. He would never, said Nixon, "surrender" even a rock of the free world to the Communist nations. This Kennedy pounced on to represent Nixon as "trigger-happy." And since these events had flowed from the Huntley question on Oct. 1 and Kennedy's answer, there was bound to be another question on it at the subsequent joint appearance of the candidates. By the time they finished their responses, the Chinese Communists had guidance as to the foreign-military policy tactic each as President would employ toward an attack on Quemoy and Matsu.

In subsequent statements both candidates have drawn back somewhat from the haste and imprudence of their original positions and this may repair some of the damage inflicted on our international relations by an aspect of the urge for votes that has appalled the diplomats of friendly nations. And the 1964 campaign is far enough away to justify the hope that the format of the television joint appearances of Presidential candidates then no longer will invite such incidents.

ELECTION CONSEQUENCES
November 9, 1960

The result of the 1960 Presidential election, and the narrow margin by which it was won, have produced several facts of prime value to the United States and the world. The victory of Senator Kennedy is proof at last that membership in the Catholic Church is not an insuperable bar to the Presidency of the United States. The close division of the popular vote will act as a restraint on legislation to carry out the extreme social-economic programs pledged by the Democrats.

For 171 years it has been commonly believed that, regardless of all else which might commend him, a Roman Catholic could not get a Presidential voting majority in the United States. Other factors—the national prohibition issue, an accent unpleasing to many trans-Hudson Americans, a Tammany-bred political career and the still-existing Republican popular majority—operated against the election of Alfred E. Smith in 1928. But the reason for his loss of some Democratic states in the South and rural areas elsewhere was palpably his religious faith. So the common belief that persisted the voters of 1960 now have dispelled, to the great benefit of their country and to the confusion of those abroad who exploited this legend to the deep disadvantage of United States foreign relations.

Big-city voting statistics yesterday make it plain that this benefit was greatly assured by a concentration of Catholic voters for Kennedy. What else could have been expected of them, and those of other minorities who joined them after evidence mounted that his faith was the principal reason why many citizens in normal Democratic areas intended to vote against him? It is also plain that Kennedy's campaign strategists, conscious that as a "sleeper" this factor could defeat him, but in the open would be an asset to him, kept it awake after certain Protestant groups had rung public bells to arouse it. But the demonstration that a Catholic birthright is not an automatic bar to the Presidency should minimize the issue hereafter.

This prospect is fortified by the additional fact established in the returns that Kennedy could not have won if Nixon had carried eight Southern states where the combination issue of Catholicism and platform was presumed to be dangerous, and in which the vote divisions show that the Republican success potential was extraordinarily strong. The eight states have eighty electors, and of these six unpledged in Alabama and eight in Mississippi were legally empowered by Democratic voters to control the Presidential choice if neither candidate got an electoral majority.

But, as now is apparent, the nomination of Senator Johnson of Texas as Kennedy's running-mate eliminated the peril of sufficient Southern state defections to defeat the Democratic ticket in an election as close as this one proved to be. Rarely has there been an instance of more cynical "practical" politics than the choice of Johnson to run on a platform pledging him to major policies and legislation he has steadfastly opposed. Just after the Los Angeles convention ended it seemed improbable that the Democratic South and its leaders would support candidates, even though one was its own, committed, at least publicly, to a political philosophy and legislative programs which Southern Democrats have been denouncing and obstructing for years.

But Johnson used his great influence to convince every important Southern party leader except Senator Byrd of Virginia that by party regularity they could restrain the "liberal" Democratic majority. Since they also depend on Democratic national victory and the seniority system for their powerful places in Congress and their state organizations, and on local party regularity for the offices they hold or seek, Johnson could use these arguments effectively. Also they "got the strong impression" (quoting one of them) and managed to persuade their resentful constituents, that Johnson would somehow see to it that the extreme proposals they bitterly resented in the Los Angeles platform would never become acts of Congress during a Kennedy-Johnson administration.

This impression will meet its supreme test when the Democratic pressure group affiliates demand redemption of the platform pledges that were designed to assure their continued affiliation. But the Johnson nomination scheme worked in enough Southern states to avert Democratic defeat in the very close election of 1960.

KENNEDY AND STEVENSON
December 10, 1960

The pressures brought on President-elect Kennedy by the host of admirers of Adlai E. Stevenson to choose their hero as Secretary of State came to their foreshadowed end Thursday in front of the Kennedy residence in Georgetown, D.C. In that public setting the President-elect made the offer to Stevenson of the post of United States Ambassador to the United Nations in which was implicit his rejection of this pressure.

It began as soon as Senator Kennedy had been nominated for President at Los Angeles. And of the groups which for months have urged, demanded, or politically maneuvered, or pleaded for, the Cabinet premiership for Stevenson, only a small miscellaneous crowd, and a few Georgetown University students still shouting, "We need Stevenson," witnessed the public collapse of the campaign.

To the west of the Kennedy doorway there is a maple tree. But even if it were an apple tree the scene would have borne no similarity to the famous occasion at Appomatox. Each principal was in effect announcing he would not surrender—the President-elect to the pressure in behalf of Stevenson to become Secretary of State; Stevenson to the proffer of another office in which there were still "unknown factors." These, he said, must be clarified by the President-elect before he will decide whether to accept or decline. And it became known that one of these "factors" was the name of the next Secretary of State that Senator Kennedy has not imparted to him, presumably because the choice was still unmade. Hence Stevenson could not be sure of compatibility with his future chief.

To some observers it seemed that, while Stevenson was at the microphone, the President-elect's facial expression betrayed an annoyance he had not quite been able to suppress. Certainly, after Stevenson made his reply there were heard in quarters close to the Senator the familiar accusation of "indecisiveness" against the former Democratic Presidential candidate. This charge has been amply documented in the eight years since his first candidacy was thrust on Stevenson by the Democratic National Convention. But a point must be conceded to a friend of his who on this occasion replied to it: "Who's indecisive now, with no Secretary of State a month after election?"

All practical aspects of executive government and personal Presidential needs were well served, however, by the failure of a campaign to force a Secretary of State on a President that ended, as this one did, in the anti-climax of a few college students and an assortment of other citizens waving worn placards and mournfully trailing Stevenson as he walked away from the Kennedy house. The practical aspects, certified by political history, are these:

A President whose choice for this post is determined by considerations of politics in any form, to which all other factors are subordinated, risks one of several adverse consequences. It is very difficult for him to attain the close personal and confidential relationship on which depends the teamwork essential to effective formulation and conduct of foreign policy.

John Quincy Adams laid himself open to the charge that Henry Clay's appointment as Secretary of State was the price of the deal by which Adams became President. The surface evidence was strong, and historians attribute Adams' defeat for re-election to its general acceptance. William Henry Harrison's choice of Daniel Webster, who had cleared the way to Harrison's nomination by withdrawing as a rival candidate, was similarly arraigned.

Woodrow Wilson, who "distrusted his [William Jennings Bryan's] political thinking" and "doubted his wisdom," nevertheless was persuaded that political expediency and repayment of a debt of gratitude for Bryan's help in getting him nominated required the Nebraskan's choice as Secretary of State. The adventure ended with the Secretary's resignation because of a fundamental difference over how the policy of neutrality toward the combatants in the First World War should be executed.

Franklin D. Roosevelt in selecting Senator Cordell Hull paid a political debt and also sought to assure to bind the Senate to the Administration. But both men became unhappy in their relationship, which was never personally intimate. And the President's growing tendency to deal directly with Hull's subordinates would have terminated their official connections earlier if the United States had not become involved in the Second World War.

Harry S. Truman's alienation from his first Secretary of State came from a different source. James F. Byrnes was a most intimate friend and political associate, and the President selected him for this and for admiration of his capacities. They fell out when the President was persuaded that his Cabinet premier was assuming prime authority. Once their close and confidential friendship and mutual trust were thus impaired, Byrnes's resignation was inevitable, so vital is this link between a Chief Executive and his State Secretary.

If the essential Kennedy-Stevenson bond ever existed, it was broken during the pre-convention primaries of 1960. Kennedy had been a loyal supporter of Stevenson's Presidential aspirations, offered his name at the 1956 convention and in the spring of 1960 almost committed himself to choose Stevenson as Secretary of State. But after Stevenson had repeatedly asserted he was not an aspirant in 1960, he acted in ways which Kennedy deemed deliberately obstructive to his own progress. Relayed Stevenson promises to declare for Kennedy if he carried Wisconsin, then if he carried all the primaries but Oregon, then if he carried Oregon—all these were unfulfilled. And at Los Angeles Stevenson tried hard for a third nomination.

A close and trusting personal relationship cannot be built on such a foundation. Moreover, Kennedy wants a Secretary of State whom he finds decisive in his thinking and follow-through. And it is not in his nature to be pressured by anyone, for anyone, into relaxing these requirements for that particular office.

TWO DIFFERENT COUNTRIES
January 12, 1961

Even with lavish allowance for the excesses of Opposition oratory, the one-track mind of task forces, and the bias of those in office toward their own records, readers of President Eisenhower's final report to Congress today on "The State of the Union" must wonder if they are simultaneously citizens of two different countries. One, according to the President, has made advances in national security and popular well-being since 1953 almost without historical parallel. In this same period, the other, according to the President-elect's campaign speeches and the implications of the reports of his task forces, has been teetering ever closer to the brink of disaster.

The President in his message agreed that the problems of the nation, deliberately and perilously deepened by the policies of international communism and by internal group pressures for special privilege at the expense of the general welfare, have pushed the United States nearer to this brink than ever before, and that many remain unsolved. But he cited numerous instances to demonstrate that he has built a protecting wall that will hold unless weakened by faulty reconstruction. The position of the incoming regime is that the barrier is inadequate because of incompetent architecture and worn-out materials, and must at once be rebuilt according to its new blueprint.

But the voters of the United States failed to make a clear choice in the November election between these flatly opposed estimates. And which and how much of the foundations of the Eisenhower structure need to be, or will be, preserved against the threats to freedom and security are questions whose answers are as yet obscured. They are obscured by the registered uncertainty of the American people and the lack of cohesion among the politicians of each party in the process of reaching the answers. And this obscurity is deepened by the fact that the public records toward these differing estimates of some of Mr. Kennedy's choices of policy-makers in his Administration run contrary to pledges in the platform on which he was nominated and to plans of immediate action he outlined in the campaign.

A striking example of this disparity is provided by comparing a campaign proposal on fiscal policy by Mr. Kennedy and a reply made to a Senate committee question yesterday by Douglas Dillon, his appointee as Secretary of the Treasury. The subject in both instances was the limitation by statute of interest rates the Treasury may offer on Government bonds of five-year maturity and upward. This ceiling the Democrats in Congress refused to raise two years ago, with the result that the Treasury has been obliged to borrow heavily on short-term paper.

"* * * We must," said Mr. Kennedy, "reverse the tight money and high interest rate policies which have choked off investment * * * and kept the small business man and farmer from getting the capital they need to survive and expand."

When Dillon was asked how he stood on maintaining this ceiling, he said that, while he had not reached a firm conclusion on this matter, "I certainly think the Treasury needs flexibility to refinance" (into longer maturities) the debt coming due in the next four or five years. "It may be," he said, "that this is a thing we shall require."

Mr. Kennedy's statement of the dire need to lower interest rates which his Treasury Secretary said the new Administration conceivably might feel it necessary to allow to rise, is only one detail that makes President Eisenhower's national portrait today seem to be that of another country. In the land he pictured, his Administration in eight years has:

1. "Carefully adjusted our economy from the artificial impetus of a hot war to constructive growth in a precarious peace." Built "a new economic vitality without inflation," while increasing expenditures to deal with new internal social and economic problems "and added international responsibilities."

2. Kept the American people in peace "in troubled times," and "consistently maintained in peacetime military forces of a magnitude sufficient to deter, and if need be destroy, predatory forces in the world."

3. "Virtually stabilized" the dollar, which in 1953 had sunk to 52 cents of purchasing power as of 1939. And generally increased the "spiritual, moral and material strength of the nation."

The Kennedy Years

The mere circumstance of having been a Washington newspaper correspondent for most of a long life accounts for the incidental fact that I have known several Presidents on terms ranging from casual to intimate. Of those in the latter category, I was best acquainted with the public talents and private characters of John F. Kennedy and Lyndon B. Johnson.

My first close associations with Kennedy occurred when, as an undergraduate at Harvard, he came to me as a long-time friend of the family for small assistance in matters of his immediate interest—to suggest a ranch where he and his elder brother, Joseph Jr., could condition themselves for athletics in their next term; to make an evaluation of the quality of his senior thesis, which became a respected book under the title "Why England Slept." So it was natural that, after he came to Washington as a member of the House from Massachusetts, and later as a United States Senator and Presidential aspirant, I saw much of him —professionally on both our parts, and socially in frequent interchanges of hospitality.

The requirements of our fundamentally hostile professions inevitably led to acts and advocacies by him, especially after he became an active candidate for the Democratic Presidential nomination, and to critical analyses of these by me on the editorial page of *The New York Times*. Though it is said that faithful are the wounds of a friend, and I felt as one to him throughout his shining career, such wounds are more likely to be taken as stabs in the back than if they were dealt by a rival or an enemy.

The more so when, as in Kennedy's case, he had to emerge into public confidence from the cloud of his tiny plurality of votes over Richard M. Nixon.

This he brilliantly achieved. But, as demonstrated by the obstruction of much of his program in Congress, the cloud was not dissipated during the Presidency, even in the sunlight of the Congressional mid-term elections of 1962. I feel as certain as anyone can whose only asset for prediction is years of close observation, that the shadows would have been swept away by the registry of a large electoral and popular majority for Kennedy's re-election if the irreparable tragedy of his assassination had not denied him even one full term. And the Great Society, built on foundations laid by T. Roosevelt, Wilson and F. D. Roosevelt, but on a realistic schedule of priorities and long-range cost commitments that his successor has lost in windy prose, would have borne in history the imprimatur of John F. Kennedy.

But, as the subsequent articles hopefully may show, much heavier and almost unbearable burdens were yet to come.

History will require a long perspective for a view of Kennedy in the round—to appraise the importance of the part he played in the world in his harshly-abbreviated time, to assess the quotients of wisdom, folly, prescience and all the other qualities by which to make a fair calculation of his statesmanship.

Already the bookshelves are beginning to groan with the weight of memoirs of Kennedy by those who served him at first-hand in the Presidency and on the route by which he came to it. Such is not the function of this introduction to day-by-day comment on his activities in that period. But throughout them runs the thread of impressions and evaluations which were formed by long and sometimes familiar acquaintance.

Style is man, said the English rhetorician. Like all generalities, however attractive, the substance of truth in this one is limited. Yet style not only helps to explain the quality which finally attracted the world to Kennedy. It also accounts for the fact that the depth of his intellect was underrated by many of his contemporaries. Youthful good looks, flashing wit and mastery of the felicitous phrase are rungs up the political ladder until the topmost round. That once attained, they become the stuff of envious or honest derogation. Hence I believe that, though these gifts of nature were greatly responsible for Kennedy's rise to the Presidency, they also explain why he was celebrated for some capacities of leadership and statesmanship he did not possess, and criticized as lacking some he did.

He compromised with Khrushchev and Castro in the "missile crisis" by yielding the point in his successful ultimatum that required "on-the-spot" checking of the sites in Cuba which Khrushchev assured him had been demolished. And, after the debacle of the Bay of Pigs expedition that his half-in, half-out support had foreordained, he blamed it on incompetent counsel of the military Chiefs of Staff whose approval, so one of them assured me, had been based on the assumption of all necessary air cover.

But he was the first President to have been confronted with decisions which carried the potential of averting or initiating a nuclear war; therefore, his compromise with Khrushchev and Castro was not the surrender imputed to him by critics but an act of the highest and most responsible statesmanship. Conversely, Kennedy's transfer of blame from himself to the Chiefs of Staff for the Bay of Pigs disaster was leaked to the press to preserve for him the reputation for resolute leadership he had definitely failed to demonstrate in this instance.

But only on that occasion, in my judgment, did Kennedy as President emphatically affirm the pertinence of the question that Truman had addressed to him in opposing Kennedy's nomination at Los Angeles: Are you sure you are ready for the country and the country is ready for you?

He was ready for the bold actions with which he sought to turn into peaceful channels the first surges of the Negro revolution. He was ready with the legislation which marked his political conversion to the "liberal" philosophy for social change. He was ready with the great Presidential instrument of public rebuke when, by raising prices, the United States Steel Company crudely exploited the influence it had welcomed, and Kennedy had exerted, on the steelworkers to make a contract acceptable to the industry.

It was a logical development of the slight and ailing youth, whom I had grown to know somewhat in his family household, to the man of Presidential stature. The independence of mind, quietly but firmly asserted before the formidable and often-differing father; the personal grace, and, above all the fortitude which triumphed over chronic ill-health, and the courage over hazards of war—all these invested his short span of maturity and power.

Perhaps the idlest and yet the most automatic of all the speculations of the finite mind is on what might have been. In any event, this element of speculation has crowded into these recollections of Kennedy. Suppose his elder brother, the family's logical choice for a career in politics, had survived his service in combat: into what channel would have been diverted the natural, brilliant equipment for the same career disclosed by the younger brother? He was a good reporter; his observations of the British election prospect in 1945 were the only ones I read that prepared me for the defeat of Churchill. Kennedy had the true scholar's grasp of the sources of human conduct which make history; this was apparent to me in his analysis of the nominees for admission to *Profiles in Courage,* Robert A. Taft in particular, that he had asked me for. Would his contribution to history have been greater as a chronicler than as a maker?

But the speculation on which I dwell the most grows out of Kennedy's comments on the problem of Southeast Asia when we were lunching together on October 11, 1961. According to notes I made immediately afterward, the President had just come from a meeting on the problem in Vietnam. He said the Pentagon generally approved a recommendation by the Chiefs of Staff to send 40,000 troops there. The President said he was not favorable to the suggestion at that time and therefore was sending General Maxwell Taylor to investigate and report what should be done. It was a hell of a note, he said, that he had to try to handle the Berlin situation with the Communists encouraging foreign aggressors all over the place.

The President said he was thinking of writing Khrushchev, urging him to call off these aggressors in Vietnam, Laos, et cetera, and asking

Khrushchev how he thought he could negotiate with Kennedy if their positions were reversed. The President still believed, he said, in what he told the Senate several years ago—that United States troops should not be involved on the Asian mainland, especially in a country with the difficult terrain of Laos and inhabited by people who didn't care how the East-West dispute as to freedom and self-determination was resolved. Moreover, said the President, the United States couldn't interfere in civil disturbances created by guerrillas, and it was hard to prove that this wasn't largely the situation in Vietnam.

I asked him what he thought of the "falling domino" theory—that is, if Laos and Vietnam go Communist, the rest of Southeast Asia will fall to them in orderly succession. The President expressed doubts that this theory had much point any more because, he remarked, the Chinese Communists were bound to get nuclear weapons in time, and from that moment on the nations of Southeast Asia would seek to be on good terms with Peking.

Suppose he had maintained these attitudes instead of giving the approval to Taylor's recommendations that initiated the active military commitment of the United States in a ground war against Asians in Asia from which no honorable exit is visible, as this is written. What would be the record and verdict of history on the Kennedy Years?

THE BEGINNING

REMINDERS OF '33
January 14, 1961

The air of excitement over the coming Presidential succession that already pervades this capital city has a quality which brings reminders of 1933 to those who were here in that year's immediate pre-inaugural period and saw Franklin D. Roosevelt take the oath of office. There are many substantial differences in the problems of the times, the dramatis personae and the general environment. But not since the same day drew near in 1933 has this community, inured to change, throbbed with the same sense of lively anticipation of things to come.

The Democrats were jubilant over Harry S. Truman's triumph over the almost-unanimous chorus of the prophets of his defeat in 1948. But he had been President for three years, and his personality, programs and reactions were thoroughly familiar. The Republicans were exultant over their return to power under President Eisenhower, after eight years of wandering without manna in the political wilderness, and the General furnished the celebration wtih the glory and clamor of a military conqueror.

But on neither occasion was there that excitement in Washington which was generated by the pledges of a young President, with the determination Mr. Kennedy revealed in a quest for the Presidency that shattered many embedded political traditions. The attendant circumstances of a young wife, small children and an intimate circle of celebrities of all types in the White House have added stimulation to the atmosphere of imminent change.

327

The state of the nation in 1933 invested the Roosevelt pre-inaugural period in Washington with a gravity not now to be sensed in the surface preparations. Then there was no schedule of gay private parties which hostesses could bait with the promised attendance of the President-elect and the most important persons in the new Administration. Then the country lay in the pit of an economic depression, with the banks closed, the industrial index touching bottom, agriculture bankrupt, and, of the thirteen million unemployed, many roaming the land as nomads.

There were clouds of war on the horizons of Europe and the Far East. Hitler was invoking Naziism in Germany and the Japanese had overcome China's main military defenses. And, though these clouds, which were to break six years later in a rain of destruction the United States could not escape, appeared to the general public as distant disturbances of the world's weather, they cast a shadow over the inaugural scene.

Instead of the current agreeable armed neutrality toward the incoming President of a strong political Opposition, it was joining the clamor that Roosevelt "do something, anything" to restore the nation's economy and social system. And this surrender emphasized the darkness of the situation. Even human tragedy attended the Administration of the incoming President by the sudden death, the day before the inaugural, of his choice for Attorney General, Thomas J. Walsh of Montana. So the flags of the city were at half-mast as Roosevelt rode to and from the Capitol and reviewed the customary parade.

Inaugural day—March 4 in that period of history—was swept by a strong, chilling wind, and the overcast was only occasionally relieved by a ray of sunlight. And, while the crowds were huge and demonstrative, eager to welcome the New Deal although unsure what it would be, mass enthusiasm was not attained until they heard the new President say, "The only thing to fear is fear itself."

More fundamental differences between that time and this also account for the holiday spirit now suffusing the town. Things again are tough all over. But, as President Eisenhower pointed out in his final message to Congress on the State of the Union, the nation has made substantial progress in his time, and during his eight years in the White House it has not reverted to the wartime status it occupied in Korea when he took office. Some of the great problems, as he also noted, remain unsolved, but except for growing unemployment none has reached the point of immediate internal emergency. Even in Cuba, where international communism has acquired its first strong foothold in this hemisphere, the new Administration will not be obliged to move instantly under the pressure of an overt act that must be met with force. The threat to the free world in Laos is grave and clear, but its more acute stage has been deferred by the Soviet's temporary policy of wait-and-see what Mr. Kennedy has in mind.

In 1933 President Hoover and Congress had been in a tug-of-war for two years. This had intensified the damage and hastened the pace of the depression. That in turn had lost to the President the influence he needed to induce business and agriculture to do voluntarily what his successor did with the plenary Government power Congress and the people gladly entrusted to him. He told them in his inaugural that he wanted enough to deal with the internal emergency as if it were "a foreign invasion." And in the inaugural period of 1933 Washington was thronged with bankers, industrialists, representatives of agriculture, politicians of both parties, and almost as many professors and Harvard men as Mr. Kennedy has been assembling, who urged that he be given this power and use it as he required.

By further contrast, the incoming President and his principal aides have discovered, in their briefing from their counterparts in the present Administration, that Executive powers—those they will have and those Congress may add—will not be the miracle tools to deal with their problems that they were for Roosevelt in 1933.

Finally, they have seen the roots of many internal problems fixed deep in Democratic Congressional as well as in Republican Executive soil, and the roots of international dangers growing through rock that cannot be shattered merely by new and vigorous leadership.

But they are young, ready, and eager to show what they can do. And Washington is as eager for the demonstration.

KENNEDY'S DRIVE
June 10, 1961

The mental and physical urge which drives President Kennedy to inspect, talk about and perform for himself so many more things than any predecessor is becoming a matter of concern in Washington. The painful strain he is now suffering from, in a spinal region not hitherto involved in his previous afflictions in that area, is only an oblique consequence of the urge. But there is at least a connection. The President dug out three spadefuls of earth in a tree-planting ceremony in Ottawa, though the ritual for these symbolic occasions calls only for one. For physical exertion his like has not been seen since Theodore Roosevelt was President. But Roosevelt had no recent record of disability except a weak eyesight which his glasses corrected. And neither Roosevelt nor any other Presidential predecessor taxed his personal equipment in any comparably brief space as Mr. Kennedy did for example, from May 27 through June 8. Since the destiny of the United States and the world will be largely shaped by his choice of policies and actions, the danger implicit in an excessive drain on his remarkable combination of vigors is obvious.

The President's activities in public view in the May 27–June 8 span certainly come within a reasonable definition of "excessive." And when it is noted that, throughout this period, his unseen activities included conversations with President de Gaulle and Premier Khrushchev that required intense preparation, concentration and vigilance over brain and tongue, plus numerous conferences on problems of government that demanded decision, the burden Mr. Kennedy assumed can be termed superhuman. The following condensed calendar supports the term:

On May 27, 28, 29 and 30 the President flew to Hyannis, to Boston, to Hyannis, to Washington, to New York and to Paris. In the course of these days he reviewed with Gen. Maxwell Taylor the very delicate business of the forthcoming report on our intelligence facilities growing out of the anti-Castro invasion failure in Cuba. He made speeches at two Democratic fund-raising dinners, one in Washington, the other in Boston, in the role of party leader and politician. In the role of world diplomat Mr. Kennedy reviewed Mideast issues with Premier Ben-Gurion of Israel. In the role of the returned native he addressed a Massachusetts group in Boston. And just before he emplaned for Paris he spoke for the great humanitarian cause of cancer research in New York.

The President's schedule for the next three days in Paris, though printed in time-table form, filled more than a column in this newspaper. Speeches, formal and impromptu, parades, luncheons, dinners, wreath-layings and answers to questions at a news conference were interspersed in breathless rapidity among five long conversations with President de Gaulle. The strain imposed on Mr. Kennedy by two extensive meetings with Premier Khrushchev in Vienna, on Saturday and Sunday, June 3 and 4, is apparent in the accounts of the grim exchanges.

The briefing of Prime Minister Macmillan in London, and the intimate social occasions there, supplied a short period of relaxation for Mr. Kennedy, and he managed to get some sleep on his way back to Washington. But after this easy interlude, the President began, at his airport welcome by a group of officials and Congressional leaders, a series of reports on his errand abroad, including an hour and a half session at the White House. And then he gave a report to the nation on the same subject by television.

The country surely would have approved if the President then had limited himself for a few days only to those things which had to be dealt with. But next morning he was early in the skies again, flying to Annapolis to redeem a promise to speak to the graduating class of the Naval Academy; back to Washington to make another speech that evening to a "Big Brother" dinner, as a gesture of appreciation to Edward H. Foley, who has served him well and unselfishly in many ways; out to the airport by helicopter the next morning to receive the visiting President of the Republic of the Congo; and thence to redeem another promise to speak, this time to the members of The United Press International.

By this time it became known that ever since he drove a spade three times in Ottawa Mr. Kennedy had been plagued by the gnawing ache of a lumbosacral strain. For days he had kept this to himself. Its comparison by his doctor to "a steady toothache" graphically describes the additional and nagging exaction on him.

These activities not only impose an extra physical burden on the occupant of an office normally overloaded: they are disorganizing in the area of administration. Often in conversation something will be said to the President on which he wants more information. Since his disposition is to seek what he wants at once, and he is extraordinarily familiar with the duties of his Administration personnel down to the sub-levels, he is likely to telephone to the quickest source. This more often is a department subordinate or a White House aide who shares a departmental field. And then either the President or the subordinate forgets to tell the departmental head man about the call.

The result is that the orderly administrative system which bureaucrats refer to as "proceeding through channels" is infracted, and intra-official jealousies or loss of self-confidence may be the consequence.

DOMESTIC DIRECTIONS

THE EXECUTIVE ORDER ON HOUSING
November 22, 1962

There are two bases of the attacks on the President's Executive order barring racial, religious or related discrimination in the admission of applicants to housing that is directly financed to any degree by the Federal Government. One, that it will disastrously depress the huge home-building industry, will be tested for validity in the market place. The other, that the order was an unconstitutional exercise of Presidential authority, will be pursued in Congress and the Federal courts.

In New York City and Pittsburgh, where the scope of anti-discrimination ordinances go much further than the Executive order by including conventionally and privately financed housing under their ban, enforcement officials assert that these have not depressed the market. Until more objective economic analyses are forthcoming, and cover at least the 13 states and 34 communities where anti-discrimination laws exist in some degree, the soundness of the forecast of the over-all economic consequence of the President's action will not be established or refuted. But the issue of legality is already plain.

It arises from the constitutional grant to Congress of the power to appropriate Federal funds, and implicitly to fix the conditions of their use; also from the several guarantees in the Constitution of individual property rights. With respect to the first, Congress has several times refused to give the statutory authority to the Executive that the President has exercised in his housing order. As for the second, the Supreme

332

Court has set certain limits to this in ever-broadening interpretations of the 14th Amendment.

In several of these interpretations the Court proclaimed as paramount a new public policy of anti-discrimination for which there was no Federal statutory warrant. And in doing this the Court struck down state and local segregation laws consonant with the "separate but equal" principle which the high tribunal had affirmed as constitutional from 1896 to 1954. The key decision in which the Supreme Court held that the overriding intent of the Constitution, as amended by the 14th Article, was that the public policy should keep pace with social-economic progress, was *Brown v. Board of Education*. This ruling invalidated all laws compelling racial segregation in the public school system of any state or community.

The social philosophy expounded and read into the Constitution in this decision by a unanimous Court has since been extended from education to other forms of racial discrimination, and therefore consistently can be invoked to uphold the President's authority as exercised in his housing order. Obviously, Mr. Kennedy strongly anticipated this when, during the campaign of 1960, he said that the next President must promulgate "the long-delayed Executive order putting an end to racial discrimination in federally assisted housing," and could do this "by a stroke of his pen."

His long delay, since he became President, in making this pen stroke is not attributable to any doubt in the Department of Justice that this 1960 anticipation was legally sound. If lower Federal court findings on the constitutional issue raised against the order are accepted by the high tribunal for review, the Attorney General will have supporting citations in plenty from the Supreme Court's anti-discrimination rulings since 1954. Mr. Kennedy delayed until Congress adjourned to avoid reprisals against his legislative program by Southern Senators.

Several of these Senators, with some sympathetic murmurs from members of Congress in other sections, have announced they will endeavor to have the Executive order reversed by statute on the ground that it represents "an audacious usurpation of power" which the Constitution reserves to Congress. In this event, which appears unlikely unless the President extends the ban to conventionally mortgaged housing and sales of private property, the Supreme Court would be confronted with a thorny constitutional issue over the separation of powers. But some lawyers who have studied its 1954 et seg. interpretations of the 14th Amendment's anti-discrimination thrust believe a majority of the justices would also strike down a statute quashing the order.

SHIFT IN CIVIL RIGHTS POLICY
July 21, 1963

With his news conference comment this week on Negro rights demonstrations in the streets, Mr. Kennedy completed a turnabout in dealing
with the problem from the position he took in his 1960 campaign for the
Presidency. In the meantime, he had tried for two years to "make the
problem go away" by means other than Federal compulsory legislation.
And as recently as May 22, 1963, the President expressed reservations
as to the need and wisdom of the street demonstrations for objectives
that he said were on their way to attainment.

But last Wednesday Mr. Kennedy spoke in warm approval of street
demonstrations as within "a great American tradition" so long as they
are not of the character that leads to "riots and bloodshed." As an example, he cited the plan of Negro organizations to assemble many thousands of their members and supporters to march through the streets of
Washington on Aug. 28. This, he said, has "developed into a peaceful
assembly" through the cooperation of its organizers with police officials;
and he personally looked forward to being in town, since he is one who
wants citizens to come to Washington if they feel their rights are not
being expressed. Because the President is pressing two programs—one
by compulsory Federal legislation, the other by pressure for voluntary
community desegregation—for the establishment of his wide concept of
what these "rights" are, it was clear he had Congress in mind as a
proper target of a street demonstration. And this, despite the feeling
among strong supporters of his legislative program that marchers may
hurt their cause in Congress instead of helping it.

The reasons for this apprehension are the product of Congressional
mail and of published accounts of brutal incidents in the steadily swell-
ing wave of Negro demonstrations. A sampling of the mail received by
members of Congress who as yet have neither endorsed nor opposed the
controversial sections of the Administration's equal rights bill have disclosed growing public indignation against the street protest policies of
the more belligerent Negro organizations. The special causes of this adverse sentiment are the public office sit-ins that blockade education and
the transaction of the business of government; also the nationwide
spread of rioting that, it was obvious in advance, would be the result of
some of the demonstrations.

Nevertheless, the President has now approved the march in Washing-

ton, which, since he has thrown all his power and prestige behind compulsory law against discrimination, he well knows is designed as pressure on Congress for total and early concurrence. Only a few extracts
from his public statements are needed to illustrate the fundamental
change in his position on the means a President and a minority group
should employ to end discrimination in all public facilities, including
those which are privately owned.

At Los Angeles, in September, 1960. Mr. Kennedy said:

> He [the President] must exert the great moral and educational force
> of his office to bring about equal access to public facilities, from
> churches to lunch-counters, and support the rights of every American
> to stand up for his rights, even if he must sit down for them.

It is significant of Mr. Kennedy's much more moderate attitude at the
time that he omitted any reference to "legislation," including the compulsory, although he had recently been nominated in the same city on a
party platform that pledged him and a Democratic Congress to enact
this in its most mandatory forms. These included a Federal Fair Practices commission with sweeping powers to enforce its finding of job
discriminations. And it is also significant of his former attitude that, as
afore-mentioned, he refrained for two years from sending to the Capitol
a program redeeming these pledges of compulsions.

By May 22, 1963, the date of a White House news conference, the
violent incidents of the street demonstrations and sit-ins had occurred in
Birmingham, Ala. But asked for comment, Mr. Kennedy said:

> I think there may be other things we can do which will provide a
> legal outlet for a desire for a remedy other than having to engage in
> demonstrations which bring them [the Negroes] into conflict with the
> forces of law and order in the community. . . . As it is today, in many
> cases they do not have a remedy, and therefore they take to the
> streets, and have the kind of incidents that we had in Birmingham.

In these remarks there is something to be noted with approval by
street demonstrators, private owners of segregated facilities and the police authorities responsible for the enforcement of local ordinances. And,
though the reference to a "legal outlet" had materialized in the Administration's compulsory equal rights bill by June 9, when the President
spoke at the Mayors' Conference at Honolulu, he still had reservations
on the necessity or wisdom of even peaceful street demonstrations, not
yet implying a close relationship between their provocations and those
listed against George III in the Declaration of Independence. But last
Wednesday he went the full distance:

I'm concerned about those demonstrations [that developed into riots], and I think the cause of advancing equal opportunities not only loses [as a result]. . . . But you just can't tell people "don't protest" . . . On the other hand "we're not going to let you come into a store or a restaurant." . . . It's a two-way street. . . . And I think the Washington march has now developed, which is a peaceful assembly, calling for the redress of grievances . . . they're going to express their strong views [and] I think that's in the great tradition.

'DUE PROCESS'
October 8, 1962

Nearly a month ago Associate Justice Black ordered the University of Mississippi to enroll a Negro, James Meredith, at the opening of the current semester, on the general ground the justice knew as a fact the state's pending appeal to the Supreme Court for formal, final review of the issue would be dismissed without a hearing when his judicial brethren reassembled. Today his forecast was borne out by the event. The Supreme Court caught up with "due process" with a formal, but *ex post facto,* order rejecting the state's appeal to be heard in support of its petition for final review.

Meanwhile, Meredith had been enrolled over official state resistance, followed by mob resistance on the university campus that cost two lives and many injuries, and was quelled only after President Kennedy sent Federal and Federalized troops to assist the United States marshals on whom he and his brother, the Attorney General, had first depended for enforcement of the Federal court orders involved. And on the day the Supreme Court passed judgment on Mississippi's review appeal, in the formal way any litigant, particularly a state, deserves from the highest tribunal when this final step is legally to be taken, 17,000 members of the national armed forces were still enforcing the order Justice Black issued after taking an informal, Gallup-type poll of his summer-scattered brethren.

Those lawyers and others, who are not at all disturbed by the casual judicial attitude toward "due process" in this instance and reject the view there was any relationship between it and the fury of the resistance on the university campus at Oxford, will probably not be in the least swayed by a differing evaluation, especially by a Southerner in political office. But a deluge of communications to this department from all parts of the United States indicates that many other lawyers and citizens are very disturbed over such aspects of the controversy. These at least will give respectful hearing to the following observations from Senator Sam J. Ervin Jr. of North Carolina, a "moderate" on the racial issue from an equally moderate state, and a former Associate Justice of the North Carolina Supreme Court.

". . . If the execution of judgment in the [Meredith] case," he writes, "had been postponed [from Sept. 10] until the Supreme Court had ruled [as it did today, Oct. 8] upon the application of Mississippi . . . for review, it is possible that the tragic events . . . within the last few days might well have been avoided. . . . Mr. Justice Black stated in substance that he would not stay the judgment in a case the [Supreme] Court had never considered because he thought the Court would probably decide the case against the applicant. . . . Mr. Justice Black's statement might be becoming to a crusader. It certainly does not befit the occupant of a judicial office.

". . . The Constitution would not have been destroyed, the heavens would not have fallen, if the efforts to force the entrance of Meredith . . . had been postponed until the Supreme Court had acted on [the state's] application . . . for review. . . ." (The postponement would have been for 28 days.)

That is a concept of due process which, by total contrast, the Supreme Court has meticulously followed in cases affecting Communist and criminal defendants. For example, in 1957 it freed one Mallory, convicted of an especially brutal rape, by a District of Columbia jury, whose death sentence was upheld in the Federal Court of Appeals here, because of "unnecessary delay" by the police between the interrogation of Mallory and his arraignment. Obedient to this vague formula, the same appellate court has just quashed the conviction for manslaughter of one Killough because his voluntary oral confession was preceded by a written one the court found inadmissible under the "Mallory rule." Killough strangled his wife and buried her in the city dump.

Chief Judge Miller, dissenting, said he was "shocked" by reversal of the conviction on such "tortured grounds" of due process. And, commented The Washington Evening Star today, the effect will be that the situation of unpunished violence now rampant in Washington will "get worse" until Congress specifies that confessions, otherwise valid, shall not be held inadmissible because of a delay in arraignment.

THE SPIRIT OF THE 18TH CENTURY
June 17, 1963

The Supreme Court's ban today on readings from the Bible in the public schools, the latest in a controversial series, derives from the American political philosophy of the 18th century. The "free exercise of religion" guarantee in the First Amendment—an article of the Constitution that is among the finest products of 18th-century liberalism—is not infringed, said the Court, when the majority which wants Bible reading in the public schools is restrained from imposing it on a protesting minority.

In another decision the Supreme Court ruled, however, that the guarantee was infringed when state unemployment benefits were denied to a person whose religion proscribed working on a scheduled working-day.

By its interpretations of the "free exercise" clause, especially in the course of the school decision rigidly construing the "establishment of religion" clause, the Supreme Court in effect sustained two interrelated concepts of Thomas Jefferson. One was that not even for the noblest or worthiest social objectives should the "wall of separation between Church and State" be bypassed. The other was stated by Jefferson in his Notes on Virginia as follows:

> [In] the first stage of education . . . wherein the great mass of the people will receive their instruction, the principal foundations of future order will be laid. . . . Instead, therefore, of putting the Bible and the Testament into the hands of children at an age where their judgments are not sufficiently matured for religious inquiries, their memories may here be stored with the most useful facts from . . . history. . . . There is a certain period of life, say from eight to . . . sixteen years of age, when . . . the memory is . . . most susceptible and tenacious of impressions.

The Court did not rest its conclusions today on this aspect of the problem with which it was dealing. Bible readings as part of a prescribed public school curriculum, it concluded, violated that clause of the First Amendment that prohibits an "establishment of religion." And it found this legal interpretation sufficient to the prohibition. But, if it is to be granted that Bible readings in the public schools have any of the substance of an "establishment of *religion*," then it follows logically that this effect is promoted by the fact that those exposed to these readings are of an age when, as Jefferson observed, "memory . . . is most susceptible, and tenacious of impressions." Hence today's decision carried into the 20th century both his understanding of the intent of the First Amendment, and his idea that children of public school age were not sufficiently mature for stimulation to "religious inquiries"— certainly among the probable effects of prescribed Bible readings.

But the composition of the majority opinion and the three concurrences might have been made easier if the authors had mentioned Jefferson's point about the ages of greatest susceptibility. To mention it might also have diminished the instant criticism of the decision. For, standing alone as legalistic fortifications of the "wall of separation" between Church and State, all the opinions are vulnerable for inconsistency.

It took Justice Brennan almost seventy-seven printed pages to explain why "other involvements of religion in public life" are "not unconstitutional" that, measured on the legal reasoning of the public school decision, appear to be equally so. The public school ban, argued Justice Brennan, sustains the First Amendment's requirement that the state be "steadfastly neutral in all matters of faith, and neither favor nor inhibit religion." But it would be "hostility" to religion, he said, if the state refused to provide military chaplains, allow tax deductions or exemptions to religious institutions, etc.—a concept into which certain forms of state financial assistance to parochial schools might neatly fit.

But the weight of 18th-century political thinking in the decision may happily start the decline of what New Frontier liberals consider an utterly crushing satirical comment on a modern conservative: "He has one of the best minds of the 18th century."

STEEL MOUSETRAP
April 14, 1962

Never have so many owed to so few words an illustration of the incapacity of some big business managers to comprehend their public obligation than when Roger M. Blough, chairman of the United States Steel Corporation, replied to a news conference question last Thursday. Asked whether he was "surprised" at President Kennedy's angry "reaction" to that company's price increase, he said:

"I think the answer to that should be that I was."

When the attendant circumstances of the price increase are considered, this reply from a business executive of Blough's experience with Government and with organized labor must either be set down as an intolerable strain of human credulity or an admission of incurable shortsightedness. But the U.S. Steel chairman has acquired a reputation for mental and other forms of integrity. Therefore, the fair assumption is that his reply was made in good faith.

Only a brief review of the events leading up to the sudden announcement by U.S. Steel is needed to explain why Mr. Kennedy's denunciation of the company's action that "surprised" the chairman was generally anticipated. Under pressure from the President and Secretary of Labor Goldberg, invoked in the name of the dominant public interest in collective bargaining in a key industry, the union had agreed to begin bargaining much earlier than usual before the expiration of a contract. In so agreeing, it laid aside the club it can wield on management in last-minute negotiations—notice of a strike in a matter of hours unless its major demands are met. And, though the industry costs of the new steel contract continued the pattern of percentage increases greater than those absorbed by gains in man-hour productivity, it was the most moderate and the least inflationary in recent years.

The industry spokesmen never conceded that the public interest urged by the Administration was paramount over the responsible function of management to fix company price structures that would return the profits it deemed required for sound business operation. Nevertheless, when Mr. Kennedy congratulated them as well as the union negotiators on the settlement for showing the "self-restraint" he had been urging, they gave no indication that U.S. Steel, the leading company, already was in the process of shattering the expectation implicit in his praise. Then, a union strike having been averted for at least a year in the most moderate contract in the industry, U.S. Steel waited in total silence, but only until the last company and its union had signed the contract, to announce its price increase.

As soon as the increase was known to the public—announcement appeared on the news ticker in this newspaper's Washington office about twenty minutes after Mr. Kennedy was informed of it—the leaders of the steel union came under heavy fire from labor critics of the contract, such as James R. Hoffa of the Teamsters, who had already assailed its terms as surrender to management. This attack made no impact in labor circles at the time. But when U.S. Steel suddenly announced a price increase, even though this was based on the added production costs imposed by prior contracts, Hoffa and some other critics renewed their attack, with the ammunition thus provided, against David McDonald, the principal steel union negotiator, whose leadership is already under challenge among his own rank-and-file.

These were the principal attendant circumstances of the move by U.S. Steel which, to its chairman's "surprise," instilled in the President a cold fury to which he gave public expression in a denunciation of those responsible for the climax, and in orders to Government agencies to retaliate with every legal weapon in the Federal arsenal—already loaded against business by pro-labor statutes and Democratic administrative policies. But, as it proved, Mr. Kennedy's angry arraignment had enlisted the much greater and preferable pressures of public opinion. This struck the steel industry as a whole when a number of other big producers immediately announced almost identical price increases, because the people have learned that the entire price structure moves upward with that of this industry.

The pressure, generated by the President, was stimulated rather than reduced by Blough's invocation of production-cost statistics to sustain the increase. Standing alone, they supported it. So does the evidence that the fiscal and labor policies of the Government have raised production costs steadily toward the peril-point.

But, in addition to the timing and other provocative acts of management that made U.S. Steel's price increase a declaration of political war against the Administration, the company was burdened by the onus of having disregarded very plain considerations of public interest; also a fair prospect of tax relief legislation to finance plant modernization. And when the immediate sequel was what Mr. Kennedy cuttingly termed the "parade" of other big companies to match Big Steel's increase, this onus grew to cover the industry as a whole and cast its shadow on the entire national management structure.

The weight of these developments broke the solid industry front on which the bellwether company relied to sell its products in a highly competitive market at the new prices. Inland Steel declined to go along, and by giving the reason that the increase was not necessary at this time demolished the base on which Big Steel had made and defended its decision. And when Bethlehem withdrew the new schedules Blough and his associates had had it.

If bitter experience has taught them what should have been foreseen they now know some important things for sure. It is one thing to base a decision solely on cost-and-earnings statistics. And this kind of decision can be ventured in circumstances which mouse-trap an unwilling competitor (Bethlehem in this case), and, for a period, even a big union. But no mousetrap will hold the President—especially this President—of the United States. Then the trapper will surely be the one to end up in the trap.

TIME TO WARM UP
THAT COLD SHOULDER
May 2, 1962

If President Kennedy had appeared before the United States Chamber of Commerce meeting here this week just after shrinking from the use on a labor union of the anti-inflation pressure he recently applied to the steel industry, the cold reception he got would have been justified. If the President had a wide vindictive streak in his make-up, and had shown it toward business generally since the steel industry episode, the chill of the U.S.C. of C. toward him would have been comprehensible.

But his speech was most conciliatory of the resentments he knew he had aroused in his audience and outside it by the methods he invoked for the vital public interest in a stable price level that is too important to be left to the private interest-serving of much collective bargaining. He used all the compulsion at his official and personal command to strongarm several big steel companies into rescinding their price increases. However, the citations he offered his audience to demonstrate good faith in an impartial pursuit of the economic objective he stated are plain in the record.

This objective Mr. Kennedy described as "an economic climate in which an expanding concept of business and labor responsibility, an increasing awareness of world commerce and the free forces of domestic competition" will "keep the price level stable and keep the Government out of price-setting." And the President listed as consistent to this purpose his resort to the courts for Taft-Hartley injunctions in national emergencies; his successful appeal to the steelworkers' union to settle for the most moderate contract in recent years; his public opposition to the twenty-five-hour week; his stand for a continued forty-hour minimum, and against labor "racketeering, featherbedding and road blocks to automation."

If he had made his speech a day later Mr. Kennedy could also have pointed to his praise of the constructive recommendations made to him by his advisory Committee on Labor-Management Policy as "a meaningful and significant document." For in their acceptance of some of these recommendations, the labor union members of the committee agreed to a diminishment of their powers over the economy.

The delegates to the annual meeting of the U.S.C. of C., whose response to Mr. Kennedy's conciliatory remarks was to sit on their hands, seemed to have no awareness that he is the first Democratic President since Woodrow Wilson to indicate by action the will to require the same consideration of the public interest from organized labor that he requires from management. The temper of the delegates was to close their minds to this most important prospect and dwell exclusively on their resentment for what many described as the President's "naked display of power" in forcing the steel industry to rescind the announcement of a price increase. And, though several delegates in talking privately to the press made no attempt to defend the timing of this action, it did not appear they realized that, if these circumstances had been designed to embarrass the President with the steel union and the consumers, they could not have been better chosen.

Mr. Kennedy, sooner or later, may encounter an economic crisis comparable to that he believed was created by the steel price increase. The creator of the crisis may be a powerful national union, or a collection of independent locals such as those which supply the labor force in the construction industry, acting in obvious collusion. If then he falters in applying the governmental and personal pressures with which he smashed the price increase in steel, and meanwhile has made no attempt to further the recommendations of his Advisory Labor-Management Committee, he will have deserted the objective he stated to the U.S.C. of C.

But nothing like this had happened when the delegates of business gave him the cold shoulder, suggesting once again that many employers share with many union leaders the herd psychology that they are being martyred as a class by injustice. Until or unless the President does desert his proclaimed economic and industrial goals, business men in any future conventions he may address would be better advised to take the olive branch he offered at this meeting.

The prospect does not seem very bright, though, that he will return with it soon to a U.S.C. of C. convention.

POLITICS AND PUNS

THE RULES COMMITTEE
February 1, 1961

The hair-breadth majority by which the House approved Speaker Rayburn's proposal to break the conservative blockade of legislation in the Rules Committee gave President Kennedy and the Speaker the power they sought. But the price both paid was in prestige.

This cost may prove to be quickly recoverable, or a small debit which will be canceled by a large favorable political balance for the Administration when its score in the Eighty-seventh Congress is computed. In politics even the narrowest victory in a struggle for power has a weakening effect on the opposition. Nevertheless, once the President and his political advisers concluded that the House battle would be lost unless his prestige at home and abroad was made the corollary issue, they required a large majority to liquidate the risk. Instead, the tally disclosed a winning margin which would have been reversed by a switch of three votes, and a defection of sixty-four Democratic members that would have been disastrous if twenty-two Republicans had not played the role of Blücher at Waterloo.

Since White House aides, for several days before the showdown, inspired reports in the local press, published under beetling headlines, that the President considered his prestige abroad to be as much at stake as his legislative power at home, how will the five-vote victory be measured on this yardstick in foreign chancelleries? The most hopeful, and perhaps a sound, answer is that the Washington diplomatic and press representatives of other countries will realize that the prestige issue was merely a political device to acquire the Congresssional power the Administration sought—hence that the President's authority over matters affecting these nations is unimpaired.

This may not be as sound an appraisal of the consequences in domestic politics. Moreover, the tabulation strongly indicates that, if threats and promises had not been lavishly employed by the Administration, the House would have voted down even its beloved Speaker to maintain the tradition of a Rules Committee independent of Administration control. And in view of the fact that the committee blockade has been against much of the "liberal" legislation urged in the Democratic platform of 1960, the rough "persuasions" required to break it demonstrate that conservatism remains a force in Congress, with ever-present potential of defeating highly controversial bills pressed by the Administration.

But those who place reliance on this potential may find that the counter-forces are more powerful and will increase in strength. The President's news conference today emphasized again his qualities of mind and personality to align the country behind him. And now he and the Administration leadership had been given legislative tools his Democratic predecessors lacked in similar circumstances. Though the enlargement of the Rules Committee is being widely characterized as a "liberalizing" process, it is not that at all. It merely transferred to the Administration the powers conferred by the House rules.

With these House allies it can block legislation reported by some insurgent committee that the Administration may wish to withhold from a vote. It can improve the chances of passage of Administration bills by sending them to the floor under rules which require the House to consider on a take-all-or-none basis legislation the majority shrinks from rejecting in their entirety.

Some observers attribute the President's narrow escape from defeat in the House, after only two weeks in office, not to conservatism, or the tradition of maintaining independence of Executive control, but to the country's disbelief that internal and external conditions require his proposed expansions in the costs and functions of the Federal Government. If so, Mr. Kennedy's failure to take notice of two grave national situations may be partly responsible. The first is the protection the law gives to picketing by which one labor union, regardless of its character or motives, can paralyze local, regional and national economy. The second is the perilously prolonged agreement to suspend nuclear testing, with a Government which has almost an unbroken record of violating its agreements.

TALE OF ONE THOUSANDTH
AND SECOND NIGHT
October 18, 1961

In the name of Lyndon, the Compassionate, the Beneficent, the Well-Publicized, here we indite the moving tale of L.B.J. and the poor Camel-Driver of Karachi:

It is related that during the days of Kennedy the King, there was a Grand Wazir, a Grandee of abundant opulence and amplest livelihood. And it is said that the King, being restless one night, sent for his Wazir and vouchsafed unto him, "O L.B.J., I am wakeful this night with the burden of thinking what new things we could do to arouse in this kingdom interest in and approval of our efforts to improve the lot of the less fortunate of the peoples of the Middle East and at the same time imprint on their minds our image as the giver of what is needed and also is good for our side."

It is written that the King said these other things to his Grand Wazir: "Alas, my heavy duties hold me here, so that I command thee to journey in my name among these peoples for the purposes aforesaid," to which the Grand Wazir made the reply, "O King, to hear is to obey, and you can count on L.B.J. to dramatize the mission thou hast entrusted to me in a manner that will imprint thy father image ineradicably upon a grateful world, and confound the Tartar hordes who are seeking to erase it."

And it has reached me that the King said in reply, "See to it that in thy loyal diligence thy extraordinarily alert instinct for personal projection will be wholly subdued, to the total suppression of any aspect of thy mission that could fall within the category of what is known as a publicity stunt." To which the Grand Wazir responded dutifully, "Of this, O King, be wholly assured."

It is written that in due course the Grand Wazir came unto the city of Karachi, in Pakistan, and set forth on a tour of the city in which vast throngs had gathered to welcome him. In strict consonance with the gravity and austerity of his errand, it is further written that the Grand Wazir made this tour of the city in an automobile of length and luxury such as the poor of Karachi had never seen, the more to imbue them with a sense of the humility of his role; that in one of the most crowded of the bazaars the gaze of the Grand Wazir lighted upon a poor man, Bashir Ahmad by name (as it turned out, the chauffeur of a camel), because of the magnificence of Bashir's mustaches. As the tale is told, the Grand Wazir halted his solid gold conveyance and engaged with this Bashir Ahmad in a conversation that ended with an invitation to visit the Grand Wazir's native land, in especial his personal fief of Texas.

The tellers of the tale relate that, no sooner did information that the camel-driver had accepted the invitation reach the domain of Kennedy the King, than many citizens quoth, "How constructively the Royal mission of the Grand Wazir has been executed. How perfectly the visit of Bashir Ahmad will serve the King's stated purpose, yet leave no ground for linking the Grand Wazir's mission with what is known as a personal publicity stunt."

And thereupon, it is further related, an airplane line in the land of Kennedy the King presented the camel-driver with a flight thereto from Karachi and back again. An airplane manufacturer supplied one of its better transports, with crew and fuel, to fly Bashir Ahmad from New York to Texas, to Kansas City and to Washington. An automobile manufacturer made Bashir Ahmad a gift of a blue truck which it exchanged for a green one, the national color of Pakistan, when he expressed this patriotic desire. And donations for the now-motorized camel-driver of shoes, clothing and rupees to the number of 2,000 flowed into the office of the Grand Wazir in the King's capital city.

But, most wondrous of all, as the story is told, Bashir Ahmad was met as he descended from the transoceanic jet airplane by the Grand Wazir himself, who acted as escort and chaperon thereafter, and also gave him a Texas horse with the brand of L.B.J.

And it is related that, in the end, when some hard-hearted persons inquired how these shenanigans comported with the King's outline of and limitation of the Grand Wazir's mission, and gave it as their opinion that Bashir Ahmad's camel would wind up at the knacker's and his owner with an incurable case of maladjustment, they were saved from the headsman only by palace gossip that the same thoughts had been indicated by Kennedy the King.

IF LINCOLN HAD INVITED 'GUIDANCE'
January 29, 1962

President Kennedy's statement at last week's news conference that even the highest civilian officials and military officers should circulate their proposed speeches through the Government for "guidance," as he did his State of the Union message, has happily brought to light an anonymous paper on this subject, worthy of having been inspired by Bob Newhart's idea of how Madison Avenue would have edited the Gettysburg Address. The anonymity is attributed to the continued presence of the author in the State Department's "speech-guidance" group.

The work is a speculation of interdepartmental comments Lincoln could have received on the Address if he and it were contemporary with present times and the "guidance" system. There is room here for only the subjoined few of these might-have-been guidelines, which seem less imaginative than they would have before the Stennis subcommittee assembled:

Comments by the State Department. (1). The phrase "brought forth on this continent," while technically correct, implies that the United States feels it owns the entire territory. This conflicts with our hemisphere policy and should be changed to "an area bounded on the north by 49 degrees N. latitude," etc.

(2). The use of "dedicate" five times is tautological, which should be corrected by the alternate use of "apotheosize." Since "nation" is a popular term without basis in international law "member state" should be substituted. On the other hand, "our poor power" implies self-admission that the United States is not a major Power, and the Secretary has directed the staff to work on a substitution. "The world will little note" invades the department's statutory assignment to make such evaluations; substitute "There probably will be only a few people who will note," etc.

(3). The requirements of international harmony call for the elimination or modification of phrases such as "conceived in liberty," "created equal," "birth of freedom," "Government of * * * for * * * and by the people," etc., because a number of our member states do not believe in liberty, freedom or equality and would properly take offense. The same objection applies to the words "under God." Also, "conceived," "brought forth" and "new birth" are open to interpretation among some of our NATO allies as offensive references to some recent irregular goings-on in their high official and motion-picture circles.

Other Departmental Comment. (1). The Department of Defense urged the elimination of "We are now engaged in a great civil war." The passage recalls to the people the cost of our military establishment, particularly undesirable in this budget-making period. The words should be changed to "We have entered upon a period of civil uncertainty involving fairly high mobilization." For the same reason "brave men, living and dead," "honored dead" and so on are ill-chosen; they unnecessarily call popular attention to a by-product of war the people don't like. And "all men are created equal" must be excised because it is highly objectionable to the Air Force.

(2). The Navy Department deplored the misleading impression, created by stress on land operations, that there were no engagements at sea. It proposed mention of air-sea rescue. The Department of Commerce reported it would take years to coordinate the interests of all its units so that they could be safeguarded in the Address, but meanwhile had compiled 253 suggested editorial changes. The Department of Health, Education and Welfare (joined by State) asked that the speech be postponed until it could locate all its officials with titles conveying supreme authority.

(3). The Budget Bureau proposed the Address be turned over for complete revision to a working-group from State, Defense, Treasury, Post Office, Labor and Commerce, explaining the bureau did not seek membership on the group because it could make whatever changes it chose later. Meanwhile, however, Budget counseled against figures of specific commitment such as "Fourscore and seven years ago"—advising "A number of years" instead—against "we cannot hallow this ground" as in conflict with Secretary Freeman's plan, and reminded the President that only Congress can "highly resolve"—or "resolve" at all.

If the luck of the United States is holding, the anonymous author of this paper is still in the State Department.

SOME CORRESPONDENCE
February 22, 1962

Because George Washington's Farewell Address to the American people (Sept. 17, 1796) was the first important example of the "muzzling" of official orators that now is under Congressional attack, its traditional

reading in the Senate to a traditionally empty chamber today should
have been entrusted to J. Strom Thurmond of South Carolina, the principal contemporary critic of the practice. But he may find a later opportunity in a purported record of what muzzlers did to the Address that
has just been turned up by Astigmatoff, famous Soviet spy in the United
States.

It may be recalled that previous products of Astigmatoff's espionage
were published in this space exclusively (he is known only to this department); also, that his reports to the Kremlin have invariably been
intercepted by American secret agents. This frustrating fate again has
attended his latest triumph of research. It consists of the following
memoranda, which Astigmatoff imputes to Washington, Madison, Jefferson and Hamilton; and to Jay, whose collaboration with Hamilton on a
second draft of the Address was rejected by its author of record.

(*Madison to Washington*): "I enclose a draft which I beg to hope
will justify the high consideration you have shewn me in asking that I
expand into formal prose the outline of your projected Address. If I
have taken too much liberty, sir, in modifying your stress on a balance
between revenue and expenditure, and in your seeming implication that
our 'detached and distant situation' from Europe will be a permanent
aspect of the cosmos, believe me that I so venture without the slightest
animation to serve the future political interests of Mr. Jefferson, or with
any persuasion of his crazy visions of airborne ships and weaponry,
steam-driven vehicles, etc."

(*Hamilton to Jay*): "You will detect, my dear Governor, from the
enclosure the cunning with which M - - - - - n, professing as always a
humility whereof he knows no jot or tittle, hath sought to insert J - - - - -
- - n's radical ideas into the address. M - - - - - n's leader, whose vault-
ing ambition is exceeded in altitude and ruthlessness only by Burr's,
hath a formula for office-seeking and holding which is rooted in the belief that, if of the publick's moneys an administration spends and
spends, it can tax and tax and elect and elect. This democratic (?)
champion of the poor and the humble—who shews it by living at Mon-
ticello in the state of a Grand-Duke of Muscovy—also would ally our
nation fast to France for eternity, and aid her instant murderous gov-
ernance in its pursuit of the endless Gallic effort to destroy the power of
England. My text of the Address excises these mischievous ideas."

(*Hamilton to Jay*): "The Great Man rejects our combined effort and
expresses a strong preference for that I originally drafted. You will not
require my assurance that I said and did nothing prompting toward this
preference, for I totally discredit the rumors to this effect and have

scourged from my ante-chamber those who sought to pour such poison into 'the porches of my ear' * * * I enclose the now-accepted text, with some examples of my revisions of passages the President said he had written himself but which exude to my nostrils something of the feral scent of T.J.'s political philosophy.

"(His) 'We should always cherish public credit, but not make it a fetish by using it as sparingly as possible.' (Mine) 'As a very important source of strength and security, cherish public credit. One method of preserving it is to use it as sparingly as possible.' (His) 'In the impenetrable future we may be obliged to interweave our destiny with some part or parts of Europe and be unable to steer clear of permanent alliances. Hence let us not foreclose our minds to a chance that the oceans and the air may yet be contracted by the ingenuity of Man.' (Mine) 'Why, by interweaving our destiny with any part of Europe, entangle our peace and prosperity in the toils of European ambition, rivalship, interest, humor or caprice. Our detached and distant situation invites and enables us to follow a different course.' "

(Jefferson to Madison): "What a flux of verbiage hath Hamilton emitted!"

But it is only fair to caution Senator Thurmond that the secret agents who, as usual, intercepted an Astigmatoff communication to the Politburo have no more doubt of its authenticity than this department has.

A SAD DAY FOR BOUNDLESS LOVE
May 30, 1962

Eros still aims his arrows from his pedestal in Piccadilly Circus, but in Alabama his bow has been broken forever. There, by the elimination of Representative Frank W. Boykin from Congress, ambition once again has proved itself "the only power that conquers love," as when the great Julius tore himself from Cleopatra's arms and voyaged back to Rome to mend his political fences and smash Pompey's.

Until Boykin ended in this week's Alabama Democratic primary as the low man among nine claimants for eight seats in the next Congress, he had been elected fourteen successive times on the slogan "everything is made for love." This slogan and Frank W. Boykin had become inseparable.

With this tender motto proclaimed as his lifetime guide, the member from the First Alabama nevertheless has managed to amass so large a store of worldly goods that once he was overheard to comment on the deduction that his wealth could be counted in millions with the amendment that he actually may be a "billionaire." This earnest of an acquisitive capacity, rarely won in the marts of Mammon by one consecrated to the spirit of brotherly (and sisterly) love, was made possible by many material activities, among them:

Manufacturer of railroad crossties. Enterprises in real estate, farming, livestock production, timber, lumber, naval stores and in politics. This last vocation he helped to make enduringly successful by inviting, to barbecues of bear and venison steaks, guests who at various times have consisted of all of Congress, public officials in charge of Federal financial handouts and the whole population of the First Alabama District.

When love seemed to the Representative to require a more solid expression than the mere devotional words he emits in divers tones on all occasions, there never was anything niggardly about the choice. It was Boykin, and Boykin alone, who amplified the news (apparently imparted to him from on high) that Commander Alan B. Shepard would be rewarded for his pioneer cosmic flight with a seat in heaven, by offering the Commander as a free gift what love's votary in Congress described as "a heaven on earth." This was a $25,000 house, with a swimming-pool and all the fixin's, in a new development at Waldorf, Md.

Cynics, who habitually question acts done in the name of pure altruism, were beastly enough to point out that Shepard's presence would give much-needed publicity to this housing project. And they noted that this publicity would accrue also to the benefit of a citizen who, before buying the land from the Representative, had served a prison term for mail and security frauds. Even when the member from Mobile explained that in trying to help this citizen he was only pursuing his dedication to prove that everything is made for love, and could not have been more surpirsed than to learn of this citizen's sojourn in stir, these cynics sneered anew. And the sadness that brought to the overflowing Boykin heart suffused both its ventricles, not to mention the aorta, when his suggestion that President Kennedy arrange to clear the offer to Shepard was ignored by the President, and when this and other acts of the Representative's compulsive generosity were used to pry him out of his seat in Congress.

So, as the poet recorded, thus "Love and sorrow both were born/On a showery summer morn" in the Alabama Democratic primary. And, come next session, the pleasingly corpulent, non-smoking, non-drinking, jolly Boykin, with a heart as big as Minnie the Moocher's but with millions or a billion in the bank just the same, will be absent from the chambers, the corridors and the House barbershop of the Capitol.

The scene will be quieter. But who would rather have quiet than a continuous and thunderous assurance of universal love? Some kind of a nut or something?

AN IMAGINARY
BUT NOT TOO FANCIFUL INTERVIEW
June 26, 1963

(The following interview with the grand master of President Kennedy's re-election strategy took place entirely, of course, in the realm of fancy):

Q. General—Do you mind being addressed as "General"?

A. Not at all. I have grown used to it in my job—it is a sort of "short title," as we lawyers say.

Q. Well then, General. It seems to me that you are getting ready to fell the Republicans in 1964 with an improved model of the old whipsaw that has cut 'em down before. I mean you will put the blame on them for the rejection or emasculation in Congress of the President's equal rights bill, and claim full credit for the Administration for whatever part of the bill survives.

A. You are correct. But if this is to be called a whipsaw, it is the implement of truth, for the enforcement of the greatest moral issue in American history—that there shall be no second-class citizens.

Q. I gather from statements made by the President, by you and by news analysts who have the privilege of daily exposure to the wonders of your thinking, that this will be a three-blade whipsaw. The third is a charge that the inside Republican strategy is to impress the G.O.P. upon the voters as "the white man's party," with the objective of solidifying the great racial majority behind its candidates of 1964.

A. Well, this charge will be self-creating, won't it, if the Republican attitude toward compulsory equal rights bill is as cool as it was at their leadership meeting last week in Denver, and if they don't give us the votes we need in Congress to get our legislation through? If the "party of Lincoln" acts that way, it will be our public duty to point it out in expounding the moral issue.

Q. General, haven't you been a little slow in fitting the teeth to that

moral issue? Won't people ask why Roosevelt never proposed an equal
rights bill, why Truman didn't fight for the one he proposed, how come
that Eisenhower's were the only ones enacted in half a century, and why
President Kennedy was in office more than two years before he got
around to legislating the 1960 platform he ran on?

A. Our answer will be that we look only forward, that to get the
country moving forward the timing has to be right, and that, so far as
Eisenhower is concerned, Lyndon Johnson was responsible for what was
passed by Congress.

Q. But, General, won't people remember that the Democrats were in
the majority in Congress at all these times, and that Lyndon Johnson
showed no pain when he cut Part III out of the Eisenhower bill to keep
it from being beaten by the votes of Democratic Senators?

A. Some may remember these purely incidental things. But you know
the old Alben Barkley story that ends, "What have you done for me
lately?" And that is what will influence the voters we need, the groups
that, when united, can carry the big states and therefore the Presidency.
We'll get them solidly for us on our new moral issue, and divide the
other groups on the political issues, as usual.

Q. But, General, isn't your strategy dependent on the choice of Goldwater by the Republicans? Suppose they pick Scranton or Romney?
And, since you have enough Democrats in the House to pass your equal
rights bill, and the exact number in the Senate needed to invoke closure,
how can you blame the Republicans for emasculation or defeat? And
how can you agree to let the Mrs. Murphys discriminate racially on
public accommodations in a bill founded on the concept that discrimination by anyone is an immorality which must be forbidden by law?

A. We'll solve those first two problems in due course. As for your
third question, there are many more Mrs. Murphys who vote than there
are Conrad Hiltons. . . . The Kennedys need at least four more years
in office to save the country, and to stay in office you've got to be practical.

THE NONPARTISAN NATURE
OF INFLUENCE PEDDLING
October 23, 1963

Of all the promises of political party platforms, the one most regularly
made and most seldom redeemed is to prevent influence peddling and
kindred violations of high official ethics. The Kennedy Administration,

like its immediate and earlier predecessors, learned this fact the hard way in several painful instances.

One was provided by the secretary of the Democratic Senate majority, Robert E. Baker, whose sideline business activities in getting Government space-contractors to install vending machines in which he was interested were so successful and lucrative that a Senate group is now reluctantly examining this miracle of salesmanship. The second instance was supplied by Navy Secretary Fred Korth. His benevolent interest in the prosperity of the Fort Worth bank he left (and plans to rejoin) impelled him to offer, on Navy stationery, to help it land rich new depositors by giving them cruises down the Potomac in his official vessel, the Sequoia, in company with persons whose names would impress the folks back home.

It may be contended that there is no factor of influence peddling in the solicitation by a Cabinet officer of representatives of corporations doing business with the Government to buy tickets to a testimonial dinner for a Senator whose re-election the Administration greatly desires. But to Representative Oliver Bolton of Ohio, who today attributed that action to Secretary of Labor Wirtz, the factor is strongly present. Though this kind of bite on business is old stuff in Washington, a great many will agree with Bolton.

On Wirtz's behalf it was said today that he sees nothing unethical in lending his name to a shakedown of lobbyists who otherwise would be most unlikely to feel the urge to feed Senator Williams of New Jersey lavishly, and his re-election aspiration at the same time. This attitude by Wirtz differs so flatly from that of Secretary of the Interior Udall in somewhat comparable circumstances a year or so ago as to suggest a growing ethical insensitiveness in the Kennedy Administration. Udall, after seeing a copy of a shakedown letter to the oil industry in which a lobbyist cited the Secretary as a sponsor, unwisely did nothing about it. But when the letter was made public, Udall penitently conceded he had allowed himself to appear in the role of an influence peddler.

In the Democratic platform of 1960, the conventional pledge appeared in these familiar words: "The Democratic Administration will establish and enforce a Code of Ethics to maintain the full dignity and integrity of the Federal service. . . ." And, with several ethical lapses during the Eisenhower Administration in mind—particularly the letters on Air Force stationery, and the phone calls from his office, in which Secretary Talbott tried to get customers for a business that, like the bank from which Korth retired to enter Government and to which he arranged to return, he was financially interested in—the Los Angeles platform piously continued:

We have drifted into a national mood that accepts payola and quiz scandals, tax evasion and false expense accounts, soaring crime rates [and] influence-peddling in high Government circles. . . . The new Democratic administration will help create a sense of national purpose. . . .

This "new Democratic administration" did not end the "quiz scandals"; that was a belated act of self-preservation by a scared industry. It has really cracked down as promised on "tax evasion and false expense accounts." And its only share of blame for "soaring crime rates" is contributed by the leniency of Democratic law officers toward juvenile urban criminals among groups affiliated with their party at the polls.

But three of the recent incidents involving Democratic "influence peddling" demonstrate not only that its urge is nonpartisan, but that the Administration "enforced" the 1960 platform pledge only in the case of Korth. A Republican, Senator Williams of Delaware, pushed the Baker case to the stage of Senate inquiry. And there is no sign as yet that the President does not agree with his Secretary of Labor about the ethics of his role in the solicitation of lobbyists to finance a testimonial dinner— in the political interest of the Administration.

FOREIGN AFFAIRS

NATIONAL DEBATE OVER CASTRO
May 10, 1961

The mounting criticisms abroad and at home of the part played by the United States Government in the invasion of Cuba by foes of its para-Communist regime have initiated what could become an adversary proceeding from which this regime and its aims would be the principal beneficiaries. Before that result becomes more of a probability, a review of the major criticisms and their basis is in order.

The charges that President Kennedy was badly informed by the Central Intelligence Agency of the prospect of a popular anti-Castro uprising, and that the C.I.A.'s operation of the venture and the favorable military judgment given the President by the Joint Chiefs of Staff were deeply at fault—these criticisms have been well established. So much so that the President himself does not dispute them, but also has assumed the blame for the final decision to take so great a risk half-heartedly. With respect to other accusations now being made, however, there are some balancing, and some refuting, factors in the record. Among these charges are:

1. The United States is under moral obloquy in the world for violating its Bogotá Treaty with other states in the Americas, specifically Article 15 of the 1948 O.A.S. Charter. The commitment of this article was that "no state or group of states has the right to intervene, directly or indirectly, for any reason whatsoever, in the internal or external

affairs of any other state, [not only with] armed force, but also any other form of interference or attempted threat * * * ."

2. The policy of this Government (in the language of a full-page advertisement published in this newspaper today and signed by a number of prominent Americans, including a great many Harvard professors) "for at least a year has been that we must crush Castro." Instead, our policy should have been "the use of our enormous economic power * * * to further Cuban democracy," and should now become an augmented effort to "detach the Castro regime from the Communist bloc by working for a diplomatic entente and a resumption of trade relations."

3. The President's "threat to impose our will in the Caribbean, whatever the wishes of the other American states [quotations from the same advertisement], has created widespread suspicion that the United States will reorient its foreign policy in the direction of Soviet-style power politics."

4. Also according to this manifesto, it was our unmistakable "determination to isolate Cuba" that "made the Soviet bloc" Castro's only source of "military and economic support."

The factual weakness of this indictment is that it begins the story of United States relations with Castro in the middle, not at the beginning. The "determination to isolate Cuba" arose after Castro had founded his policy on arousing popular hostility to the United States. Behind the shield of this agitation Castro, from the very start of his regime, engaged in all kinds of economic aggression against United States interests; made it a merit for Cubans to buy from other nations; and accepted aid from outside the American continent for purposes clearly in violation of the Resolution of Caracas (1954). He had set up an iron dictatorship, and a police state apparatus never before seen in this hemisphere that by now has jailed at least 50,000 Cubans as political prisoners. And this dictatorship and police state apparatus Castro effected and has enforced with arms obtained from the Soviet nations.

It is a fact that, by training, equipping and transporting the anti-Castro rebels, the United States violated (1) Article 15 and perhaps to a degree (2) the Caracas Resolution requirement of prior consultation. But Castro's acts, only a few of which are enumerated above, pose the open threat of the establishment in this hemisphere not only of a Moscow-directed state, but one affiliated for the first time in our history with a world system dedicated to the overthrow of Western free institutions. And that threat invoked a superior obligation of the United States. That is to preserve from violation, and consequent inevitable corrosion, the principle of the Monroe Doctrine. Though now a Pan-American commitment, it has remained the basic foreign policy of the United States —to be applied unilaterally when there is a clear risk it will not be enforced otherwise.

In a national debate over Cuba, consideration of these items also is material to popular judgment of the issues.

KENNEDY'S JUDGMENT ON CUBA QUESTIONED
May 27, 1961

Seldom if ever, and certainly never as early in an Administration, has the soundness of a President's judgment in matters of foreign policy, and twice in rapid succession, become a hot controversial issue. Yet this has been the experience of President Kennedy, growing out of (1) his approval of an invasion of Cuba by anti-Castro forces under United States supervision; and (2) his sponsorship of an American citizens' committee to finance the swap proposed by Castro of 500 tractors for the prisoners captured in the invasion.

Though the President's decisions in both instances have been attributed to faulty information and counsel from advisers, this has not lessened the concern manifested in Congress and its constituencies over Mr. Kennedy's quality of judgment. And many of those in Congress, including Democrats personally devoted to him, who argue that no President can be expected to possess a sixth sense to warn him against projects overwhelmingly recommended by trusted aides, seem to think he should replace them.

In this view the replacement should include the Joint Chiefs of Staff at the latest when their terms expire—the director and other policy-making officers of the Central Intelligence Agency, and several of the young and enormously self-confident college teachers to whom the President has assigned administrative and policy-making powers on the top level of Government. Among the latter the names of McGeorge Bundy, Walt Rostow, Arthur Schlesinger Jr., and Richard N. Goodwin most often are mentioned. Though Professor Schlesinger seems to have been unique in the President's inner circle in opposing the Cuban invasion project, he and Goodwin are credited with persuading the President, and thus implicitly the United States Government, to become a principal in the prisoner-tractor swap which was cynically and almost casually proposed by Castro.

The President's decision to sponsor the swap has many stout defenders, in contrast with his approval of the Cuban invasion program that was equipped and directed by the United States Government. It is being contended on Mr. Kennedy's behalf that he merely responded to the prompting of the highest moral and humanitarian impulses when he took measures to provide for the effective organization and leadership of an effort to free prisoners for whose plight his official act was responsible. In that opinion also, this response has had the very useful effect of impressing on other peoples of Latin America the brutal cynicism and barbarity of Castro (not the less so if the offer struck him as a good joke at the expense of the United States Government) in contrast with the deep humanitarian instinct of the American President and people.

This evalution may ultimately prevail, especially if the fund for the tractors is raised, the regulations obstructing their delivery to Castro are removed, and Castro then welches on his offer. Currently, however, both the project and the President's intervention to promote it are under intense critical fire. Members of Congress report that their correspondence is heavy with protests against what the writers term "surrender to Castro's blackmail." And the correspondence strongly supports another criticism which has been widely expressed at the Capitol. This is, that to accept Castro's proposal will establish the blackmail principle as a United States policy which other dictators and assorted tyrants can invoke as official sanction of comparable proposals.

The President's intervention to collect and pay the ransom was a positive action. Observing (or more likely having been so informed by the advisers who generated the idea) that the native American "dogood" impulse was creating many fund-raising groups where one was indicated for effectiveness, he moved to consolidate the effort. He personally telephoned Mrs. Franklin D. Roosevelt and Walter Reuther a request that they take over, added Dr. Milton Eisenhower for politically-neutralizing purposes, and on the suggestion of one of these asked Joseph M. Dodge of Detroit to act as treasurer. But, disposing of points raised in the apparently very brief period he gave for consideration of the idea, the President also expressed the definite opinion that the contribution would be ruled tax-exempt, and assured the group it could proceed without fear of being held by the Administration to have infringed the Logan Act (forbidding negotiations with foreign nations by private persons).

Because the President served fourteen years in Congress, having been a member of both branches, his personal assurance of tax exemption particularly disturbed the legislators. They felt that his experience, at least, should have told him to consult the fiscal committees of Congress on the legality of this ruling before he gave it. And it seemed to many also that his failure to do so marked a defect of judgment.

So in two incidents, each with an important bearing on world opinion toward the United States, President Kennedy's judgment and his choice of advisers have come into open question. In some quarters this question has gone to the point of anxiety over the play of these elements in his forthcoming meetings with DeGaulle and Khrushchev.

That concern is not general. But its early arrival in the life of the Administration, and the circumstance that the incidents which engendered it came in such rapid succession, make this apprehension unusual in the annals of American politics.

TRUCE WITH THE BEAR IN CUBA
October 29, 1962

Unity between the American people and the President of the United States over a Government policy in a critical time has never in our history been manifested more clearly than in the public response to Mr. Kennedy's moves to disperse the threat to national security created by the offensive Soviet military build-up in Cuba. And by the same token this unity extends to the President's cautious evaluation of the Soviet backdown as merely "So far, so good."

But on that limited appraisal, which a long postwar record of broken agreements by Bolshevist Russia has taught this nation in the 20th century and other nations learned in prior dealings with Czarist Russia, President Kennedy should in consistency have maintained full surveillance by sea and air of the pledged dismantling of the offensive missile installations in Cuba.

Pravda today quoted a "Soviet worker" as saying: "Let nobody take our peacefulness as a sign of weakness." It is more to the point that, by all tangible evidence, neither does the President nor the American public take the Kremlin's promised retreat from Cuba as tantamount on its face to a sign of sincere and new resolve to remove the world tensions which long have been the designed product of Soviet foreign policy.

All that has occurred thus far seems superficially to have been a simple chain reaction from a miscalculation by the Kremlin. This miscalculation apparently was that the Government of the United States would indefinitely continue the policies of delay and concession whenever and wherever the U.S.S.R incited a situation that posed a risk of world nuclear war if forcefully opposed. Such an error of judgment could have been induced, for instance, by this Government's promotion of a surrender of Dutch West New Guinea to Sukarno's militant blackmail on the official explanation, which became a Washington routine, that this was necessary to "prevent a warlike confrontation of the great powers."

Miscalculation could also have been fostered by this Government's policy of allowing its international positions to be importantly shaped by considerations of "world opinion" (an imaginary element it equates with the voices of a majority in the heterogeneous Assembly of the United Nations). Probably the multitude of postwar treaty strings with which the United States bound itself to act in concert with allies was also relied on by Premier Khrushchev to "sickly over" this nation's action in crises with, as Hamlet said, the "pale cast of thought."

But miscalculation alone cannot be accepted as the sole factor when these plain facts are considered: that (1) Cuba is within the geographical center of the United States' sphere of security interest; (2) the effectiveness in reconnaissance of its cameraxlin planes is well known to the Kremlin, (3) and hence the presence of an offensive missile build-up in Cuba could not be concealed up to a trigger-ready stage. Therefore, the President's restrictive judgment of the "peaceful" portents of the U.S.S.R.'s retreat from its reckless military adventure in Cuba is statesmanship as strong and wise as his decision to dismantle the installations and their weapons by any force required. But not for months, maybe for years, will the actual purposes and reasoning of what appears to have been the Kremlin's gross, face-losing blunder be soundly established.

However, even if Premier Khrushchev's retreat from his offensive missile armament of Cuba shall eventully prove reparable in matters more substantial than loss of face, it may be that he risked the latter to the extent he did because of reliance on faulty intelligence. Perhaps he was twice surprised by the American people: first, when they brought heavy pressure on the Administration to act in advance of the action that was taken; second, when they so coldly received the proposal of Presiding Bishop Lichtenberger of the Episcopal Church that President

Kennedy repay Turkey's faithful and courageous alliance with a trade of its security for our own. Perhaps, also, Premier Khrushchev depended on the United States record of U.N. "cooperation" to assume that the President would swallow U Thant's proposal that he remove our Cuban blockade and allow the U.S.S.R. to keep its offensive missile establishment on the island pending the outcome of another Kennedy-Khrushchev "talk."

YOU CAN'T KEEP A GOOD SPY DOWN
November 26, 1962

In the glittering and fur-bearing published list of those attending U Thant's dinner in New York City tonight for the United States and U.S.S.R. negotiators of the Cuban crisis one name of vast significance was missing. That is not because there was any intent to deceive on the part of the host or his guests. It is because nobody knew the intruder was there.

How could the security agents responsible for the complete privacy of this momentous dinner conversation have been expected to penetrate the disguise of the celebrated spy who, during his long span of activities in the United States, has made a unique record? Unique in that, though every report he has written has been intercepted by United States intelligence units, the Great Informer himself has continuously eluded capture by changing identities the moment one report was completed and another begun. For instance, when the F.B.I. was hot on the trail of the elderly office boy in the latest series of law firms to which John J. McCloy at various times has belonged, the elderly office boy had transformed himself into one of the Nubian slaves who come on in "Aïda" at the Metropolitan.

Perhaps any regular readers of this department there may be will immediately realize from the above that it can describe only one secret agent, Astigmatoff. And in the subjoined extracts from his report of conversations he said he heard at Thant's dinner tonight—where he claims to have impersonated a framed Picasso on the west wall of the salon—

an old mystery about Astigmatoff recurs: since every report he had made to the Kremlin has been intercepted (many were published here), is his real mission to mislead the United States Government into the dangerous delusion that all Soviet spies are *duraks* (that is to say, schlemiels)? Or is this maybe true?

Whichever the fact, the following is the first section of Astigmatoff's report of the Thant dinner, dropped from the Picasso onto a bear-rug that was in fact one of the Cuban experts of the C.I.A.:

"(*Yost to Mikoyan*) Was the climate nice in Cuba during your stay?"

"(*Interpreter Gerebcov to Mikoyan*): He seems just to be asking whether the climate was nice in Cuba during your visit, which maybe with Stevenson or McCloy would only mean what it seems to mean. But this is a pretty smooth baby, boss, and we had best be careful. How about answering that the climate there was pretty hot for some people?"

"(*Mikoyan to Gerebcov*): But that is a bourgeois joke, a kind of pun. It could mean war. If this Yost is as sharp as you say—how did he get on the delegation, anyhow?—he will suspect this. We must hurry, because I see Kuznetsov looking at his watch, and the Politburo is monitoring it. So just say I said, in the words of the old Russian proverb, 'Heat and cold are relative unless you are thinking of your mother-in-law.'

"By the time Gerebcov made this reply, Yost had forgotten his question. But it was clear that the word 'mother-in-law' alarmed McCloy, Stevenson, Thant and U.N. military adviser Brig. Indar Jit Rikhy. I do not think Mikoyan handled this very well. One of your own old Russian proverbs would have been perfect, 'When it is hot on the hill it is cool in the valley.'

"The conversation then took a serious turn, and Mikoyan did better. The host quoted an old Burmese proverb, 'One dreams when one is awake.' Stevenson and McCloy menacingly quoted two old American proverbs, 'Don't take any wooden nickels' and 'The bigger they come the harder they fall.' Loutfi quoted an old Egyptian proverb, 'He who builds on another's land brings up another's child.'

"So far, as Your Excellency can see, the dinner is being fraught with great significance. But my assistant, Serge the bear-rug, is signaling me for copy. More to come. *Astigmatoff*."

As we go to press this meaningful document is being analyzed by the Department of State and the C.I.A.

LAST DRIPPINGS
FROM THE GREAT CERTIFIED "LEAK"
December 6, 1962

Probably it was just luck, but maybe it was that sixth sense called "a nose for the news," which was responsible for the unplanned encounter of this department today with one of the many reporters who were given a fill-in of the secret discussions among the nine top security officials of how the recent Cuban crisis should be dealt with by President Kennedy. But, whatever the reason, this colleague generously supplied these extracts from the transcript of who said what:

(*McG. B.*) "Let's run all the ideas up the flagpole and see who salutes. What we need is a spell-out, everything-wise, and expertise, definitize, maximize and optimize escalation-wise until we finalize. In other words, let's put the ideas on the train and watch which one gets off at Westport."

(*T. S—n.*) "You mean toss it in the well and see what kinda splash it makes; follow it into the high grass and see if it eats; get things down to where the rubber meets the road. Remember, what the job will be and when it will be done is still a row of apple trees away."

(*McN.*) "So right! Let's be sure we have plenty of options and be certain there will be no overkill. And then, I think, after these options are mirror clear, and to pursue this further would be counter-productive, we can melt this ball of wax and move the hardware from the shelf. Suppose I start batting up the fungoes. How's about this opener—a kind of gradual naval blockade in the Caribbean, just the Honey Fitz and the Marlin at first, and wait for the Schmerdovolsk to heave in sight——"

(*Himself.*) "The word is 'hove.' "

(*McN.*) "Okay, hove. Now you well may ask, what do we do then? Of course, our vessels will have Russian-speaking skippers. I repeat, what will we do then?"

(*McC.*) "I thought *you* were going to tell *us*. But, interimwise, let me feed this one into the computer. While the Schmerdovolsk, with (according to our latest intelligence) a cargo of seven Kropotkin IRBM's is getting within bow-shot of the Honey Fitz and the Marlin, Castro (also according to our latest intelligence) will be in the barbershop of the Nacional having his whiskers curled. While he is entangled with the curlers, we'll launch an air-strike on the factories that make his cigars. I predict this will cause utter demoralization of the regime; news of this situation will be passed by radio to the Schmerdovolsk; she will turn back; and the Honey Fitz and the Marlin can return to their stations, mission accomplished."

(*D.D.*) "Sounds inexpensive. I'm for that."

(*A.E.S.*) "No, John and Doug, we gotta negotiate first. I'll negotiate with Kusnetsov. Norstad can negotiate with the Warsaw powers, our bases for theirs. Dean (I mean the one that doesn't get up every day breathing fire through his mustache) can negotiate with the O.A.S. And if all this doesn't come to much, we can negotiate a swap of Ft. Knox for the offensive Soviet weaponry in Cuba."

(*Voices.*) "He wants a Munich" . . . "That soft stuff again" . . . "Boss, we're eyeball to eyeball with you-know-who, and I think the other fellow just blinked" . . . "If they get away with this one we'll be a paper tiger, a second-class power."

(*R.F.K.*) "Now, don't lets us get divided into hoves and dawks . . . . No, I am *not* lugging in Brumus again; I said 'Dawks.' . . . My brother will never be a party to a Pearl Harbor, will you, sir? But we may all be fighting for our lives in two weeks, according to how hairy it is, as Larry always says."

(*Himself.*) "Whichever way the decision goes, those who are against it will be the lucky ones. I don't want the Honey Fitz or the Marlin to intercept a single Russian ship until absolutely necessary. Send that order in the clear. Now all we have to decide is the definition of 'absolutely necessary.' But, as someone just said—oh, it was my brother— we're all agreed, or anyhow we better be, that if the Russians are ready to go to nuclear war, we might as well have the showdown now as six months later . . . Any questions? [After a show of one hand] I'll get back to you later."

According to this authoritative fill-in, the only possible inaccuracy in the above is that this last remark could have been "I'll get *at* you later."

STRONG WORDS AND FIRM ACTIONS
July 26, 1961

The speed with which President Kennedy projected his verbal promises last night of a military build-up into a detailed legislative program for Congress today, and the speed with which Congress is operating its machinery to produce this program, could furnish a more effective deterrent to nuclear war than any since Soviet Russia broke the West's monopoly of atomic weaponry.

For unless Premier Khrushchev believes that a surprise nuclear attack by the Communist forces can paralyze the power of the Western allies to retaliate in kind, the swift, stern combination of words and deeds in Washington has made certain one prospect of militant resistance he may have doubted. This prospect, as Mr. Kennedy expressed it last night, is "We cannot and will not permit the Communists to drive us out of Berlin—either gradually or by force."

Premier Khrushchev, therefore, must now in good faith join the Western allies in exploring even the most remote possibilities of negotiating the West Berlin dispute he has provoked, or he must take a gamble far greater in its threat to his own people as well as to others than Wilhelm II and Hitler took and lost. Among the promptings of such a gamble, in addition to his acceptance of Soviet military reliance on the theory of a quick victory accomplished by surprise nuclear attack, would be these:

An East-West war over Berlin can be limited to being fought with conventional weapons, with Soviet victory assured by easier access to greater combat manpower; the NATO alliance will disintegrate in the actual confrontation of war, or there is a fundamental defect in the Premier's own mentality (of which there have been no signs so far) which causes him to reject even this week's demonstration by the President and Congress that the United States will not retreat from its rights and commitments in Berlin.

In his speech last night the President, on the excellent principle that space for maneuvering should always be left to the party who has gone to extremes, offered this room to Premier Khrushchev. "We recognize," he said, "the Soviet Union's historical concern about their security in Central and Eastern Europe after a series of ravaging invasions." And he suggested that "arrangements * * * to meet those concerns" are possible, so that "both freedom and security" can be brought to this troubled area. One such arrangement would be the exchange of an allied-controlled corridor from West Berlin to West Germany for a permanent Polish-German boundary on the Oder-Neisse Line.

This was drawn at Yalta and confirmed at Potsdam. It added to Poland—as compensation for war sufferings and Soviet land grabs— former German territory, in which about seven million Poles have now established their homes. West Germany has repeatedly declared the line is provisional; so have the United States and Great Britain; and West Germany's position also is that the problem of German unification cannot be settled without rectification of the line. But the Soviet Union has treated it as permanent, an essential protection of the Communist nations from an upsurge of German militarism. And the puppet East German Government has signed an agreement with the satellite Government of Poland accepting the line as the final Polish-German border.

The allied position is certainly negotiable, since unification is not visible in the foreseeable future. Even General de Gaulle, after meeting with Chancellor Adenauer in 1959, in endorsing unification as "the destiny of the German people" added the powerful reservation that "they do not call into question their present frontiers."

Any search for negotiable factors, however, will have to be a long one. And it will be under heavier burdens of the rearmament forced by Soviet policy on the American people than the President prepared them for last night. Such as the choice he probably must make between (1) ruinous inflation and (2) more taxes, economic controls and rigid cuts in non-military spending.

HOT COPY FOR IZVESTIA
November 22, 1961

Presidents of the United States in the past have included foreign press correspondents in the very few exclusive interviews they have given, and these rare journalistic items have been published in full and generally reprinted. One of the handful was the famous interview of Woodrow Wilson by George Adam, Paris correspondent of The Times of London, soon after the President arrived in France for the Allied summit peace conference after World War I.

But the forthcoming interview President Kennedy has granted to the editor of Izvestia is unique in the short series for these reasons: The Moscow newspaper is an arm of a government, and one whose relations with the United States are strained. Its editor, like the rest of the staff, is a Government employe and subject to totalitarian official controls. And in the case of Izvestia this official control is the shortest and surest of any such chain of command because the editor, Aleksei I. Adzhubei, is the son-in-law of the controller in chief, Premier Khrushchev.

Yet these very circumstances impose an obligation on the Government of the Soviet Union to publish the whole of the interview, although a consequence may be to apprise the Russian people of events in United States–Soviet relations that have been withheld from them or officially distorted. It is true that the meanings in English of many words have no precise Russian equivalents in even the most meticulous translation; and that many English words and phrases which have precise equivalents express entirely different political concepts: for examples, "freedom," "democracy," "peaceful coexistence," "a free press."

But President Kennedy is very much aware of these linguistic obstacles. The evidence is his remark at a news conference that the first requirement in exploring the prospects of constructive negotiation of East-West differences is to "see if we can get a more precise definition of the phrases and words and thoughts which the Soviet Union has expressed in the matter of Berlin, Germany and Central Europe." He can be relied on in his conversation with editor Adzhubei to make his own definitions clear in the context of Russian readers of the whole interview. Consequently, assuming that the questions from Izvestia will be pertinent to the conflict between East-West international policies, the product of the interview will justify Mr. Kennedy's decision to make probably the first Presidential use of Government-controlled journalism as the vehicle of a major public information medium developed by the free press.

Viewed from any aspect, this is a bold venture into democratic practice by Izvestia, which is to say, the Kremlin. For there can be no question that the approval of highest authority was necessary before the project could be undertaken and the preliminaries of feeling out the attitude of the White House begun. And, since the risks to Soviet anti-American propaganda and Moscow's selective public informational method were plainly visible, it is certain that these were fully reviewed, and the questions to be asked of the President most carefully processed, before the go-ahead signal was given to Adzhubei. But Premier Khrushchev is a bold man, and his son-in-law gives the same impression. On the other hand, the interview presents Mr. Kennedy with an opportunity he and press secretary Salinger were prompt to see and the President is wholly capable of exploiting.

While the White House in this instance has agreed to an exclusive Presidential interview which has no precedent because of the governmental status of the journalistic medium and the interviewer, the action conforms to an informational policy Mr. Kennedy has greatly expanded from that of his predecessors. Press requests for legitimate information that used to stop at the desks of subordinates are being fielded to the President in greater numbers than previously when he alone can supply authoritative answers and the news conference channel is not shortly available. And Mr. Kennedy's evaluation of the merit of such questions is fair and even generous.

In further conformity to this policy the President has given occasional exclusive interviews to British, French and United States representatives of press and radio-television—a past practice so rare that each use of it was an important event in journalism. But for the reasons stated the Izvestia interview can become that.

HOPE IN THE CONGO
January 17, 1962

The Administration is cautiously organizing a case on which to claim a triumph in the Congo of the United Nations policy of sustaining its mandates by armed force that the United States Government first opposed, then "reluctantly" endorsed and finally rescued from disaster by financial contributions and an internal airlift.

The caution is prudent because the actions of Congolese politicians and of the troops of the central Government are unpredictable from day to day. This volatile quality has just been emphasized by the delayed report of the beatings and murder of a group of Catholic missionaries at Kongolo by troops which, despite the central Government's description of them as partisans of the deposed pro-Communist provincial leader, Antoine Gizenga, nevertheless were one of its detachments.

Since the common objective of the United States and the Acting Secretary General of the U.N. is to restore peace and order, and establish a stable non-Communist government in the Congo, all signs of progress toward these goals are highly desirable. But the U.N.-U.S. record of Congo policies and methods will make it very difficult for the Administration to establish its claim of sound, consistent, long-range statesmanship.

This estimate is about to receive the powerful political and publicity assistance of Chairman Gore of the Senate inquiry subcommittee who, though he can be depended on to give a fair hearing to its critics, approves the U.S.-U.N. procedure. But no service to political interest or publicity power can erase from the record a number of events which badly damage the case being organized to prove that the Administration was right all along in act and in foresight. Some of these occurred in the United Nations during November, 1961.

In the early part of that month United Nations forces, which had been dispatched to Katanga to bombard President Tshombe into line with the central Leopoldville regime, were routed by Tshombe's army. In this setback the U.N. saw a threat to the regime, which incidentally had been formed by an alliance with the pro-Communist Lumumba (since deceased) on his condition that Katanga be reunified with the rest of the former Belgian Congo by military force. On the same day Leopoldville ordered Lumumba's provincial successor, Gizenga, to return to the capital within three days, which order was followed by a rampage of the Government troops at Albertville, the massacre of a U.N. Italian contingent, and a pro-Gizenga mutiny at Kindu in favor of the separatist Gizenga government.

As the U.N. in New York prepared to consider resolutions—including proposals by the United States and by a Ceylon-Liberia-United Arab Republic trio—to deal with the situation, Adlai E. Stevenson, the American chief delegate, stated that Gizenga rebels were "much more defiant and dangerous" than the Katangan, and created "a situation of no less gravity, perhaps in the long run even greater gravity," than that in Katanga. By Nov. 16 Stevenson had entrenched this official United States position so deeply that the press generally forecast we would either abstain on the vote for the trio resolution, which authorized combat sanctions against Tshombe only, or oppose it.

Stevenson maintained his fundamental objection to this unilateral thrust of Congo military sanctions until the Security Council delegate of the Soviet Union had vetoed our corrective amendments of the proposal. Then, after a twenty-minute recess for consultation with Washington, he voted—"reluctantly," he explained—for the resolution which he had characterized as ignoring a threat in the Congo "much more dangerous" than Tshombe's resistance (which is now being politically negotiated) to the total subordination of Katanga to the Leopoldville Government.

The fall of Gizenga controverts, temporarily at any rate, our official judgment of Nov. 24, 1961, that his rebellion carried even graver potentials than that of Tshombe. But this tentative demonstration is cited by the State Department as proof of a U.N.-U.S. policy founded in flawless foresight. That is only one of several weaknesses in the claim. The record abounds in others, which are readily susceptible of development in the Senate subcommittee hearing.

SANCTIONING AGGRESSION
IN THE PACIFIC
August 16, 1962

The expulsion of the Netherlands as administrator of West New Guinea, and its replacement by the Government of Indonesia, is the latest of the triumphs of the threat of armed force as a means of territorial aggression. And in this particular instance it was the United States which supplied the pressures by which this triumph was attained.

The explanations offered, on and off the record, by officials here is that, if the Dutch had longer resisted Sukarno's ambition, he would have carried out his threat to attain it by military measures, and there would have been war in the Pacific. And, the explanation continues, the only way to avert this dangerous prospect was to let the Dutch know in advance that the United States would close the channels through which their forces in that distant area would have to be supplied; and that also it had obtained pledges from the British to follow the same policy. This perforce immobilized Australia, which administers the remainder of New Guinea, from lending any assistance to an armed stand by the Netherlands against the Indonesian aggressor.

But this explanation serves to emphasize that it was the threat of military aggression against another nation's territory, to which in this instance the aggressor has neither an ethnic nor historical claim, that was the means by which the threat accomplished its purpose. And in congratulating themselves on what the State Department hailed today as "the resolution of the West New Guinea dispute through peaceful negotiations," the U.N. was celebrating a member's violation of the U.N. Charter, and the department the abandonment of a policy which the U.S. has long proclaimed.

(1) The signatories to the U.N. Charter, of which Indonesia is one, pledge themselves to "refrain . . . from the threat or use of force against the territorial integrity . . . of any state." In threatening to occupy the Netherlands' territory of West New Guinea by force unless the Dutch ceded its administration to Indonesia, and in landing troops there while the above-styled "peaceful negotiations" were in process, Sukarno fractured this pledge in several places. (2) Refusal to abet external aggression or to give official recognition to its success have been the historic policies of the United States which the Kennedy Administration has often reiterated. But in forcing the Dutch capitulation to Sukarno, the United States laid this policy on the shelf.

To those who feel that the threat of an aggressor to go to war is sufficient cause for the United States to abandon this historic policy, and even assist him to gain his objective, this justification by the Government of its courses in the Dutch-Indonesian dispute will be sufficient. But the longer this reasoning controls the foreign policy of the United States, the weaker will be its influence in preserving the peace of the world which is the proclaimed goal of all its international activities. And the oftener the United States brings pressure on its friends and allies to surrender to such aggression as Sukarno's, the feebler will be the alliances with free world nations that are the foundations of United States security. Moreover, history offers overwhelming proof that aggression cannot be successfully compromised; that compromise leads inevitably to larger wars than those it is relied on to avert.

At the U.N. yesterday, negotiators were felicitating one another on the "peaceful" outcome in West New Guinea, and were thanking the United States Government and the Acting Secretary General of the U.N. for a result in which both abjured their sworn principles. But last night the Premier of the Netherlands dispelled this artificial atmosphere with a blast of the truth. Holland, he said, "could not count on the support of it allies, and for that reason we had to sign" the capitulation to the aggressor. And the UPI dispatch which carried this quotation reported that the Dutch Government feels bitterly disappointed at the strong-arm activities of the United States, which accomplished the humiliation of one of its stanchest allies in the world contest with militant communism.

Also, how many believe that, after Sukarno has administered West New Guinea for seven years, the promised U.N. plebiscite will bring independence to the Papuan natives, even assuming they still will have the courage to vote for it?

KENNEDY'S FORESIGHT AT AP BAC
January 7, 1963

There is a special reason why the lack of will to fight for their own independence that the Vietnamese troops displayed at the battle of Ap Bac a few days ago merits fundamental Administration review of its current policy of military aid in South Vietnam. That special reason is found in a citation of conditions in which such a policy is "doomed to failure" that President Kennedy made April 6, 1954, to the Senate of which he then was a member.

"I am frankly of the belief," he said, "that no amount of American military assistance in Indochina (South Vietnam is now a separate state therein) can conquer an enemy which is everywhere, and at the same time, nowhere, 'an enemy of the people' which has the sympathy and covert support of the people."

Mr. Kennedy believed then, as did former Representative Judd of Minnesota (whom he approvingly quoted), that "only for such a cause as their own freedom" would the Indochinese "make the heroic effort necessary to win this kind of struggle." And the Senator urged France to grant this freedom as a *sina qua non* of this "historic effort."

South Vietnam, as one of the four areas into which Indochina has divided, has enjoyed this freedom in the sense Mr. Kennedy and Mr. Judd used the term in 1954. Its people have rejected, for a Western type of semi-dictatorship, the Chinese Communist export type of government that dominates their North Vietnam neighbors and former fellow-countrymen.

But for some years the population, and lately the armed forces, of South Vietnam have failed to show willingness to make the "heroic effort" necessary to maintain their independence against the spread of

Communism in Southeast Asia. And their latest indication of this, at Ap Bac, confronts President Kennedy with the 1954 thesis of Senator Kennedy. It was, specifically, that "no amount of American military assistance" can preserve independence for a people "who are not willing to die for it." And generally the thesis was that U.S. military involvement on the Asian mainland in any degree was a most dubious policy.

At Ap Bac last week, our Jan. 6 dispatch from Saigon reported, "attacking South Vietnamese troops were badly beaten by Communist guerrillas. At several crucial moments during the battle . . . with reinforcements on the way, and the eastern flank open, the Americans pleaded for reinforcements to come in on the east to close a ring around the Vietcong. But Vietnamese, at a high level, disregarded this, refused to take or attack certain positions, reinforced on the west, and gave the (outnumbered) Vietcong an escape route."

These circumstances not only expose our military assistance policy to very serious question, they also strongly suggest the existence in South Vietnam of the very situation that led Senator Kennedy in 1954 to foresee as "doomed to failure" the policy he as President is pursuing in 1963. And among their consequences was the killing, wounding and capture of American members of the armed forces—probably not 375 as the North Vietnamese claim, but more than the 30 casualties our official sources concede.

It will be very difficult for the President to find an alternative to the U.S. policy that has proved ineffectual, and trends to deeper and deeper military involvement in Southeast Asia. This policy is the product of starry-eyed diplomacy and even more ingenuous commitments, all with the congenital weakness which in 1954 Senator Kennedy diagnosed as fatal when it appears.

His Administration took the venture of a sensible alternative to the previous Administration's attempt to make Laos a firmly allied pro-Western nation. No important new threat to our security has resulted. But there would be heavy political and popular resistance to repeat this Laos policy in South Vietnam, because the plausible "domino theory" still is widely accepted in this country. And this, despite the fact that whenever Communist China gets nuclear weapons, most of Southeast Asia will turn its face to Peking.

This venture in South Vietnam, however, may have to be taken by the President. And in more difficult circumstances than he foresaw in 1954, or could have foreseen.

INTRA-ADMINISTRATION WAR
IN VIETNAM
October 2, 1963

The Central Intelligence Agency is getting a very bad press in dispatches from Vietnam to American newspapers and in articles originating in Washington. Like the Supreme Court when under fire, the C.I.A. cannot defend itself in public retorts to criticisms of its activities as they occur. But, unlike the Supreme Court, the C.I.A. has no open record of its activities on which the public can base a judgment of the validity of the criticisms. Also, the agency is precluded from using the indirect defensive tactic which is constantly employed by all other government units under critical fire.

This tactic is to give information to the press, under a seal of confidence, that challenges or refutes the critics. But the C.I.A. cannot father such inspired articles, because to do so would require some disclosure of its activities. And not only does the effectiveness of the agency depend on the secrecy of its operations. Every President since the C.I.A. was created has protected this secrecy from claimants—Congress or the public through the press, for examples—of the right to share any part of it.

This Presidential policy has not, however, always restrained other executive units from going confidentially to the press with attacks on C.I.A. operations in their common field of responsibility. And usually it has been possible to deduce these operational details from the nature of the attacks. But the peak of the practice has recently been reached in Vietnam and in Washington. This is revealed almost every day now in dispatches from reporters—in close touch with intra-Administration critics of the C.I.A.—with excellent reputations for reliability.

One reporter in this category is Richard Starnes of the Scripps-Howard newspapers. Today, under a Saigon dateline, he related that, "according to a high United States source here, twice the C.I.A. flatly refused to carry out instructions from Ambassador Henry Cabot Lodge . . . [and] in one instance frustrated a plan of action Mr. Lodge brought from Washington because the agency disagreed with it." Among the views attributed to United States officials on the scene, including one described as a "very high American official . . . who has spent much of his life in the service of democracy . . . are the following:

The C.I.A.'s growth was "likened to a malignancy" which the "very high official was not sure even the White House could control . . . any longer." "If the United States ever experiences [an attempt at a coup to overthrow the Government] it will come from the C.I.A. and not the Pentagon." The agency "represents a tremendous power and total unaccountability to anyone."

Whatever else these passages disclose, they most certainly establish that representatives of other Executive branches have expanded their war against the C.I.A. from the inner government councils to the American people via the press. And published simultaneously are details of the agency's operations in Vietnam that can come only from the same critical official sources. This is disorderly government. And the longer the President tolerates it—the period already is considerable—the greater will grow its potentials of hampering the real war against the Vietcong and the impression of a very indecisive Administration in Washington.

The C.I.A. may be guilty as charged. Since it cannot, or at any rate will not, openly defend its record in Vietnam, or defend it by the same confidential press "briefings" employed by its critics, the public is not in a position to judge. Nor is this department, which sought and failed to get even the outlines of the agency's case in rebuttal. But Mr. Kennedy will have to make a judgment if the spectacle of war within the Executive branch is to be ended and the effective functioning of the C.I.A. preserved. And when he makes this judgment, hopefully he also will make it public, as well as the appraisal of fault on which it is based.

Doubtless recommendations as to what his judgment should be were made to him today by Secretary of Defense McNamara and General Taylor on their return from their fact-finding expedition into the embattled official jungle in Saigon.

THE TEST-BAN
July 28, 1963

From the moment science made it known that as a result of fallout from indefinite testing of nuclear weapons in the atmosphere, the earth's inhabitants could be born cancerous and eventually eliminated, the public pressure on statesmen of the atomic powers for a test-ban agreement has mounted steadily.

When it became a common-sense conclusion that no thorough shelter system could be devised for the masses of population within the radius of a nuclear bombing attack, this pressure moved the Governments of the United States and Great Britain to a momentous decision. It was that the necessity of concluding a test-ban treaty with Communist Russia far outweighed the risks implicit for the West in any treaty whose effectiveness is dependent on the sincerity of the Kremlin's professed veto of nuclear war as a means to conquer the world.

Now this decision has materialized in the test-ban articles signed at Moscow between the three principal nuclear powers, to which a fourth—France—has the option of adhering. And, though the fifth great nation with a rising nuclear weapons potential—Communist China—is not considered in the least likely to avail itself of the same option, the Moscow articles, if carried out in good faith by all the signatories, will strongly restrain that potential in time and degree—perhaps even confine it to its present primitive status.

Viewed from the humanitarian aspect, the test-ban treaty takes its place in history as a step toward what conceivably could become one of the greatest accomplishments of civilized statecraft. If duly ratified, and scrupulously executed by the immediate signatories, it could rescue earth's creatures from the threats of extermination—one, by nuclear warfare; the other, by slow but sure deterioration of the fiber of all life on the planet. And, in these circumstances, history would add the names of President Kennedy, Prime Minister Macmillan and Premier Khrushchev to the small top roster of statesmen who have permanently advanced the condition of mankind.

But the agreement must also be inspected from the standpoint of the political gain it may contribute to the first two heads of state, and perhaps even to the third (although the closed Soviet society makes impossible a reliable assessment of this, or Khrushchev's need of it). And the logical conclusion from this inspection is that the signing has given a powerful lift to the present political influence of the President and the Prime Minister; and that this effect will be lasting if the treaty attains its stated objectives. Should it do that in their time, and also supply a foundation for general, though gradual and practically-limited, disarmament, there can be little question that the constituencies of Mr. Kennedy and Mr. Macmillan will give them generous political reward.

Both of them need it, which was not the case with President Eisenhower. He sought a test-ban treaty for a much longer period, and against a series of obstructions by the Kremlin that even his endless patience and firm resolve could not dispel. A test-ban treaty was not a campaign issue when the General was elected to his first term. And, when Adlai E. Stevenson in the 1956 campaign proposed a halt to testing—he shifted from his proposition that this be done unilaterally by the United States—Washington-Moscow relations were so hostile that President Eisenhower's rejection of his opponent's idea as an obvious threat to national security was overwhelmingly endorsed by the American people.

But in his second term, by Constitutional fiat his last, Eisenhower pursued the goal of a test-ban treaty as persistently and patiently as if his official tenure depended upon the outcome of the enterprise. It was he who first proposed the formula of agreement on which is based the treaty that has now become a part of the executive record of the General's successor. Since there was no political gain for Eisenhower in the terms of keeping or holding office, this record qualifies him for a share in whatever benefits to humanity the test-ban treaty eventually may bestow.

These benefits, as the enormous loopholes in the text disclose, are very far from assured. For example, the text can be read to commit the signatories against the use of nuclear weapons in war, even as retaliation against an attack with conventional weapons. It can be read to assert national jurisdictions in outer space—a principle which the United States entirely rejects. The Constitutional duty of the Senate is to examine the treaty microscopically, and in that period it might be disclosed that the Administration paid a price for the signature of the U.S.S.R. that, as former Vice President Nixon remarked, could be too high for the merchandise, and dangerous as well. In the judgment of many, such a price would be new "understandings" in Europe and elsewhere by which the U.S.S.R. would consolidate all that it has seized by external aggression and internal subversion.

But the Administration is certain to wait on the Senate before conferring with Soviet Russia on the "non-aggression" pact the Kremlin seeks as a supplement to the test-ban treaty. And the forces for Senate approval would seem to be the stronger than those opposing. While the text makes it obvious that any of the signatories can cheat, perhaps successfully, in outer space, and also employ the three-month notice of withdrawal in secret preparations for new testing, thus shattering the heart of the treaty, the factors which create the pressure for Senate approval appear to be much more powerful as political considerations.

It has been a long time since Bernard M. Baruch, representing the

United States, offered the U.S.S.R. the "choice between the quick and the dead" that he said was presented by our proposal of a nuclear weapons test-ban, effectively supervised. The total absence of this proviso from the Moscow compact demonstrates, not only that time has passed, but also the whole concept that our national security can never be risked on the good faith of the U.S.S.R.

THE FUNERAL

November 25, 1963

For the first time since leaders of the nations assembled at the bier of another, to pay final tribute to him and to his people, all have been able to make the pilgrimage within two settings of the sun. Only three days had elapsed from the death of President Kennedy in Texas to the hour when his requiem was intoned in Washington. Yet so complete has been man's conquest of time and distance that the requiem mass and the following interment were attended by the heads or plenary representatives of more than 100 states in the six continents of the world.

If grief had not been uppermost among those who watched the magnificent funeral ceremonies, these manifestations of ever-expanding human genius might have been accented, as in Hamlet's meditation: "What a piece of work is a man! How noble in reason! How infinite in faculty, in form and moving! How express and admirable in action! How like an angel in apprehension! How like a god! The beauty of the world! The paragon of animals!" But submerging the incidence of the scientific miracle was the thought of the ancient and abiding curse of violence which these potentates and princes from afar had come to mourn.

The young President lay dead in his coffin under his country's flag because not even the enlightened system of freedom and self-government of which he was the shining symbol has exorcised this curse from the human heart. "At his best," said Aristotle, "man is the noblest of all animals; separated from law and justice he is the worst." At Dallas both law and justice had been trampled upon by the President's assassin, by their civic guardians, and by the maddened avenger who took law and justice into his own hands.

This is the shame which all the elegiasts—at the Capitol, in the press, and throughout the world—lamented. And the theme common to all the elegies may eventually be sustained by factual evidence. This theme is that the violence of political differences that is current in the United States stimulated the fanaticism that expressed itself in the murder of the President. But the American people have always been violent and often venomous in political debate; fanaticism bred in personal or doctrinal grievances has taken the lives of three earlier Presidents and unsuccessfully attempted the assassination of four who were, were to be, or had been Presidents. Hence, there is no merit in the implication of some of the orators that Mr. Kennedy's murder should be related to the area where it occurred because of the intensity there of the controversy over his policies.

This implication especially lacks merit by reason of the only facts known about the only suspect, Oswald. He was a Marxist; at least a sympathizer with the religion of communism; emigrated to and married in the Soviet Union; and was trying to return. This is certainly not the dossier of the "Right Wing extremists," a stigmatic label of Dallas which some members of the Administration are too prone to affix.

That inclination was revealed by the Voice of America broadcast at 1:59 P.M. last Friday of the ghastly tragedy in the city. "Dallas," the V.O.A. explained to the world, "is the center of the extreme Right Wing." This gratuitous, and as it proved false, suggestion that such was the affiliation of the assassin was deleted from the broadcast at 2:10 P.M. but it was grist to Moscow's mill, which has been grinding it ever since.

The Johnson Years

There may have been a more complex human being, or a more political animal, in the White House than Lyndon B. Johnson, but I have not been able to find him in the mass of biographical matter about Presidential predecessors, or in more or less intimate acquaintance with several. Johnson matches others in frequent revelation of both pettiness and greatness of act and spirit, in the strength with which he exerts his awesome powers, and in the avidity with which he seeks their increase. He makes enemies, as Jackson did, by yielding to the urge of a very bad temper. But, unlike Jackson, he feigns a sad surprise at a show of reciprocal ill will by the enemies he deliberately has made.

Like most of his predecessors, Johnson's resentment has grown steadily at the assertion by Congress of its constitutional role as disposer of what a President proposes. But in this he has displayed his greatest inconsistency, made more so by the evidence that he seems unaware of it. This inconsistency derives from the fact that no official spokesman for Congress ever emphasized its coordinate function set forth in the Constitution, or guarded it more zealously, then Senate Majority Leader Johnson. And his was not a purely partisan attitude, to be abandoned if a Democratic President succeeded General Eisenhower. I base that judgment on many intimate conversations with the President before the generally unexpected event of his nomination as the Democratic candidate for Vice President at Los Angeles in 1960.

Of the White House predecessors who openly resented dissent to their programs by Congresses where their party was in the majority, none who had been invested with leadership in either branch did so more visibly than Lyndon Johnson. Wilson was a political scientist, and had been Governor, but never a member of the national legislature. The two Roosevelts saw no service there. Lincoln served only one term in the House. Cleveland, like the two Roosevelts, went to the White House from the Governorship of New York. (In Theodore's case, by way of the Vice Presidency.) Washington, Grant and Eisenhower were military victors and national heroes. Taft's prior public-service training was that of a judge and a pro-consul. Truman and Kennedy were two-term Senators, the first prominent, the second much less so, in the scope of their legislative activities.

But this shift in assessing the proper role of Congress in dealing with Presidential programs, being a familiar occupational mutation, is nothing as violent as another change which began to show in Johnson when he was nominated for Vice President. This is his now passionate devotion to the political philosophy of ever-expanding centralization of Government to create a welfare state in the mold of advanced socialism. The change is also manifest in his alliance, with unexpected fervor, with special-interest groups whose pressures he publicly fought and privately denounced as Senate Leader.

I am thinking particularly of that part of this philosophy which sets up, with costs rising by geometrical progression, a super-state as the regulator of every detail of the life of its citizens, sacrificing individual incentive and distributing the yield of personal ability and industriousness on an officially-computed standard of need, regardless of merit.

During the President's tenure as Senate leader, in many conversations and close observation of his activities and concepts of Government, I never found any basis for the explanation now being made that, as a congenital Populist, this was always his basic political philosophy, that he was only waiting for favorable timing and the power to put it in operation. My files are choked with memoranda from him contradictory to this claim. All of these documents reflect the thinking of the Greeks in the Age of Pericles and of the moderates in American politics: that art, in and outside of government, is restraint, that the half is better than the whole when honest differences are fundamental, and especially that free enterprise under public regulation restrained by the rule of reason is the genius of the American system.

He was a New Dealer, but never of the super-radical persuasion, so far as I could see. He resented as an impractical nuisance the organization naméd Americans for Democratic Action whose programs he as President has so warmly embraced. He strongly opposed, as an expression of political principle, those sumptuary infringements by statute of the rights of others. And, by excising proposals to this effect from the Administration drafts of the Civil Rights Acts of 1957 and 1959, he made it possible to enact the first laws of their kind since Reconstruction. Now he is chiefly responsible for the enactment into law of the very sections he had strongly opposed as a repudiation of the principle of equal treatment of all citizens.

As Senate leader, he reserved some of his harshest criticism for the "liberals" for paying no heed to the cost, in relation to the national capacity to pay, of those social and economic reforms they incessantly were urging. Now he has made these reforms his own, and amplified their socialistic concept.

But in all this ringing cycle of change (for which I at least was unprepared) certain *modi operandi* of the President have not altered from those of his Senate leadership days. Johnson's method of trying to "manage the news" is to withhold news he particularly wants to be favorably received until he is ready to become its first conveyor to the public. The purpose is to invest even minor announcements with his unique prestige. But his passion for this practice has grown into an obsession. He still reacts angrily to criticism, even in the mold of amiable satire. As the author of one example of that (it is the first of the appended extracts) I have abundant and direct evidence to support this judgment.

Not until the President has completed his record in the White House, which may not occur until January 20, 1973, can history appraise whether he succeeded in his great aims: Whether, and if so at what expenditure of the human and material resources of the United States, he prevented the U.S.S.R. and China from expanding the area ruled by Communism by the use of force against the weaker nations on their perimeters. Whether, by deficit spending and related fiscal and financial policies, he strengthened or emasculated the economy on which depends the creation of the Great Society; and increased or reduced the influence the United States can exert in the solutions of world problems.

Nature endowed Lyndon Johnson with great gifts—strength of purpose which does not falter under the heaviest fire, a fine intelligence, an instinct for mastery and leadership, a simple gospel faith, an unappeasable thirst for excellence, an incredible capacity for whatever may be the mental and physical labor required for the performance of any task he sets himself. Denied the bright pinions of personality and physical appeal on which Kennedy soared rapidly to the heights, Johnson has had to climb to his pinnacle. But, once won, he has fortified it with the stuff of practical experience, and the skills of one of the greatest political artisans in American history.

Perhaps a great man—the measurement is not yet possible to make. A strong President, who may prove himself a great one. A brooding, restless and yet at all times a determined man. A ruthless man, with a streak of vindictiveness, but with a wider streak of compassion. A man in whom insecurity alternates with confidence in his star, and vanity with humility.

Such is Lyndon B. Johnson, as he has appeared to me.

In the many years which have passed since Justice Douglas introduced me to the brand-new, young, skinny Representative from Texas, our personal relations have followed an undulating curve. High when he was the Senate leader, a receptive candidate for the Presidential nomination and in the first year of his Presidency, because my published commentaries pleased him. Low, during the campaign of 1960, his tenure as Vice President, and since his election as President in his own right, because my commentaries did not.

But *c'est la guerre* in Washington where nine lives are none too many for the newsroom cat who takes a good hard look at political royalty.

THE TRANSITION

JOHNSON'S SPEECH
November 30, 1963

The most "remarkable" aspect of President Johnson's speech to the joint session of Congress Wednesday is that his perfect matching of construction, content and delivery to the solemn occasion was so frequently described as remarkable. For, though he was addressing Congress, the nation and the world for the first time in the capacity of President of the United States, Mr. Johnson has displayed all these qualities—dignity, emotional fitness and eloquent prose—many, many times as majority leader of the Senate and as Vice President.

In these roles he has for many years sensed the oratorical requirements of an event. In times when satire, direct attack, a plea for support and cooperation, arm-twisting or a carrot-and-stick combination have been the best means to the end he had in view, he has used them alternately and with true perception of the needful. This sixth sense marks the masterly politician. And it is the explanation of the most brilliant and successful Congressional leadership of recent times, originally undertaken in the difficult period of 1953, when one major party controlled the Executive and the Congress and maintained during the following eight years when divisions in his own party weakened the power of its regained majorities and assured that the vetoes of the Republican President would almost always prevail.

Those commentators and others who hailed the speech as "remarkable" with an air of discovery must, therefore, in the mists which inevi-

tably veil the Vice President, temporarily have lost sight of Mr. Johnson's repeated demonstrations that he possessed the potential of national
leadership at the highest level. President Kennedy had recognized this
when, during the Democratic pre-convention campaign of 1960, he said
that Mr. Johnson was perhaps the best qualified by experience of all
the Presidential aspirants. This judgment greatly influenced the choice
of his only strong rival for the Presidential nomination as his running-
mate, and also Mr. Kennedy's association of his Vice President in all
the major decisions he made.

As for the first "state of the union" message, there also was nothing
in its reaffirmation of President Kennedy's legislative priorities that was
"remarkable" in the sense of revelation. Ever since he accepted the Vice-
Presidential nomination, Mr. Johnson has committed himself to President Kennedy's political principles and programs.

In witness, here is the new President, who as Senate majority leader
twice incurred charges of "liberal" Democrats that he had extracted the
teeth from equal-rights bills to be able to claim credit for the first legislation in this area in half a century, speaking to the Governors' Conference at Miami Beach, July 23, 1963:

> Whatever the legalisms or traditions, it is wrong that tax-paying,
> arms-bearing, vote-casting Americans should be unable to find a bed
> for the night or meals for their children along the highways of our
> free and decent society . . . It is wrong that Americans who fight
> alongside other Americans in war should not be able to work alongside
> the same Americans, wash up . . . eat . . . win promotions alongside
> them, or send their children to school alongside children of other
> Americans.

This is the same Lyndon Johnson who had negotiated passage of an
equal-rights bill from which were excised Federal compulsions to penal-
ize the commission of some of these very "wrongs," and in August,
1957, said to the Senate:

"This is not the first time that I have agreed to accept proposed legislation less than completely satisfactory, and it will not be the last time.
All of us must realize that men have strong convictions on this issue
. . . and must bow a bit if we are to have a reasonable solution rather
than a burning issue." But the provision he was discussing concerned
only denial of the right of trial by jury for minor equal-rights offenders.

From the time he accepted the Vice-Presidential nomination on a
platform which rejected even "bowing a bit" on casting this legislation
in drastic form, and included a labor plank specifically repudiating

labor legislation for which he had voted as a Senator, Mr. Johnson has given other evidence that this acceptance carried the obligation of full adherence to President Kennedy's proposals for the term to which they both were elected.

President Johnson has changed some political attitudes since he became a candidate for national elective office and the Presidential tenure will change them again, more tangibly, when and if he is elected in his own right. But his speech to Congress last Wednesday was totally consistent with the commitment of his 1960 candidacy, his Vice-Presidential record, and with the estimate he earned before that as uniquely well qualified for the highest office in the land.

THE PRESIDENT'S MESSAGE TO CONGRESS
January 8, 1964

The State of the Union will be utopian if ever it attains the level to which President Johnson today urged Congress and the American people to aspire. And this will be the first nation of its size to stand on that peak in the history of civilization. Also, if Congress makes even a long start on the eight tasks he assigned it for performance "by this summer," the United States will have climbed at least to the foothills of heights President Johnson envisages as common goals, and all within the reach, of this heterogeneous people.

But, partly because these aspirations have been voiced before, by other Presidents to other Congresses, and are yet far from realization, and partly because deep differences exist among the people and the legislators on the political philosophy by which their consummation should be attempted, they came under instant challenge. Some were challenged as not feasible, some as undesirable.

Most Republicans and a few Democrats wondered aloud, and with incredulity, at Mr. Johnson's firm assertion that the eight items of major legislation he proposed to Congress, for completion by "this summer . . . , can be done without any increases in spending." Southern Democrats, joined by some Northerners of both parties, opposed his sweeping endorsement of the equal rights bill supported by his predecessor, since that includes Federal compulsions against racial or other discrimination in the choice of patrons by private owners of certain types of public facilities.

In this reference, the President prefaced his call for the abolition of "not some, but all, racial discrimination" with these words of reservation—"as far as the writ of Federal law will run." But one section of the Kennedy Administration bill he supported in full stops this writ only at the thresholds of neighborhood groceries, and of privately owned lodging-houses with five rooms or less to let, by an owner living on the premises. And this assured a bipartisan dissent to that part of Mr. Johnson's message—on constitutional grounds which several as yet unreversed Supreme Court decisions have fortified.

The most popular section of today's message, of course, was the President's report of his cuts in the costs of Federal housekeeping and his pledge to follow "frugality" as a permanent principle. The Democrats applauded because of strong evidence that there is danger to their party in the Republican issue of ever-expanding Government at Washington, at an ever-increasing cost and deficit spending. The Republicans applauded because they have been attacking Democratic spending for years, and they believe they can successfully claim credit for its reduction.

Two other features of the President's message came under immediate and critical inspection on both sides of the party aisle in the House and Senate. He called on Congress to allow "each important proposal" at least to come to a vote, either for approval or rejection. And this could be and was construed as reserving to the President, and excluding Congress from, the judgment of what measures are "important." Mr. Johnson also used "must" 31 times in citing the legislation he desires. This is a Presidential record in the employment of a term which Congress finds as unpalatable as Mr. Johnson did when he was the majority leader of the Senate.

However, his first State of the Union message was remarkable for the wide sweep and bold idealism of his programs, for its eloquence in composition and the masterly manner of its delivery. And Congress, despite the political and philosophical differences of some of its members with the programs the President urged upon it for achieving the aims he expounded, received him with the warmth inherent in the consciousness that he is its own high honor graduate.

He was especially effective in the places where he used the sentence form known to grammarians as "antithesis." The outstanding example of this, as was demonstrated by applause which, except for the gloomy abstention of the Ambassador of the U.S.S.R. would have been unanimous, was:

"We intend to bury no one—and we do not intend to be buried."

THE 'LBJ' BRAND
April 13, 1964

In an astonishingly brief time, Lyndon B. Johnson has put his famous brand firmly on the Presidency and the leadership of his party and the nation. By this accomplishment, in unusually delicate circumstances, he has developed next November's popular referendum into a judgment on the *Johnson* Administration and his own performance as President.

He has executed this masterly political feat without major deviation from the programs of President Kennedy because of a highly individual style and administrative method. Although Mr. Johnson has had only a few months—in a year when he must submit his claims for direct election—to demonstrate that his is not a "caretaker" Administration, he has achieved that objective.

Among his predecessors who succeeded from the office of Vice President, Chester A. Arthur made the same attempt and failed, despite the fact that he had three and a half years of President Garfield's unexpired term for the purpose. Calvin Coolidge, in a period of Presidential succession only a few months longer than Mr. Johnson's, made small effort to identify himself as a new national leader of the people or of Congress, taking positive positions only when extreme political exigency compelled him to. And, though Mr. Truman ultimately stamped his Administration as his own, and not just an extension of President Roosevelt's, he was in the White House many months longer before he established this than Mr. Johnson will have served of President Kennedy's unexpired term when he will submit his record to the electorate.

It required a remarkable man to cast the Presidency in his own image so firmly and so rapidly after the three years of its identification with John F. Kennedy, and in the first stage of the worldwide mourning for Mr. Kennedy's tragic death that will not soon abate. But Mr. Johnson is a remarkable man. He proved this by his extraordinary skill in getting from a Senate, in which his party followers were divided, the first significant antidiscrimination measures since Reconstruction, and in inducing a Democratic Congress to cooperate constructively with a Republican President. But full national comprehension of these and other natural talents of leadership was limited by the scope of his Senate office and the Vice Presidency, important as these are.

Now, supplied by a cruel stroke of destiny with the powers of the

Presidency that he was denied by the normal electoral process, Mr. Johnson is exercising their powers in a protean political performance of many diverse roles. One day he is the patient arbitrator of a stubborn and protracted management-labor dispute which threatens to culminate in the collapse of the national economy. The next he is coercing a balky Congress with a highly professional mixture of ruthless arm-twisting and cajolery in which the rewards and punishments at his disposal are unmistakably implied.

Another day, the President is dangerously relaxing from the *ex officio* confinement of his native high spirits by driving an automobile as if he were a juvenile with a hot-rod. Still another day, and the President is impulsively opening the gates of the White House grounds to a group of tourists that has happened along; then leading them in an inspection of the august premises. But when the occasion demands a show of the dignity befitting his great office, no President has excelled him.

Then he stands tall and grave of voice and manner behind the lectern that bears the Presidential medallion on its face—a TV prop that has become as closely associated with Mr. Johnson as the desk across which Franklin D. Roosevelt conducted his news conferences without benefit of instant video.

When Mr. Johnson's acute political perception apprises him that he has left himself vulnerable to criticism he shrewdly turns the tables on his critics with a homespun wisecrack or by drawing the mantle of the Presidency around him, according to the occasion. And in these shifting roles as a Lincoln trying to bind up the nation's wounds, as a Jackson whipping his party and Congress to his will, as a Theodore Roosevelt defying Presidential conventions, he still manages to remain Lyndon B. Johnson, the poor country boy from the wide Southwest, the Alger hero who bettered himself in the admired American way.

JOHNSON'S SIX MONTHS
May 23, 1964

The most political animal to occupy the White House since Andrew Jackson, if not since the creation of the Federal Government, has just completed the first six months of his Presidency. The man of action has succeeded the man of contemplation, and Congress and the American people are moving under his pressures in the direction he wants them to go.

These are generalities, with the weakness of all generalities, which is that they are subject to major exceptions. President Johnson often takes a long look before he leaps. And President Kennedy sometimes acted on impulse.

President Johnson has given weeks to contemplation of the risks of military action which would check the steady erosion of anti-Communist resistance in Southeast Asia, but he has not yet brought himself to assume them. President Kennedy reacted instantly and aggressively when most of the largest units in the steel industry announced an increase in prices. But the over-all difference in their personalities and administrative methods is the difference between the activist politician and the politician whose decisions are guided by a sense of history.

Congress, also being a political animal, has responded to his pressures to legislate measures it denied to President Kennedy or deeply abridged in granting. Tensions with the U.S.S.R. have been relaxed, however superficial and transient this development may prove. Mr. Johnson not only has charmed the proprietors and managers of private industry and finance with his personality and his attitude of sympathetic co-operation, in large degree they appear to view with favor the prospect of his election to a four-year term.

Organized labor, although declining to abide by his economic guidelines, is planning to become his open political ally in the Presidential campaign. His apparent popularity with the ethnic minorities is enormous, especially among the Negroes.

There is little new, and much that is politically-motivated, in his "war on poverty"; moreover, its administrative structure promises inefficiency and waste. But the President has imbued this "war" with a persuasive show that his heart is more deeply involved than the obvious consideration of the votes to be accrued.

All this has covered the nation with promises of something for everybody at the punitive expense of nobody, with general gain for the social and economic order and the military establishment of the United States, and with a descending rate of Government expenditure. The President has been candid in conceding to the people that unforeseen events, including war, could force a suspension of his programs in general and a long postponement of some units in particular. He has not satisfied many qualified authorities that he can make good his promises, even if the status quo at the end of his six months as President lasts long enough for a thorough tryout. But insofar as unanimity among those who make a business of "sampling" public opinion can indicate the trend, the majority of the American people approve his efforts and are willing to gamble he will redeem an impressive percentage of his claims.

A very important explanation of this phenomenon seems to be a nation-wide belief in the sincerity of Mr. Johnson's expressed wish to be the best President in history for the people as a whole; and their acceptance of his flagrantly-professional politicking as the method experience has shown him to be necessary to his purpose.

But this experience has also taught the President that his acclaim at the end of six months carries no guarantee of durability, even through Election Day. He knows that unforeseen events could reverse the dismal prospect of any contender for the Presidency who might emerge from the fratricidal conflict current in the Republican party. He knows that candidates seemingly as far in the lead as he is now have made blunders which caused their defeat at the polls—a possibility always inherent in his own natural exuberance.

He is acutely aware of disaster factors in the involvement of the United States in Southeast Asia that a strong Republican campaigner could successfully attribute to Administration policy, and could require him to make the fateful decision he hopes to postpone until the election is over. And he also realizes that, if race rioting is the bitter fruit of the equal rights bill on which he has staked so much of his power and prestige, he and many of the members of Congress who stand with him could go down to defeat at the November poll.

But as yet these possibilities are casting only light shadows on the horizon of his popularity at the end of the half-year in which the President so quickly and firmly established that this is "the Johnson Administration." And he does not share the fear of some friends that he is taking too heavy a toll of his incredible energy, and has already incurred whatever political peril there may be in "overexposure."

"The Twelfth Amendment," one of these friends ironically remarked to him the other day, "does not require you to get *all* the votes to be elected, not even a popular majority, only a majority of the electors." But there is no sign the President was listening.

THE POLITICAL MAN

THE 'INFORMAL' NEWS CONFERENCES
December 19, 1963

The only law which obliges the President to hold news conferences with members of the press is the political law of self-preservation. The format of these dispensaries of public information at the highest level is for the President to determine. Also, when and whether he shall make himself personally accessible to the press.

Thus far President Johnson's chosen format is a modernized reversion to the procedure of the Chief Executive, Woodrow Wilson, who instituted the first formal and regular White House news conference. The reversion is the limitation of the group to those reporters who are on constant duty at the White House. The modernizations include partial visual coverage by movie cameras minus a soundtrack; reportorial freedom to ask questions of the President without prior submission; the issuance of transcripts of the dialogue (these are furnished as soon as they can be turned out); and the summoning of the group without advance notice.

But Mr. Johnson has not substituted these informal news conferences for the large, televised assemblages before which Presidents Truman, Eisenhower and Kennedy appeared for general questioning. It is understood that he, too, will schedule these in advance on occasion, and, like Mr. Kennedy, permit them to be broadcast in full on television as soon as they have ended. The combination would reflect a sound decision on his part, because there are flaws in both the *omnium gatherum* and selective types of news conference that would be minimized by variation.

In the come-all-ye type, the flaws derive from the number of interviewers seeking a share of the usual time limit of thirty minutes, and the TV exposure that impels some reporters to personal exhibitionism instead of news-gathering. The result is that a number of questions asked of the President deal with trivial matters; and one matter of importance cannot be fully explored except to the exclusion of inquiries about others.

The selective type of news conference, limited to reporters who are regularly stationed at the White House, lacks these particular defects. But it has a serious set of its own. There is no time for the preparation which is required for well-stated questions. The intimacy of the setting —in the President's private office, with Mr. Johnson officiating at the coffee urn—acts as a restraint on inquiries about subjects to which he has a personal relationship, yet are within the legitimate bounds of essential public information. This restraint is absent from the mass news conferences in the State Department auditorium, where few of those present have their principal sources of information in the White House Staff.

The selective method also excludes the large majority of Washington correspondents, because it is available only to the representatives of the press associations and those newspapers which can maintain a regular staff member at the White House. Another of its defects is that reporters who have special knowledge of major government operations in the fields of science, finance, business, agriculture, military programs, etc., are stationed elsewhere in Washington. Consequently, the selective method precludes informed questioning of the President on some of the most important activities of Government, consuming huge portions of the budget and greatly influencing the future of the American people and their institutions.

The only medium which affords an opportunity for this group of specialist reporters to enlighten the public through the President, on problems and events in these vital areas of human affairs, is the general White House news conference. Clearly, the selective news conference cannot satisfactorily substitute for the larger gathering, summoned with advance notice whenever the President decides that it is time for a broad review of Government operations. Doubtless, that decision will be frequently made.

President Kennedy also appeared on television with two or three questioners, and granted a number of interviews to individual reporters, in which he could give more time to the discussion of a single subject than is possible at a general news conference. To what extent Mr. Johnson will use these outlets is not yet known.

A QUIET CHRISTMAS
AT THE WELL-KNOWN RANCH
December 24, 1964

"The President expects to spend a quiet Christmas," according to the
last dispatch from Texas before this department went to press. This
strongly suggests that the reporters whom duty called to Austin from
their holiday hearths will not cross the Pedernales tonight or tomorrow.
But in fancy, bred by rereading familiar poems by Bret Harte and
Longfellow, this is what happened:

Christmas at the Ranch—I

Above the pecan-trees the moon was slowly drifting,
The Pedernales crept below
The lawn where smoking barbecues were lifting
Aromas in the evening glow.

Their fires to each upraised face imparted
An aureate rosy hue,
Which made its owner look and seem warm-hearted
Whate'er his political view.

Then rose the host, smiling beneath his Stetson,
Whilst silence fell like a pall
So deep it was it also fell his pets on—
Him, Blanco and Y'All.

And then while nearby mooed the long-horn cattle
And spareribs passed around,
He read of victories won without a battle,
Of budget waste he'd found,
Of cuts much thicker than the festal sirloins,
And cheaper by the pound.

Christmas at the Ranch—II

Under a spreading pecan-tree *
The great Panjandrum stands,

* The morning the verses were published, Jon Vondracek, a *Time* magazine correspondent, asked President Johnson if he had read them. The President replied that
if the author had taken the trouble to look for himself, he would have known the
trees were oaks, not pecans.

The Pan a mighty man is he
Here and in foreign lands,
Both nuclear and fiscal are
The powers he commands.

Tall in the saddle and afoot,
Browned by the Texas tan,
The foe of waste and undue haste
In worrying out a plan.
And when it comes to saving face
He outsmarts any man.

Week in, week out, from morn to night
You see him on TV,
You hear him make most things seem bright
That don't seem bright to me,
Yet 'neath the spell he weaves so well
I hanker to agree.

The nearby cattle mooed and bellered,
Whose folks were being et,
And scampering on the grassy sward
Was each L.B.J. pet—
Also the horse that Hubert grasped
By mane lest he should fall
(And hurt his public image bad,
In Minneapolis and St. Paul).

And then were heard the well-known words
"I have a statement here."
It told of things amazing planned
Within the coming year;
How poverty will vanish
And with it fear of fear;

Of victory without battle won,
Of budgets shorn of waste,
Of the virtue which is "prudence,"
Of the error which is "haste,"
Of Congo and the Vietnam
Where our programs got misplaced.

Though fancy has this vision drawn
Of Yule with President J.
It's reasonably conceivable

>   That he'd talk thataway,
>   And this the faithful listening press
>   Would to the world convey.

In that conveyance, of course, is always the risk of having the product termed "speculative." Like maybe U.S. policy in Southeast Asia?

THE GOVERNMENT
OUTSHAVES THEM ALL
April 7, 1965

In one of his most learned and longest opinions, Chief Justice Warren sustained the judgment of the Federal Trade Commission that the televised "sandpaper" commercial of the Colgate-Palmolive Company misled the viewers. They were induced to believe the company's claim that "Rapid Shave Outshaves Them All" by the substitution of a slab of plexi-glass sprinkled with sand for the "tough, dry sandpaper" the slab was represented to be.

Hence, said the Chief Justice, the viewer was led to believe that an application of Colgate's cream would make it instantly possible to shave sand off sandpaper; but, the Chief Justice went on to say, the "evidence . . . disclosed" that sandpaper must first be soaked for eighty minutes in the Colgate product.

This aspect of the case, however, despite its intended and probable effect of increasing the sales of the cream at the expense of the competitive producers, was not the one which "concerned" the Court. "An advertiser has himself conducted a test . . . he honestly believes will prove a certain product claim, he may not convey to television viewers the false impression that they are seeing the test . . . for themselves, when they are not because of the undisclosed use of mockups." And on this basis the commission's conclusion of the illegality of this particular commercial was sustained.

The principle is now established in the law. But fortunately for government at all levels, the courts have no power to apply it to official representations. Fortunately, because government habitually encourages impressions as misleading as any ever created by the claims of industry.

Start with the celebrated tax reduction of 1964. An incalculable number of taxpayers have been obliged to go into debt to meet the levies on their 1964 incomes in the final reckoning on April 15. There are several reasons why this situation was so widely unanticipated. But foremost among these reasons is that, in order to get the highest possible return in voters' gratitude in a Presidential election year, the Administration concentrated on extolling the fact it had reduced income taxes, and muted the other fact that cutting the withholding tax from 18 per cent to 14 per cent would leave the taxpayer with a larger cash obligation to the Treasury on April 15, 1965, than in previous years.

Thereby the Administration at least allowed a false impression of the benefits of the tax reduction to exist without doing much to correct it. In the business world this is a form of overselling to which the fake sandpaper test bears a family relationship.

The Administration can, and does, claim that a high purpose of the tax cut was to stimulate the national economy, and the psychological effect could only have been diminished by stressing a factor of restraint which was obvious to anybody who owned a pencil and paper and could add and subtract. But the shaving-cream maker could, and did, argue that, since sandpaper can actually be shaved as claimed, why load down the sales pitch by using the real article (which looks like mere stained paper on television)? In the same framework of statesmanship, the Administration omits or blurs the pricetag on legislation for the Great Society.

The speech by President Johnson tonight deals with another matter on which Government has greatly misled the American people. With each successively broader commitment to aid South Vietnam in resisting forcible annexation by its Communist neighbor, official prophesies of success took on a rosier hue. Time after time Secretary of Defense MacNamara or some other high Government spokesmen returned from an inspection of the situation with optimistic appraisals which in turn were rapidly shattered by events in Vietnam.

President Kennedy, whose position as a Senator was that the United States must never engage in ground war on the Asian mainland, was persuaded to actions which increased the risk of this involvement. Until very recently the inheriting Johnson Administration was insisting there was no need to expand the war to the degree to which it has now been expanded.

If Government were subject to the principle asserted by the Chief Justice for industry's selling practices, it would have been the leading defendant in the Colgate case.

AT BREAKNECK SPEED
April 10, 1965

Of the activists who have served as President of the United States, none has set and maintained such a driving pace as Lyndon B. Johnson. His incessant urgency for speedy action pervades the executive and legislative branches of the Government, and only in wartime have they responded to the present degree over so broad a range of problem areas.

During Franklin D. Roosevelt's Hundred Days, to which the Johnsonian period from last Jan. 20 has been compared, executive and Congressional action were centered on rescuing the national economy. Now every sector of American life is stirring with the President's activity.

In his time-table for rapid and simultaneous action he is involving the government and the people in his concepts of social and political reform, the conservation of natural resources, eradication of the physical blights of progress that scar the cities and the countryside, and the military and diplomatic policies required to stem the tide of world Communist aggression—while maintaining the ever-growing, sound civilian economy. The President is sweeping toward these goals like a great wind, with confidence it will not raise the whirlwind that often in human experience has devastated public policies pressed too far too fast.

He is sweeping Congress along with him, and, insofar as the prevalent tests of public opinion are dependable, the American people, too. Under the spell of the President's evangelism when he urged Congress, in joint session, to approve sight-unseen his voting reform bill without material change, even several of the members of the Supreme Court—five of the nine—who thought it proper to attend applauded his outline of legislation they also had not seen, and would surely be asked to review for constitutionality.

In the last few days Congress has advanced to the enactment of spending measures (for the President's Great Society) whose long-range costs could exceed speculative estimates by tens of billions. Yet if the disregard in the automobile industry's wage settlement of the Administration's anti-inflation guidelines is repeated in the steel industry, inflation could increase the eventual cost of these programs by additional tens of billions that no forced growth of the Gross National Product would supply.

Although foreign economic aid is being examined in Congress with more dubiety than ever as to the effectiveness of its concept and the wisdom of its administration and allocation, particularly in Southeast Asia, members of the majority expressed the greatest enthusiasm for the President's offer to invest another $1 billion in this area as soon as the Communist aggressors there make possible this "peaceful cooperation." Only from members of the small Republican minority, rendered more ineffectual as an Opposition by the divisive political lure of Mr. Johnson's Great Society programs, was any question raised either of the financial soundness of the proposed venture on the test of "Gresham's law," or of the political psychology of a proposal reminiscent by its attendant circumstances of the crude era of American "dollar diplomacy."

The President has attained this pace and speed, on a path free of the usual political obstacles, partly because of the overwhelming vote cast for him last November. It was not so much the size of his popular majority, however, as its centrifugal effect on the makeup of Congress that is responsible for the success of his multi-faceted program.

The voters of 1964 elected 38 more Democrats to the House than there were in the 88th Congress; and nearly all of these owe their seats to his candidacy on the same ticket and share his commitment to the political philosophy of the Democratic national platform. But the changes in the House personnel also changed the membership of the committees where the measures now sailing through were scuttled when President Kennedy launched them. Moreover, at least thus far, a majority of the most influential spokesmen of Big Business and Big Finance are going along with the "new economics" to which both Mr. Kennedy and Mr. Johnson were converted.

But there are points to which even the most tractable and happy-go-lucky Congress cannot be driven. And an easing of criticism of government by the press is a condition no President can count on. Therefore, Mr. Johnson is busier than even he has been before in cultivating good relations with both.

No birthday or other anniversary of any member of Congress passes without a congratulatory note or a telephone call from the President. The same is true of deaths, funerals and illnesses. Hardly a member hasn't had his photograph taken with Mr. Johnson, and received a copy inscribed by his "good friend." The President's famous individual "treatment"—the warm handclasp, the whispered "secret," etc.—has been administered in the White House to every legislator, with a tour thrown in for their wives, if any, conducted by Mrs. Johnson. And, unlike other Presidents, Mr. Johnson's "liaison" with Congress is himself, in person and by telephone.

The President's unexampled access to the press was described in this space last Sunday. This week, in one of his fits of annoyance with news treatment, he shook off his reportorial escort for a few hours by slipping away to Texas. But he repeated the performance in which at his command, members of the assembled Cabinet stand up like schoolboys before a group of reporters and make dull little speeches about their doings.

CIVIL RIGHTS

'THE SANCTITY
OF PRIVATE PROPERTY'
October 21, 1964

President Johnson expressed a reservation when a few days ago he signed the legislation designed to aid the recovery by private owners of property worth $1 billion-plus that was expropriated by the Castro Government. He was concerned over the section of the bill that transfers to the United States the ownership of certain assets of the Castro regime now held in this country. In noting his reservation the President wrote: "The United States strongly adheres to the sanctity of private property."

It all depends on Mr. Johnson's definition of what is "the United States." For in a number of the states which are its components in the Federal Union, the sanctity of private property rights has been deeply abridged by public laws sponsored by the political groups of which the President is the national leader. Unless "sanctity" has ceased to have its dictionary meaning of "inviolability," examples of this abridgment are provided by what are euphemistically known as the "fair housing laws."

Under these laws the private owner of a house is forbidden to discriminate among applicants for its purchase for personally preferential reasons—such as race, national origins, etc. If an applicant charges that
406

his bid has been rejected for any of these reasons, the burden of establishing disproof before a state agency rests upon the private property owner, and if the agency finds discrimination to be the cause of rejection, the owner must conform to the law or suffer its penalties.

A proposal to repeal this statutory violation of an ancient private property right that is a basic principle of the democratic system will be voted on in California on Nov. 3. The statute at issue affects not only all public housing, but 60 to 70 per cent of all private housing in the state by covering all publicly assisted single-family dwellings that are occupied by the owner. The law enjoys the advantage of identification as a "fair housing law," thanks to the semantic skill of the political liberals in this country. But it merits the designation of "fair" only if it be agreed that the right of preferential disposal of private property is no longer one of those "human" rights to which bipartisan liberalism professes dedication. And this concept is the antithesis of the fundamental liberal philosophy of government.

This philosophy was best stated by Voltaire to Helvetius: "I disapprove of what you say, but I will defend to the death your right to say it." Paraphrased to fit the referendum proposal in California, it would read: "I disapprove of the grounds on which my neighbor discriminates in choosing those to whom he will sell or lease the house he owns, but I will defend to the death his right to make this discrimination." Jefferson expressed this same basic principle of liberal political philosophy when he wrote: "It were contrary to freedom, and indeed ridiculous, to suppose that a man had less right in himself than in one of his neighbors, or indeed than all of them put together. This would be slavery, and not that liberty which the Bill of Rights has made inviolable."

In the shrewdly named "fair" housing laws, several state governments among those constituting "the United States" have breached that "sanctity of private property" to which, according to the President, this nation, represented in his context as a unit, "strongly adheres." The representation is accurate only if his reference was to the Federal Government with respect to the disposition of privately owned housing. In the Civil Rights Act of 1964 this was prudently left to state action because its inclusion would have brought about the defeat of the measure.

In California, the sample polls indicate that a large majority will support Proposition 14, the official label on the proposal to repeal the state housing law. But here, as elsewhere, the candidate supported by the national Democratic liberals—in California this is Senator Pierre Salinger—is defending the statute that is a travesty of basic liberalism.

Considering the opinion sampling on Proposition 14, this is an act of courage and of fealty to the dominant national Democratic faction. In unadmirable contrast is the "neutrality" on the issue of his Republican rival, George Murphy.

FAIR EMPLOYMENT
November 21, 1964

An example of the extent to which a politically-oriented Government agency could interfere with equitable hiring policies of private management has just been provided by the Illinois Fair Employment Practices Commission. After delaying its ruling in the so-called Motorola Company case until after the Nov. 3 election, thereby crippling the effort of the Republican candidate for Governor, Charles H. Percy, to make the case a clear issue with his Democratic opponent, Gov. Otto Kerner, the Commission in effect fined the company for the hiring practices it simultaneously left undisturbed.

The consequences of this mixed-up finding by a bureaucracy conceived and influenced by partisan political considerations are:

Private management in Illinois may continue to use an aptitude test by which the capability of job applicants is determined by private employers throughout the United States. But when the Board agrees with the claim of a rejected applicant that a test is discriminatory to a "culturally deprived and disadvantaged group" of which he is a member, the employer must pay him a sum fixed by the Commission as compensation for incidental expense and embarrassment," and "possible" loss of the job he held elsewhere at the time. In this instance, the commission ordered Motorola to pay $1,000 to the applicant who failed the capability test for employment.

He is Leon Myart, a Negro. Last February the State Commission referred his complaint to a Negro examiner, who ordered the Motorola company to hire him, despite his failure to pass its aptitude test; and to stop using the test because its effects were group-discriminatory, as asserted by the complainant. The Commission, composed of persons appointed by Governor Kerner in 1963, found various excuses to defer the ruling until his re-election. On Nov. 20, the Commission reversed its examiner's order that Myart be hired; and nullified his order that the test be dropped, for the reasons he assigned, by holding that these matters were beyond its jurisdiction. Motorola has appealed to the courts the concomitant order to "compensate" Myart with $1,000.

Several aspects of the decision support the comment of a Motorola vice president, Kenneth Piper, that it was "doubletalk." For instance, the company was directed to cease "unfair labor practices," but none was specified either by the board or its examiner. And the reference could not have been to the aptitude test because the Commission ruled this out of its purview. Also, the board warned Motorola that it was going to keep a close and critical watch on company hiring policies for a pattern of discrimination. Yet neither the board nor its examiner pointed out any "discriminatory act" committed by Motorola.

Typical of the confusion created by this specimen of official pretense that an issue was being met that in effect was being evaded were conflicting appraisals of the ruling. The Motorola spokesman concluded it would have no "substantial effect on the hiring practices in the state." But the Illinois Manufacturers Association saw in it an "unfair" slant against management and "a real threat to sound employment practices" in that area.

The outcome of the Illinois case has been a matter of acute interest to management in general because of the establishment of the Equal Employment Opportunities Commission in Section VII of the Civil Rights Act of 1964. This creates a Federal bureaucracy to prevent or punish job discrimination for reasons of race, color, etc., all specifically forbidden by the new statute. Section VII assigns a 60-day priority to state commissions (where they exist) for disposal of these complaints before they can be laid before the E.E.O.C. The concern of employers growing out of the Motorola case is that the partisan politics and political ideology served in its processing by the Illinois Commission may infect the Federal agency.

This will not happen if President Johnson's appointees to the E.E.O.C. are as determined it shall not as is Hobart Taylor, Jr., the executive vice-chairman of President Johnson's Committee on Equal Employment Opportunity. His influence over policy-making in this field is enhanced by the fact that he also is Associate Special Counsel to Mr. Johnson, with offices in the White House. A good, though not absolute guide, to Taylor's thinking on fair employment standards is his commendation of a study of the subject by Harold Mayfield, prepared for the American Management Association. The following is a pertinent passage:

> With all their weaknesses, properly-validated psychological tests are the best predictors of job success we have. Moreover, they are free from personal bias. . . . Not all under-privileged people do poorly on employment tests. Despite their handicaps, the more capable usu-

ally do quite well enough to qualify for most industrial jobs, and those who do poorly are actually difficult to fit in anywhere.

The application of this to the Motorola case is that the test which the Negro job applicant failed to pass was prepared by the Illinois Institute of Technology; and that during the hearing before the state commission expert witnesses with indisputable anti-discrimination records supported the job selection formula.

"Some well-meaning people," Mayfield's pamphlet continues, "are so intent on getting jobs for underprivileged people that they tend to overlook the other side of the coin. Placing a man on a job he cannot really handle is no favor to him or to the cause. . . . The worst thing, surely, is for us to abandon tried-and-tested selection procedures simply in order to place as many on the pay-roll as possible. . . . But other steps employers can take to assure that applicants with poor backgrounds are given a fair deal are to re-examine job requirements, particularly arbitrary employment standards; to re-examine other phases of the selection process . . . for all kinds of curious prejudices that may never come out into the open; to intensify recruiting efforts . . . beyond the convenience of the moment to certain long-range goals and the good of society in general . . . without weakening [a company] competitively."

If these become the White House guide-lines for the E.E.O.C., as Taylor's general approval of them indicates to be his objective, private business management could dismiss its fear that the ruling of the Illinois F.E.P.C. in the Motorola case will infect the Federal administration of Section VII.

COURT SANCTION FOR MOBOCRACY
January 18, 1965

Having recently proclaimed a new public policy in the Southern sit-in cases—that due penalties for acts which were illegal when committed shall not be enforced because the acts were legalized thereafter—the Supreme Court majority today consistently tortured another law to expand its protections of violations of local public order in the name of racial equality. It did this by upholding the appeal of the Rev. B. Elton Cox from a 1961 conviction under a Louisiana law.

Cox had taken command of a group of 2,000 who were demonstrating "near" the Baton Rouge courthouse in protest against what they considered the "illegal" arrest of 23 Negro college students, incarcerated in the building for picketing stores which maintained segregated lunch counters. The Supreme Court majority today agreed that the demonstration was located where it was to influence the courts and peace officers of Baton Rouge to release the prisoners. All were in agreement also that a Louisiana statute, patterned on a 1949 act of Congress, prohibits such an activity "in or near a building housing a court."

The problem for the Supreme Court majority, then, was to find a judicial basis for the particular defiance of this statute that was led by Cox, without voiding the state law or its Federal model. Justice Goldberg proved equal to the task. To do so he employed the following rationale:

The chief of police of Baton Rouge, harassed like all his kind by trying to carry out his duty to enforce the laws against public disorder, and at the same time keep from running afoul of the Supreme Court, had informed the demonstrators as they reached the vicinity of the courthouse to confine themselves "to the west side of the street," which was 101 feet from the courthouse. Justice Goldberg concluded that Cox and his followers properly considered this "official permission" to demonstrate there, and hence an official interpretation that 101 feet from the courthouse was not "near" in the meaning of the statute.

"After the officials acted as they did," summed up Justice Goldberg for the majority, "to sustain [Cox's] later conviction for demonstrating where they told him he could . . . would be to sanction an indefensible sort of entrapment by the state." Moreover, disapprovingly wrote the majority's deft spokesman, "it is clear that the statute, with respect to the determination of how 'near' the courthouse a particular demonstration can be, foresees a degree of on-the-spot administrative interpretation by officials charged with administering and enforcing it."

As proof that this latitude was subject to abuse, he ruled that on-the-spot interpretation infringed Cox's constitutional rights; therefore, the contrary ruling of the Louisiana courts must be reversed on the "near-the-courthouse" conviction.

The following extracts from opinions of 2 of the 4 justices who dissented to the ruling provide ample ground for the judgment that the majority of 5 today tortured another law to fit the public policy the Court initiated in the public school cases in 1954:

"I fail to understand," wrote Justice Black, "how the Court can justify the reversal of these convictions because of a permission which testimony in the record denies was given, which could not authoritatively have been given, anyhow, and which even if given was soon afterwards revoked. . . . Government under the law as ordained by our Constitution is too precious, too sacred, to be jeopardized by subjecting the courts to intimidatory practices . . . fatal to individual liberty and minority rights. . . ."

"I have always been taught," wrote Justice Clark, "that this nation was dedicated to freedom *under law*, not under mobs, whether they be integrationists or white secessionists. . . . For the Court to place its imprimatur upon [mobocracy] is a misfortune that those who love the law will always regret."

The imprimatur was given nevertheless. And also despite the facts that the location of Cox and his demonstrators was "near" enough to the courthouse to create turmoil in the whole area and impel one judge to suspend his work and leave the building.

THE WASHINGTON RIOT
April 13, 1966

The professional apologist for the spirit of lawlessness their own preachings have stirred are searching busily for other provocations of the riot of Negro juveniles that began at an amusement park in neighboring Maryland two nights ago and erupted onto the streets of the nation's capital. This customary effort began the next day when the Negro director of the Washington Urban League expressed the view that the probable cause was "youthful restlessness," colloquially called "spring fever," and that the outbreak of vicious vandalism was not a riot but merely a "disturbance."

Yet what happened was this:

On Easter Monday evening a youthful crowd, overwhelmingly Negro, swarmed into the amusement park, greatly overtaxing its facilities. When the mass seeking places on the "rides" became a menace to their own safety, the rides were shut down. This produced a perilous human traffic jam, whereupon the park was closed as a measure of protection of the installations and the park's patrons.

Since this was several hours before the regular closing-time, only a couple of buses were available. That incited a scramble for transport which the bus operators, unable to supply—and made justly fearful by experience—resolved by driving off. Almost 2,000 of the approximately 7,000 juveniles, now taking on the character of a mob, retaliated by smashing the windows and pillaging the contents of a store and a bank nearby, as they began the long walk back to their homes. On the way they threw rocks through the windows of houses and the windshields of private and police cars, and even stoned two ambulances taking their own injured to hospitals.

Even though, as the Washington police believe, the riot was planned and incited by a small cadre, the other alibis with which bemused do-gooders and deliberate exploiters of Negro grievances seek always to account for such outbreaks cannot be credibly offered for this one. The vandals among the group at the park site and on the way home had the money for admission and for the amusement facilities within. There was no "police brutality" at any juncture; to the contrary, the Maryland county officers and those of the District handled the riot with a very dubious moderation in the circumstances. They arrested only four among the hundreds of offenders, three of whom were released to their parents as too young for the processes of the law.

But in the search for causes that ten Negro clergymen and civil rights group leaders in Washington, including the one who described the anarchy as a mere "disturbance," undertook today, it is highly unlikely that the following will be cited, despite their obviousness:

¶ The preachment of Dr. Martin Luther King that individuals have a right to select the laws they will obey on their judgment of which is or is not just and nondiscriminatory.

¶ The encouragement of public "demonstrations" as a method to redress grievances, including those which infringe the constitutional rights of others and violate existing laws.

¶ The various encouragements and protections of illegal demonstrations by vote-seeking legislators, executives and judges—among these encouragements being judicial decisions which protect criminals at the expense of the social order, and quash sentences imposed for violations of law-and-order statutes that were in legal force at the time.

¶ The special condonation of such infractions by Negroes, on the ground of the injustices and discriminations they have suffered.

This latter and ever-recurring alibi is a particular favorite of the Washington Post, as witness the following in an otherwise objective editorial assignment of "blame" for the Easter Monday riot: ". . . the abyss that divides two worlds of this vicinity—the world of the affluent and middle class from the world of the dispossessed and disinherited." This is a typical sample of the highly emotional projection of a past that is rapidly disappearing, particularly in this community where Negroes constitute the popular majority.

And disrespect for the rights of others, of which riot is only the most violent expression, is hardly discouraged by the current deep engagement of Negro leaders in a boycott movement against merchants who decline to associate their stores in the pressure for home rule in the national capital, on the excellent point that this is a political issue for citizens to resolve for themselves as individuals.

THE GOLDWATER CAMPAIGN

PRIMARIES ASSAYED
May 9, 1964

The Presidential preference primaries in the states have seldom come even close to attaining the design of the Republican Progressives of the Nineteen Hundreds who invented them. This purpose was to supersede the decision-making power of the state organizations at the nominating conventions with the composite will of the party rank-and-file as expressed in state-by-state referendums.

But the limited use of the method among the states, and the fact that in some which employ it the convention delegations are not bound by the results of the referendum, have blocked the path to the objective the system was created to achieve. And this particularly describes the Presidential prenomination condition in the Republican party this year.

On the face of the returns, Senator Goldwater has acquired a commanding lead over the Republicans who actively, or as more or less inactively "receptive," are involved in the contest for the party Presidential nomination of 1964. The positive reasons for this situation include (A) the strong preference for the Arizona Senator by the year-round organization leaders and workers in most states, especially in the midlands, the South, and Southwest and the Northwest; (B) the fact that he has run unopposed in others; and (C) the choice of delegates in still others by the convention system.

Nevertheless, the outcome of a single primary—in California—not only could overcome this composite of national party choice. It could even cancel Goldwater's increment of power, implicit in his lead at this

415

point, to be the convention kingmaker if he is denied the crown. And this negative impact of a single primary, in a state however populous, on a candidacy put so far in the lead by a succession of victories, was neither foreseen nor intended by the Progressive Republicans who originated the Presidential primary system.

They even indulged the hope, if not the belief, that a composite of freely-expressed state preferences—the bulk of it in primaries—could prevent an incumbent President from being nominated over party opposition thus strongly indicated. Though President Taft was renominated over powerful party opposition in 1912, they continued to believe in their theory because his majority over Theodore Roosevelt had its source in the boss-controlled and subsidized Southern delegations of that period. But Harry S. Truman thoroughly disproved it at the Democratic National Convention of 1948 by getting the nomination despite his defeat in the first Presidential primary of that year—in New Hampshire —by the late Senator Kefauver.

The remaining expectation of the authors of the Presidential primary —that its composite preference would at least prevail in the Opposition party—crumbled at the Democratic Convention of 1952 to which Kefauver came with a heavy bag of delegates won at the primaries, and the nomination went to Adlai E. Stevenson, who started with none.

In alignment with this negative history, Wendell L. Willkie abandoned his attempt for renomination in 1944 because of his defeat by Thomas E. Dewey in a single primary—Wisconsin's.

This record exposes the weakness of a system which devolves man-killing labor, and huge expenditures of time and money, on the Presidential aspirants who, like Goldwater and Rockefeller, seek the nomination through extensive use of its mechanisms. The basic flaw is apparent in the agreed destructive potential of the California primary. But the alternative of a national party preference referendum, in which the system would include all the states and supervene the selection of delegates by any state convention, has even deeper defects. Current candidates for the party nomination at least can make a selection of the primaries they will contest, thereby limiting the drain on their time, their physical stamina and their financial resources. Also, if the preference primary were made a national medium of choice, binding on the convention delegates of every state, either the colossal cost would have to be met by the American people as a whole, or only multi-millionaires could contest it.

With all the imperfections of the limited system, however, the one use has revealed a number of interesting aspects of the state of politics in this country. Among them:

(1) Although there is no doubt that President Johnson will be over-whelmingly nominated for election to the office he fills by succession, the existence of the primary system enabled a Southern Democrat opponent of the President's programs to expand his effort in the North. The entrance of Gov. Wallace of Alabama in the Wisconsin, Indiana and Maryland Presidential preferences tests confronted the party organizations in those states with the necessity of drafting fictitious candidates for the Presidential nomination, since Mr. Johnson could not be put in the position of contesting primaries with the Governor of Alabama. So Gov. Reynolds of Wisconsin, Gov. Welch of Indiana and Senator Brewster of Maryland were obliged to pretend to be contenders against the President to keep the state preferences from being registered for Wallace by default.

(2) The primary system provided non-Southern Democrats with their only means of registering protest against the pending equal rights bill—through the "candidacy" of Wallace—since both major parties in that area are committed to the measure.

(3) To express their opposition to Senator Goldwater's nomination in their section of the Indiana primary, more than 100,000 Indiana Republicans were obliged to vote for Stassen, whom the overwhelming majority of these voters neither wish nor expect to be nominated at San Francisco.

(4) In other states, for the same reason or because write-ins are authorized by the primary laws, anti-Goldwater Republicans either had to stay at home, scatter their support, or try to concentrate on an undeclared party eligible to contribute to the "stop Goldwater" effort. Such maneuvers are as artificial as the "Presidential candidacies" of Reynolds, Welch and Brewster, except for the write-in for Ambassador Lodge and Richard M. Nixon. These are generally expressions of sincere and definite preference.

So much at the midway point of the seventh decade of this century for the "great reform" of the Republican Progressives fifty years ago.

THE G.O.P. RIFT
July 18, 1964

With two sentences in his speech of acceptance, Senator Goldwater reopened the wounds inflicted on the Republican party by the contests over its platform and Presidential nomination during the national convention of 1964 that former Vice President Nixon and Governor Scranton of Pennsylvania had sought to bandage and to heal. Thereby a convention, already notable because it reversed a philosophy of government that as practiced had been the party's guiding principle for 25 years, entered the category reserved for landmark events in history.

Why Senator Goldwater, on the instant of assuming his roles as Presidential nominee and national party leader, deliberately chose language which was bound to reopen and intensify the most acute cleavage among the Republicans must await development by the fuller explanation department. And, even accepting the underlining of this language as sufficient proof of its deliberate employment, why did the Senator in effect commend the coercive mass demonstrations in the streets that he and the all-Goldwater convention platform had arranged?

His statement that "extremism in the pursuit of liberty is no vice . . . and moderation in the pursuit of justice is no virtue" was, it is true, the principle of conduct of those who established the Republic by armed revolution. But it also is a precise statement of the justification by which CORE and other pressure groups for Negro rights have taken the issue to the streets and to the offices of government, and have impeded citizens in the exercise of their daily concerns.

Moreover, in praising by usage the word "extremism," Senator Goldwater was demolishing the principal argument he and his leaders made for excluding it from the platform. This argument was that the word was misleading semantics, because it could be distorted to mean what any doctrinaire might want it to mean.

Since it was obvious also that these two sentences in the speech of acceptance would rub salt into the sores of the defeated liberal faction in the convention, they virtually invited the angry and amazed reaction of which Governor Rockefeller's explosion was typical. Therefore, for the time being logic is on the side of the politicians here who read into these sentences a decision by Goldwater that to win the Presidency he must create a distinct national cleavage on the conservative-liberal line; and could do this without fear of a Republican bolt of proportions anything like as serious as that led in 1912 by Theodore Roosevelt on the independent Bull Moose ticket.

The immediate developments here have sustained this judgment insofar as a nationwide Republican bolt is concerned. But there also were indications that more of the party candidates for seats in Congress in the Northeast will campaign independently of the national ticket than intended to do this before the speech of acceptance was delivered. And a broken party front in a state with a large bloc of electoral votes can be costly to the Presidential candidate of that party beyond the capacity of several small states in another region to liquidate. The potential loss to Goldwater could conceivably be overcompensated in the states of the former Confederacy. But an obstacle exists in the Presidential candidacy of Governor Wallace of Alabama on an independent Democratic ticket, a candidacy which Goldwater again reasserted here he will make no move to eliminate, and Wallace has declared he will expand to all other sections of the country where he can manage to get on the ballot.

Thus the Republican national gathering of 1964 has been added to the list, rare in political history, of conventions in which the speech of acceptance by its Presidential nominee and not the platform presented the major issue of the campaign to the people of the United States. The platform identified this issue as "collectivism" through the steady growth of centralized Federal power, financed by excessive and ever-growing deficit spending; and a foreign policy that, as rephrased by Goldwater, "cringes before the bullying of Communism" throughout the world. The candidate put the emphasis on the procedure by which he will seek a popular mandate to dispose of this issue by destroying its roots.

As he stated his indictment of the party in power to the convention, it was a serious and solid challenge of facts and conditions which trouble millions of good citizens, a challenge which cannot readily be sneered or laughed away, or shouted down, as nostalgic longings for a dead or imaginary past. Not until he implicitly justified "extremism" as the method of enforcing change and reform did his bill of particulars provoke the strange, unexpected and still inexplicable renewal of the intra-party controversy that the convention had so overwhelmingly resolved in his favor.

NEVER ANYTHING LIKE IT
August 27, 1964

When President Johnson retired from the front to the rear of the podium of the 1964 Democratic National Convention last midnight, his path was littered by so many shattered traditions of these events that it seemed he had exhausted the supply.

No Presidential nominee ever before had made an informal speech of acceptance in advance of the scheduled formal occasion. None had nominated his choice for second place from the convention platform; and augmented the triumph of his own nomination by true—as opposed to managed—"acclamation" by gaining it for his running mate also.

But there was more tradition-shattering to come. The echoes of the benediction, which marks the close of convention sessions, had scarcely died away in the high vault of the hall when Mr. Johnson was bounding down from the platform to the floor to mingle with the delegates of Texas. From these, after much back-slapping and howdying and joyous "abrazos," the gregarious and elated President extracted Price Daniel, quondam Governor and Senator of his home state, and bore him off to the airport. There another friend, James A. Farley, had been summoned to return to the White House to keep the President company on his night of nights.

This act of impulse is characteristic of Mr. Johnson, and so are the compulsions which made it impossible for him to carry through his determination not to reveal the name of his choice for the Vice-Presidential nomination until he appeared before the convention.

Yet he also presents the paradox of possessing the discipline which enabled him to explore so long and intensely the problem of choosing a Vice-Presidential candidate with the highest ratio of the principal qualifications he sought. As listed by the President to the convention last night, these qualifications were: Capacity "to assume the office of President . . . should that day come"; experience in the technique of elective politics and of legislative management; knowledge of the international and domestic realities of today; compassion for the needs of others and respectful understanding of convictions opposed to his own.

But undoubtedly Mr. Johnson was seeking qualifications he did not mention on the first occasion in American political history when a Presidential nominee not only informed a convention in person of his choice of a running mate, but virtually placed that person in nomination and gave an outline of what the acceptance speeches of both would subsequently be.

These other qualifications were: A Vice-Presidential candidate whose selection could not be ascribed to the consideration that he would attract a vital voting group of co-religionists, as in the case of his Republican opposite number; a nominee who would gratify the truculent "liberal" Democratic groups whose support is vital to the success of the ticket, but whose liberalism had been prudently tempered to avert mass desertion by the Democratic conservatives, most importantly those in the South; and a man with an impressive record of victory in closely contested areas.

Even if, as many believe, the President's exploration had chiefly been for reassurance of an original choice of Humphrey, it remains an example of looking long and hard before leaping that contrasts sharply with the impulsiveness, or compulsiveness, he has so often disclosed.

And never was the revelation more visible than in Mr. Johnson's restless activities yesterday, with its shifts in schedules, its darts in and out of public exposure, its frequent, invariably televised, garrulous and ambulatory exchanges with the press, and the final breakdown of his self-imposed discipline to keep his great "secret" until he could invest it with its highest dramatic effect—on the podium of Convention Hall.

THE GREAT DISCOVERY
OF 'THE VITAL CENTER'
October 12, 1964

Many political scientists with access to all the media of public communications are portraying President Johnson as standing in "the vital center" of political philosophy in the United States and as the choice of a popular "consensus." According to the dictionary, this is saying that his supporters are linked by a consideration common to them all.

To test the accuracy of this pronouncement, it might be imagined that the Presidential election is over, and an opinion-sampling organization, for which the name of Predetermined Pollsters might not be amiss, has assembled a group of citizens and asked them why they voted for the Johnson-Humphrey ticket. Assuming all the answers to be the product of objective self-examination, no additional strain on the imagination is required to anticipate the following responses:

(A normally Republican farmer in the Midwest.) The Soil Bank has paid my taxes. I don't like the crop controls, but I couldn't figure out what Goldwater would have substituted for them.

(The parents of young children.) We think Johnson can be better relied on than Goldwater to prevent a nuclear holocaust. He is softening up the Soviets, and this will keep us out of a shooting war.

(An advocate of "hot pursuit" in Southeast Asia.) I voted for the President because he told the Navy to fire on suspicion in the Gulf of Tonkin. That will also teach the Commies we don't go for any of that nonsense about "international waters."

(A Washington representative of veterans' groups.) We have a better chance with Johnson of keeping our service-unconnected benefits and getting more.

(A big business defense sub-contractor, echoed by his banker and his legal and legislative representatives in Washington.) The Federal Government is our biggest client; we are making nice money; and sound management doesn't take chances on a change in the executive power.

(A union leader in Big Business plants.) Especially when Democratic liberals are in control of the Government, we can count on remaining immune from the antitrust laws, which gives us the whip hand in collective bargaining, and enables us to strike a nationwide industry until it substantially accepts our terms. Those Administration "guidelines" on wage increases? Don't make me laugh.

(An advocate of the sumptuary Federal equal rights law.) Didn't Johnson put all his political weight and the prestige of the Presidency behind it, and didn't Goldwater vote against it?

(A senior citizen.) Many of us need and all of us deserve free Government medicare and bigger Social Security payments. Johnson agrees it's only right that the younger generations should be taxed more to provide them. Goldwater says this eventually will make the Social Security system insolvent. But I'm interested in "now" and not "eventually."

(A Southern Democratic political leader.) The South has most of the major chairmanships in Congress. This is very helpful to our sectional interests, and if we stay regular we can keep those committee chairmanships much longer than if we don't.

(A cross-roads oracle.) The President has got to be a skilled politician to be a successful leader of this diverse nation. This requires wheeling and dealing and arm-twisting at times, and knowing when and when not to burn your bridges. Johnson is a professional in that field; Goldwater is an amateur; and this is no time for amateurs in the White House.

(A first-hand observer of the Governmental process.) It was clear from all the pre-election indices that, even if Goldwater refuted them and was elected, he would have to contend with a Democratic Congress and a badly split Republican party. It was clear that only with Johnson could there be orderly government. And, good or bad, we can't afford a stalemate in Washington.

The composite of the above is a *pool* of different reasons for reaching a common decision. But, unless the dictionary is wrong, it certainly is neither a "vital center" nor a "consensus" of political thinking.

THE JENKINS CASE
October 17, 1964

It would be inhuman not to feel the deepest sympathy for Walter Wilson Jenkins, whose exposure as a sexual deviate on two occasions during his long and faithful service to the public and to President Johnson ended in the ruin of his career and the deep affliction of his wife and six children. And sympathy in such circumstances is a foremost trait of the American people.

But it would be irresponsible if the American people felt no anxiety over the fact the exposure has established that a Government official to whom the most secret operations of national security were accessible, moreover the President's enforcer of security within the Administration itself, is among those unfortunates who are most readily subject to the blackmail by which security secrets are often obtained by enemy agents. This anxiety is augmented by Mr. Johnson's statement that he was totally unaware of Jenkins' deviation until it was about to become a matter of public knowledge, after the failure of two of his closest intimates to prevent publication.

Therefore, it is now the right of the American people to ask and be given adequate answers to these questions the tragic revelation has invoked:

(1) Why, after Jenkins' first arrest for sexual deviation in 1959, and the forfeiture of collateral that obviated his presentment for trial on the charge, did the Washington police, in forwarding his finger-prints to the Federal Bureau of Investigation, conceal the nature of the offense? And why did they omit the identification of the accused as the chief of staff to the Majority Leader of the United States Senate? The first concealment has the vague description of the cause of the arrest as "investigation, suspicion" (of what not stated). The second concealment has the identification of Jenkins merely as "clerk," omitting the vital word "Government" that surely would have alerted the F.B.I.

(2) Does the explanation that the Secret Service "goofed" fully account for its negligent handling of Jenkins' file in checking his application for a White House pass in 1961? The negligence included failure to

check the F.B.I. notation of his arrest in 1959, and to notify higher authority of this.

(3) Why, after the second arrest on the same charge Oct. 7, 1964, did the Washington police repeat the same vague descriptive, clerk, with respect to one who by then had attained such prominence that, even if the arresting officers were unaware of his identity and his previous arrest for the same offense, their superiors in any efficient police department would have known of both?

There are many other questions to which the interest of national security requires full public answers. So does President Johnson's interest. This would be obvious even if he had not stressed, during the campaign, his responsibility for all actions by members of the Executive Department in pursuance of his theme that Senator Goldwater would dangerously delegate some of this obligation and is generally too irresponsible to be entrusted with any of it.

Yet, it was not for want of effort by two of his closest personal advisers to prevent publication of the Jenkins disclosure that the entire press did not join the three Washington newspapers last Wednesday in agreeing temporarily to withhold the fact of the Oct. 7 arrest and the previous one in 1959. Had not the United Press International persisted in checking a tip to examine the veiled police record of Oct. 7, and had Republican National Chairman Dean Burch not publicly charged that a scandal involving national security was being swept under the rug, no one can say how much longer the President, and the people in the final stages of the pre-election campaign, would have remained in ignorance of both the immediate and earlier incidents. Although these advisers, Abe Fortas and Clark M. Clifford, are not members of the Administration, Mr. Johnson has deputized them for so many important personal and political missions that in Texas they would be described as "wearing the brand of L.B.J."

There is no shred of evidence that Jenkins revealed any national security secret to anyone. And most of those who know him at all share the certainty of his intimates that this pitiful victim of what is properly being accepted as an authentic mental disease never has. But the enormity of the disservice to the President by those, including Jenkins, whose concealment of his weakness from Mr. Johnson is implicit in the President's Thursday statement, can be measured by an event of last September. This was a memorandum to all high-level Government officials, issued by Jenkins in his capacity as the Administration's top security officer.

After recommending that these officials have the F.B.I. check all prospective Federal appointees before they were informed they were being considered for appointment, Jenkins made these comments:

"It would be unfortunate if undesirable individuals were put on the public payroll simply because sufficient precautions were not taken prior to their appointment. . . . These procedures can prevent considerable embarrassment both to the Government and to the potential employe himself. . . . We have been somewhat concerned about our own procedures in requesting security name checks [and] it would be desirable for all departments to examine [them] in the above regard. This practice is in effect at the White House now and will be strictly adhered to in the future."

The political professionals are agreed that the scandal, compounded by the President's laissez faire attitude in the Bobby Baker case, will in some degree damage his prospect of an overwhelming victory at the polls on Nov. 3. If the Jenkins incident has proved nothing else, it has disclosed alarming flaws in the Administration's stewardship of national security and a policy of suppressing the evidence. But political history suggests that the damage from these will not be fatal if the President avails himself of the means for reparation at his command, as he is expected to do.

His administrative capacity where close associates are involved, but not his own character, have been put heavily on the defensive. But no Presidential election has demonstrably been lost on such an issue. However, none before has been merged with the issue of national security within the White House itself.

GOLDWATER OPPOSITION
October 24, 1964

As a campaigner for the Presidency against heavy tangible odds, and the psychological handicap created by the sample polls, Senator Barry Goldwater is bucking what is perhaps the strongest opposition tide ever encountered by a candidate who was the free-will, overwhelming choice of his party's national convention.

With every day that brings nearer the Presidential election of 1964 the critical assault on Goldwater increases from his own party; from a large majority of the metropolitan press which generally supports Republican nominees; from leaders of the politically independent, academic, professional and foreign policy groups who normally divide on Presidential candidates; and from leaders of the business-financial communities who usually favor the Republican nominee. The pounding Goldwater is taking from these in combination would discourage any candidate for office.

It is a "must" of campaign strategy that the Senator should give no public indication of this discouragement. But, considering the fact that all the daily samplings of voter intent are adverse to him, his ability to maintain an appearance of optimism is phenomenal. For he is too much of a political realist to be unaware that his chance of defeating President Johnson is slim, and depends only on the existence of some subterranean resolve among the American people, or one of those eleventh-hour campaign disclosures.

In private conversations, Goldwater has conceded this prospect cheerfully. Probably the fundamental reason for his attitude is that the Republican party workers and conservative groups, on the plea that if he did not run he would "let them down," pushed him into a candidacy he did not want to undertake after the death of President Kennedy. But another reason deducible from these private conversations is he firmly believes what he deplores. This is, that, if President Johnson is elected, events will sustain the soundness of the Senator's campaign challenge.

Meanwhile, everything Goldwater reads is bad news. Several conscientious reporters sniffing the political air in Midland, Mountain and Southern states, where the strongest impulse for his domination was centered, detect a shift to the President. Direct or indirect defection of Republican officeholders in states he must carry to be elected endures and grows with the approach of Nov. 3. The chorus of Republican newspapers "supporting a Democrat for the first time" is incessant. Under the skillful shepherding of James H. Rowe, McGeorge Bundy and Henry H. Fowler, Republicans in business, finance, corporation law, and in public service, in international affairs and in scientific work concerned with national defense, have been assembled in committees supporting the candidacy of President Johnson.

The Republican party is in a state of disarray, not only because of rank-and-file defections, but because men elected to high office on its ticket, who participated in the decisions of the San Francisco convention and whose proposals were rejected in procedures conducted strictly according to party rule, have refused to abide by these decisions. Among these Republicans are Gov. George Romney of Michigan, Senators Keating and Javits and Representative John Lindsay of New York, and Senator Case of New Jersey. Without the discipline which was enforced by the "loyalty" requirement at the Democratic Convention of 1964, a political party as such loses its identity as a responsible group accountable to the people.

Presidents Taft in 1912, Hoover in 1932 and Truman in 1948 also encountered party defection. But in those years Taft was nominated in close combat and Hoover and Truman by reluctant conventions; whereas the large majority of the San Francisco delegates were enthusiastic in their choice of Goldwater. In Truman's "Memoirs" he wrote:

I was confronted [in 1948] not with one major defection in the Democratic party but with two bolts of sizable proportions. In addition to the . . . alternate candidate on the platform of States' Rights Democrats, there were the so-called Progressives under the leadership of another Democrat, Henry Wallace. . . . Approximately 90 per cent of the press and radio . . . supported the other candidates. [But] my chief objection was to the commonplace practice of distorted editorials and slanted headlines in the press and of outright misrepresentation in the daily offerings of the columnists and commentators.

He was elected, however, because, undeterred by these conditions, he sought and won the support of the rank-and-file of his party in key states, of Republican farmers and roving ethnic groups in large cities. But the parallel with Goldwater fails, since in all these quarters his struggle is uphill. Also, the opposition to his candidacy in the normally Republican press is much larger than was the anti-Truman percentage in the normally Democratic press.

So the miracle of President Truman's election in 1948 against heavy tangible and psychological odds would become minor compared to the miracle Goldwater's election would be.

PROBLEMS
IN THE GREAT SOCIETY

AN ECONOMIC NEW JERUSALEM
February 5, 1966

The American society, more nearly than any great human complex of the past, would fulfill the vision of St. John the Divine of "a new Jerusalem coming . . . out of heaven" if the recommendations of the Presidential Commission on Automation could become the state of the Union without wrecking it. But the American form of government would have been supplanted by a Socialist system in which public power is totally federalized.

President Johnson's programs for the Great Society derive from the same egalitarian concept. In recommending a national guarantee of a minimum standard of living for all persons and families, whether or not they have attempted to the limit of their capacities to earn it, the commission provides a logical supplement to these programs. However, it would expand them with detailed proposals which go far beyond the philosophy of classic Socialism. And some of these, in operation, would effectually depress individual initiative and sap the incentive of economic reward commensurate with character, ability and effort.

Among the recommendations of the commission are: expanding the present high rate of Government spending to provide public service jobs for the unemployable as well as the unemployed; furnishing a college education for all who are "qualified," a word certain to be most liberally interpreted; increasing the present generous rates of social insurance;

428

and contributing from the general tax revenues the differences between the income of every family, if any, and the income required to meet a Government-fixed minimum standard of living.

For the sake of producing unanimous recommendations, the commission deleted one favored by the majority. This was, that seniority protections in labor contracts should be eliminated because they have been the vehicle of racial discrimination, and because they reduce the job mobility required to adjust employment to the new technology of automation. The commission, for the same reason, also backed away from registering the opinion of the majority that a shorter work week would restrain the full productivity its recommendations assume.

These concessions to labor members in the interest of a unanimous report impaired the commission's general conclusion—that automation will not become a basic threat to employment if the present rate of Government spending to "stimulate" the economy is substantially increased. Nevertheless, the commission retained tax cuts among its major recommendations.

The group of fourteen was created by Congress in 1964, "to be appointed by the President . . . from among persons outside the Government with a competency in the areas to be dealt with . . . [to be] broadly representative [and include] not less than four members drawn equally from labor and management." Mr. Johnson's choices in the latter category included two whose credentials are undisputable: Thomas J. Watson Jr., chairman of I.B.M., and Walter Reuther, president of the Auto Worker's Union. But few would have believed that they, as well as other members presumably divided sharply in political philosophy, would have united on proposals which outrun even those of the Great Society in moving the American Government toward total centralization and the ideals of advanced Socialism.

The President has reason to be gratified by the outcome of the commission's deliberation. Even his recommendation to Congress to finance a rent-supplement program—making up the difference between what low-income families can pay and the cost of what the Administration conceives to be "adequate" housing—looks conservative in contrast with the commission's proposal of a direct, guaranteed income for every family that would cut deeply into what remains of the American capitalist system.

One need only read the report of the McCone Commission, growing out of the anarchy in the Watts section of Los Angeles, to find substantial evidence of a tendency in human nature to exploit government when it finances deliberate idleness, and puts a rising premium on children produced, even without benefit of clergy, in plain disregard of the inability to care for them.

Congress, reflecting public opinion, may be coming to the point of disapproving the more radical of the Great Society legislative proposals. In which event the commission's recommendations have no immediate future. But if any of them become law, it is to be hoped Norman Thomas will still be around to administer them.

He is the only citizen in sight who is both learned in the philosophy of Socialism and knows the responsible limit to enforcing it in the American society.

LET'S YOU AND HIM
CURB INFLATION
April 2, 1966

He stood up there before the representatives of Big Business and urged them to cut down their programs for plant expansion. He stood up there before the group of White House "interns" and accented increases in corporate and individual income taxes over other anti-inflation measures available to the Government, such as meaningful reductions and project postponements in the domestic budget.

He besought the heads of city governments to defer public works projects and other capital expenditures. He moved in and out of White House press briefings, and held impromptu news conferences, to suggest that American housewives could check the leaping cycle of food prices by shopping for cheaper "substitutes." And he put Congress on the spot as a prodigal spendthrift, though it has added not more than a fraction to the swollen Federal budget of $113-billions that includes a $3.3-billion increase in the costs of building the Great Society.

But not until President Johnson had finished a full round of these comments and exhortations did he disclose his acceptance of the fact that a basic source of the current inflation is his policy of sustaining and increasing the vast flow of concurrent Government spending for a welfare state while the cost of the war in Vietnam is steadily rising in terms of billions. Then he announced he had ordered the Administration to try to cut current Federal spending in an amount which, with anticipated greater revenues, could be as much as $1.1-billion. Before issuing that order the President seemed to be saying "let's you and him provide the anti-inflationary curbs."

He stood up there, "Texas-tall and pencil-thin," like the character in the cigar ads, and urged on the private sector and local governments the initiative for spending restraints he has rejected as Administration budgetary policy, the most effective means by which they can be successfully imposed. Moreover, just a few hours before the President began his exhortations he had successfully employed his unmatched political power to induce a reluctant House of Representatives to start two other Great Society programs with an immeasurable potential of ultimate costs—rent supplements to low-income groups out of the general revenues, and a Federal Teachers Corps.

Also, while the President was calling on these groups, in the name of the public interest, to practice what he and his Administration are merely preaching, his agents in Congress were putting the finishing touches on a minimum-wage increase bill which breaks his designated anti-inflation "guidelines;" and he was maintaining silence toward a strike of the railroad firemen's union, in defiance of a Federal court order, which was crippling the economy of 38 states, notably by idling the huge automotive industry. But the President's only comment in that quarter was that he is arranging a meeting in which he will exhort organized labor leaders to join in the economic restraints he is urging on industry, and on the women who buy the food for their families.

Furthermore, Mr. Johnson quickly retreated from the two most nearly definite positions he had indicated—that his probable choice among the inflationary checks open to the Government would be a rise in the income tax rates, and that he favored a form of "buyers' strike" by American housewives. He used the impromptu news conferences to try to modify these natural assumptions which his original statements had invited. He would not ask for a tax increase, he said, "until the fiscal advisers and the men in the Administration and in Congress whose judgment I respect consider that we need it." And perish the thought he was suggesting a "buyers' strike"—only that housewives "take out their lead pencils and put on their glasses and look at some of these price lists, and see where shortages were occurring . . . and say good-by to those products that insist on going up and up."

Since a tax increase is the last thing Congress wants to do in an election year, the President's inclusion of that body as a source of the "judgment" on which he would base an affirmative decision inevitably checked the impression he had given just previously of being on the verge of that decision. But, with respect to a houswives' buyers' strike, he may not be able to limit it to the "selective" dimension he proposed on second thought. As the events of 1921 demonstrated, when this movement begins it spreads rapidly to all the items which make up the cost of living. In 1921 people quit paying their rent and declined to buy new clothes, shoes, household work-saving devices, etc., which would play hob with the perpetual-boom theory of the new economics with which Mr. Johnson has become entranced.

In finally ordering a cut in spending he had long insisted was fixed at an irreducible minimum, the President moved to spike an issue the Republicans in Congress have sought to make paramount in the 1966 election campaign. But they had already damaged their position, for the first opportunity to check Great Society spending-as-usual, despite the exactions of the Vietnam war, was lost in the House when six Republicans supplied the majority for the rent-supplement plan which the President could not muster in that overwhelmingly Democratic body. And, though the Republican leaders call for a reduction of $5-billion in the domestic budget, and declare it can be done without impairment of any service essential to progressive and enlightened public welfare, they have yet to bring in a bill of particulars.

Resentment of inflation, and of the conduct of the Vietnam war, may and probably will gain the Republicans some Congressional seats in the 1966 elections. But thus far, as the Opposition party, they have not earned them.

TOO LATE AND TOO EARLY
April 20, 1966

Four reasons account in varying degree for the refusal of the Senate once again to submit a constitutional amendment to the states removing from the Supreme Court its asserted power to require that the districts which elect members of each branch of the state legislatures contain an approximately equal number of eligible voters.

1. Thirty-seven states have already complied with the requirement, or are proceeding to do this, so that their legislative function would be temporarily paralyzed if and when the amendment was ratified.

2. The one-man, one-vote principle on which the Supreme Court ruling is based has the quality of those political slogans which appeal to the strong streak of idealism in the American people.

3. The constitutional issue—that the Court exceeded both its specified and inherent jurisdiction—is too complicated to evoke an emotional

popular response, especially since the Court's ruling gives greater weight to the votes in the urban communities in which 80 per cent of the people reside.

4. The contention that the effect of the ruling will be legislative control by urban political machines in disregard of the constitutional rights and legitimate interests of the non-urban 20 per cent might have persuaded the Senate to submit the amendment if it had been demonstrated in practice on either of the occasions when the vote was taken; but there has been insufficient time for that.

Even so, the Senate favored submission by an emphatic majority of seventeen among the 93 who voted, but seven short of the two-thirds required to lay a proposed constitutional amendment before the states.

But, in addition to the four specific reasons listed above, the proposed Dirksen amendment failed for the second time to get the constitutionally required two-thirds because of the innate reluctance of the American people to impose curbs on the Supreme Court. Primarily, they see no constructive alternative to its assertions of power and jurisdiction, however greatly these may lack the definite warrant of the Constitution or stretch it beyond the breaking point. Currently, as from time to time in the past, a Court majority has unilaterally amended the Constitution when this has not been done by the prescribed method and the majority believes it should have been. The majority has legislated on the same belief when Congress has failed to exercise its function. And, though the formulation of public policy is constitutionally reserved to the Federal legislative and executive branches, the Court majority has proclaimed it in the absence of such action.

These are not just the conclusions of public and political critics of the current Court majority, or even of members of the bar who have voiced them. All can be found in dissenting opinions by members of the Court itself, and often by a maximum minority of four. But, as Chief Justice Hughes once put it, in the period between his retirement and return to the Court, "The law is what the judges say it is." And, though this concedes judicial supremacy among three Federal branches set up by the Constitution as separate and equal in the Government provinces assigned, the American people have accepted the fact as the only practicable working arrangement, despite its frequent judicial abuses.

This attitude makes it hard going to acquire a two-thirds Senate majority for a proposal definitely designed to overrule a decision of the Supreme Court, particularly one which resounded with the rhetoric of democratic equality at the polling place. But the seven more affirmative votes the Constitution requires might have been forthcoming on this second try if so many states had not already complied with the one-man, one-vote dictum with respect to their legislative election districts. For the proposal was more consistent with this dictum than the Court's rulings based on it, because it authorizes the voters in a state to decide whether they want to choose one legislative branch on considerations other than just population equality in the voting districts. And the Court majority has rejected "one man, one vote" on that proposition as unconstitutional.

This extraordinary limitation of the Court's own asserted principle, plus the development of injustices to the non-urban population that are inherent in its reapportionment formula, could swell the Senate's emphatic majority to two-thirds in the not distant future. But the first test came too early, and today's both too early and too late.

FOREIGN AFFAIRS

THE CRISIS IN THE U.N.
December 3, 1964

If the peacemaking potential of the United Nations had not been over-sold from the beginning, if the Charter had been invoked impartially against violators and its specific limitations respected, the U.S.S.R. would not now be in the position of offering the U.N. a single choice between yielding to blackmail or risking disintegration. And the U.N. policies of the United States have the largest share of responsibility for this situation.

The overselling to the American people of what this international association could do to establish a peaceful, durable world order was initiated by the Truman Administration and continued by the Eisenhower and Kennedy-Johnson Administrations. President Kennedy went so far as to assert in his Inaugural Address that the United Nations is "our last best hope for peace in an age where the instruments of war have far outpaced the instruments of peace." And the majority of the General Assembly naturally read sanction of the irresponsibility it was display-ing in his pledge of support of the U.N. "to strengthen its shield of the new and the weak . . . to enlarge the area in which its writ may run."

This irresponsibility of the Assembly soon expanded into such resolu-tions as the demand that all the African peoples be granted "immediate independence," regardless of their capacity for self-government. And the representative of the United States voted "aye."

On one notable occasion this Government took the lead in assuring the success of a flagrant violation of the Charter by a U.N. member in the form of military blackmail. It blocked the only channels through which the Netherlands could strengthen the defenses of West Irian against Indonesian occupation by force of this Dutch territory to which Indonesia had no shred of historical or ethnical claim.

On another occasion of Charter violation by a member, the United States Government stood aside when Prime Minister Nehru sent military forces to seize the Portuguese enclave of Goa. The American representative, Adlai E. Stevenson, made an eloquent speech of protest and warning. But, though he described the issue as fundamental, this Government shrank from submitting it to a vote in the Assembly on the not-so-noble ground that a motion of censure was foredoomed to failure.

The outstanding example of U.N. disregard of specific limitations on its function in the Charter, with the indispensable support of this Government, was the bloody war to suppress the establishment of Katanga as a separate state by Moise Tshombe. He was the only pro-Western leader in the vast territory which Belgium, under the pressure of an "anti-colonial" foreign policy to which the United States was a principal subscriber, was forced to grant independence before its inhabitants were in the least prepared for this status. Moreover, Katanga had the only viable economy and public order in the Congo; other provincial chieftains had repudiated an agreement with Tshombe for a loose federation; and Article 1 (7) of the Charter banned U.N. intervention in "domestic matters," which described the civil war between the central Congo "government" and Katanga.

By June 1963, at a cost to United States taxpayers of about $73 million, Katanga was, as the State Department put it, "peacefully reintegrated" and Tshombe was in flight. But the U.S.S.R., disappointed in its hope that the manhandling of Article 1 (7) would end with its pet, Lumumba, in charge of the Congo, decided that it could do some manhandling of its own of Article 19, which prescribes the loss of votes in the Assembly of members two years in arrears for nonpayment of assessments for such U.N. activities as the intervention in the Congo civil war.

Confronted with the threat of Moscow to withdraw if the U.N. applies Article 19 with a fidelity it has casually breached in other sections of the Charter, other members led by the United States are seeking an undercover way of paying the price of the vulnerability of the organization for which their own overselling of its peacemaking potential, their abettance or toleration of other violations of the Charter, and unauthorized wars invoked in the name of peace are basically responsible.

But the blackmail-bluff of the U.S.S.R. and its willingness to parley indefinitely with Washington disclosed that—despite threat of withdrawal, shoe-pounding and all that—the Kremlin finds the U.N. very useful and wants to stay aboard.

THE LARGER STAKE
IN SANTO DOMINGO
May 1, 1965

When President Johnson interrupted a televised news program Friday night to acknowledge at last that the mission of our military intervention in the Dominican Republic was to forestall a Communist take-over as well as to rescue endangered Americans and other foreigners, he confirmed a fact which for two days the highest Administration spokesmen had curiously refused to concede. And implicit in this confirmation was the conclusion virtually everyone here had already made. This is, that he is determined there shall be no spread, especially in the Caribbean, of regimes oriented to or controlled either by Moscow or Peking; and that the end has come of the evangelistic and faltering United States policy which assisted Castro to power in Cuba and led to the calamitous episode of the Bay of Pigs.

Having in effect delegated enforcement of the Monroe Doctrine to the ponderous, divided and uncertain agency of the Organization of American States, the Administration had at first apparently deemed it a diplomatic necessity to insist in the face of clear evidence to the contrary that the only purpose of the United States military landings in the Dominican Republic was to rescue Americans and other foreigners who were in the line of fire between the Dominican rebels and the armed forces loyal to the government. This line of diplomacy was fortified by the following passage in the President's announcement of his dispatch of the first contingent, the Marines, of the American military rescue expedition:

"The United States Government has been informed by military authorities in the Dominican Republic that American lives are in danger [and that] they are no longer able to guarantee their safety."

But it is historically routine for this Government to respond, by sending troops or other forms of assistance, to Americans whose lives are endangered in the Caribbean area. Why, then, the Congressional leaders, suddenly summoned to the White House to hear the President's announcement, asked of one another, did he cloak the occasion in emergency atmosphere associated with a turning-point in American history?

An obvious explanation was implicit in the summons of the Congressional leaders only a few hours after Mr. Johnson had individually made the decision to land the Marines in the Dominican Republic. Protests from Latin-American nations and certain domestic groups that the United States had returned to "gunboat diplomacy" were certain; and the President wanted to nail down Congressional approval before these protests began. This explanation tightly fits the pattern of his constant search for a "consensus," especially with respect to any foreign policy and steps taken in its pursuit.

But the fact that several of the leaders at the meeting revealed great curiosity as to whether the Dominican rebellion was infiltrated by Communists, and particularly Castro-Communists, indicated their feeling that the obvious purpose was not the entire one. Although Administration aides, including Rear Admiral Raborn, the new C.I.A. director, made small reference to the "Communist angle," the feeling persists that it was much more importantly involved in the President's decision.

An event earlier in the day stimulated this impression among several of the Republicans who were called to the White House. They had attended a "breakfast" of Congressional Republicans whose guest was Jack Hood Vaughan, the Assistant Secretary of State for Inter-American Affairs. Most of his discourse concerned what he described as strong, Castroist-Communist infiltration in Latin America, most currently conspicuous in the Dominican rebellion. According to members of the group, Vaughan emphasized that this infiltration was advanced by the use of money and by guerrilla fighters trained in Cuba. And when asked whether Moscow or Peking was the most probable source of the financing, he had replied "Moscow."

Also, the day after the dramatic White House meeting, the State Department heightened the impression of a dual objective in the American military landings by one of those familiar official performances in which the right hand points one way and the left hand another. On the highest levels of the department the insistence was maintained that the only purpose was to safeguard the lives of Americans, and of other nationals who desired the protection. On the lower levels a voluntary contribution was made to the press of the names of individuals known to be active in the rebellion, where and by what Communist regime they were trained, etc.

But on the reasonable assumption that the theatrical setting of the

President's meeting with the Congressional leaders was designed to give the widest possible publicity to their support of the decision he already had taken and executed, it was an example of the technique the President employs in his constant search for "consensus." By the time the leaders reached the White House, they were psychologically conditioned to go along with whatever was the objective. "During my taxi-ride to the White House," said one, "I speculated tensely over what the emergency could be—an attack on Hanoi, perhaps, or even on the Communist China nuclear works. When the President made his anticlimactic announcement that the Government was doing what it has never failed to do, especially in the Caribbean, my relief was so great it took me a while to take a second look for the real message.

"This, I hoped and believe, is that the President intends never to let the Communists set up another government where the U.S. is in shooting range."

BY ANY OTHER NAME, IT'S STILL WAR
June 9, 1965

In retrospect it would appear that when the President dispatched regular combat forces to Vietnam, their commitment to ground warfare would be generally foreseen as inevitable. To Prime Minister Menzies of Australia this foresight has always been "a simple matter," as he remarked today. The only reason for the stir created in this country by the confirmatory announcement from the State Department is the Administration's evasive rhetoric on every occasion when our military role in Vietnam was expanded from the original limitation of providing strategic counsel and technical assistance.

The first expansion was the landing of Marines and regular Army paratroopers. The Administration's explanation was that they were to provide "perimeter defense" for United States military installations. Since effective perimeter defense requires that the Vietcong guerrillas over a wide area be prevented from concentrating to attack in depth, American ground combat action naturally ensued. But this was officially differentiated from the actual involvement of United States armed forces on the Asian mainland.

But at that juncture it became apparent that this fine distinction was

about to be swept away by developing conditions. One was the advent of
the monsoon when the advantage would rest with the Vietcong if the
United States military role continued to be limited to a holding action.
Another was the conclusive evidence that the cautious, selective United
States air strikes in North Vietnam had failed of their purpose to
produce a cease-fire and bring the Hanoi Government to the conference
table. The only alternatives being (1) to escalate the airstrikes to the
point where the aggression from North Vietnam would be paralyzed,
(2) to commit our forces to ground war, or (3) to pull out of the area
—the Administration chose the second.

Then was initiated the kind of public relations operation that is
marked for confusion from the start because of faltering at the controls.
The operation began last week at Saigon where United States sources
gave the press a strong hint designed for publication, that a conventional ground war was shortly to be expected. Over the weekend the
State Department not only encouraged, but affirmed, suggestions that
the Saigon forecast had materialized. Yesterday, in a full-circle swing
from gobbledygook to realism the department spokesman affirmed this
officially, and seemed glad to do it.

Yes, he said, it was true that for some time the United States military
command in South Vietnam had the President's authority to commit our
ground forces to combat whenever so requested by the South Vietnam
Government. Today the White House volunteered that this authority
extended to occasions when, in the "judgment" of the command, "the
general military situation urgently requires" the commitment.

But the self-evident purpose of the White House statement was to
modify one consequence of the public relations operation. This was the
only possible public conclusion—that the primary mission of United
States troops in South Vietnam had been fundamentally changed. "Not
recently or at any other time," said the White House, has the President
given any such order to General Westmoreland. The General has always
been authorized to do "whatever is necessary," just as Congress gave
advance approval in those very words to the President's judgment of
whatever may be needed to repel the aggression against South Vietnam.
"Any such change of primary mission," said the White House, "would
obviously be a matter for decision in Washington."

Thus the Administration reverted to a semantic quibble after officials
in Saigon and Washington, who could only have been acting under orders from on high, had initiated Operation Candor. For there is certainly fundamental "change" in a "mission" which begins as strategic
counsel and technical assistance within a government territory, proceeds

to bombing outside that territory by the Air Force and the Navy, moves onward to "perimeter defense" that inescapably leads to ground combat, and finally is given authority for expansion into formal ground warfare.

"The question is," said Alice to Humpty Dumpty, "whether you *can* make words mean so many different things." "The question is," said Humpty Dumpty, "which is to be master—that's all."

TRYING TO GET LOOSE
FROM THE TAR BABY
July 24, 1965

The means employed by President Johnson and his principal advisers on the conduct of the war in Vietnam to call public attention to the urgency of their deliberations are justified by the gravity of the problem and the need to prepare the American people for whatever new sacrifices may be required of them. This atmosphere has been intensified for the purpose by daily official emphasis on the secrecy by which the President has bound the participants to reveal no detail of the conferences.

This elaborate public relations technique would lose its justification only if it should develop that the decisions of the conferences are not for the deeper involvement of the United States in the war, with the much graver portent the expansion would create. But the general impression among qualified observers is that that is the most unlikely outcome of the White House meetings.

The decisions which have been in the making, or have been made, may be public property by the time this dispatch appears in print. But while they may encourage, and eventually fulfill, hope of at least moderating the desperate nature of the problem of Vietnam, their immediate product will be a more realistic coming-to-grips with its true magnitude than the Administration has publicly conceded before.

The ways and the plights of men and of nations have been recorded, examined, analyzed and adjudged in countless works of history and fiction. And, as in the instance of Vietnam, contemporary writings and oratory have dealt with them in millions of words. But often the serious character of these plights has been made more comprehensible to humanity by humorous fable than by solemn exposition. Such a fable, uncanny in the comparison it invites with the involvement of the United States in Vietnam, is "The Wonderful Tar Baby Story."

Like the other nursery tales Uncle Remus told to "the little boy" in Georgia long ago, this one concerned the unending effort of Brer Fox to catch and eat Brer Rabbit. An unusual series of errors of foresight by the rabbit had for the first time put him in a predicament from which no exit was in sight except down the fox's gullet. This menacing situation arose after Brer Fox, smarting under Brer Rabbit's recent success in making him look foolish in the matter of the "calamus root" hoax, fixed up a contraption of tar and turpentine that the fox named The Tar Baby, set up in the big road, and lay in the bushes to await developments.

He didn't have long to wait, as the tale was told, because very shortly Brer Rabbit came pacing down the road, lippity-clippity, clippity-lippity, as sassy as a jay bird. Brer Fox lay low. When the rabbit spied the Tar Baby he reared up on his hind legs in astonishment, and then, remembering his social obligations, wished it the time of day, praised the weather and inquired how the Tar Baby's symptoms seemed to segashuate that morning. No reply was forthcoming, and Brer Fox winked his eye and laid low.

At this point the offended Brer Rabbit lost his temper and proceeded on actions without looking ahead to their potential consequences. Continuing to get no response from the Tar Baby—to an inquiry whether deafness was the cause of its refusal to talk, or to information that Brer Rabbit could holler louder if this was necessary, or to the stated conclusion that the Tar Baby was stuck up and the obvious cure was to bust him wide open—Brer Rabbit fit the action to the word.

First he blipped the Tar Baby on the side of the head, and his hand got stuck. The Tar Baby went on saying nothing and Brer Fox went on laying low. Second, the rabbit fetched a blip with his other hand, and that got stuck. The rabbit lost the use of his feet in the same way, and then the use of his head when he butted the Tar Baby cranksided, after getting no response to a demand to be turned loose.

At this planned-in-advance strategic moment Brer Fox arose from the bushes, looking as innocent as a mocking bird; observed that the rabbit appeared to be sort of stuck up that morning; rolled on the ground and laughed and laughed until he could laugh no more; and gasped out that this time Brer Rabbit would dine with him, to partake of some calamus root the fox had thoughtfully laid in, and no excuse would be accepted.

"Did the fox eat the rabbit?" the little boy asked Uncle Remus. He might have and he might not, was the reply: at any rate that was the end of the story for the present, though "some say" that "Jedge" Bear came to the aid of the rabbit, and some say he didn't. Which pretty closely matches the conflict in speculations of the outcome of Averell Harriman's mission to Moscow.

Thus once more a fable serves as an excellent means to make a complex situation clear—in this instance one which could not even have been imagined at the time of the telling as a situation in which the United States would ever find itself. Certainly it is stuck hard in a tar baby. Certainly its own errors of foresight have stuck it deeper than was intended. Certainly one of the responsible factors is the concept of the mission of the United States as morally and militarily obligated to oppose the spread of Communism anywhere in the world, single-handed if necessary, and whether or not beyond our reasonable sphere of national security and interest.

But fables are not necessarily conclusive as analogies to the courses of men and nations, only of the durable origins of the human tendency to err. If Brer Rabbit had been a real member of his species instead of the quasi-human Uncle Remus suggested by giving him speech, he would never have assumed the arrogant role of lord of the highway in "The Wonderful Tar Baby Story."

THE ORIGINAL QUIZ KID
December 1, 1965

It was a great surprise today when Rollo—the boy nuisance of American literature, whose endless demands for the "why" of everything made him the Brat of All Time—appeared in this office, still a child despite the passage of 131 years. It was in 1834 that Jacob Abbott created the character who has been described as the "inquisitive type in juvenile fiction." And, true to type, he refused to leave until he asked the questions and got the answers that follow:

Q. Our teacher says Americans are fighting in Vietnam to save the free world from being overrun by Communist aggression. What is the free world?

A. It is composed of the United States and all other anti-Communist and neutral nations.

Q. What are they doing to help us save them by preserving the independence of the South Vietnamese, whether they want it or not?

A. Our allies constantly assure us of their support of the war we are fighting for them in Southeast Asia with a ground army nearing

200,000, the Air Force and the Seventh Fleet. The Australians have sent 1,000 troops, and South Korea has promised a division. So, you see, the free world is very appreciative that we are protecting its independence.

Q. But our teacher says some of our allies are regularly delivering to North Vietnam the shiploads it has to have to carry on the war. And I read that Senator Bobby Kennedy believes Americans should send blood, to make the wounded Communist soldiers well enough to shoot our men again. Why?

A. Those allies, Rollo, are maintaining the sovereign right of independence we are fighting to maintain for the people of South Vietnam. So it would be inconsistent policy for the United States to challenge the right of independent action by these allies on the self-centered argument that they are helping our enemy to equip more soldiers to kill more of ours. As for Bobby, he explained he was merely asserting a noble American tradition.

Q. Did we send blood to restore to fighting form the Germans, Italians, Japanese, North Koreans and Chinese Communists when they were killing our soldiers?

A. No, but traditions have to begin somewhere, and who can start one with more authority than a Kennedy?

Q. Why did the State Department in late 1964 deny that North Vietnam had proposed a peace conference about Vietnam when the opposite was the truth? Did Secretary Rusk get static on his antenna?

A. No. But if he had interrupted President Johnson's campaign broadcasts by telling the facts to the American people, Rusk would have lost not only his antenna, but his head, too.

Q. Our teacher says we are able to do everything at once without real inflation—making war in Southeast Asia while garrisoning Europe; spending whatever it takes to establish Mr. Johnson's Great Society throughout the world, while committing more and more billions of deficit money to the war in Vietnam. How is this possible?

A. The President hasn't said. But he must know how. Because only today a White House spokesman in Texas announced Mr. Johnson felt "no undue concern" over the steady inflation in living costs that the latest official statistics disclosed; that he didn't view it as a "major threat at this time," and was fixing to take care of it if and when.

Q. Why, then, has he summoned to Texas what our teacher calls his Quadriad of economic advisers?

A. Well, he probably thinks it a good idea to assure the people again that the shrinking purchasing power of the dollar isn't inflation at all; it just feels like it.

Q. The papers say this Quadriad is composed of Secretary Fowler, Chairman Martin, Budget Director Schulze and Chairman Ackley. How can Mr. Johnson be sure this Quadriad will agree with him that Government policy is not chiefly responsible?

A. Rollo, you obviously don't know what this President can do with a deck stacked three-to-one on his filling a hand.

Q. Our teacher says the supply route of the North Vietnamese and the Vietcong passes through a part of Laos. Why did the Administration pull out of Laos in 1961 at the very time it decided on a vast expansion of our military role in South Vietnam?

A. Rollo, you are obviously subversive. And you use words too big for a child of 13½. Clear out before you ask why Ambassador Goldberg views a protest march around the White House in which the Vietcong flag was shown as just another proof of our national "virility."

BELEAGUERED POLICY
April 9, 1966

The violence and anti-American direction of the riots against the Ky military junta government in Vietnam support the official finding that Communists are exploiting the popular unrest to further their design to dominate Southeast Asia. But that is merely the latest exercise of a settled policy. And it does not remove the fact that what is occurring is the ripening of the seeds of civil war that tend to be nourished by the military intervention of a totally alien foreign power, however benevolent and high-minded its purpose.

The threat to the attainment of this purpose by the United States, the totally alien foreign power involved, is stimulated by the Administration's judgment on the highest civilian and military levels that a military junta is the only type of regime which can be entrusted with the government of South Vietnam at this juncture. And the threat was further intensified at Honolulu by President Johnson's dramatic identification of Marshal Ky as the symbol of the American interest.

Whether or not Ky's purge of the most popular member of the junta, and the other personal power-plays which followed, were direct consequences of this Presidential laying on of hands, they at least were productive of the turn to violence by the dissident faction. And, since Ky was the prime target of this dissidence, his certification as the United

States' chosen leader was sure to imbue the protest with strong anti-American coloration. That combination presented the Communists with a rare opportunity to exploit both, and naturally they have taken full advantage of it.

Between the time this is written and appears in print, order and some show of unity by the South Vietnamese people toward their government may have been established. But the outbreak of what has been described by some American observers as "a civil war within a civil war" disclosed an internal condition which challenges the concept that it was and would remain negligible. And on that estimate the intervention policy of the United States was based.

The steady increase in our military involvement has automatically increased the difficulty of modifying the policy, once undertaken. And this painful paradox, accented by the violent and anti-American character of the riots in South Vietnam, has laid on President Johnson the enormous task of trying to extricate the United States from this predicament without the loss of national honor, international prestige or an undeniable bastion against Communist domination of Southeast Asia.

As Senator Fulbright usefully noted the other day, this predicament developed from a very limited foreign aid program. President Eisenhower transferred it to the new states of Indochina, set up at Geneva, when they gained their independence from France. In holding expansion of the South Vietnam aid program to a small group of military and technical advisers, after the invasion threat from the North became formidable, General Eisenhower was influenced by his professional estimate that greater involvement imposed a strong liability of encountering the condition in South Vietnam that now has come to pass. And for the first few months of President Kennedy's Administration, this policy was maintained.

In May, 1961, the President was still riding herd on the outlines of a South Vietnam assistance program he had assigned to the then Deputy Secretary of Defense, Roswell Gilpatrick. And in a conversation with this correspondent he said he saw no wise alternative to a "neutralist" government in Laos in which Communist representation was most probable. In a similar discussion on October 17, 1961, the President repeated what he had said in a Senate speech in 1954—that United States troops should never become involved in a war on the Asian mainland. As for the armed conflicts between population groups in South Vietnam, the President remarked that they appeared to be guerrilla warfare; and, if so, this was the type of civil disturbance in which the United States must not become militarily involved.

But the President added he had just left a meeting at which "the Pentagon" generally approved a recommendation by the Chiefs of Staff to dispatch 40,000 troops to South Vietnam, where external military aggression and internal subversion from the north had taken on increasing proportions. He was not, he said, favorably disposed to the recommendation, but was sending General Maxwell Taylor (accompanied by Walt Whitman Rostow of the White House staff) to appraise the proposal on the basis of an on-the-spot investigation. The result was adoption of the recommendation of the Chiefs of Staff, and a military involvement of the United States that has since grown to nearly 300,000 members of the armed forces.

It was not until much later, after Lyndon B. Johnson had succeeded to the Presidency, that this fateful commitment was asserted to have been in discharge of a specific obligation imposed on the United States as a signatory to the Southeast Asia Treaty (SEATO), negotiated by President Eisenhower's Secretary of State, John Foster Dulles. The principal spokesman for this sudden and new interpretation, designed as an answer to the widespread criticism of our mounting military engagement, is Dulles's present successor, Dean Rusk.

But its wholly expedient nature is established by the flatly opposite understanding on the basis of which the Senate approved the treaty. As stated by Dulles to the Foreign Relations Committee, and emphasized in the committee's explanation to the Senate, SEATO was not in any way a commitment in the area by the United States, collectively or unilaterally, beyond "having mobile striking power and the ability to use that against the sources of aggression if it occurs . . . [and] not to build up a large local force, including, for example, United States ground troops . . . but rely on the deterrent of our mobile striking force."

RIDDLES
April 18, 1966

The common report of some members of Congress, after sampling the sentiments of their constituents during the Easter recess, is that the Administration's conduct of the war in Vietnam has spread confusion and discontent among the American people. The discontent derives from a widely voiced judgment that our deep and growing military involvement

448

reflects a colossal blunder of statesmanship, and can therefore be expected to persist. But the confusion could be removed if the Administration faced up to the riddles of policy that have created it.

This would require the substitution of candor for the official evasions and outright misrepresentations of current and prospective conditions of the war. It would also require the admission of gross miscalculations, largely the product of public appraisals of the military situation by Secretary of Defense McNamara. But political considerations make it unlikely that this Administration would depart from the pattern of governments on the defensive by meeting these requirements, especially when the nation is at war.

However, the reports of a number of members of Congress of identical questions they encountered in their constituencies support the view that certain conflicting directions of the policy with which the war is being pursued are a main source of the people's confusion. Such as:

¶ The Administration long rejected proposals that the offices of the United Nations be enlisted in bringing about a cease-fire in Vietnam. But when it reversed this position, the Administration simultaneously resumed the bombing of North Vietnam. What is the explanation of a timing which paralyzed the U.N. function while it was being solicited?

¶ A statement by Secretary of State Rusk before the House Committee on Foreign Affairs, prophesying and encouraging eventual friendly relations with Communist China, was released for publication last Saturday. Such releases, and their timing, are always by mutual consent. The day after this release United States aircraft bombed the environs of Hanoi for the first time. This bombing, calculated to intensify the hostility of the present Government in Peking, requires days of preparation. What is the explanation of the timing of the Rusk release and an action certain to defer any possible attainment of its objective?

¶ The same question applies to the proximity of the date of the bombing of the Hanoi suburb to the conciliatory announcement of the State Department that a number of Chinese scholars would be admitted to the United States to participate in university programs.

¶ Since it has always been obvious that missile sites in North Vietnam were a major threat to United States military operations, and their whereabouts was known, why were those in the Hanoi area spared from air attack until the other day? And why was the attack timed in the context of official conciliatory gestures to Communist China?

¶ The publication in this country of well-documented reports of United States weapons shortages was swiftly met by denials from McNamara; and by the statement that the only shortage was in the limited unloading facilities in South Vietnamese ports. Immediately thereafter, it was disclosed that the Defense Department had bought back, at a higher price, a consignment of bombs sold to West Germany. If there was no shortage, what was the reason for this transaction, especially since more bombs would increase instead of reduce the pile-up at the docks?

¶ Senator Mansfield, the majority leader in his branch of Congress, proposed a summit conference in Asia of all the parties with interest in the Vietnam war. Since Mansfield had just returned from a trip to Mexico with President Johnson, and is not given to irresponsible policy proposals, it is reasonable to assume the proposal meets with the approval of the President. But Communist China continues to demand withdrawal of the United States forces in South Vietnam and Formosa, and recognition of the Vietcong as the sole spokesman for South Vietnam in any peace negotiation. In the circumstances, how can the Mansfield proposal be taken as more than another unrealistic approach to the hard facts of the war?

The President acts on a body of information which no one else in the Government has in its entirety. He may have sound answers he cannot possibly give to all these and other questions. But until or unless he can and does, the public confusion reported by the members of Congress will continue.

In Conclusion

The foregoing commentaries on events, and on people closely involved in them, are reprinted unchanged, with all their imperfections on their head. Subsequent developments have left them even more exposed than when they were written to any criticisms which were tenable at the time—lack of insight, prejudice inherent in my belief in a certain philosophy of Government, miscalculation of men and measures. But the only editing has been the elimination of paragraphs and sentences giving reportorial details which the passage of time has made dispensable.

But, if the design of these commentaries was achieved, they register the trend of the Federal Government and of United States foreign policy in the decades they cover. This period beheld the vastly expanding exercise of the powers of the President to commit the American people, in advance or absence of their specific sanction or that of Congress, to global evangelism and war; the recurring abdication by Congress, when it is overwhelmingly composed of members of the President's party, of its coordinate constitutional function; the mounting assumption of authority to impose crippling controls of the free enterprise system by Executive agencies which look to the President rather than to the statutes which created them.

The articles which deal with judicial decisions represent an effort to keep pace with the ever-broadening interpretations of its constitutional function and responsibility by the Supreme Court. Beginning soon after

the re-election of Franklin D. Roosevelt, the Court moved out of the era
when it construed the Constitution as a static document. Increasingly,
the Court has, in effect, inserted judge-made amendments into the Constitution. And it has found inherent constitutional warrant, particularly
in the 14th Amendment, to proclaim and impose new public policies
when the units of Government to which this power was reserved—the
Federal Executive and Legislative Branches and the States—have failed
to initiate them, and when, in the judgment of the Court, the day for the
policies has arrived.

On this concept of its actual and implied authority, the Court, for examples, has:

Desegregated all public facilities without statutory warrant, years before Congress provided it;

Despite the constitutional provision (Art. 1, Sec. 4-1) leaving reapportionment to the States and to Congress, ordered all voting districts
which choose State and Federal legislators to be reapportioned on the
basis of equality of population.

And, by arbitrarily making retroactive the provisions of the Civil
Rights Act of 1964, quashed penalties imposed on deliberate violators of
the laws of trespass which were in full force at the time the violations
were committed.

Moreover, the American people and the press have come to accept as
a matter of course the presence of an applauding Chief Justice of the
United States in assemblages whose purpose is to further the specific
political ideology he shares by the enactment of programs already on
public notice of legal challenges which only the Supreme Court can finally resolve. These assemblages have ranged from public dinners to
Presidential presentations to Congress of proposals on which there is
deep political and popular division.

"Every man who takes office in Washington," said Woodrow Wilson,
with the experience of four years in the Presidency, "either grows or
swells. . . ." Since the impact of an apothegm is measured by its brev-
ity, he did not expand the observation to include others not in public
office who are stationed near the seat of power. They include the spokes-

men of trades and professions, of special-interest groups and causes, who readily become disposed to mistake themselves for the institutions they merely represent.

And I plead *nolle contendere,* in advance, to a finding by any reader that, among the principal victims of this self-delusion, are the commentators of the press.